ASTD's Ultimate Performance Management

Training to Transform Performance Reviews into Performance Partnerships

ASTD Ultimate Series

Linda Russell

Jeffrey Russell

ASTD PRESS

Alexandria, Virginia

ASTD Press is an internationally renowned source of insightful and practical information on workplace learning and performance topics, including training basics, evaluation and return on investment, instructional systems development, e-learning, leadership, and career development. Visit us at www.astd.org/ASTDPress for more on our publishing program.

Ordering information: Books published by ASTD Press can be purchased by visiting ASTD's website at store.astd.org or by calling 800.628.2783 or 703.683.8100.

Library of Congress Control Number: 200892326

ISBN-10: 1-56286-543-9
ISBN-13: 978-1-56286-543-6

ASTD Press Editorial Staff:
Director of Content: Dean Smith
Manager, ASTD Press: Jacqueline Edlund-Braun
Manager, Acquisitions and Author Relations: Mark Morrow
Senior Associate Editor: Tora Estep
Associate Editor: Maureen Soyars
Editorial Assistant: Georgina Del Priore
Full-Service Design, Editing, and Production: Aptara Inc., Falls Church, VA, www.aptaracorp.com
    Development/Production Editor: Robin C. Bonner
    Copyeditor: Sarah A. Bonner
    Indexer: Kidd Indexing
    Proofreader: Sarah A. Bonner
    Interior Design: Lisa Adamitis
Cover Design: Ana Ilieva Foreman
Cover Illustration: Shutterstock.com

Printed by Versa Press, Inc., East Peoria, Illinois, www.versapress.com

The ASTD Ultimate Series

ASTD Press's *Ultimate* series is a natural follow-on to the popular *Trainer's WorkShop* series. Like the *Trainer's WorkShop* series, the *Ultimate* series is designed to be a one-stop, practical, hands-on road map that helps you quickly develop training programs. Each book in the *Ultimate* series offers a full range of practical tools you can apply or adapt to a variety of training scenarios. As in the *Trainer's WorkShop* series, you will find exercises, handouts, assessments, structured experiences, and ready-to-use presentations, along with detailed facilitation instructions. So what's the difference? The *Ultimate* series aims to present the full scope of various topics, offering today's overcommitted training professionals even MORE practical and scalable help: More practical exercises, handouts, assessments, and other ready-to-deploy training solutions. More detailed instructions. Broader topic coverage. More downloadable material. In short, more value for your training budget dollars.

Contents

Preface vii

Chapter 1   Introduction—How to Use This Book Effectively 1

Chapter 2   An Introduction to Performance Management 9

Chapter 3   Assessing Your Performance Management Culture and Competencies 43

Chapter 4   Turning People on to Learning 51

Chapter 5   Evaluating Your Training Program Results 63

Chapter 6   One-Day Workshop on Establishing a Coaching Relationship for
Great Performance 69

Chapter 7   One-Day Workshop on Performance Goal Setting 91

Chapter 8   One-Day Workshop on Diagnosing Employee Performance
Problems and Developing Improvement Plans 109

Chapter 9   One-Day Workshop on Conducting Performance Coaching and Annual
Performance Analysis and Planning Conversations 129

Chapter 10   Half-Day Workshop on the Employee's Role Within the Partnership
for Performance and Performance Coaching Conversations 149

Appendix A   Using the Accompanying CD Materials 165

Appendix B   Handouts 175

Appendix C   Training Instruments 213

Appendix D   Training Tools 251

Appendix E   Learning Activities 259

For Further Reading 337

About the Authors 341

Index 343

Preface

Let's face it. Performance reviews have a bad reputation. For a variety of reasons, too many people approach the review with trepidation, even dread. Without the right mindset or tools, managers tend to put them off until the last minute, whereas performers often approach them with anxiety—not sure how their performance over the past year will be judged. It's time that we step back from this often negative perception of performance reviews and begin seeing the review as an important opportunity to strengthen the partnership between a performer and his or her manager. When approached with the proper mindset and a new set of tools within the larger context of *performance management*, the review can be transformed into a powerful conversation that will result in insight and learning by both the performer and the manager. This new perspective, in turn, leads both the manager and performer to take constructive action toward achieving future-oriented performance outcomes. It also builds employee commitment to achieving *great* performance.

Dozens of books describe how to prepare for and survive performance reviews. Many of these books offer model performance review forms, step-by-step strategies for giving feedback, and methods for diagnosing performance problems. You can even buy phrase books that suggest words and sentences to use when giving constructive feedback to a performer. All these books have an appropriate place on a manager's shelf as he or she approaches the task of guiding the work of another person. It is essential, however, that any of these specific skill-building, strategy, or phrase books be used within an overarching, comprehensive, and integrated approach to performance management. Conducting performance reviews without this larger framework is like filling your car's gas tank, changing its oil, rotating its tires, and beginning a journey without knowing where you're going, having no map to guide you, and neglecting to check the speedometer, oil temperature, and gas gauges as you wander around aimlessly looking for your ill-defined destination. And we wonder why too often it's a frustrating process!

Ultimate Performance Management is a different kind of book. It presents an approach to performance management and performance reviews that includes the larger context within which all performance occurs and then seeks to develop the skills in managers and performers for navigating the landscape of this framework. We wrote this book to help organizational leaders, consultants, human resource professionals, and organization development specialists create a comprehensive yet practical approach for performance management and performance reviews. Our goal was to write a book that described this larger framework of performance management and then to present an array of supporting models and tools, and a flexible set of interactive training modules that readers could customize as they design or redesign their organization's performance management system.

Our journey to find a better approach to performance management and reviews and to create the innovative models, tools, methods, and approaches that you'll find within *Ultimate Performance Management* began with our own personal frustrations with giving and receiving performance reviews. Both of us have permanent performance review scars that have shaped the way we approach this topic today. This book represents the results of our efforts to find a better way. It also benefits from our years as consultants to a diverse clientele—many of whom have, in the past, struggled with the implementation of effective performance management and review systems. Our models and methods have been field-tested by our clients and by the thousands of managers and employees who have participated in our performance coaching and performance management workshops over the years.

One of our core objectives in writing this book was to create an approach to performance management and performance reviews that can be layered on any organization's current performance management system. We believe that the models and tools we introduce in this book will work effectively with any existing performance management systems. At the same time, we also hope that readers will reflect on our approach to performance management and then take steps to refine, adjust, or redefine their own systems to reflect the ideas embedded within this book.

The CD-ROM that accompanies this book offers handouts, training instruments, a detailed facilitator's guide, and PowerPoint slides that are ready for immediate use. With these powerful tools, you are encouraged to either use the training program designs as outlined in the book or custom-design your own workshops around your organization's performance-management system. The greatest strength of *Ultimate Performance Management* is that it enables you to construct your skill-building workshop around our models and tools and to design the right program to meet your specific needs.

Because much of the work you see in these pages has evolved from our consulting practice and our skill-building workshops on performance coaching and performance reviews, we want to thank our many clients who have helped us learn what works and what doesn't when it comes to performance management and coaching. Their collective enthusiasm kept us active in the search for effective models and approaches to this crucial ingredient in helping organizations achieve and sustain their *great* performance outcomes.

Our greatest thanks go to Mark Morrow, the book editor at the American Society for Training & Development and to Robin Bonner, of Aptara, Inc. Mark recognized the importance of this book as one of the first volumes in ASTD's Ultimate series and encouraged us to undertake this sometimes daunting subject. His patience with us as the book evolved and his enthusiastic support for our innovative approach to performance management and reviews kept us at the task. Robin helped us clarify our thinking and thereby enabled us to effectively translate our ideas onto the page. Of the many editors we have worked with over the years, Robin's careful and sensitive approach demonstrated perhaps the best understanding of what we were trying to achieve with a great respect for our work. We could ask for nothing more than this.

We hope that this book moves you and your organization toward a new approach to performance management and performance reviews. We also hope that it enables you to build the critical skills in your workforce that, in turn, enable your managers and performers to transform the traditional performance review into a new and powerful *Performance Coaching Conversation*. If this book starts you on your own journey toward improving this process within your organization, then we will have accomplished one of our most important goals: ensuring that performance reviews are a value-added process benefiting the performer, the performer's manager, and the larger organization.

We would like to hear from you as you use *Ultimate Performance Management* to build a new set of performance management skills in your workforce. Tell us what did and didn't work with any aspect of our approach. We welcome your ideas, suggestions, and questions. We would like to begin an ongoing dialogue with our readers on strategies for effective performance management. Please email us. We look forward to hearing from you.

Linda and Jeffrey Russell
RCI@RussellConsultingInc.com
www.RussellConsultingInc.com
Madison, Wisconsin
July 2009

Introduction—How to Use This Book Effectively

What's in This Chapter?

- Discussion of the value of conducting performance reviews within a larger performance management context

- Explanations of our workshop designs for performance coaching, goal setting, diagnosing performance problems, and conducting effective performance reviews

- Instructions on how to use this workbook most effectively

- Description of what's included in this workbook and what you will find on the accompanying CD

You've been given the assignment to design and develop one or more workshops on performance reviews, and you're beginning to wonder why *you're* the lucky one. Who actually *likes* a performance review, you wonder? Isn't the performance review the most feared encounter between an employee and his or her supervisor? How in the world will you be able to design a workshop that actually gets people excited about doing something that they currently run away from? Well, be prepared to transform your own thinking about performance reviews and performance management!

This book turns the conventional approach to the performance review on its head. Based on the principles and models that we share in this book, you'll soon begin to view the performance review in a more positive light. As a result, you'll begin to see how our workshops can be used to help transform your entire organization's thinking and approach to the performance review process.

A thought revolution, of course, begins with learning a few bedrock perspectives on performance management and then exploring the role that the performance review plays within this larger context. This is where we'll start our journey.

The two main purposes of this book are to present an innovative framework and approach to conducting the performance review and to offer a series of integrated workshop designs that will enable you, in turn, to engage leaders, managers, and frontline employees in learning and adopting this new practice. Naturally, first you'll need to find your own way through this approach. Some of what we have to offer may be "aha!" moments for you. Or, you may find you disagree with some aspects of our approach, methods, or principles. Our approach to facilitating learning may not always gel with yours—or perhaps it will be a perfect match! That's what we believe is the exciting part of making this book work for you: weaving together the different threads that, once integrated in your own mind and practice, form the warp and woof of both a fresh approach to performance management and reviews and a suite of highly customizable workshops to deliver to your organization.

At a minimum, our goal is to alter your perspective on performance reviews and to give you the tools for developing performance review competencies in leaders, managers, and employees at all levels. Our goal is to enable you to begin a process for guiding your organization through a larger transformation in its approach to performance reviews and performance management.

Value of Performance Reviews

The simplest definition of the performance review is that it is a process for providing retrospective feedback to a performer on that performer's performance over a given period. This definition is only partly right. Yes, the review does provide an important feedback loop to the performer on his or her past performance, but the performance review must be much more than this. More than anything, the performance review is a small, though critical, part of a much larger dialogue between the performer and the individual to whom the performer is accountable. The major task of the review is to focus the energy and attention of the performer and reviewer on a deeply reflective process that explores four fundamental questions:

- *What went well?* Looking back over the performance period, what has he or she done *well*? What performance outcomes have been achieved? What performance successes have been realized? In general, what is the *good news* about the employee's performance?

- *What didn't go well?* What hasn't gone well? What performance outcomes weren't met? Where did the employee fail to meet expectations? In general, in which areas is there a need for improved performance?

- *What are the causes of success and failure?* What are the *causes* of the employee's successes and failures? What are the forces that both *support* and *undermine* the employee's performance? What factors contribute to understanding why the employee did or did not accomplish all that he or she set out to achieve?

- *What should stay the same and what should change?* Given what has gone well, what hasn't gone well, and the forces that have influenced these results, what might both performer and reviewer need to *continue doing*, and what might each need to *change*? What needs to happen next to sustain great performance and to improve less-than-ideal performance?

Although the purpose of the performance review is to answer these questions, the review is neither the place nor the time to *begin* exploring them. Exploration begins at the very onset of the performance partnership that must be forged between the performer and his or her supervisor or manager. The nature and quality of this performance partnership forms the backbone of not only the performance review but also the entire performance management process. It also forms the backbone of this *Ultimate* series book. By the time you have finished studying the approach and workshop designs in this book, you will see the importance of both the performance review and the performance partnership in helping the organization realize its bottom line objectives.

The goal of this book is to help you understand the broader context within which the performance review takes place and then to present an array of skill-building workshop designs that prepare managers, supervisors, and the frontline employees themselves for translating performance reviews into great results for the performer, manager, customer, and organization as a whole.

Something for Everyone

This book is written to directly address a variety of needs. If you are new to your training role, we provide you with a solid foundation in some of the basics of training program design, including assessing needs (chapter 3), facilitating learning (chapter 4), and evaluating results (chapter 5). Veteran workplace learning facilitators may want to review these chapters for a refresher or to pick up some new ideas or approaches.

If you are new to performance reviews and performance management, you'll find our overview of performance management, performance coaching, and performance reviews in chapter 2 particularly useful. This chapter lays down the philosophical and methodological foundation upon which our subsequent workshop designs are based. We hope that you'll find this chapter helpful in your efforts to design your own skill-building workshops.

The main focus of this book is to provide you with an array of half- and full-day interactive workshops that integrate these performance management and review philosophies, methodologies, and skill practices in the classroom. You'll find that these customizable workshop designs are great opportunities for creating a fresh approach to performance reviews—a fresh approach that engages both the reviewer and the reviewed in a new dialogue around performance and its outcomes.

How to Use This Workbook Most Effectively

Whether you are a novice instructor or an experienced trainer, you will find this book an invaluable resource for designing, developing, and facilitating a variety of workshops geared toward preparing for and conducting the performance review. Based on our chapter 2 discussion of the broader context within which the performance review takes place and the training modules in chapters 6 through 10, you will be able to custom-design all the skill-building training programs you may need to present to audiences from your chief executive officer or president to frontline staff.

To benefit most from this book and the associated CD, we recommend that you follow these steps as you begin to design your performance review and related performance review preparation training programs:

1. *Skim the book.* Take a quick read through its entire contents. Study the "What's in This Chapter?" lists at the beginning of each chapter. Get a good sense of the layout, structure, and content of each chapter and the book overall. This will enable you to decide where you should begin your own efforts toward building an integrated approach to performance reviews.

2. *Immerse yourself in the foundation of the performance review: the performance management system.* Read chapter 2 for an overview of performance management and performance coaching as well as the role and importance of the review within this framework. In this chapter, you'll also discover some powerful new tools for strengthening the entire performance management and coaching process—tools that are integrated into the workshop designs in subsequent chapters.

3. *Assess the organization's readiness for and receptivity to an effective performance management and review system.* Chapter 3 introduces some approaches for better understanding the environment within which the performance review training and the reviews themselves will take place. Knowing how receptive or ready the organization is to take performance management and reviews seriously—seriously enough to do them right—will be key to the success of your skill-building efforts. Understanding this context and designing your training programs with this context in mind are critical to the success of your efforts. The needs and readiness assessment methods that we share with you in this chapter will help steer your own design efforts in the right direction—and increase the likelihood of positive performance review outcomes.

4. *Review the basics of how to facilitate a positive learning environment.* By reading chapter 4 you will learn ideas, approaches, and strategies for effectively teaching adults, preparing them for learning, supporting the "transfer" of learning to practice, and designing effective training programs. If you are an experienced trainer, review this chapter to reinforce what you are already practicing and to perhaps add a few more tools to your approach to instructional design.

5. *Make sure that you build evaluation into your training program design.* Read chapter 5 for some ideas on measuring learning, behavior change, and results as an integral part of your larger performance review training and development strategy.

6. *Explore the training modules.* Chapters 6 through 10 offer a variety of training programs that you can draw on as you design a program to fit both your organization and your various target audiences. These chapters include everything from a half-day program for frontline employees on the performance review process and their role in the process, to a number of half- and full-day workshops covering different aspects of preparing for and conducting the performance review. Use these carefully designed workshop modules as a foundation for developing your own series of performance review skill and knowledge training workshops.

7. *Design your suite of performance review training programs.* Based on the foundational approaches to performance management and performance coaching, effective strategies for facilitating learning, techniques for needs assessment and learning evaluation, and the array of workshop designs in this book, you can then create your own customized suite of training programs.

What's Included in This Workbook and on the Accompanying CD?

All assessments, checklists, course handouts, and PowerPoint slides referenced in this workbook are included on the accompanying CD. (Thumbnails of the PowerPoint slides also appear at the end of the chapter in which they are referenced—chapters 6–9.) Follow the instructions in the appendix "Using the Accompanying Compact Disc." The book and CD include these training materials:

- tools and strategies for assessing the readiness of your organization for performance management and performance reviews (chapter 3 and CD)

- training workshops that can be used as is or modified in response to the organization, its challenges, and your own teaching style (chapters 6–10)

- learning activities and supportive training instruments and handouts that are designed to fit into the training modules (appendix and CD)

- tools for facilitating training workshops that encourage active learning and integration of content, and also strengthen learning application once attendees are back on the job (appendix and CD)

- printable documents that can be used as workshop handouts (CD)

- Microsoft PowerPoint presentations and slides for your use in guiding participant learning and focusing their energy (chapters 6–9 and CD)

- additional resources for future reference, including books and websites that you may find helpful in designing effective training programs and in understanding strategic planning.

Icons

For easy reference, icons are included in the margins throughout this workbook to help you quickly locate key elements in training design and instruction. Here are the icons and what they represent:

CD. This icon indicates materials included on the accompanying CD.

Clock. This icon indicates recommended time frames for specific activities.

Discussion Questions. This icon highlights questions you can use to explore important issues as part of a training activity.

Handout. This icon indicates handouts that you can print or copy and use to support training activities.

Key Point. This icon will alert you to key points that you should emphasize as part of a training activity.

PowerPoint Slide. This icon indicates PowerPoint presentations and slides that can be used individually. These presentations and slides are on the CD accompanying this workbook. Instructions for using PowerPoint slides and the CD are included in the appendix.

Learning Activities. This icon introduces learning activities that are structured or guided to facilitate participant insight, application, and learning. The learning activities are noted in the training workshop agendas in chapters 6 through 10, detailed in the appendix and included on the CD.

Training Tools. This icon introduces tools for facilitating training workshops that encourage active learning and integration of content and also strengthen learning application once attendees are back on the job (appendix and CD).

Training Instrument. This icon identifies specific tools, checklists, and assessments that are used before, during, and following the training seminars.

What to Do Next. This icon highlights recommended actions that you can take to transition from one section of this workbook to the next, or from a specific training activity to another within a training module.

The next chapter presents a model for performance management and identifies the role that the performance review plays within this model. It discusses the roles of both the performance coach and the performer, within the great performance management model and during the performance review itself. This chapter also introduces a powerful framework for constructing a healthy and productive performance partnership between the reviewer and the reviewed, based on an innovative approach for mutual learning.

What to Do Next

- Review the next chapter to better understand the organizational context within which performance reviews are conducted. Study the innovative models and approaches for an effective review and discover some new tools to help strengthen the performance partnership.

- Reflect on your own experience with performance management and performance reviews in your current or former organizations. What assumptions and biases do you bring to the topic of performance reviews? To what extent does your own positive or negative experience with reviews influence your perspective? How open are you to a different approach to reviews than those you have experienced?

• Begin thinking about the responses you are likely to hear from managers, supervisors, and employees when you talk to them about designing a new approach for conducting performance reviews.

An Introduction to Performance Management 2

What's in This Chapter?

- Performance management as a *process* rather than as an event
- The Great Performance Management Cycle
- The purpose of performance reviews
- Common problems with the traditional performance review process
- An innovative alternative: the Performance Coaching Conversation
- The foundation for an effective dialogue around performance: mutual learning
- Governing values, assumptions, and behaviors that support an effective Performance Coaching Conversation

▲   ▲   ▲

Many people report that the performance review is one of the most dreaded events of the year. Whether preparing for and giving the review as a manager or steeling oneself to receive it as a performer, the annual review is rarely perceived as a positive event. Why is this event so ill-favored? Why is it that, too frequently, both sides of this particular interaction find it distasteful? Is there a better way to structure this event such that both the manager and the performer benefit from the experience?

This chapter explores the answers to these questions. We'll first step back from the performance review itself and examine this signature event within a larger performance framework. In doing so, we'll uncover the foundations of effective performance management and explore the role that the performance review should play within this larger context. Unfortunately, too often the traditional performance review fails to fulfill this important role. We discuss why this is so and offer an alternative approach—the Performance Coaching Conversation.

The Performance Coaching Conversation is structured in such a way that it addresses many of the problems with the traditional review, which we will identify, while actually strengthening communication, understanding, and trust between the manager and the performer. The quality and effectiveness of the Performance Coaching Conversation depends on a strong partnership for performance. This partnership is based on a mindset of mutual learning embraced by both the manager and the performer.

Wrapping your mind around a new approach to performance reviews will be easy. We are confident that the philosophy and methods that we reveal in this chapter will strike you as relevant, useful, powerful, and transformative. Once you "see the light" with this new approach, you'll be able to use the subsequent chapters of this book to design a suite of educational sessions that will transform the way both managers and performers view the performance management process and give all parties a new set of tools and skills to transform the nature, type, frequency, and quality of the ongoing performance management dialogue.

Managing Performance Is a Process, Not an Event

Whenever you talk about performance management, people tend to immediately think about performance reviews and performance feedback. Although conducting performance reviews and providing performance feedback are fairly central to performance management, it is critical that we step back from these "events" and see the larger context within which they occur. Providing specific feedback on and appraising the quality of someone's performance are important pieces of this larger performance management framework, but, in reality, they are no more important than any of the other elements of this approach.

"The performance review is no more important than the other elements of performance management?" you ask. Absolutely! You may have a great performance review methodology in place to guide managers in conducting great reviews, but if your managers haven't mastered all the other key components that contribute to performance, their performance reviews are likely to be failures.

The Great Performance Management Cycle

Let's take a look at this larger context, within which the performance review event takes place. Figure 2-1 depicts this larger performance management framework and gives it a name: the Great Performance Management Cycle. We'll spend some time with this mindset, because it is the foundation for everything that needs to happen throughout the entire performance cycle and profoundly influences what happens during the performance review.

Define Great Performance Outcomes

The very top of the Great Performance Management (GPM) Cycle is where performance management begins and where the *purpose* or *aim* of the performer's work is defined. The word *great* is used here intentionally. The purpose of every performer's work should be to make a significant and positive contribution to the organization. We use the word *great* to help elevate this purpose to a higher level, to help ensure that we envision the purpose or aim of a performer's contribution as far beyond

Figure 2-1. The Great Performance Management Cycle

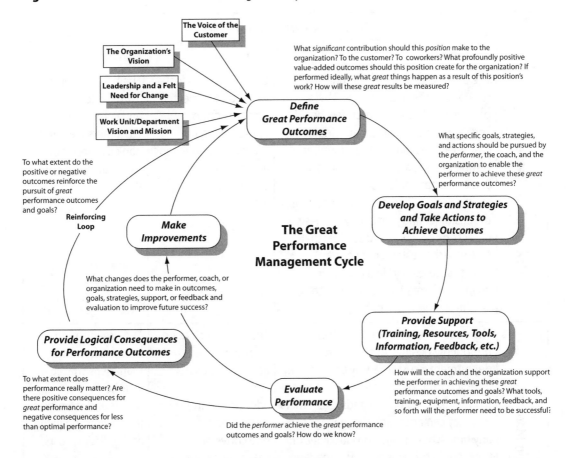

an ordinary, just-get-by performance. In this first step of the GPM Cycle, our goal is to define the profoundly positive outcomes that should become the target of the performer's efforts. By helping the performer imagine what great performance outcomes actually look like, the performer is more likely to create these significantly positive results.

It might be useful to think of great performance in terms of three types of profoundly positive outcomes: those that benefit the *customer*, those that benefit the *team* or co-workers, and those that benefit the *company* or organization as a whole. Table 2-1 offers examples of some great performance outcomes for a mortgage loan officer at a financial institution and for a department manager.

In addition to the great performance outcome expectations for the organization, customers, and team, the employee should also focus on the five dimensions of great performance. These are quality, quantity, cost, timeliness, and impact on the team. Those additional dimensions provide greater depth to our emerging definition of great performance and help focus the employee's efforts toward achieving great results in each of these areas.

Table 2-1. Examples of Great Performance Outcomes

GREAT PERFORMANCE OUTCOMES			
	CUSTOMERS	**TEAM**	**ORGANIZATION**
MORTGAGE LOAN OFFICER	The officer creates value through strong customer partnerships. These partnerships help customers feel heard and respected. The officer anticipates customer questions and communicates complex financial information in clear and understandable ways. The officer anticipates additional financial needs of the customer and proactively suggests other bank products and services that may ease the customer's financial anxieties. Customers feel that their financial information was dealt with sensitively and confidentially.	Coworkers also feel heard and respected and are comfortable approaching the officer with questions and customer problems.	The bank benefits from the loyalty and commitment customers feel for the bank as a result of their partnership with the officer.
DEPARTMENT MANAGER	The department manager creates profoundly positive outcomes for the department's customers by anticipating, listening to, and proactively responding to emerging customer needs. Customers feel they can approach the manager at any time when quality, productivity, or timeliness problems arise. The manager continually seeks out ways to exceed customer expectations through routine dialogue sessions, where emerging issues are explored and the partnership is strengthened.	The manager's team members' needs are anticipated and anxieties are addressed through routine one-on-one conversations that strengthen the performance partnership.	The organization benefits from the manager's strategic insight on future trends and strategies for maximizing value and reducing costs.

How does one decide on great performance outcome expectations? As depicted in figure 2-1, these profoundly positive outcome expectations naturally reveal themselves when you explore with customers what matters most to them, when the performance outcome implications from the organization's vision are clearly articulated for each position, when the performer's leader or manager has clear performance outcome expectations, and when the vision or mission of the performer's department or work area suggests specific performance outcomes.

A critical next step in defining great performance for a position is the integration of these specific performance outcomes within an individual's position or job description. Because the position description is the keystone for defining everything that is expected of a performer, the great performance outcome expectations must be spelled out in that document. If a performer is to be held accountable for achieving great performance, then the position description must reflect these outcome expectations. Unfortunately, position descriptions usually focus on describing behaviors and activities or offer general outcome statements about the role and function of a position. Although behaviors, activities, and general statements about the position's role are important, by themselves they are not sufficient for providing performers with the clear and compelling direction that's needed.

By making an effort to use the position description to spell out the specific great performance outcome expectations that emerge from these behaviors and activities, the purpose or aim of the performer's work becomes much clearer. To provide greater clarity of purpose and to ensure that performers focus on what matters most to customers, co-workers, and the company as a whole, it is essential that position descriptions be written in ways that reflect these great performance outcome expectations.

Note how the examples in table 2-1 focus on the results of the performer's work rather than on the processes, behaviors, or activities used to achieve those results. Although processes, behaviors, and activities are important, in the first step of the GPM Cycle, it is critical to focus on outcomes rather than on how the performer achieves these results.

The first step of the GPM Cycle also involves identifying how performance results will be measured. To have the greatest positive effect on performance, every great performance outcome should have a predefined performance measure that enables both the performer and the manager to know if and when the outcome has been successfully achieved. Without a method of measurement, both the performer and the manager may have a hard time knowing if the outcome has been achieved. Establishing outcome metrics early on in the GPM Cycle reinforces accountability and provides for a built-in feedback process that will be used later in the cycle.

Develop Process Goals and Strategies

In the first step of the GPM Cycle, the objective is to develop a clearly defined vision of the great performance outcomes that represents the aim or purpose of the performer's contributions to the company. The second step in the cycle involves defining the specific *process* goals, strategies, actions, and steps that the performer and the company will take to ensure that the great performance outcomes are accomplished.

The great performance outcomes deal with *results*, whereas the goals, strategies, and actions defined in this second stage of the GPM Cycle tend to deal more with *processes*—the "hows" of moving from the performer's current performance level to the desired great performance level:

- improving key work processes or procedures

- increasing individual effectiveness by pursuing training and development in specific competencies

- reducing error rates or problems with quality

- building stronger partnerships with customers

- strengthening working relationships with peers

- being more innovative in work methods and processes.

The process goals, strategies, and actions identified in this step of the GPM Cycle should include any goals, activities, and behaviors that will help move the performer toward achieving the desired great performance outcomes. Each of these goals, strategies, actions, and so forth should be *measurable*, such that both performer and manager will know if and when each has been successfully achieved.

As with defining the great performance outcomes, these process goals, methods, behaviors, and so forth must be firmly anchored in the performer's position description. The position description should be reviewed at least once annually to ensure that it accurately spells out both the great performance outcomes and the position's essential job functions. Because the essential job functions form the backbone of each employee's performance, every performance expectation, goal, strategy, and behavior that is spelled out in the second step of the GPM Cycle must be linked back to these functions.

Provide Organizational Support

With the performer now pointed in the right direction—toward great performance outcomes—and working with a set of process goals, strategies, and actions, the next step in the GPM Cycle comes into play: organizational support. Providing organizational support involves both identifying and delivering the information, training, resources, and other forms of support that the performer requires to translate his or her effort into the desired great performance outcomes.

In this step of the GPM Cycle, the performer, his or her manager, and the organization work together to ensure that a supportive infrastructure focuses on generating the desired results. Although this supportive infrastructure is always specific to each performer and the great performance outcomes he or she is expected to create, here are some of the most common broad areas of organizational support:

- providing skill and information development and training

- ensuring access to critical job-related information

- ensuring access to essential tools and equipment

- identifying and removing obstacles to performance

- ensuring frequent communication and interaction between the performer and his or her manager

- ensuring frequent updates on emerging issues and challenges affecting the performer's efforts or results

- providing ongoing feedback on performance.

Providing organizational support is a central contributor to great performance in that it enables and facilitates the performer's effort. When the manager and the organization follow through by providing this supportive infrastructure, the likelihood that the great performance outcomes will be achieved increases. Doing so also lets the performer know that the manager and organization want to see the performer succeed in his or her efforts.

Evaluate Performance

The next step within the GPM Cycle is the step we usually focus on whenever anyone brings up the subject of performance management. As we have learned in this chapter, however, the performance review is only a single step within this larger performance management framework. This evaluation step is a moment when the performer and his or her manager reflect on the original performance target (the great performance outcomes and the supporting suite of goals and behaviors) and then compare the original goal with the actual results achieved.

With skillful guidance from his or her manager during a dialogue called the "Performance Coaching Conversation," the performer explores his or her performance results and the likely causes of these outcomes. We'll dig deeper into the Performance Coaching Conversation later in this chapter, but for now we want to make the point that the success of this performer-centered interaction depends on everything that preceded it:

- a clear and compelling great performance outcome

- a supportive set of goals, strategies, and behaviors to help achieve that outcome

- a strong organizational infrastructure that provides the support the performer needs to achieve his or her great performance outcomes.

With these elements in place, the performance evaluation is a natural next step as both the performer and manager keep their eyes on the great performance outcomes and explore opportunities to improve and strengthen the performer's work toward them.

Make Improvements

The final step of the GPM Cycle extends the Performance Coaching Conversation and, with the manager's skillful guidance, identifies specific opportunities where the performer can strengthen his or her performance. In this step of the process, the performer and the manager mutually identify a set of actions to be taken by the performer and manager, to build on the performer's past success and address improvement areas.

This step targets these improvements:

- clarifying, adjusting, strengthening, or modifying the great performance outcomes in such a way that they may be clearer, easier to measure, easier to attain, and so forth

- adjusting and modifying existing process goals and strategies—or adding new ones that reflect improvement areas and new work priorities

- identifying new ways in which the manager or the larger organization can provide organizational support or adjusting the level of support provided in the past to reflect new priorities, challenges, or constraints

- changing the nature, focus, frequency, or structure of the evaluate performance step of the process, including refining the Performance Coaching Conversation process, and strengthening the dialogue between performer and manager.

It is in this critical final step of the process where insight and learning emerge from the dialogue. The "make improvements" step is also when a performance improvement plan is developed with an eye toward moving the employee's performance closer to achieving his or her great performance outcomes.

The make improvements step is the final step in the GPM Cycle, but there remains one additional component of the cycle that acts as a reinforcing loop to help focus the performer's efforts on his or her great performance outcomes: providing logical consequences for performance results.

Provide Logical Consequences for Performance Results

People aren't Pavlovian dogs that salivate on cue (that is, waiting for a juicy steak to suddenly appear after hearing a bell), but they do pay attention to the consequences that occur based on their contribution to the organization. Whether the organization actively manages it or not, both the planned and unplanned consequences that a performer experiences following performance have a profound effect on his or her future behavior.

When a performer receives positive consequences or rewards following a performance that moves his or her outcomes closer to great performance, then the employee is encouraged to behave similarly, to ensure the continuation of these positive outcomes. When a performer receives negative consequences following a performance that misses the great performance target, then the performer tends to change behaviors to stop these outcomes. The overarching purpose of providing positive or negative consequences for performance is to reinforce the desired behaviors and discourage behaviors that run counter to great performance. Table 2-2 offers several examples of positive and negative consequences that a manager might use to influence performers' behaviors.

Managers who want their performers to engage in positive behaviors and discontinue undesired behaviors need to take this reinforcing loop within the GPM Cycle seriously. This loop involves the manager directly providing clear and meaningful consequences (both positive and negative) for performance.

Table 2-2. Examples of Positive and Negative Outcomes From Performance Discussions

EXAMPLES OF POSITIVE CONSEQUENCES	EXAMPLES OF NEGATIVE CONSEQUENCES
• A financial bonus • Advancement opportunity • Greater independence and autonomy • A letter of commendation • Recognition for a job well done • Flexible work schedule • Approval to work from home • Opportunity for high visibility or status project assignments	• Loss of autonomy and independence • A withdrawal of an opportunity for a financial bonus • A corrective action letter or memo documenting the need for the performer to improve performance • Reduction in flexible work schedule opportunities • Withdrawal of opportunities to work on high-visibility or high-status projects • Discipline—up to and including termination

It also requires that the manager is aware of other forces that may be influencing the performer, such as the responses of co-workers and customers, other teams with whom the employee interacts, the larger organizational culture (which may sometimes work at cross-purposes to the manager's goals), and even the employee's family and friends.

Unfortunately, managers often have little control over many of these other influences. They should, however, at least be aware of them to reinforce the positive pressures and counterbalance those that contradict their aims for their employees.

A key factor in using the power of providing logical consequences as part of the GPM Cycle is that the performer must see the logical connection between his or her own behaviors, the performance outcomes from these behaviors, and the positive or negative consequences that he or she receives. The performer needs to see that positive consequences naturally follow the right behaviors and outcomes and that negative consequences naturally follow the wrong behaviors and outcomes.

Who's in Charge of the Great Performance Management Cycle?

We've spent a good deal of time walking you through the GPM Cycle and have identified a set of activities that need to occur at each step of the process if truly great performance is to occur. One question we haven't yet answered, however, is this: Who is in charge of this process?

When we ask this question in our workshops, the answer is almost always "the manager!" This is understandable. When it comes to actually managing the performance of another person, it seems that the process of management would fall to the manager, as he or she is the person the organization looks to when an employee fails to contribute in the expected way. In reality, the person who is most responsible for moving along the GPM Cycle is the performer him- or herself. Each employee is always fully responsible for his or her own performance, whether it is good or bad. Although the manager must take an active role in guiding the performer throughout the GPM Cycle, at the end of the day, it is the performer who needs to define the outcomes, set the goals, identify the resources required to accomplish the outcomes, evaluate whether or not he or she has met the target, and identify opportunities for improvement or change.

Within the GPM Cycle, the manager fulfills the role of a coach: guiding, shaping, challenging, questioning, provoking, supporting, encouraging, and inspiring the employee to take on the challenge of great performance. As in the sports arena or the performance stage, however, the manager, as coach, never walks onto the field or steps onto the stage to get the job done—that is the duty of the performer. Doing the job, engaging in the right behaviors, gathering performance data, self-assessing and correcting performance as necessary, and so forth are all the responsibility of the performer. When it comes down to setting and achieving the goal, it is up to the individual athletes, musicians, actors, or employees to do the work. The coach should never do it for them.

Although the employee is primarily responsible for his or her performance and the resulting outcomes, the manager as coach still plays a critical role. Together, the manager and employee forge a *partnership for performance* that focuses on guiding and supporting the employee toward achieving the great performance outcomes. Who actually takes the lead within this partnership at any given time,

Figure 2-2. The Dynamic Partnership for Performance

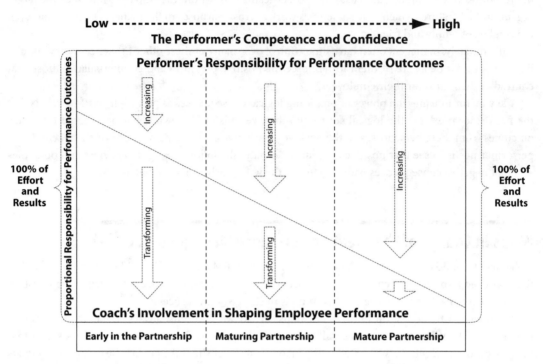

however, is a function of the skill, knowledge, and experience of the performer, and the coach responding with the correct amount of direction, guidance, support, feedback, and reinforcement.

Figure 2-2 highlights the nature of this dynamic partnership for performance. As shown in this
figure, early on in the partnership the manager (depending on the skill, knowledge, and experience level of the performer) may take the lead role in defining performance outcomes, establishing
goals, identifying supportive resources, providing feedback on performance, and suggesting improvement goals. Even in this early stage of the relationship, however, the performer remains fully
engaged in each of these key steps in the GPM Cycle and remains fully responsible for the resulting
performance.

As the performer gains competence and confidence in his or her work, however, the manager
as coach downshifts his or her role. This downshift includes moving away from defining great performance, setting goals, identifying resources, and so forth for the employee and moving toward
guiding the performer to take full responsibility for these steps. The coach determines the best
approach to take, based on an assessment of the competence and confidence of the performer. The
coach then shifts to a more supportive role through skillful dialogue, probing questions, encouragement and suggestions, and constructive feedback. Figure 2-2 displays what this shift in responsibility might look like as both the performer and coach transition their roles to a new performance
partnership.

Examining and Improving the Performance Review

With the Great Performance Management Cycle providing our framework and the dynamic nature of the partnership for performance between the performer and the coach delineated, we can now shift our attention to the structure of the face-to-face performance review. We'll first look at the purpose of the performance review, highlight some of the problems with traditional methods of review, and then present an innovative employee-centered approach to reviews that both eliminates the problems and strengthens the partnership with performance.

The Purpose of the Traditional Performance Review

Confusion over the *purpose* of the performance review is where everything begins to go wrong. If we're not clear about what we're trying to accomplish during a performance review, then the results will be worse than muddled—we may end up diminishing our performance partnership with the employee, resulting in a decline in communication, confidence, trust, and, eventually, performance itself.

Traditionally, performance reviews—also known as performance appraisals—focus on an employee's past performance. They provide an opportunity for managers to present their assessments or appraisals of their employee's work over a defined performance period—typically a year. The core purpose of this traditional performance appraisal is judging the quality and effectiveness of the employee's contribution to the organization and often to the team, co-workers, and customers as well. This retrospective judgment of the performer's contribution often involves rating the employee on a narrow range of performance dimensions, leading up to an overall rating of the employee's performance.

When well-designed, each of these performance dimensions links back to the employee's job description, the organization's goals or core values, activities related to department or team goals, or specific performance improvement goals identified in the previous year's performance review. In addition, a well-designed appraisal system provides feedback to the performer, using specific and measureable performance dimensions. Each dimension is described in terms of both behavior and outcome to give the performer useful feedback on what was expected and how well he or she met these expectations. In contrast, poorly designed appraisal systems and their supporting forms tend to define these performance dimensions in overly broad terms (for example, team player) that often result in an overall rating that is imprecise and subjective.

For the overall performance rating, the better review processes use a Likert-type rating scale, with a set of clearly defined anchors, such as these: fails to meet expectations, meets expectations, and exceeds expectations. Although the actual scale used may be made up of three, five, or 10 options, the end result, regardless of the scale, is a comprehensive rendering of judgment as to the employee's overall performance.

When designed well, the results of the employee's annual performance review are forwarded to the human resources department and then used for such actions as salary increases (if any), determining the employee's career advancement potential, and flagging the employee for possible coaching and assistance if warranted. In some circumstances, a sufficiently negative appraisal would form the foundation for subsequent actions, which might include progressive discipline, leading up to and including termination. Even in this well-designed system, however, the results from the annual review are often just filed away by HR and forgotten. One year later, the process repeats itself and another appraisal document is added to the archives.

In a well-designed performance review process, the results from the one-on-one performance appraisal are also used by the manager as a key source for defining the performance outcomes and goals for the upcoming performance period—again, typically one year in duration. This future-oriented performance planning process should reflect continuing or new organizational and team priorities and outcomes, identify emerging issues and challenges, and spell out an improvement plan to address any performance deficits identified in the past-oriented performance appraisal. The improvement plan may also identify specific performance improvement goals and spell out the desired employee behaviors to achieve these goals. Finally, this future-oriented plan identifies the steps the manager and the organization will take to support the employee's performance. This might include detailing a development strategy that could include training, mentoring, coaching, and other activities to assist the performer in reaching the goals spelled out in the plan.

The purpose of the traditional review is historical in perspective, evaluative and corrective by nature, and a key driver for human resource decision making and actions.

Problems with the Traditional Review and a Reframed Purpose

Although the traditional review can play a positive role in providing feedback to the performer, guiding the development of a performance improvement plan, and influencing key HR decision making, too often these positive aspects are diluted by how the review is conducted. The "how" is all important here because the success of a performance review depends on the quality of the interaction between the manager and performer. If either approaches the review without the proper mindset—something we'll explore later in this chapter—the resulting interaction is likely to fall far short of the key objectives for the review.

Table 2-3 highlights the most problematic characteristics of the performance review and proposes higher purposes for the review that should become the driving force behind a reformulated review process.

One-way communication vs. two-way dialogue. The traditional review is hampered in its effectiveness because it tends to focus on what the manager has to say to the performer rather than on developing a true dialogue. The limitation of one-way communication is that the manager may need to listen more than talk to discover the best way to assist the performer toward great performance.

Focus on the past vs. improvement for the future. The performance review, by definition, looks backward at the employee's past performance. Although a historical assessment is a good place to begin, looking only at the past fails to build a foundation for *future* performance. In a well-designed process—or in the radically transformed process that we'll explore later—the manager uses a historical assessment only as a stepping stone for exploring ways to strengthen performance for the future. This shift in focus moves from problem orientation toward improvement orientation.

Table 2-3. Reframing the Performance Review

PERFORMANCE REVIEW PROBLEMS	A PROPOSED HIGHER PURPOSE
One-way communication ◄──────►	Two-way dialogue
Focus on the past ◄──────►	Improvement for the future
Appraisal, evaluation, and judgment ◄──────►	Learning and development
Focus on financial implications ◄──────►	Learning and development
Focus on filling in forms and checking boxes ◄──────►	Developing understanding
Assumes that the manager knows and sees all ◄──────►	Both parties to the review have knowledge and insight to share
Focus on the performance review as an event ◄──────►	Performance management as a process
Over-reliance on some measurements while ignoring others ◄──────►	Using a holistic approach to performance measurement
Being overly influenced by recent events or personal characteristics ◄──────►	Using objective data when analyzing and assessing performance

Appraisal, evaluation, and judgment vs. learning and development. When the focus of the review is purely evaluation and appraisal—a rendering of judgment on the employee's work—the result is often defensiveness and denial. This response is natural when a person's entire year's work history is reduced to a single check-box on a five-point scale! The resulting defensiveness is a major barrier to communication, understanding, and dialogue. When the performer shuts down, gets defensive, and runs for cover, the manager's goal of better understanding the causes of less-than-optimal performance becomes elusive. If, however, the focus of the review shifts away from judgment and toward learning and development, defensiveness tends to fall by the wayside, as both the manager and performer examine the range of causes of performance problems and explore ideas for addressing these causes.

Focus on financial implications vs. learning and development. If the higher purpose of the performance review is to facilitate understanding leading to performance improvement, then everything that the manager says and does in the review should focus on that purpose. Unfortunately, there's nothing like linking the performance rating of an employee to the resulting pay raise (or lack thereof) to shift the review's focus away from understanding and communication. When there are fiscal consequences for a performer based on which "box" is checked on the review form, the conversation is suddenly about the manager defending why a certain box was checked and the performer arguing for a more favorable rating.

It is possible for the manager to link the performance review with the employee's pay without compromising the review. The solution rests on how this linkage is made and when this discussion occurs. By simply separating the discussion of the employee's overall performance rating and its pay implications by at least a day, much of the financial distractions can be avoided. The focus of the review process must remain on communication and understanding as a pathway to learning, development, and performance improvement.

Focus on forms and checking boxes vs. developing understanding. Nothing that occurs during the performance review should interfere with the overarching goal of developing understanding between the manager and the performer. Too often, however, the form designed to document the review becomes a barrier to communication and understanding. When the focus of the performance discussion shifts to what's on the form or which box is checked rather than on the quality of the dialogue between the manager and performer, the form needs to be temporarily set aside. The official review form may still need to be completed by the manager, but it should be done *following* the performance dialogue. This delay allows the manager to learn new information that he or she wouldn't have known without the Performance Coaching Conversation.

A post-review form completion step ensures that the final written document submitted to HR reflects the best thinking by the manager—informed by open dialogue with the employee. Once the form is completed by the manager, a brief follow-up meeting with the performer can be scheduled to discuss the final document, the overall rating, and any pay-related consequences.

Assumptions that the manager knows and sees all vs. both parties of the review have knowledge and insight to share. One of the biggest mistakes a manager can make as he or she prepares for and conducts the performance review is assuming that what he or she sees or understands about the employee's performance represents all the facts. Making this assumption becomes a problem when the manager's "all knowing" perception is taken as a fact, leaving little room for the employee to offer his or her own perspective. In reality, the manager has a perspective on the employee's performance and the factors influencing it, but the employee's perspective is just as important. Understanding and honoring each other's perspective is one of the key functions of the performance review.

When these two perspectives agree, the conversation shifts to building on this consensus. When either the manager or the performer has knowledge or insight that the other doesn't have, however, the performance conversation shifts to identifying and understanding these differences. Both parties in this performance partnership have important information, knowledge, and insight to share. The higher purpose of the performance review is to mine these diverse perspectives toward the goal of strengthening the partnership and improving the employee's performance.

Focus on the performance review as an event vs. performance management as a process: The performance review is certainly an event, but if this event is viewed in isolation outside of the larger framework of performance management, then its full benefits will never be realized. As we noted earlier in this chapter, great performance doesn't happen by accident and it certainly doesn't happen because of one performance review each year. When the manager and the employee see the performance review as one of *many* conversations throughout the year, then this annual event takes on its proper role and function. Viewing performance management as a process and the review as an integral part, but only a single step, of this process helps ensure that both the manager and the employee focus on performance every day of the year.

Over-reliance on some measurements while ignoring others vs. use of a holistic approach to performance measurement: It's easy to document the duration and number of calls an employee in a call center makes; it's harder is to measure the *quality* of these interactions. Therein lies one of the major challenges of performance reviews: measuring easily accessible information vs. measuring information that is harder to document but may be more important. Performance reviews are a time of measurement and assessment, when both the performer and manager look back on great performance expectations (outcomes and goals) and determine if and to what degree these expectations were met. The tendency in the traditional review is to over-rely on the data that is the easiest to gather—such as the number of times something was done, the frequency with which the performer's output met certain specifications, the conversion ratio between attempts and results (for example, closed deals compared with total sales calls made), and so forth.

A more effective performance review takes a more holistic approach to measurement. At the beginning of the performance period and the GPM Cycle, the performer and manager explore ways to measure, and subsequently assess, if and to what extent the performer achieved or moved closer to the great performance outcomes. Part of this discussion certainly should include the easier quantitative measures such as numbers, frequencies, completion rates, and so forth. This initial discussion should also include how to assess more qualitative data, such as the *quality* of the interactions with customers, the *quality* of the information being communicated by the performer, the *quality* of the written reports, and so forth. Developing clear measures of these qualitative aspects of a performer's work is rarely easy, but it is essential if the final review is to accurately capture and assess whether or not the performer has accomplished his or her great performance outcomes.

To paraphrase the British mathematician and physicist Lord Kelvin, "If you can't measure it, you can't manage it!" (Van Der Zee, 2003). The challenge for both the performer and coach within the GPM Cycle is to figure out a way to measure all of the aspects of performance that matter most to achieve great performance. Once there is agreement on these more holistic measures of performance, the conversation in the performance review about the measures that matter is more likely to be clear and focused.

Excess influence by recent events or personal characteristics vs. use of objective data when analyzing and assessing performance. Our final problem with traditional performance reviews has more to do with psychology than with the nature of the performance conversation. Two psychological characteristics are especially problematical during a performance review. The first, called the "recency effect," finds that people are cognitively biased toward recent stimuli or observations and away from earlier stimuli or observations. For performance reviews, this means that a manager who is unaware of this effect might focus on key events that happened last week or last month rather than on events that took place at the beginning of the performance period. Regardless of whether the recent event was a positive or negative one, the event would tend to loom larger in the manager's viewpoint and would therefore be given greater weight. The recency effect is defeated by a strong performance partnership where the employee and the manager meet and discuss performance on a regular basis, with the final performance review being only the last of a long line of conversations. Recency can also be addressed by ensuring that performance throughout the year is documented by both the employee and manager and then integrating that documentation into the performance review.

The other psychological characteristic that may get in the way of a traditional review is the "halo/horn effect." This situation finds that people are cognitively biased to view a single dimension of an employee's performance—such as interacting well with customers or co-workers—as representative of the employee's performance in all other areas. In other words, when an employee does something right, the resulting angelic "halo" causes the manager to not see or to ignore problem areas. The corollary to the halo effect is the "horn" effect. In a reversal of the halo effect, when an employee does something wrong—such as missing a mission-critical deadline—the resulting demonic "horn" causes the manager to not see or to ignore areas where the employee is performing well (Thorndike, 1920).

For either of these psychological tendencies, the antidote is for the manager as coach to again develop a strong partnership with the performer, to use objective data when analyzing and assessing performance, to document positive and negative performance events when they occur, and to have numerous performance conversations throughout the performance period.

An Employee-Centered Alternative to the Traditional Review

We've spent some time dissecting a number of the major problems associated with the traditional review, and we've offered some suggestions for reframing the purpose of the review to reflect a new approach. Let's now bring this new approach into sharper focus with the introduction of the "Performance Coaching Conversation" and the "Annual Performance Analysis and Planning Conversation." The employee-centered mindset is based on the GPM Cycle and is deeply anchored in the belief that the performer should take the lead during the review process. As noted in figure 2-2, however, performance management is a shared process between the manager and the performer. Although this also holds true for the Performance Coaching Conversation and the Annual Performance Analysis and Planning Conversation, one of the manager's key goals is to actively encourage employee ownership of the process toward assuming the major role throughout both conversations.

The Performance Coaching Conversation and the Annual Performance Analysis and Planning Conversation both comprise four steps: the manager's preparations, the performer's preparations, conducting the conversation and coming to agreement, and following up and following through. Let's look at each of these steps and identify the role of the manager in each.

The manager's preparations. Before the face-to-face Performance Coaching Conversation or Annual Performance Analysis and Planning Conversation takes place, the manager does his or her homework. This homework involves several activities:

- reviewing the employee's job description and ensuring that it is still an accurate portrayal of the job

- reviewing the great performance outcomes and goals that the employee, in partnership with the manager, established at the beginning of the performance period

- reviewing the ongoing performance log that the manager has maintained on the performer's work (as well as on all other performers)

- reviewing other available documentation of the performer's work

- reviewing notes from past Performance Coaching Conversations held throughout the performance period.

If this is a periodic Performance Coaching Conversation session, then, based on this retrospective review of the performer's work, the manager prepares a bullet-point summary of key findings of the employee's performance strengths and weaknesses, potential causes of performance problems, and elements of a preliminary plan for maintaining and strengthening the employee's performance.

If the get-together is for the Annual Performance Analysis and Planning Conversation, the manager prepares a more extensive written summary of key findings of performance strengths and weaknesses, potential causes of performance problems, and elements of a preliminary plan for maintaining and strengthening the employee's performance. This summary and action planning might also include completing an initial draft of the formal performance review form required by the organization. Although the form must not be the focus of the subsequent Annual Performance Analysis and Planning Conversation, it can help clarify the manager's thinking and perspective and serve as a useful summary document of key findings and next steps for moving the employee's performance closer to his or her great performance outcomes.

The employee's preparations. In preparation for the Performance Coaching Conversation or the Annual Performance Analysis and Planning Conversation, the manager invites the employee to do something very similar. Specifically, the manager meets briefly with the performer prior to the conversation and asks the employee to reflect back on the performance period and develop some answers to the following critical reflection questions:

- *What is going well in your job?* Reflect on your job description and the great performance outcomes that we defined at the beginning of the performance period, and identify those aspects of your work and the results of your work that have gone well for you. Also consider these related questions: *What in your performance over the period do you feel most proud of? What "stand out" performance results have you achieved this period?*

- *What isn't going as well in your job?* Again reflecting on your job description and the great performance outcomes, identify those aspects of your work that haven't gone as well as you had hoped. Also consider these related questions: *In which performance outcome and goal areas have you fallen short of the desired end result? Which performance areas have created the most difficulty for you? What aspects of your job have been the most frustrating? What disappointments and setbacks have you experienced during the performance period?*

- *What lies behind your successes and setbacks?* What are the factors that led to the positive outcomes you identified in response to the first question? What are the factors that led to the less-than-ideal results that you identified in response to the second question? Also consider these related questions: *What's behind the success that you've experienced? What's behind some of the failures you've experienced? What factors supported or undermined your performance during the performance period?*

- *What actions can you take to build on your successes and address areas of performance weakness?* Based on your assessment of the causes of your successes and setbacks, what actions can you take in the future to maintain your successes and improve your areas of weakness? Also consider these related questions: *How might you use your performance successes to further strengthen your great performance outcomes? What could you do to address the causes of things that are not going well, thus improving your future performance outcomes and goals?*

- *How can I (your manager) help you be even more successful and productive in your job?* What actions would be useful for me to take to help sustain your great performance results? What actions would help you address performance areas that aren't going as well for you? This question can include this variation: *What can I do more or less of to enable you to achieve your great performance outcomes and goals?*

- *What do you see as performance areas that may need new responsibilities and future growth in performance?* This question can include these variations: *Given your understanding of your job and role in this organization and department, what new responsibilities or growth areas do you see for your position? Given our organization's strategic goals, what are you learning from your customers? What new responsibilities or job growth areas do you see for yourself given new technologies and their effect on your work? What new directions do you see for your position in the future?*

The six "critical reflection questions" engage the performer in a process designed to encourage deep reflection on his or her past work with the resulting insights becoming a key driver for both the Performance Coaching Conversation and the Annual Performance Analysis and Planning Conversation with the manager. If this is the annual or semi-annual review, these questions should be accompanied by a copy of the performance review form. The manager should encourage the performer to complete his or her version of the review form based on what he or she learned after reviewing the critical reflection questions.

To help focus the performer's attention on these questions in advance of either coaching conversations, the manager should give the performer these questions in writing. It may also be useful for the manager to create a simple critical reflection questions worksheet that provides space for the employee to jot down his or her thoughts and responses.

Conducting the conversation and coming to agreement. Up to this point for the Performance Coaching Conversation and the Annual Performance Analysis and Planning Conversation, both the manager and performer have done some pre-work. The next step of the process involves the face-to-face conversation. Given all the analysis and reflection that both the manager and performer have done, this step—the one most feared by both managers and performers alike—should be relatively easy. This is how it should work: The manager welcomes the performer into the conversation with language along these lines:

> *Thanks for coming in today. As I mentioned to you the other day, today's Performance Coaching Conversation/Annual Performance Analysis and Planning Conversation is an integral part of my approach to performance management and performance reviews. It's my hope that our conversation today will help me better understand your concerns, needs, and issues related to your contributions here. It also gives me a chance to clarify my own thoughts and*

expectations and to identify ways that I can help you achieve your great performance out-comes. All of this, I hope, ensures that the formal review of your performance is both accurate and helpful in moving you toward great performance.

As you recall, several days ago I asked you to think about a number of questions in preparation for today's conversation. My intention in asking you to think about these critical reflection questions was to encourage you to do a self-assessment of your own performance, encourage some critical reflection on your past work, and get you thinking about things that both you and I could do to support and enhance your performance in the future.

My preference is to have you *start things off—I'd first like to hear your thoughts about your performance—and then I'll add my comments and thoughts when you're done. Does that sound okay to you? I'm willing to share my analysis of your performance first, if that's what you'd like me to do, but my preference would be to hear your perspective first. Are you willing to kick things off?*

Okay, to start things off, I'd like to hear your thoughts on the first question I asked you to think about: What is going well *in your position?*

Following this employee-centered Performance Coaching Conversation or Annual Performance Analysis and Planning Conversation, the performer takes the lead role by sharing his or her self-assessment. Why encourage the performer to go first? Our goal is to build greater employee ownership within the GPM Cycle, and we believe that this is best accomplished by having the performer take the lead for each of the six critical reflection questions. This is never done unilaterally, however. The manager explains the reasoning behind *why* he or she prefers the employee to go first and then works with the performer to mutually decide the approach to use during the conversation or annual review conversation. If the employee insists on the manager going first, the manager comes to a mutual agreement with the performer as to how they will proceed after exploring the employee's own reasoning behind this preference.

Assuming that the employee is the first to answer each of the six critical reflection questions, the manager then follows with his or her perspective on what the performer has already shared, and offers new insights and perspectives. This includes building on and agreeing with the employee's self-assessment when there is a shared perspective on a given performance dimension or outcome. It also includes adding new insights, perspectives, and observations that go beyond what the employee may have shared. By following instead of preceding the performer's self-assessment, the manager may gain important insights into the quality of the employee's critical reflection and thinking skills. This also enables the manager to gain new insights concerning strengths, improvement areas, and their underlying causes that the manager did not or could not see. Another key value of the performer presenting his or her self-assessment first is that it tends to reduce defensiveness because the employee has named performance problems first, instead of reacting to the manager's doing so. This is especially important for the second critical reflection question: *What isn't going as well for you?*

By using the six critical reflection questions as the core of their coaching conversation, both the performer and manager should arrive at a shared understanding of the employee's performance strengths, areas for improvement or growth, and action plans for both the performer and the manager to support the employee's future performance.

We have only scratched the surface of the steps for conducting these two critical coaching conversations. For more details and suggestions on how a manager might successfully navigate the Performance Coaching Conversation or Annual Performance Analysis and Planning Conversation, see **handout 28**. This is one of the many supportive training handouts we have incorporated into the workshop designs in the chapters that follow.

Following up and following through. This is the final step in both the Performance Coaching Conversation and the Annual Performance Analysis and Planning Conversation. In this step, the manager finalizes his or her assessment and, for the Performance Coaching Conversation, summarizes his or her understanding in a follow-up e-mail or memorandum. For the Annual Performance Analysis and Planning Conversation, the manager schedules a follow-up meeting with the performer to discuss and explain the final assessment rating (if required). The most important part of this step is the assurance that the manager and the organization do their part to support the employee's performance by providing the training, information, equipment, and other organizational support identified during either performance conversation.

The support of the manager includes observing the employee's performance, documenting performance events in an ongoing performance log, and holding periodic Performance Coaching Conversations as warranted, based on mutually agreed on frequency and emerging issues related to the employee's performance. It will also require that the manager recognize, reinforce, celebrate, and reward efforts and results that move the performer toward *great* performance. For employees experiencing performance problems, this affirmation means recognizing *any* degree of improvement—even if is simply that the employee is failing at a lesser rate!

Looking back at the Great Performance Management Cycle explored earlier in this chapter (figure 2-1), we can see that both the periodic Performance Coaching Conversation and Annual Performance Analysis and Planning Conversation naturally occur at the "evaluate performance" and "make improvements" phases of the cycle. If conducted well and frequently enough, however, the Performance Coaching Conversation becomes the core conversation upon which the partnership for performance is based and through which all phases of the GPM Cycle are routinely explored. Beyond simply the "evaluate performance" and "make improvements" phases of the cycle, the periodic Performance Coaching Conversation is the main vehicle through which the manager and the performer interact throughout the performance period.

How frequently should the Performance Coaching Conversation occur? Figure 2-3 highlights two hypothetical performance scenarios. The one scenario, for a performer named John, is based on the traditional "annual" review, where the intensive assessment and appraisal of John's past performance is conducted just once during the year-long performance period. Note that, in John's performance improvement path, the big improvements really happen only once during the year—immediately after the annual assessment. Although some improvements may occur in the intervening times, because the coaching conversations with his boss occur infrequently, John isn't always able to recognize or take advantage of improvement opportunities.

Figure 2-3. The Performance Paths of Two Employees

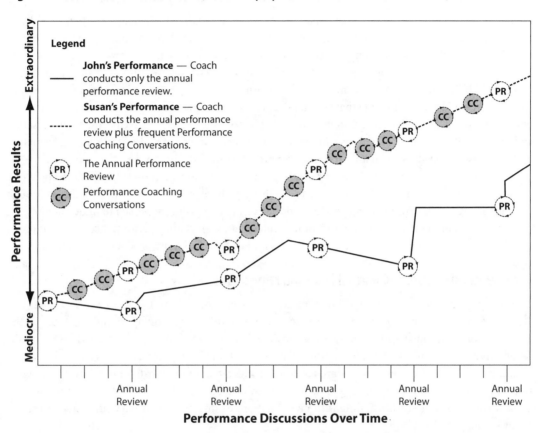

The second scenario displays the performance improvement path for Susan. In this scenario, frequent Performance Coaching Conversations take place in which Susan conducts a self-assessment and receives additional feedback on her *current* work from her manager. Note the emphasis on *current*. Whereas John's review looks back on the past 12 months, all the Performance Coaching Conversations with Susan look at what she is doing now. Only one of these coaching conversations—the Annual Performance Analysis and Planning Conversation—is the official "assessment," yet all conversations throughout the year contributed to her ongoing and incremental improvement in performance. The key issue here is that frequent coaching conversations between Susan and her manager led to frequent and ongoing adjustments and realignments of energy and effort over the course of the entire year by both Susan and her manager. When you compare Susan's improvement path to John's, the differences between the pace and angle of these hypothetical improvement trajectories is significant.

The Foundation for Effective Performance Coaching Conversations

We have provided you with a rough template that you can use with your managers to help establish a broad framework for effective employee-centered Performance Coaching Conversations and Annual Performance Analysis and Planning Conversations. This framework by itself, however, isn't enough to truly lead to the transformational approach to performance reviews that we think is vitally important. If you want to build a transformational mindset for performance management and reviews in your organization, then you'll need something that goes far deeper than our Great Performance Management Cycle or even the six critical reflection questions embedded in both the Performance Coaching Conversation and the Annual Performance Analysis and Planning Conversation. What's called for is a transformation in the mindsets of leaders and managers and, over time, the mindsets of those on the front line.

Fortunately, you don't have to invent or create this transformational mindset. We, with the help of a number of thought leaders who have preceded us in this area, have provided you with a roadmap through this important terrain. Our roadmap presents a powerful and compelling approach to understanding the origins of what often goes wrong in our daily human interactions—including performance conversations—and then offers a path for rewiring these interactions for healthier and more productive outcomes.

The Unilateral Control and Mutual Learning Mindsets

Our roadmap builds on the ground-breaking work of Chris Argyris and Donald Schön, which was continued by Roger Schwarz and others. The foundation of this new roadmap to understanding is the identification of the underlying mindset or worldview that we tend to carry around with us. Our mindset tells us how to act in a variety of situations that we face. From his research, Argyris has deduced that we draw on this mindset whenever we are confronted with situations that call for quick action or when we're under pressure to do something. Our working mindset is especially useful to us because it gives us a shorthand way of quickly dealing with new situations or threats rather than being forced to create a new strategy on the spot.

Argyris suggests that we each have two theories of action that we routinely call upon when we are presented with a situation that requires us to respond: our "espoused theory"—what we say we will do in this situation—and our "theory-in-use"—what we actually do in this situation. The problem with our theory-in-use, argues Argyris, is that it almost always operates below our own radar. We are unaware that it is steering our behaviors and actions; yet there it is, nudging us to act in ways that actually run counter to what we *say* we believe and intend to do. An example of this is when we *say* we value another person's perspective, but, when this person shares a perspective that is contrary to our own thinking, what we actually *do* is act in ways that may be dismissive and discounting of the other person.

The disconnect between what we say and what we actually do is especially prevalent when we find ourselves in difficult, stressful, or uncomfortable situations, such as when we feel threatened, exposed, or vulnerable—or when we experience a perceived loss of control. When we are embarrassed or psychologically threatened, we tend to activate a theory-in-use that, unfortunately, leads us to defensiveness, denial, blaming, rationalization, and justification. These feelings, in turn, lead to higher levels of misunderstanding and conflict with others. The deteriorating relationships that result further impair our ability to make the right decisions. As if this wasn't bad enough, our actions are worsened by the fact that most of this occurs outside of our consciousness. The net effect is significant erosion of our personal effectiveness and continuing deterioration of our relationships with those who are involved in the situation.

In their book *Theory in Practice* (1974), Argyris and Schön label this counterproductive theory-in-use Model 1. Robert Putnam, Diana McLain Smith, and Phil McArthur at Action Design, as well as Roger Schwarz in his book *The Skilled Facilitator* (2002), renamed this theory-in-use the "unilateral control model." Building on these earlier efforts, we have translated the key elements of these action science models, integrated insights from our own practice as consultants, and renamed this theory-in-use the "unilateral control mindset." The unilateral control mindset is characterized by defensive reasoning, a desire to win not lose, and an absence of insight and learning. *Mindset* is defined as a set of beliefs that determine a person's behavior and outlook. When our mindset is focused on unilateral control, especially one that flies below our radar, we are predisposed to a relatively narrow range of interpretations of and responses to various situations.

Figure 2-4 displays the unilateral control mindset and explores the set of predisposing values and assumptions, enacting behaviors, and consequences that are likely to occur when we, unthinking, bring this mindset into our relationships.

When we are in stressful, embarrassing, or psychologically threatening situations, our unilateral control mindset tends to kick in. As noted in figure 2-4, this mindset includes a set of governing values

Figure 2-4. Unilateral Control Mindset

Governing Values and Assumptions		Enacting Behaviors	Consequences
• Achieve your goals	• I am right, those who disagree with me are wrong	• Withhold information from others that may cause me embarrassment or expose a vulnerability	• Poor communication and limited understanding
• Win, don't lose	• Only I have a complete understanding of the facts	• Don't test assumptions, inferences, and judgments about others	• Root causes of challenges/difficulties are unexplored
• Minimize the expression or generation of negative feelings	• There is only one right answer—and it is mine	• Keep reasoning and intentions private	• Erosion in working relationships
• Act rationally	• Being open to another's perspective raises the possibility that I may be wrong—which I can't entertain	• Don't inquire into others' reasoning and intentions	• Lower levels of trust
• Be indifferent to others		• Decide and act unilaterally	• Higher interpersonal conflict
	• I have pure motives; those who disagree with me do not	• Be blind to inconsistencies in your reasoning and behavior	• Limited compassion
	• My feelings are justified	• Be blind to the effects of your decisions and actions on others	• Less than optimal results (e.g., productivity and performance)
		• Suppress feelings	• Shallow conversations
		• Prevent others from being hurt by covering up, withholding information, and "easing-into" difficult or sensitive issues	• Self-fulfilling, self-sealing processes
		• Don't question deeply held beliefs and behavioral patterns	• Limited or no learning

© 2009, Russell Consulting, Inc.

that are focused on achieving our goals, winning not losing, minimizing the expression or generation of negative feelings in ourselves and others (because negative feelings might lead to greater discomfort and to a loss of control), acting rationally and objectively (for example, the *facts* are on my side), and being indifferent to others and their interests. These governing values translate into a set of assumptions about ourselves and others, which, in turn, leads to a set of enacting behaviors that tend to be counterproductive to our relationships and what we want to achieve:

- believing in the rightness of our position

- keeping our thinking and reasoning private

- failing to test the assumptions we make about others, not inquiring into others' reasons and intentions

- withholding information that may lead to embarrassment

- assuming that we know all of the relevant facts

- refusing to hear alternative views

- feeling justified in our beliefs

- being blind to inconsistencies in our own reasoning and behavior

- mistrusting the motives of others

- preventing others from being hurt by "easing in" or covering up embarrassing information

- acting unilaterally.

Observing and taking action based on the unilateral control mindset, unfortunately, gives us false comfort. Although we unconsciously believe that sticking to the unilateral control mindset will help us achieve our goals, in reality the results that we hope to achieve for ourselves and our relationships become harder to attain. The harder we push using the unilateral control mindset, the less likely it becomes that our goals will be realized. Even if we experience a "victory" using this approach (when we "get our way"), the array of negative consequences spinning out of this illusory victory lead to a longer-term erosion in our effectiveness, leadership, authority, credibility, and relationships with others.

How does the unilateral control mindset work within performance reviews? Given the stressful and often psychologically uncomfortable nature of the traditional performance review, it is almost inevitable that both the manager and employee end up using the unilateral control mindset in his or her approach to the review. Acting rationally, being right, minimizing negative feelings, being in control, and winning seem to be part of the natural mindset that both the manager and the employee are likely to assume, especially if the focus of the review is on delivering or receiving constructive feedback or bad news. Unfortunately, as we can see in figure 2-4, when both the manager and the employee use the unilateral control mindset, they actually move farther away from the communication, understanding, and the partnership for performance that is so essential for knowing the right thing to do and executing it.

Fortunately, another theory-in-use mindset is available to all of us that can lead us in the opposite direction of the unilateral control mindset. This alternative mindset, which Argyris and Schön call

Figure 2-5. Mutual Learning Mindset

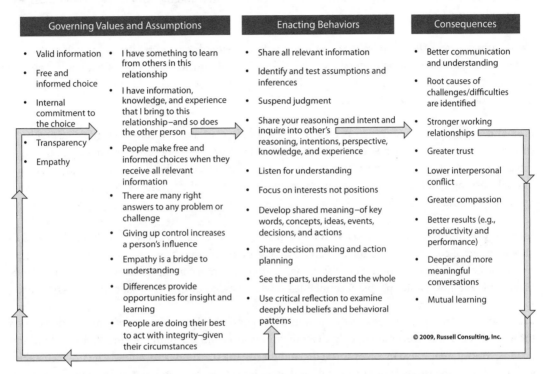

Governing Values and Assumptions	Enacting Behaviors	Consequences
• Valid information • Free and informed choice • Internal commitment to the choice • Transparency • Empathy	• I have something to learn from others in this relationship • I have information, knowledge, and experience that I bring to this relationship–and so does the other person • People make free and informed choices when they receive all relevant information • There are many right answers to any problem or challenge • Giving up control increases a person's influence • Empathy is a bridge to understanding • Differences provide opportunities for insight and learning • People are doing their best to act with integrity–given their circumstances	• Share all relevant information • Identify and test assumptions and inferences • Suspend judgment • Share your reasoning and intent and inquire into other's reasoning, intentions, perspective, knowledge, and experience • Listen for understanding • Focus on interests not positions • Develop shared meaning–of key words, concepts, ideas, events, decisions, and actions • Share decision making and action planning • See the parts, understand the whole • Use critical reflection to examine deeply held beliefs and behavioral patterns	• Better communication and understanding • Root causes of challenges/difficulties are identified • Stronger working relationships • Greater trust • Lower interpersonal conflict • Greater compassion • Better results (e.g., productivity and performance) • Deeper and more meaningful conversations • Mutual learning

© 2009, Russell Consulting, Inc.

"Model II" and "Action Design," and Schwarz calls the mutual learning model, represents the set of values, assumptions, and actions that facilitate insight, learning, and growth. Our term for this approach is the "mutual learning mindset"—a mindset premised on a set of values, assumptions, and behaviors that are profoundly different from the unilateral control approach. Because the mutual learning mindset starts from a different set of governing values and assumptions than the unilateral control mindset, the end result is profoundly different. Figure 2-5 summarizes the key components of the mutual learning mindset.

Governing Values and Assumptions That Support Mutual Learning

The governing values and assumptions of the mutual learning mindset represent a significant shift away from the unilateral control approach. The broad focus of the mutual learning mindset is embedded in a pervasive openness and receptivity to alternative perspectives and learning. As a result of this different orientation, there is also a critical shift toward an array of significantly positive outcomes. For a manager or performer facing the Performance Coaching Conversation or Annual Performance Analysis and Planning Conversation, moving toward mutual learning leads to a stronger performance partnership, better communication and understanding, an earlier identification of performance challenges, and more effective solutions to these challenges.

Let's first take a detailed look at the governing values and underlying assumptions that enable these positive outcomes from the Performance Coaching Conversation and the Annual Performance Analysis and Planning Conversation.

Valid information. All information relevant to the issue being discussed is shared in such a way that all parties to the conversation understand what they need to know to make a decision. For the mutual learning mindset to work, the decisions people make and the actions they take must be based on valid information that is anchored in facts and observable behaviors, actions, and results.

Free and informed choice. When people have valid information, they can then make an *informed* choice. When they do so in an environment that is free from pressure, coercion, and manipulation, and is based on trust instead of fear or defensiveness, then their choice is likely to be a *free* choice. For the mutual learning mindset to work, each party to an interaction makes choices freely and willingly that are based on valid information.

Internal Commitment to Decisions Made. When people participate in decision making, they tend to have an internal commitment to the decisions made. As a result, they tend to display a greater willingness to be held accountable for their decisions and actions. Internal commitment to decisions in the mutual learning mindset holds people accountable for what they say or do—or what they *don't* say or do.

Transparency. Transparency asserts that people make good decisions and take informed actions when those involved in a conversation openly share the motivation and reasoning behind their thinking and actions. Transparency also involves surfacing and discussing the "undiscussables." The undiscussables are those topics and issues in our relationships that we don't talk about and that, in keeping them silent, create barriers to communication, understanding, empathy, and informed action. When people operate from a mindset based on transparency, they tend to be more open, honest, and direct about what they think and why they think that way.

Empathy. People who practice empathy in their relationships bring a willingness to reach out to others to understand their differing viewpoints and have compassion for other people's circumstances. When understanding, empathy, and compassion are present in a relationship, each person displays a genuine concern for the other's perspective. When people act based on empathy, they tend to be more open and receptive, less defensive, and better able to appreciate where others are coming from.

These governing values collectively shape a set of assumptions that complete the affirming and open mindset of the mutual learning mindset. Following the assumptions described in figure 2-5, a manager using the mutual learning mindset in both the Performance Coaching Conversation and the Annual Performance Analysis and Planning Conversation should approach this interaction with several assumptions:

- I have something to learn about the employee's performance and about the employee in general, if I pay attention.

- I have some information about the employee's performance, and the employee also has information from his or her perspective. Each of us may see things related to the employee's performance that the other may not see.

- The employee makes conscious choices about his or her performance based on the information that he or she has available. These choices make sense to him or her even when they may not make sense to me. In making these informed choices freely and voluntarily, the employee is more likely to be committed to great performance, take ownership for his or her own performance, and conduct an objective self-assessment of his or her performance.

- There are actually many right ways to achieve performance goals, overcome challenges, and so forth. By being receptive to these alternative ways of moving forward, new pathways and solutions will reveal themselves.

- If I give up the need to control the outcomes of this performance conversation and focus instead on listening and understanding with empathy, my ability to influence the employee's future behavior will be strengthened.

- If I bring understanding and empathy into my relationship with this person, this empathy can form the foundation of a working relationship based on appreciation of differences.

- The differences in perspective, knowledge, expectations, and so forth, between me and the performer provide us both with opportunities for insight and learning. This insight and learning can lead to more effective action planning for improving performance in both of us.

- The employee is doing his or her best to act with integrity in his or her situation. The employee has good intentions and motives—even when these intentions and motives aren't clear to me.

Imagine how the traditional performance review is transformed when the manager consciously moves away from the unilateral control mindset and instead takes up the mutual learning mindset. The focus of the review shifts away from the traditional appraisal that only renders the manager's judgment of the employee's performance and toward an open and constructive conversation that seeks to uncover, understand, and address obstacles to performance. The overarching purpose of the mutual learning mindset fits perfectly with the focus of the Performance Coaching Conversation and the Annual Performance Analysis and Planning Conversation, which is to strengthen the partnership between the manager and the performer through communication, understanding, insight, and learning. When both parties embrace the values of valid information, transparency, free and informed choice, internal commitment to decisions, transparency, and empathy, each will experience performance gains. The employee's performance improves because he or she is working on the right things and feels the support of the manager, and the manager's performance improves because his or her coaching conversations are having positive effects on employee performance. This, in turn, reflects positively on the manager's approach to leading and guiding others.

Behaviors that Support Mutual Learning

The governing values and assumptions of the mutual learning mindset form the backbone of the Performance Coaching Conversation and the Annual Performance Analysis and Planning Conversation. Translating these values and assumptions into the interactions between the parties of this partnership is the required next step if mutual learning is to occur, which leads to performance improvement. Let's end this chapter by examining these enacting behaviors, which are deeply anchored to the values and assumptions of mutual learning and which enable the manager to successfully guide the employee toward great performance through well-crafted Performance Coaching Conversations and Annual Performance Analysis and Planning Conversations.

Based on the work of Argyris, Schön, Putnam, Smith, and Schwarz, we have identified 10 enacting behaviors or strategies that, when practiced by those interested in mutual learning, have a profound and positive effect on both the individual's effectiveness and the individual's relationships with others.

Share all relevant information. Managers and performers can only make informed decisions with the GPM Cycle when they have all the necessary information. Good problem solving and decision making within the GPM Cycle depends on a full airing of information regarding expectations, measurement, frustrations, anxieties, opportunities, hopes, and so forth. This requires both manager and performer to actively participate in dialogue with each other to say what they are thinking, what they know, and how they each view the situation before them. Within a coaching conversation, sharing all relevant information also involves either party saying "I don't have an opinion" or "I don't have anything to add to what you have offered" rather than remaining silent and causing the other person to *wonder* if the person is sharing all relevant information.

Identify and test assumptions and inferences. This enacting behavior pushes back on the common tendency for us to make assumptions and inferences about others and then fail to actually verify whether these assumptions and inferences are true. The mutual learning mindset requires that when we make an assumption about someone else's motivation or intentions, we stop and verify whether we have assumed or inferred correctly instead of taking our assumptions and inferences as fact.

Within the GPM Cycle, when a manager observes a performer making statements, making decisions, or taking actions, it is essential that the manager not make assumptions or inferences about or speculate on the performer's intentions or motivations. The manager needs to verify his or her assumptions and inferences about the other person. This enacting behavior first involves the manager *identifying* when he or she is making an assumption or inference, then testing the assumption or inference directly by asking the other person for more information. The best way to do this is simply by asking the performer for more information: *"When you missed the deadline for completing the report, I assumed that you didn't understand the importance of the due date. Was that a correct assumption on my part or have I missed something? What caused you to miss the deadline?"*

Suspend judgment. In our normal conversations, we tend to make quick value judgments about what others have said or done. We view others' statements or actions as good, bad, right, wrong, foolish, bold, brutish, bullying, caring, and so forth, often without hard data behind our conclusions. When we fail to suspend our judgments about others, we tend to create a self-sealing, self-fulfilling unilateral control mindset that becomes a barrier to insight, learning, and the discovering of the real factors underlying problems and challenges. Using the mutual learning mindset within the GPM Cycle, an effective manager must test his or her assumptions and suspend his or her judgments about the performer. By suspending judgments, the best managers put enough distance between their judgments and themselves to free them from having to act on or be influenced by them.

Share your reasoning and intent, and inquire into others' reasoning, intentions, perspective, knowledge, and experience. When we share our reasoning and intent with others and inquire into others' reasoning and intent, we honor the governing value of transparency. When both party's thinking and reasoning are transparent, we are far more likely to discover common ground and fields of mutual interest.

When used by a manager within a coaching conversation, this enacting behavior enables the performer to see how a manager reached his or her conclusions and judgments and to then explore areas of the manager's reasoning, especially when the performer may have reasoned differently. When managers explain to their performers *why* they think the way they do about something or why they made the statement they did, it enables the performers to better understand the basis for the managers' words and actions and their purpose or reasons for doing something. The second half of this behavior involves managers actively *inquiring* into the performer's reasoning, intent, perspective, and so forth. When people genuinely inquire into another person's reasoning and intentions, they are able to better understand and appreciate what lies behind the other person's words and actions. Mutual learning naturally evolves from the rich dialogue that emerges from this sharing of reasoning and intentions and an appreciation of divergent experience and backgrounds.

Listen for understanding. The mutual learning mindset depends on the skill of reflective listening, with a focus on understanding and appreciating another's perspective. When we are engaged with others in conversation, true understanding of each other's perspectives and interests is only possible through reflective listening.

During a coaching conversation, reflective listening involves paying attention to what lies behind the words of the other party. The listener then "mirrors," or paraphrases, what is learned back to the speaker in such a way that demonstrates his or her understanding. Reflective listening enables the speaker to confirm or disconfirm what the listener understood, leading to a deeper understanding of what the other was saying and thinking. A manager benefits from reflective listening behavior by gaining insight and a better understanding of why the performer is thinking and acting as he or she does. An employee benefits from this critical behavior in two ways: by knowing that he or she has been truly heard and by better understanding why the manager is thinking and acting as he or she does.

Focus on interests, not positions. Rather than focusing on positions (which we tend to defend and hold), this enacting behavior helps us focus on better understanding by sharing our *interests* and exploring the interests of others. Our interests reflect the underlying needs and desires we have in a given situation. When we focus on exploring interests, we are more likely to end up with win-win solutions. Based on the important work *Getting to Yes* (1991) by Roger Fisher and James Ury of the Harvard Negotiation Project, this behavior, if practiced well, enables us to move beyond argument, posturing, and win-lose dichotomies and toward win-win outcomes.

When both the manager and the performer focus on understanding each other's *interests* during the coaching conversation, uncovering root causes of and discovering solutions to performance problems is far easier. If, instead, both parties focus on their *positions* (for example, I am right, I am your boss, You are wrong, My view is what counts, and so forth), they would tend to *defend* and protect these positions, which profoundly limits their understanding, agreement, and learning, and makes a win-win outcome much less likely.

Develop shared meaning of key words, concepts, ideas, events, decisions, and actions. Giving specific examples in our interactions with others (for example names, dates, times, places, the meaning of key terms or concepts, and so forth) assists in providing information that is relevant to the conversation and enables people, in turn, to clarify their understanding and make an independent judgment on the validity of the example. As a result, when we use specific examples in our conversations with others, we are more able to have an informed discussion on the issues before us.

Within Performance Coaching Conversations, one of the most critical behaviors for both the manager and performer is developing shared meaning of specific dates, times, places, and key words or concepts (that is, for vague terms such as commitment, success, *great* performance, or acceptable) related to the employee's performance. When there is agreement on these events, words, concepts, and so forth, both the manager and performer are able to work from a shared understanding of the events and words instead of drawing different conclusions and going off in different directions. On matters related to employee performance, going off in different directions can have serious consequences for both the performer and the manager.

Share decision making and action planning. When we act unilaterally, we attempt to impose "our way" and our will on others. Unfortunately, although we may feel righteous and true in our actions, this approach does little to build effective relationships with others. Even when we act unilaterally using softer language and actions, if we insist that our way is the only way, communication, understanding, empathy, and trust will inevitably deteriorate. Bringing shared decision making and action planning into managing the performance of others involves managers working *with* their employees to jointly decide on a plan of action.

Rather than imposing their way of thinking on the performer, then, managers share their own ideas and the reasoning behind them and invite the performers to share their thoughts and inquire into their supporting reasoning. Based on the shared understanding that emerges from this conversation, the manager and performer then jointly decide the next logical steps that each should take. This enacting behavior is premised on one of the core tenants of Goal Theory, by Edwin Locke, which postulates that involvement in setting goals, rather than having goals imposed without explanation, tends to form a higher commitment to the goal (Locke and Latham, 2002).

You might wonder why a manager, with all of the organizational authority to be unilateral in this relationship, would choose anything other than the unilateral approach—especially on matters related to performance improvement. Although a manager certainly has the right to choose the unilateral approach, it is not an approach that leads to a strong partnership for performance, good communication and understanding, or increased commitment by the performer to great performance. Our objective in all of our coaching conversations and in the entire partnership for performance is to guide the employee toward great performance; therefore, we need to use a collaborative decision-making approach that maximizes the employee's participation in and commitment to their own improvement plan. Yes, the unilateral approach is always an option for a manager—but it should be the option of *last* resort.

See the parts, understand the whole. By gathering all valid information in a given situation, we can appreciate the pieces of the larger puzzle and make an informed choice about what to do next. Mutual learning, however, moves beyond the parts, to consider the larger context and the fabric of the whole. People are moved to make decisions and take action in their lives based on pieces *and* the whole. By understanding the whole, instead of looking only at the parts, we can begin to appreciate why people do what they do. The larger context of their lives is as much responsible for their decisions and actions as a specific event or circumstance. When we see things holistically, we tend to be more empathetic and understanding toward others and, therefore, more open to their experience, perspective, insights, and so forth.

Within Performance Coaching Conversations, it is essential that the manager sees the performer's decisions and actions in this larger context. Focusing on specific behaviors and actions is an important part of every Performance Coaching Conversation, but understanding the larger context can help the manager gain greater insight into the array of causes that leads the performer to think, decide, and act in specific ways. When the manager understands the whole—all of the forces and factors that influence the performer as he or she approaches a task—the manager will be able to know how best to intervene and help the performer get back on track.

Use critical reflection to examine deeply held beliefs and behavioral patterns. Critical reflection is the capacity to think deliberately about something in such a way that our underlying beliefs are open to challenge and change. Socrates once said that "the unexamined life is not worth living." When forced by his prosecutors to choose between giving up his life or being banished from society and dialogue with others, he chose death (Plato, *The Apology of Socrates*, 28c). Socrates valued a close examination of his beliefs and the beliefs of others more than his life. He challenged us to critically examine our deeply held beliefs and behavioral patterns in such a way that we are aware of their power and role in our life and are then able to entertain and explore alternative beliefs and behaviors that may be more facilitative of understanding and learning.

Critical reflection, when used by managers within their Performance Coaching Conversations, compels those managers to challenge closely held beliefs (about themselves and others) and question the behaviors that they tend to use without thinking. The result of such deep inquiry can lead managers to personal insights as well as openness and receptivity to different ways of thinking, acting, and relating to others. Through the opening created by critical reflection, managers can learn new information from performers and entertain alternative ways of seeing their performers and the performance challenges that they face.

The Challenges of Achieving the Mutual Learning Mindset

Most of us readily use the mutual learning mindset in our everyday relationships. We want to infuse our relationships with honesty, compassion, open-mindedness, and learning. Somehow, though, in the actual reality of most of our lives, our behavior tends to belie our words: We are generally unable to consistently act in ways that truly focus on mutual learning. Although most of us want to replace the unilateral control mindset with the more forward-thinking mutual learning mindset, doing so is often very difficult. In spite of themselves, people tend to use the unilateral control mindset because they have been socialized by their families, schools, and workplaces to use this approach to human interactions. Despite the misunderstandings, false assumptions, illusion of control, and erroneous judgments that spiral out of the unilateral control mindset—and the resulting conflict, frustration, discord, and unhappiness it creates—we continue to use this counterproductive approach. This happens because most people remain unaware of an alternative, such as the mutual learning mindset, and their surrounding culture tends to operate from a unilateral control perspective (Argyris, Putnam, and Smith, 1985). Finally, moving toward a mutual learning mindset is difficult because it involves more than just adopting a short list of behaviors to memorize. Changing from a unilateral control mindset to a mutual learning mindset involves altering the underlying set of values and assumptions that structure how we engage the world. Changing our behaviors is relatively easy; changing the underlying values behind these behaviors is far more difficult.

As a result, introducing the mutual learning mindset will not be an easy task. A great way to begin pushing back against the unilateral control mindset autopilot for your organization is to introduce a compelling alternative. Performance Coaching Conversations are a key strategy for creating understanding and providing direction to people throughout your organization, so this is the place to begin. By integrating the mutual learning mindset into the conversations throughout the workshops that follow, you begin laying down fundamental infrastructure that reinforces an alternative to the unilateral control mindset. The transformational alternative you will offer managers and employees alike through these workshops will significantly improve the quality of the performance conversations that occur throughout the organization.

In this expansive chapter, we have explored the Great Performance Management Cycle, discussed the role of manager and performer within this cycle, examined the purpose of performance reviews, and identified some common problems with the traditional review. We then offered an employee-centered alternative to the review process called the Performance Coaching and Annual Performance Analysis and Planning Conversations—conversations that are centered on communication, understanding, and mutual learning, leading toward great performance. Finally, we introduced a new mindset that, if adopted by both managers and performers, has the potential to transform the quality of the interactions, decisions, and intentions that occur within the partnership for performance. Our mutual learning mindset, as well as the governing values, assumptions, and enacting behaviors that bring this mindset to life, represent a powerful new approach to dialogue that strengthens the working relationship between the manager and the performer and leads to improved performance in each.

Once you have assessed your organization's performance management culture and infrastructure and defined the key competencies you'll focus on developing in leaders, managers, supervisors, and employees, you're ready to take the first steps in designing your performance management, performance coaching, and performance review programs.

 ## What to Do Next

- Develop your strategies for gathering data on leader, manager, supervisor, and employee perceptions of performance management, coaching, and reviews as practiced in the organization.

- Work closely with the team that is responsible for managing or designing the organization's overall performance management system. Share what you are learning through your assessment and offer your insights into ways to strengthen the performance management system. Work with this team to decide on the core performance management competencies to be developed in your training initiative.

- Begin developing ideas for integrating the key insights, mindsets, and approaches from this chapter into your performance management research. Your challenge will be to bring together the best thinking on performance management and reviews with your organization's culture and current practices.

Assessing Your Performance Management Culture and Competencies

3

What's in This Chapter?

- Strategies and approaches for needs assessment

- Strategies and approaches for assessing the organization's culture and infrastructure

- Strategies and approaches supporting meaningful performance reviews

- Strategies and approaches determining the core performance management competencies that need to be developed in leaders, managers, supervisors, and frontline employees

▲   ▲   ▲

Assessing the Organizational Culture and Infrastructure

You have been given the task of designing skill-building workshops on performance reviews, and you think you have a good sense of what your boss wants. Perhaps you even have an idea of how you might design and develop a set of integrated workshops that will give your managers and supervisors the skills they need to conduct an effective review.

Not so fast! This chapter asks you to slow down a bit to look into the heart of the request for a training program on performance reviews and ask some bigger questions. The first set of these questions aims at gaining a better understanding of the organizational culture in which the performance reviews will take place. Is this culture a performance-oriented culture? To what extent might the cultural beliefs, values, and norms *reinforce* or, worse, *undermine* your skill-building efforts?

Another set of questions explores the existence or absence of a supportive performance infrastructure. Your approach for designing performance review workshops for an environment in which good systems are already in place for measuring organization, work area, and individual performance will be quite different from your approach for work environments in which these systems are absent. To help you find the answers to these questions, we'll guide you through a process of documenting your organization's performance management infrastructure.

The final set of questions relates to the performance management, coaching, and review skills that are most critical for development. We will offer you some ideas for discovering the core performance competencies that should become the focus of your performance review training and development efforts.

Your first step must be to assess these issues—organizational culture, performance infrastructure, and performance management competencies—*before* you design the performance review training program. The answers you find from these assessments will shape every part of your training program design. From defining your desired outcomes and deciding on the key skills that need development to timing training program delivery and reinforcing the application of learning, you will use the results from this assessment to guide every step you take.

Gathering Information on Your Organization

We'll discuss three approaches for gathering information on your organization's culture, the performance management infrastructure, and the core performance management competencies: interviews, focus groups, and surveys.

Structured Interviews

One-on-one interviews are an especially effective way to explore all of these organizational issues. Generally, the interviews should be structured such that approximately the same questions are asked of all participants. You should identify a sample of people who represent a cross-section of your organization. This should include, at a minimum, representatives from the executive leadership team, managers, frontline supervisors, and employees from different work areas. If your organization has individuals who telecommute or who work or are managed remotely, understanding and integrating this perspective into your data is especially important. Each interview should last no more than 45 minutes to an hour and should provide an opportunity for participants to offer their thoughts both in response to your questions and on their own initiative (in the context of the interview's focus). After you complete the interviews, you will summarize the results by highlighting key themes and trends emerging from this qualitative data.

Focus Groups

Focus groups allow you to probe many of the same issues that you explore in your interviews, but in a far more dynamic and interactive way. In response to the questions you pose to the group, you can facilitate participants' reactions to each other's comments and move beyond your initial questions to explore their ideas, approaches, and solutions at a deeper level. Your purpose in using focus groups is more on identifying and exploring diverse perspectives and issues rather than developing consensus around a given issue or proposal.

The interactivity within the group and the opportunity to explore the issues in greater depth are the strongest selling points for using focus groups as a source of your information. As with interviews, you should draw your participants from a diverse cross-section of your organization. Whether you create homogeneous (similar in kind) or heterogeneous (diverse and dissimilar in kind) groups, each group should be asked the same set of core questions, with an opportunity for deeper exploration as necessary. Similar to your objectives within the structured interview, your goal in analyzing the focus group data is to highlight the key themes and trends in what people are saying.

Online or Paper Surveys

The survey—whether distributed and completed online or using paper and pencil—provides a fast and relatively inexpensive way to gather information from a large number of your organization's staff. As with the other forms of gathering information identified in this chapter, you should ensure that you have sampled a diverse cross-section of your organization. This increases your confidence that you can generalize your findings to the entire organization.

Although surveys are the most effective approach for reaching the greatest number of people, they are largely a one-way feedback mechanism. It isn't easy to ask survey respondents follow-up or clarifying questions when what they have written isn't clear or is incomplete. Without the back and forth that's possible in the interview and focus group, exploring the depth of respondents' ideas is difficult.

Constructing a survey can sometimes seem intimidating. Getting the wording of your questions right, such that you actually measure what you think you are measuring (question validity) can indeed be tricky. Keep in mind, however, that your goal is simply to gather information on employees' perceptions of performance reviews, performance management, and the organization's culture. We encourage you not to fret about validity and instead focus on asking a few simple questions that get people thinking and responding. Open-ended questions are always a good way to find out what people are really thinking (for example, *In general, how could this organization improve its performance review process?*). Questions or statements that use a forced-choice Likert-type scale are especially useful for zeroing in on specific issues (for example, indicate the extent of your agreement with the following statement using the six-point scale: *My manager gives me specific feedback on my performance at least twice a year.*). It is not as difficult as you may think to develop good questions that help you achieve a better understanding of employee attitudes and perceptions.

For all of these forms of data gathering, the quality and usefulness of the data you receive depends on the quality of the questions, the diversity and distribution of the sample of people you involve, and how you analyze the resulting data. We recommend that you use all three methods of data gathering in your research. This approach, which we call *triangulation*, helps you understand a single construct—employee and manager attitudes toward and perceptions of performance reviews—using three different data collection methods. Each method explores the same issue in a slightly different way, and each contributes to a more holistic understanding of the topic. Although we recommend this three-dimensional research approach, you will need to decide what to do based on the information you want to collect, how much interaction you want with your participants, the importance of gathering information from as many people as possible, the need to gain a deep understanding of key stakeholder perceptions of the issues, and how much time and resources you have available.

Questions to Explore in Your Research

The specific issues and questions you decide to explore in your needs assessment and research depend on the primary focus of your training and development efforts as well as how much information you believe you need to design and deliver a program that matches your organization's requirements. The questions that follow, organized by the area of exploration, can be modified to be included in any method you use for data collection.

Assessing Your Performance-Oriented Culture and Infrastructure

Before you design your training program for performance reviews, you need to explore the extent to which the organization's culture supports or undermines effective performance management. When you explore the organization's culture, you examine the underlying beliefs, principles, values, and actual behaviors that influence overall behavior up and down the organizational chart.

Our experience is that you ignore culture at your peril. You may roll out a top-notch skill-building program that gives people a new set of tools for management performance, only to have the new tools undercut by a set of underlying values that may say: *When push comes to shove, it's who you know, not what you achieve, that determines your success here* or *People on the front line are accountable for their daily performance; those with power aren't.* These and any number of other beliefs can quietly work to undermine your skill-building efforts.

Similarly, if your organization doesn't have a strong, consistent, and effective set of policies, methods, practices, and reinforcers—all elements of the performance management infrastructure—then your top-notch development program may again fail. This time, however, failure may be attributable to the lack of an integrated system that makes managing performance comprehensive, consistent, easy, and effective.

Exploring both the culture and infrastructure is perhaps best done through focus groups and interviews—but there are a number of issues here that may also be examined through written or online surveys. Here are our ideas for possible areas to include in your inquiry:

- In general, are people at all levels of the organization held accountable for their performance? Please explain your answer.

- What do you see as the *assets*, or strengths, of this organization when it comes to achieving desired performance outcomes at either the individual or group level?

- In this organization, what are the most significant obstacles or barriers to holding people accountable for their performance?

- What words would you use to describe the performance review process here?

- On a six-point scale (with 1 = Strongly Disagree and 6 = Strongly Agree), indicate your level of agreement with each of the following statements:

  ◦ My annual/bi-annual performance review gives me useful feedback on my performance.

  ◦ My manager/supervisor gives me formal feedback on my performance at least twice a year.

  ◦ I look forward to (either *giving* or *receiving*) performance reviews.

- The standards by which my performance is evaluated are objective.

- My manager/supervisor asks me to rate my own performance prior to conducting my performance reviews.

- My manager/supervisor and I have frequent informal discussions about my performance throughout the year.

- The annual/semi-annual performance review provides me with an opportunity to identify obstacles and barriers to my performance.

- The annual/semi-annual performance review provides me with an opportunity to discuss my professional and career goals.

- In this organization, we tend to focus on blaming rather than exploring the causes of problems.

- In this organization, employees tend to be intimidated by those who have power.

- In this organization, people who do good work are rewarded and those who don't do good work experience negative consequences.

- In this organization, effective measurement systems provide useful quantitative performance feedback to teams and individuals.

- In this organization, what you accomplish determines your success.

- In this organization, people are held accountable for the results they achieve.

- Who you know in this organization determines your future far more than what you accomplish.

- My performance goals are clear to me.

- My performance goals reflect the organization's vision and strategy.

- I am actively involved in setting my own performance goals.

- I have the resources, tools, technology, and equipment that enable me to do my job well.

- If you were to design the "perfect" performance review and feedback system, what would it look like?

- What, from your perspective, are the key performance drivers in this organization? In other words, what measures of performance are the most important here?

- In general, are all people in this organization held to the same performance standards?

- If the leaders of this organization could do one thing to support an effective system for managing performance here, what would it be?

- Give me a *positive* example of how this organization manages performance at the group or individual level.

- What do you see as the greatest barrier to an effective performance management system in this organization?

- What could this organization do to reinforce managers and supervisors effectively using the skills and knowledge of performance management, coaching, and reviews?

Assessing Performance Management and Review Competencies

The core competencies that support effective performance management and reviews should be explored using all three data-collection methods that we have identified. Surveys are especially useful for assessing the skill levels on a wide variety of performance management and performance review behaviors of both managers and employees.

Let's first look at a range of issues that lend themselves to an online or paper-based survey. *On a six-point scale (with 1 = Strongly Disagree and 6 = Strongly Agree), indicate your level of agreement with each of the following statements*:

- My manager/supervisor is skilled at giving me constructive feedback on my performance.

- My manager/supervisor asks me to rate my own performance prior to conducting my performance reviews.

- My manager/supervisor and I have frequent informal discussions on my performance throughout the year.

- My manager/supervisor works with me to set specific and challenging performance goals.

- My manager/supervisor listens to my perspectives, ideas, and concerns related to my performance.

- My manager/supervisor provides honest feedback to me on my performance.

- My manager/supervisor's expectations for my performance are clear to me.

- At least twice each year, my manager/supervisor discusses my performance goals and my success in achieving these goals.

- My manager/supervisor recognizes my accomplishments.

- There is good two-way communication between my manager/supervisor and myself.

- I feel free to approach my manager/supervisor with my work-related questions and concerns.

- My manager/supervisor provides the assistance and support I need to achieve my performance goals.

- My manager/supervisor supports me when I take appropriate risks—even those that fail.

- My manager/supervisor encourages me to increase my knowledge and grow in my work.

- My manager/supervisor has taken steps to ensure that my work-related skills are updated in a timely fashion.

- If I were to have problems accomplishing my performance goals, I would feel comfortable asking my manager/supervisor to help me get back on track.

- My manager/supervisor encourages my participation in managing my performance.

- My manager/supervisor is able to adjust his/her management and coaching style based on what I need to perform at my best.

As we indicated earlier in this chapter, focus groups and interviews are especially good for exploring issues at a deeper level. You can use this deeper approach for exploring performance management competencies by investigating these issues:

- What are the strengths of this organization in relation to performance management, performance coaching, and performance reviews? How have these strengths been expressed? How are they evident and visible?

- What skills and knowledge are most important for us to develop in our *managers* and *supervisors* to enable them to effectively manage performance and conduct performance reviews? Why are these skills and knowledge the most important to develop?

- What skills and knowledge should be developed in *employees* to enable them to be effective participants in their performance reviews and in managing their own performance?

- What is the best way to develop these skills and knowledge areas in managers and employees? Some approaches include half- and full-day workshops, online learning modules, informal supervisory forums and "brown bags," and coaching and mentoring of individual managers.

- Identify someone who, in your experience, has nearly perfected the art of managing and coaching others. Describe for me what this person does so well that enables him or her to be especially good at this important role?

- What do you see as the biggest obstacles or barriers to managers and supervisors *applying* what they learn back to their job and in their everyday coaching relationships with their employees? How might we reduce or eliminate this obstacle?

Once you have assessed your organization's performance management culture and infrastructure and defined the key competencies you'll focus on developing in leaders, managers, supervisors, and employees, you're ready to take the first steps toward designing your performance management, coaching, and review programs.

 ## What to Do Next

- Develop your strategies for gathering data on leader, manager, supervisor, and employee perceptions of performance management, coaching, and reviews as practiced in the organization.

- Work closely with the team responsible for managing or designing the organization's overall performance management system. Share what you are learning through your assessments and offer your insights into ways to strengthen the performance management system. Work with this team to decide on the core performance management competencies that will be developed in your training initiative.

- Review the next chapter to learn how to design and facilitate dynamic educational programs that encourage participant involvement in and ownership of their own learning.

Turning People on to Learning 4

What's in This Chapter?

- The fundamentals of adult learning
- Strategies for supporting the transfer of training
- Strategies for designing effective training programs
- Keys to effective facilitation

▲ ▲ ▲

Training doesn't ensure that learning occurs, but it is a powerful tool for developing the critical competencies needed to meet the challenges facing any organization. This chapter offers some key insights into how people learn best, which will enable you to design training programs that actively engage people in their own learning and growth. This involvement, in turn, will enable them to successfully do their work, make decisions, solve problems, and contribute to creating great results for the customer.

The Fundamentals of Adult Learning

Although learning has always been a part of the human experience—often through necessity as much as desire or aspiration—some broad principles for guiding and facilitating adult learning in particular have emerged over the past 40 years. Drawn from the work of Knowles, Brookfield, and others, these core principles, along with implications and suggestions for the learning and teaching environment, are outlined in table 4-1.

Table 4-1. Key Principles of Adult Learning and Their Implications for Teaching and Training Design

ADULT LEARNING PRINCIPLE	IMPLICATION FOR TEACHING AND TRAINING DESIGN
Adults bring life experience and knowledge to the learning environment. This experience and knowledge includes work-related, family, and community events and circumstances. Adults learn best when they can relate new knowledge and information with previously learned knowledge, information, and experiences.	Provide opportunities for learners to reflect on and share their existing knowledge and experience. Create learning activities that involve the use of past experience or knowledge. Ask learners to identify the similarities and differences between what they are learning and what they already know.
Adults tend to prefer self-directed, autonomous learning—but this is often not an expectation of educational institutions and society.	Design training around participants' needs and goals. Ask participants what they want to learn. Learners learn best when they establish a specific learning objective or goal for themselves. Provide learner action planning tools and templates to help develop and focus their self-directed efforts and facilitate learning. Provide opportunities for learners to direct their own learning through guided inquiry and self-facilitated small-group discussions.
Adults have self-pride and desire respect. They need their experience, beliefs, knowledge, questions, and ideas acknowledged as important.	Because learning involves risk and the possibility of failure, design training to minimize each learner's risk and embarrassment. Provide opportunities for learners to share ideas, questions, opinions, experiences, concerns, etc., and to create an environment that honors and respects everything that is appropriately shared. Create flexible training programs that honor participants by accommodating their contributions and questions as much as possible. Make it safe for learners to express their confusion, anxieties, doubts, and fears.

continued on next page

Table 4-1. Key Principles of Adult Learning and Their Implications for Teaching and Training Design, *continued*

ADULT LEARNING PRINCIPLE	IMPLICATION FOR TEACHING AND TRAINING DESIGN
	Provide opportunities for "small wins" and little victories in the learning process—to build competencies incrementally.
Adults want practical, goal-oriented, and problem-centered learning that can immediately help them deal with life's challenges.	Ask learners to identify what they would like to learn about a topic.
	Establish clear learning objectives that make the connection between participant's needs and the learning content.
	Share examples and stories that relate the learning content to participant's current challenges. Ask learners to share their own examples that make this linkage.
	Engage learners in identifying the challenges they face and the value of learning in addressing these challenges.
	Follow theories with practical examples and applications to demonstrate the relevance of the learning.
Adults desire feedback on the progress they are making at learning something new.	Provide opportunities for learners to get immediate feedback to their own learning through case examples, role-playing, quizzes, and responses to trainer questions.
	Encourage learners to self-evaluate and assess their own learning and performance.
	Praise any level of learning improvement and encourage continued learning.
Adults have preferences for the way in which they learn. Some prefer learning by doing (kinesthetic), others prefer learning by observing (visual), whereas still others prefer learning by listening (auditory).	Recognize that not all learners will respond to a given teaching method or technique.
	Use a wide variety of methods that tap into all learner preferences in training delivery.

continued on next page

Table 4-1. Key Principles of Adult Learning and Their Implications for Teaching and Training Design, *continued*

ADULT LEARNING PRINCIPLE	IMPLICATION FOR TEACHING AND TRAINING DESIGN
	Use all three learning modes (kinesthetic, visual, and auditory) in every 20-minute teaching interval.
	Make trainers aware their own learning preferences and wary of favoring this approach in their own teaching.
	Free learners to learn in the style that best suits them by using small group work, dyadic discussions, and individual activities.
Adults learn best through collaboration and reciprocity—an environment in which people learn with others while sharing what they already know.	Provide a low-risk environment for learning while capitalizing on the different levels of knowledge and skill within a group by using small group work and dyadic discussion.
	Strengthen learner self-esteem through team-based learning, based on mutual trust and respect.
	Use small-group learning to more accurately reflect the participants' interdependent and collaborative work environment back on the job.
Adults are motivated to learn by a wide variety of factors. These are the most common: personal aspirations, externally imposed expectations, internal desire or interest, escape from a situation (boredom or fear), growth and advancement, and service to others.	Inquire into the reasons participants are interested in learning.
	Invite learners to identify the link between learning and the satisfaction of a personal need or a reduction in an external stress or threat.
	Make a connection between the learning content and each learner's long-range objectives (in work and life).
	Ask participants to discuss in pairs and small groups the short- and long-term benefits of learning the program's content.

Supporting the Transfer of Training

The goal of training involves more than simply teaching essential skills and knowledge to participants. It also involves ensuring that what is learned in the workshop is "transferred" to the workplace. The transfer of training should be of the utmost importance to the trainer because if a trainee learns what is desired but is unable or unwilling to apply this new learning back on the job, the trainer's time and the organization's resources have been squandered. For this reason, the "transfer problem" has been the focus of considerable debate and research.

In their book *Transfer of Training* (1992), Mary Broad and John Newstrom offer a powerful model to better understand and influence the transfer of training. They designed and tested a transfer of training matrix that combines the three key roles involved in the learning experience (trainee, trainer, and manager) and the three time phases associated with training delivery (before, during, and after). The results of their research offer some important insights into the best roles and times to support the maximum transfer of learning to the workplace.

As shown in table 4-2, Broad and Newstrom's research revealed that the most powerful influence on the effective transfer of training from the workshop to the workplace is the manager's support for the learning *prior* to the training event. The second most powerful role and time period is the trainer taking steps to prepare the trainee prior to the training event. The third most powerful impact on effective transfer was found to be the manager's support and reinforcement of learning following the skill training.

Broad and Newstrom's research, which was based on interviews with expert trainers, indicates that ensuring both the manager and the trainer are doing the right things at the right time will provide the maximum benefit. With this in mind, here are a few suggested actions for managers, supervisors, and trainers that will help facilitate the transfer of training before, during, and after the training session.

Table 4-2. Perceptions of Most Powerful Role-Time Combinations for Using Transfer of Training Strategies

	Before	**During**	**After**
Manager	1	8	3
Trainer	2	4	9
Learner	7	5	6

Key: 1 = high to 9 = low effectiveness/potency
Source: Broad and Newstrom (1992).

Before the Training

Managers and supervisors can support the transfer of training before the training session by these actions:

- communicating learning outcome expectations to the trainer to ensure that the training session develops the right knowledge, skills, and abilities

- discussing the importance and benefits of the skills that will be learned in the training session to the trainee, to his or her own work products, and to the broader performance of the work area or team

- involving the trainee in developing the learning goals and objectives for the session to help him or her understand the benefits

- supporting the employee's participation by providing assistance or backup for covering workload

- ensuring that this is the right person for the training at the right time (there's no point sending someone who doesn't need the training or sending someone who does but who may be working under distracting pressures)

- attending the training program in advance of the trainee, or attending with the trainee

- developing a learning contract with the employee to reinforce learning goals and the value of skill acquisition

- sending the trainee to the session with others, to facilitate and reinforce team learning.

Trainers can facilitate the transfer of training in advance of the training session by:

- ensuring that the training objectives match the skill requirements of the organization, department, and individual participants

- piloting the training session with subject matter experts to ensure that the right knowledge, skills, and abilities are being developed in a meaningful way

- sending information to trainees highlighting the program's goals and the session's relevance to their work and the challenges they face

- requesting that training participants complete pre-session work, conduct research, or complete readings.

During the Training Session

Managers and *supervisors* can support the transfer of training during the session by these actions:

- ensuring that the trainee's workload pressures don't distract the trainee from active engagement in the session

- arranging for back-up support to the trainee to cover phone calls, e-mails, and other requests that, if directed to the trainee, might distract him or her from the session.

During the training session, the *trainer's* responsibilities for facilitating the transfer of training include following the principles of adult learning and ensuring that the seminar content and instruction relate directly to the participant's workplace. Here are some specific activities that facilitate transfer during training:

- asking participants to develop specific learning objectives for the skill or knowledge area

- providing cases, scenarios, and role-plays based on participant examples and situations

- communicating and selling the on-the-job benefits of learning

- providing "job aids" (for example, checklists, tools, models, reminder cards, and so forth) that trainees can use back on the job and that aid learning and application

- facilitating action planning to guide training participants in developing specific "next step" application goals following the training session.

Following the Training

Managers and supervisors can support the transfer of training following the delivery of training by

- meeting with the trainee to discuss what he or she learned and how he or she will use and apply the learning to their work or behaviors

- providing opportunities for the trainee to practice the new skills and behaviors

- giving positive reinforcement to the trainee when he or she observes the person practicing the learned behaviors or skills

- establishing a formal "debriefing" following the training to provide feedback and additional learning to help sustain the new practices

- encouraging the trainee to summarize key insights, methods, tools, and approaches learned during the session at a future work unit meeting.

The *trainer* can facilitate and support the transfer of training following the training session by

- following up with the trainee to check for understanding, questions, and progress in using the new practices or skills

- distributing tip sheets, check sheets, and other job aids to trainees as a follow-along reminder and reinforcement of key learning outcomes, tools, behaviors, and methods

- conducting refresher mini-sessions or discussions at specific intervals to facilitate, integrate, and sustain learning and application and provide opportunities for additional feedback and reinforcement

- being available to answer follow-up questions, provide additional feedback, and give further direction to trainees.

Simply honoring the principles of adult learning and taking the right actions to facilitate the transfer of training will be enormously helpful in the design of the training program. Before we move on to the performance management and review training modules, we want to offer some additional tips that will further help you build and deliver a dynamic and effective training program.

Designing Effective Training Programs

Training program design is more art than science, in that a perfectly designed training program with all of the right content will fall flat if it doesn't make room for both the participants' learning preferences and the teaching style of the trainer. The program should reflect the suggested content and modules in this book as well as your own personal style and approach to learning and teaching. Within this approach, here are some specific suggestions for effective training program design:

- Ensure that you do a thoughtful needs analysis of the organization and prospective learners before designing and delivering the training. The suggested strategies for conducting this analysis in chapter 3 will start you off in the right direction.

- Stay flexible in your design and delivery. If you need to change gears in response to what you're seeing and hearing, don't be afraid to do so. This means, however, that you must go into the session with a deep understanding of the content, which will enable you to pivot when necessary. Be prepared.

- Actively involve participants in their own learning. Use a variety of interactive training methods: small groups, pairs, role-playing, action planning, pop quizzes, practice time, brainstorming, games, and guided inquiry are some common methods. Be adventurous and take some risks to help make learning happen.

- Break up the allotted training time into segments, focusing on a specific learning outcome in each.

- Design each learning segment with a clear beginning, middle, and end. Ensure that the training methods and activities you use help achieve the specific learning objective of each segment.

- At the beginning of the session, give trainees the "big picture" of the topic and the issues you'll be exploring with them during the program.

- Solicit participant questions and integrate a process of addressing these questions into your training delivery.

- Provide sufficient time for learning integration. Pace your learning objectives and supporting activities to allow time for trainees to reflect upon their learning insights and integrate them into their future practice.

- Provide supplemental worksheets to facilitate the trainees' recording of key learning insights ("aha! moments") gleaned from session discussions and applications.

- Build trainee action planning into your training program. Developing a specific action plan of what the trainee will do back on the job helps ensure that what is learned is applied to daily tasks and responsibilities after the training session.

- Strive to integrate all three ways in which people learn (auditory, visual, and kinesthetic) when teaching each of your learning outcomes. For example, when delivering a specific learning objective to trainees, tell a revelatory story (auditory), give people a checklist or graphic that displays key learning points (visual), and engage the learner in some "doing" activity—such as role-playing or action planning (kinesthetic). By using each of the three learning modes to teach every learning objective, the trainer increases the likelihood that each trainee, regardless of his or her preferred learning style, will remember the learning objective.

- End your training session with a recap of the key learning points and a final restatement of the value of translating the insights gained into daily practice.

Facilitating Versus Teaching

Facilitating learning involves more than just teaching or instructing participants. Facilitation includes creating and managing an environment that makes learning easy and invites the trainee into a learning opportunity by giving him or her the choice to learn and the decision on how to learn. The internal commitment to learning that results from the trainee *choosing* to learn increases his or her learning retention and helps sustain the application of learning back on the job.

Here are some suggestions for facilitating participant learning:

- Warmly greet people as they arrive at the training room. Find out where they work, what they hope to get out of the session, and some of the challenges they face.

- Write key questions, quotes, and provocative statements related to the topic on flipchart pages and post them around the room.

- Create a comfortable aural environment by playing soothing music (we recommend classical or light jazz) as people enter the training room.

- Establish the expectation of participant involvement early in the session. For example, you might begin a session by asking the large group a provocative question about the topic, to immediately engage trainees in the content and encourage active participation.

- Have participants formally interact with each other within the first 10 to 15 minutes. This "ice-breaker" can be an exercise in goal setting, sharing key questions, or simply getting to know one another. The point of the ice-breaker is to create a safe and welcoming environment and to set the expectation that this will be an interactive and engaging seminar.

- Find a way to value every contribution, no matter how far off the subject or difficult to comprehend the trainee's comments or questions might be. People are taking a risk when they volunteer ideas or offer questions. Honor and respect what people offer by establishing a link between what they have said and the key point you are making.

- Establish ground rules for discussions and information sharing that help create confidentiality and safety. Encourage people to state their honest perceptions, experiences, and thoughts without fear that what they share during the session will be used against them.

- Establish the expectation early in the session that participants are responsible for their own learning. Indicate that you will provide a framework for learning and offer them useful information, tools, and tips, but let them know that learning is primarily their responsibility.

- Stay connected to the group. Watch for signs of involvement or boredom and respond accordingly by sustaining the energy or dealing with the boredom by switching gears or changing direction.

- Use breaks to interact with participants. Find out if they are engaged, learning, frustrated, energized, or anxious. Talk to a variety of people to gather multiple perspectives.

- Use people's names when calling on them or when responding to their questions or comments.

- Refer back to specific comments, ideas, questions, or suggestions offered by participants earlier in the session (for example, "Earlier this morning, Steve gave an example of where there wasn't sufficient focus on performance accountability and performance results didn't seem to matter in his area. How might we use the tools we've just learned to help Steve deal with this issue?").

- When asked a content question by a participant, use the question as a teaching opportunity. Turn the question back to the group to answer (formulating your own answer while the group responds).

- Vary the pace and methods of your instruction. Use different techniques throughout the session to engage participants in new ways.

Many additional training design and facilitation tools, tips, and resources are available. For more information, check the For Further Reading section at the end of this book and join professional associations, such as the American Society for Training & Development (ASTD). ASTD and other human resource professional associations are a rich reservoir of knowledge and skills that will be an invaluable resource as you develop and deliver training programs.

The next chapter explores ideas and strategies for evaluating your workshops' learning outcomes. The chapter will also enable you to make improvements to your training program design based on participant reactions.

What to Do Next

- Join the local chapter of ASTD or another human resources professional association, such as the Society for Human Resource Management.

- Get leadership approval and commitment for the proposed training program or set of training programs. Ensure that your learning outcomes match their objectives and expectations.

- Begin planning your performance management and performance review training sessions using the session design suggestions in the chapters that follow.

- Adjust and modify the suggested training program designs based on your objectives, audience, and available time, and on your own teaching style and preferences.

- Practice. Use your first session as a field test "pilot" with a smaller group of participants. Debrief the pilot session with participants and gather their perspectives on the learning outcomes, models, tools, methods, and exercises to help you make adjustments to the training content and design.

- Facilitate the transfer of training by encouraging managers to support trainee participation prior to and following the session.

- Read the next chapter on evaluating learning outcomes.

Evaluating Your Training Program Results

5

What's in This Chapter?

- The role of evaluation in assessing the effects of your training program
- Approaches for measuring participant reactions, learning, behavior change, and organizational results
- Development of your evaluation methods

▲   ▲   ▲

Role of Evaluation in Assessing the Effects of Your Training Program

Gone are the days of taking the effectiveness of a training program at face value. In a time of lean operations and increasing demands for demonstrating the positive organizational impact of the training cost, you will need to incorporate evaluation into the very heart of every one of your training programs. This chapter offers you a quick overview of training program evaluation and presents you with a few ways to assess the multiple levels of your training program effectiveness.

Kirkpatrick's Four Levels of Training Evaluation

Attempts to measure the value and effectiveness of your training program should begin with the classic four levels of training evaluation first defined and developed by Donald Kirkpatrick in 1959. His four levels, published initially as a four-part series entitled "Techniques for Evaluating Training Programs" in the *Training Director's Journal* and more recently in his book, *Evaluating Training Programs: The Four Levels*, 3rd edition, are the standard that almost all training evaluation efforts follow.

Kirkpatrick's four levels are

- *Level 1—Participant Reaction and Intention*. This level of evaluation focuses on the reaction of participants to the training program. Although this is the lowest level of measurement of a training program's effectiveness, it remains an important dimension to assess. If people are unhappy with the learning environment, the instructor, the pace of the workshop, the physical environment, and so forth, they may be less able to learn what they need to learn.

- *Level 2—Participant Learning.* The focus of this assessment level is on whether the participants actually learned what you expected them to learn as a result of attending the training session. This level seeks to measure the participant's acquisition of cognitive knowledge or behavioral skills as a result of the workshop. Learning can be demonstrated by a participant's ability to describe the Great Performance Management Cycle and the role of the supervisor, or coach, within this model. To show learning from a performance goal setting workshop, a participant could develop a set of performance goals for an employee as an in-class exercise.

- *Level 3—Participant Behavior Change.* This level focuses on the degree to which training participants were able to transfer their learning to their workplace behaviors. For example, if participants learned the elements of the Performance Coaching Conversation in your workshop, were they able to actually conduct a performance coaching session with their employees back on the job?

- *Level 4—Impact and Results.* The last of Kirkpatrick's levels moves beyond the training participant to assess the *impact* of the training on organizational performance. For training sessions on performance management and performance reviews, you would explore these fundamental questions: Did the new performance review process lead to measurable improvements in employee performance as compared with previous approaches or as compared with a control group of employees who did not benefit from the new review process? Measuring the impact and return on investment (ROI) of a training program is a way to ensure that your training effort generates the results that are needed for the company to succeed in our global economy.

The American Society for Training & Development's *2006 State of the Industry Report* presented benchmark data on the levels of evaluation practiced by organizations. Approximately 38 percent of ASTD's 2006 BEST Award Winners (39 companies selected for their excellence in linking learning with performance) used or were moving toward using Kirkpatrick's four-level model.

Assessing the effectiveness of your training—by using at least the first three levels—should be an integral part of your training program design. Assessing Level 4, although less common because of the difficulty of measuring the cause-and-effect relationship between training and organizational outcomes, should also be undertaken to the extent that you are able.

Table 5-1 highlights each of Kirkpatrick's four levels, notes when each can and should be used, and suggests some possible strategies you can use to conduct your assessment.

Developing Your Evaluation Methods

To gauge the effectiveness of your training through evaluation, your assessment methods should be integrated into your training program design. This means that as you design your training program, you should identify specific opportunities and methods for assessing the various levels of evaluation outlined in this chapter.

Table 5-1. Strategies for Evaluating Your Training Program

Evaluation Level	When Conducted	Training Evaluation Ideas and Strategies
Level 1: Participant Reaction and Intention	Level 1 assessment can be done during the training program and at the conclusion of the session.	**During the session:** • Learning temperature or "pulse" reading cards (one word that describes what you're feeling, thinking, and learning) • Participants post reactions on flip chart pages: *content* and *methods* • Observation: Are people engaged? Having fun? • Mid-course key insights sharing (are they learning the right things?) • Action planning: What are their *intentions* following the session? Do they take the action planning process seriously? **At the end of the session:** • End of program reaction sheet: learning environment, useful content and tools, areas for improvement, relevance of content, etc.
Level 2: Participant Learning	Level 2 assessment can be done during the training program and at the conclusion of the session.	**During the session:** • Observation: Are people doing and saying things that reflect the content of the training? Use role-playing, case studies, presentations, etc. • Action planning: Do participant action plans reflect an integration of the course content? **At the end of or following the session:** • Pre- and post-tests or quizzes: Measuring the participant's acquisition of core content • Follow-along surveys: What learning do participants report *following* the training?
Level 3: Participant Behavior Change	Because the focus of Level 3 assessment is on measuring the impact of the training on participant behavior, this level is generally done following the training session.	**Following the end of the session:** • Self-reports: Do participants report changes in attitudes and behaviors? • Surveys of others: Do the participants' supervisors, staff, or peers report changes in core content attitudes and behaviors? • Observation: Do participants demonstrate the new behaviors in their daily work?

continued on next page

Table 5-1. Strategies for Evaluating Your Training Program, *continued*

EVALUATION LEVEL	WHEN CONDUCTED	TRAINING EVALUATION IDEAS AND STRATEGIES
Level 4: Impact and Organizational Results	Level 4 evaluation is conducted after the training has been provided and after sufficient time has been allowed for the behavior change of Level 3 to lead to positive impacts on organizational results.	**Following the end of the session:** • Gather organizational data: Collect performance data on outcomes that are positively affected by the training's content. This data might include such things as reductions in employee turnover, reduced defects, less overtime, more on-time deliveries, higher customer satisfaction, less wait-time for customer service, less machine down-time, increased sales, time-to-market data, greater employee commitment to performance improvement, etc. *Note:* Demonstrating the impact of the training on the organization's performance is a research question—one that requires a thoughtful process that uses proven social science research methodology. At a minimum, this requires that you track key organizational performance data *before* the training is offered. In addition, the best research design would be to establish a "control group" that didn't receive the training and then compare the performance differences between the groups that did and did not receive the training. • Conduct surveys or interviews of customers, supervisors, staff, peers, and other stakeholders • Compare pre- and post-training performance outcomes • Compare performance results of who received the training with those who didn't

To assist you with assessing Level 1, we have included a sample reaction sheet that you may find useful. This sheet is located in Training Tool 4, in the appendix and on the accompanying CD. For assessing Levels 2 and 3, you'll need to spend some time developing quizzes or tests to assess learning and identify a method for gathering data on post-training behavior change. For assessing Level 4—the most difficult level to assess—you are encouraged to begin documenting the performance indicators that your training program intends to influence. You may also want to consider exploring the return on investment (ROI) of your training dollars. Calculating ROI—one way of measuring the impact of your training—can be a powerful way to document the value of training to your organization's long-term success.

Some of the best work in calculating ROI has been done by Jack L. Phillips. His efforts at highlighting the importance of ROI and providing some tools for doing so have made a significant contribution to the training world. His book *Return on Investment in Training and Performance Improvement Programs,* 2nd edition (Butterworth-Heinemann, 2003), is perhaps the best text on the process of calculating ROI and demonstrating the value of training. You may find these additional books on ROI useful:

- *ROI at Work* (ASTD Press, 2005), by Jack and Patricia Pulliam Phillips

- *Return on Investment Basics* (ASTD Press, 2006), by Patricia Pulliam Phillips

- *How to Measure Training Results, 1st Edition* (McGraw-Hill, 2002), by Jack Phillips and Ron Stone

Another resource that might be useful to you in your efforts to explore ROI is the ROI Institute (http://www.roiinstitute.net).

The next chapter is the first of several that offer suggested workshop agendas for your training program on strategic planning and decision making. With your pre-work done and a plan for evaluation in place, you're ready to begin your workshop design.

 ## What to Do Next

- Design an approach for training evaluation that addresses all four levels.

- Review **training tool 4**, in appendix D and on the accompanying CD, for possible assessment issues to include in your workshop evaluation process.

- Explore methods for calculating the return on investment for your training program.

One-Day Workshop on Establishing a Coaching Relationship for Great Performance

6

What's in This Chapter?

- Objectives of the one-day workshop establishing a coaching relationship for great performance workshop

- Designing the workshop

- Workshop agenda and facilitator's guide

▲   ▲   ▲

This chapter introduces the first of several workshops focused on developing the performance management, coaching, and assessment competencies of both managers and employees. We believe that performance management is a two-way street—both the manager and the employee have a key role to play in the process, and competencies need to be developed in both; therefore, it is essential that you develop a plan for growing these competencies in everyone. Most of the workshop designs in this book are geared primarily toward managers. Each, however, with only a few adjustments, can easily be modified to develop these competencies in employees as well as managers.

Our first design lays the foundation for an effective partnership for performance: the manager develops a coaching relationship with those he or she manages. This is the foundation because everything that a manager does to shape the performance of an employee—including conducting the performance review—must be grounded in the mutual learning mindset and a relationship of communication, understanding, compassion, and trust. When these qualities and characteristics are present, there is an important shift in the focus of the performance review away from appraisal and judgment and toward learning and improvement. We believe that the core purpose of the performance review is learning and improvement.

One-Day Workshop: Establishing a Coaching Relationship for Great Performance

Objectives

As a result of participating in this one-day workshop on establishing a coaching relationship, participants will be able to accomplish these goals:

- Describe what performance coaching is and why it's important to performance management.

- View performance management as a *process,* not as an event.

- Apply the Great Performance Management Cycle to their own performance partnerships and identify the role of the coach within this cycle.

- Describe the roles of a coach and determine when each role is appropriate.

- Analyze a performance management situation and identify the most appropriate coaching role for this situation.

- Apply a new mindset for performance coaching and its supportive values, assumptions, and behaviors to their own performance partnerships.

- Develop a personal action plan for integrating the lessons of performance coaching and the mutual learning mindset into their daily practice.

Materials

For the instructor:

- Learning Activity 1: What Is a Coach?

- Learning Activity 2: Goal Setting

- Learning Activity 3: Performance Coaching and the Roles of a Coach

- Learning Activity 4: Coaching Cases—Using the Right Coaching Role

- Learning Activity 5: The Great Performance Management Cycle

- Learning Activity 6: Personal Action Planning

- Learning Activity 7: Sharing "Aha!" Moments and Questions/Goals Review

- Learning Activity 8: Unilateral Control and Mutual Learning Mindsets—Two Approaches to Managing Relationships With Others

- Learning Activity 9: Case Studies—Unilateral Control vs. Mutual Learning

- Learning Activity 10: The Ladder of Inference

- Training Tool 1: Training Room Configuration/Layout
- Training Tool 2: Learning Goal/Objective ➔ Outcomes
- Training Tool 3: "Aha!" Sheet
- Training Tool 4: Training Program Reaction Sheet
- Training Tool 5: Selecting Group Leaders
- flipchart and marking pens

- PowerPoint slides 6-1 through 6-49

For the participants:

- Handout 1: The Definition of a Coach
- Handout 2: The Roles of the Performance Coach
- Handout 3: The Dynamic Nature of the Coaching Relationship
- Handout 4: The Great Performance Management Cycle
- Handout 5: Defining Great Performance
- Handout 6: Actions for Encouraging Employee Ownership
- Handout 7: The Role of the Coach in Shaping Great Performance
- Handout 8: Unilateral Control and Mutual Learning Mindsets
- Handout 9: Values and Behaviors for Mutual Learning
- Handout 10: The Ladder of Inference
- Training Instrument 1: What Is a Coach?
- Training Instrument 2: Responsibilities of the Performance Coach
- Training Instrument 3: Selecting the Best Coaching Roles
- Training Instrument 4: Which Coaching Role Is Best?
- Training Instrument 5: What Enables Great Performance?
- Training Instrument 6: Building Employee Ownership for Great Performance
- Training Instrument 7: A Personal Plan for Action
- Training Instrument 8: Responding to Threat or Embarrassment
- Training Instrument 9: Mutual Learning and Coaching Cases

Using the Accompanying CD Materials

Materials for this training session are provided as electronic files on the accompanying CD. Further directions and assistance in using the files can be found in the appendix, "Using the Accompanying CD," located at the back of the workbook.

Preparations

Before the Workshop:

1. If appropriate, meet with a representative or representatives from the executive leadership team to discuss their expectations for the Establishing a Coaching Relationship for Great Performance Workshop.

2. Decide on your target audience for this workshop. This workshop is a foundation session that introduces some key concepts: coaching, great performance, mutual learning mindset, and so forth. Because subsequent workshops build on these fundamentals, we strongly encourage making this program a prerequisite to the workshops that follow. Although the focus of this workshop is primarily on the manager, employees would benefit equally, if the workshop were modified slightly.

3. Schedule the session and secure a training room for the workshop. If additional follow-up workshops are planned, schedule these additional sessions at the same time.

4. Design the program around the organization's culture, methods, and systems for managing employee performance. If some aspects of the organization's culture and practices conflict with the approaches introduced in this workshop, work to reconcile these potential conflicts and get executive leadership approval for the resulting design.

5. Prepare training materials (handouts, training instruments, instructions, training program evaluation form, PowerPoint presentation, and supporting audio-visual materials).

6. Send a memo, letter, or email invitation to participants, reiterating the purpose of the Establishing a Coaching Relationship for Great Performance Workshop and the importance of this workshop in managing employee performance and conducting performance reviews. It may be helpful to have this communication come from your CEO or COO to reinforce the importance and value of their participation in this program.

7. Order food and beverages as necessary.

The Day of the Workshop:

1. Arrive early at the training room.

2. Verify room setup, using **tool 1**.

3. Set up and test equipment, such as flipcharts, markers, LCD projector, overhead projector, and so forth.

4. Prepare and post flipchart pages titled "Your Questions/Goals," if desired, and any additional flipchart pages as detailed in the Learning Activities. You may also want to post another flipchart page highlighting key questions that you plan to address during the workshop and that relate to the objectives.

5. Place participant materials on tables.

 6. Display PowerPoint **slide 6-1** as a welcome and greeting to participants as they enter the training room.

7. Greet and connect with individual participants as they enter the training room. Inquire into their department, role, time with the organization, and so forth.

 ## Sample Agenda

8:30 a.m. Welcome (5 minutes)

Welcome participants to the Establishing a Coaching Relationship for Great Performance Workshop. Introduce yourself and highlight the key questions concerning performance management and performance coaching as you move into **learning activity 1.**

You can post these questions on a flip-chart and highlight them for the group:

- How can managers help maximize employee contributions to great performance?

- What is the work of a performance coach?

- What characteristics of a coach enable employee performance?

- Who is responsible for managing employee performance?

 8:35 **Learning Activity 1: What Is a Coach?** (25 minutes)

This activity gets participants to immediately begin to think about performance coaching and the role a coach might play in guiding someone toward great performance. This activity engages participants in the fundamental question about what a coach is and the role the coach plays in the partnership for performance. You may want to use **tool 5**, if appropriate, to help the table groups decide on who will lead their small group discussions. For subsequent table group discussions, you can continue to draw from this tool's list of ideas.

 9:00 **Learning Activity 2: Personal Learning Goals** (25 minutes)

Using **tool 2,** make the transition from the opening activity by suggesting that today's workshop focuses on reframing the work of a manager to become more of a coach—with the goal of bringing out the employee's best efforts.

 9:25 **Learning Activity 3: Performance Coaching and the Roles of the Coach** (30 minutes)

 Guide participants through this activity to develop an understanding of the characteristics of effective coaches, when coaching is appropriate, the five coaching roles, and the methodology for selecting the right coaching role.

9:55 Break (15 minutes)

10:10   **Learning Activity 4: Coaching Cases—Using the Right Coaching Role** (30 minutes)

This activity asks participants to diagnose different employee performance situations and then decide which coaching role is appropriate to use in each one.

10:40   **Learning Activity 5: The Great Performance Management Cycle** (60 minutes)

This activity introduces the Great Performance Management Cycle and guides participants in exploring the role of the coach in shaping and influencing how employees move through this cycle.

11:40   **Learning Activity 6: Personal Action Planning** (20 minutes)

In this learning activity, participants begin building a personal plan to help integrate the lessons from the workshop into their actions beyond the workshop.

Noon   Lunch (60 minutes)

1:00 p.m.   **Learning Activity 7: Sharing "Aha!" Moments! and Questions/Goals Review** (25 minutes)

This activity reinforces the key learning objectives from the morning session and provides an opportunity for participants to make connections between their questions and learning goals and the content of the workshop. It also helps you gauge the extent to which the participants understood and absorbed the key lessons from the morning session.

Note: This activity is optional. If you choose to skip this activity to focus more time on the Great Performance Management Cycle, developing a coaching relationship, or the mutual learning mindset, then take steps to address connections between the participants' questions identified in **learning activity 2** and the content of the workshop at other times throughout the day. Discussing participant questions can occur at any time—whenever a specific question seems relevant to the topic at hand or in the final integration and conclusion activity.

1:25   **Learning Activity 8: Unilateral Control and Mutual Learning Mindsets—Two Approaches to Managing Relationships With Others** (50 minutes)

In this learning activity, you introduce the two mindsets that a manager as coach might bring into his or her coaching relationships. Participants will learn the perils of the unilateral control mindset and why people tend to use this mindset in spite of the problems it creates for us. You will then highlight the mutual learning mindset as a far more productive and constructive approach for the coach to use throughout the Great Performance Management Cycle. This activity also explores the underlying values, assumptions, and enacting behaviors of the mutual learning mindset. Participants will ask and answer questions about these values, assumptions, and behaviors.

2:15   Break (15 minutes)

2:30   **Learning Activity 9: Case Studies—Unilateral Control vs. Mutual Learning** (30 minutes)

Introduce this activity by suggesting that these two different approaches for managing our relationships with others might be a bit easier for them to understand if they applied them to some coaching situations. This activity asks participants to describe the different approaches that a unilateral control manager and a mutual learning manager might use for solving an employee performance problem.

3:00   **Learning Activity 10: The Ladder of Inference** (30 minutes)

The final activity of this workshop introduces the powerful ladder of inference as a tool to help participants become better performance coaches by not making assumptions and inferences or rushing to judgment. This activity is strengthened when you can use real examples from your own experience or examples out of the organization's collective experience. Participants will gain an appreciation of the roles that assumptions and inferences play in undermining coaching effectiveness.

3:30   **Learning Activity 6: Personal Action Planning (conclusion)** (20 minutes)

Participants should once again turn to this activity and to their Personal Action Plan (**training instrument 7**), and complete Parts C and D. Note that these last two parts of the plan ask them to apply key insights from the mutual learning mindset and ladder of inference to their situation.

3:50   Integration and Conclusion (35 minutes)

Bring together the various elements of the workshop content and review any of the remaining unanswered questions from the personal learning goals activity flipchart pages. As time permits, ask participants to answer any question that has not yet been addressed during the workshop. Depending on the time available, you can either assign questions to the small groups to address or facilitate a group discussion of unanswered questions.

Your concluding remarks should highlight these key points as you display **slides 6-46 through 6-48:**

- Performance coaching involves building effective relationships with employees, such that they are challenged, supported, guided, and inspired to do their best toward achieving their great performance outcomes.

- The best coaches are effective because they are thoughtful about selecting the most appropriate coaching role to meet the requirements of the performer, the task, and the environment.

- All employee performance happens within a process—whether that process is managed or not. The goal of the performance coach is to actively facilitate the Great Performance Management Cycle through a variety of strategies that include encouragement, support, providing tools and training, and asking questions that provoke critical reflection.

- Highlight the GPM Cycle on **slide 6-47** as a summary of the role of a coach in guiding and shaping an employee's performance. Reiterate that although the employee is primarily responsible for his or her own performance, the coach plays an active role to ensure that the GPM Cycle moves in the right direction.

- When managers and coaches come from a unilateral control mindset, their ability to coach effectively and do the right thing is significantly impaired.

- If managers and coaches were to adopt a mutual learning mindset, however, their working relationships with employees would be strengthened. Most important, their coaching interventions would involve behaviors that support employee ownership and responsibility for performance.

- The mutual learning mindset's governing values of valid information, free and informed choice, internal commitment, transparency, and empathy are transformational in nature. If each of us can fully master and integrate them into our daily behaviors, all of our working relationships will become healthier and more productive.

- The ladder of inference is a powerful tool that helps us slow down and reflect on the basis of our beliefs. It also compels us to gather more information about someone else's intentions before we pre-judge their motives.

Encourage participants to take the next step and integrate the various elements of the action plan that they developed throughout the day into their daily work. If this workshop is the first in a series of performance management workshops that they will be attending, make note of the dates of these follow-along workshops. If appropriate, give a preview of the next workshop in the series.

4:25   Evaluation (5 minutes)

 Display **slide 6-49**. Thank the participants for attending the Establishing an Effective Coaching Relationship for Great Performance Workshop and for their active involvement throughout the session.

 Distribute **tool 4** and encourage participants to leave the completed forms at their tables or a designated location.

4:30   Close

The next chapter includes an agenda and learning activities for a workshop on performance goal setting. This follow-along workshop builds on the Great Performance Management Cycle framework and the mutual learning mindset introduced in the coaching relationship workshop.

 ## What to Do Next

- Prepare for the one-day session.

- Compile the learning activities, handouts, training instruments, and PowerPoint slides you will use in the training.

- Decide the timing of this session in relation to the one-day workshops on performance goal setting, diagnosing performance problems, and conducting the performance review, which are introduced in the following chapters.

PowerPoint Slides

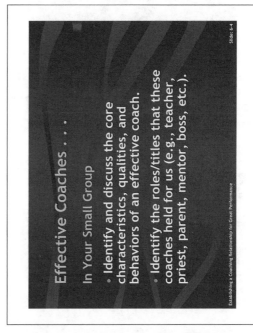

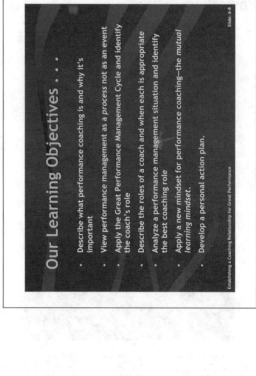

An Effective Coach . . .

- Guides, facilitates, and supports a person toward realizing his potential
- Helps a person overcome challenges to achieve her goals by enabling her to achieve her best
- Enables a person to achieve a level of accomplishment that wouldn't have been possible without the coach's guidance, prodding, and encouragement.

Establishing a Coaching Relationship for Great Performance

Slide: 6-6

Our Learning Objectives . . .

- Describe what performance coaching is and why it's important
- View performance management as a *process* not as an event
- Apply the Great Performance Management Cycle and identify the coach's role
- Describe the roles of a coach and when each is appropriate
- Analyze a performance management situation and identify the best coaching role
- Apply a new mindset for performance coaching—the *mutual learning mindset.*
- Develop a personal action plan.

Establishing a Coaching Relationship for Great Performance

Slide: 6-8

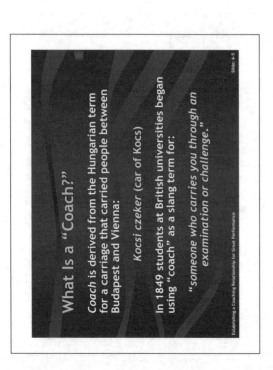

What Is a "Coach?"

Coach is derived from the Hungarian term for a carriage that carried people between Budapest and Vienna:

Kocsi czeker (car of Kocs)

In 1849 students at British universities began using "coach" as a slang term for:

"someone who carries you through an examination or challenge."

Establishing a Coaching Relationship for Great Performance

Slide: 6-5

"When you need me, but do not want me, then I must stay. When you want me, but no longer need me, then I have to go."

— Nanny McPhee

Character in the movie *Nanny McPhee*. Screenplay adaptation by *Emma Thompson* from the *Nurse Matilda* books by *Christianna Brand*

Sharing Objectives and Questions

- Share your personal objective(s) for the day.
  - As a group . . . identify some common goals/issues of interest to the group.
- Develop two or three questions about performance coaching or performance management that your group would like to have answered by the end of today.

Slide: 6-10

Coaching Responsibilities

1. Guide and facilitate a person towards achieving his or her potential.
2. Encourage his/her personal and professional growth.
3. Increase an employee's long-term commitment to the organization.
4. Assess an employee's competence and confidence levels.
5. Guide employee in discovering and applying his or her knowledge and skills.

Slide: 6-12

Your Goals/Objectives . . .

What are your goals for this session?

1. What is your *learning objective?* What behavior do you want to learn/change?
2. What is the *benefit* of achieving your objective? What outcomes might you expect?
3. How much do you *value* this outcome?

Slide: 6-9

Coaching Is a *Relationship,* Not an Event!

Slide: 6-11

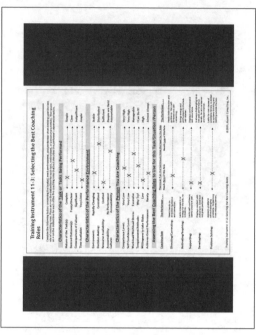

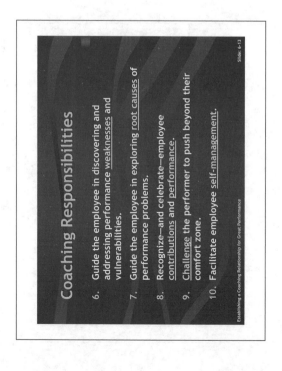

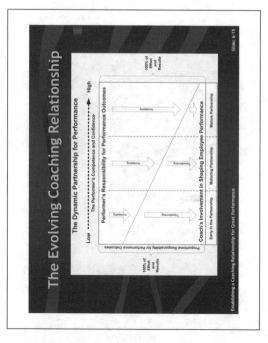

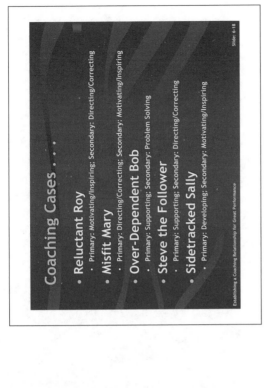

Coaching Cases . . . .

- **Reluctant Roy**
  - Primary: Motivating/Inspiring; Secondary: Directing/Correcting
- **Misfit Mary**
  - Primary: Directing/Correcting; Secondary: Motivating/Inspiring
- **Over-Dependent Bob**
  - Primary: Supporting; Secondary: Problem Solving
- **Steve the Follower**
  - Primary: Supporting; Secondary: Directing/Correcting
- **Sidetracked Sally**
  - Primary: Developing; Secondary: Motivating/Inspiring

Establishing a Coaching Relationship for Great Performance

Slide: 6-18

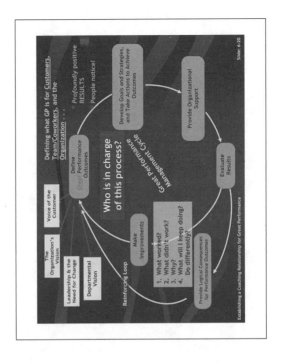

Coaching Cases

In your small group . . . .

- Read your assigned case(s).
- Using handout 2 and instrument 3, identify the primary coaching role or roles your group thinks best meets the needs of the situation and person.
- If more than one coaching role is identified, which would you start with?

Establishing a Coaching Relationship for Great Performance

Slide: 6-17

Enabling GREAT Performance

- What enables someone to consistently meet or exceed performance goals?

- What actions by the performer support achieving great outcomes?

- What actions by the coach support achieving these outcomes?

Establishing a Coaching Relationship for Great Performance

Slide: 6-19

⑤ Make Improvements

Transforming Role of Employee . . .

- Reflect on past results.
- Be a critical thinker.
- Focus on <u>cause</u>, not blame.
- Explore system issues.
- Ask great questions.

Transforming Role of Coach . . .

- Ask questions to generate reflection.
- Listen.
- Inquire and challenge.
- Focus on <u>cause</u>, not blame.
- Explore system issues.
- Be receptive to receiving feedback.

Establishing a Coaching Relationship for Great Performance

Slide: 6-26

Developing Your Plan . . .

Complete Parts A and B of your Personal Plan for Action:

- Part A: Identify key insights from the definition of coaching, the five roles of the coach, and diagnosing the best coaching role.
- Part B: Identify actions to build greater employee ownership for great performance.

Establishing a Coaching Relationship for Great Performance

Slide: 6-28

④ Evaluate Performance

Transforming Role of Employee . . .

- Take the lead.
- Determine the frequency.
- Make assessment part of the work process.
- Use valid GP measures.
- Talk to customers, co-workers, and coach.
- Focus on trends, not incidents.

Transforming Role of Coach . . .

- Establish the expectation that the employee is responsible.
- Share expectations regarding frequency.
- Model the process.
- Keep in touch.
- Observe.
- Inquire.
- Ask great questions.

Establishing a Coaching Relationship for Great Performance

Slide: 6-25

⑥ Provide Logical Consequences

Transforming Role of Employee . . .

- Be clear about what is important to you.
- Identify intrinsic rewards.
- Tell the coach.
- Negotiate customized rewards.
- Recognize resource limitations.

Transforming Role of Coach . . .

- Find out what the employee values.
- Follow through.
- Be consistent.
- Let people know that performance DOES matter (and reward accordingly).
- Don't promise what you can't deliver.

Establishing a Coaching Relationship for Great Performance

Slide: 6-27

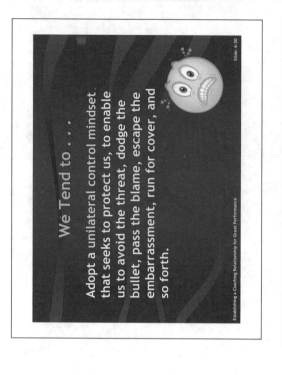

We Tend to . . .

Adopt a unilateral control mindset that seeks to protect us, to enable us to avoid the threat, dodge the bullet, pass the blame, escape the embarrassment, run for cover, and so forth.

Establishing a Coaching Relationship for Great Performance

Slide: 6-30

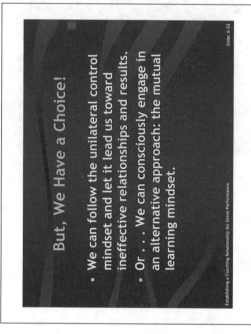

But, We Have a Choice!

- We can follow the unilateral control mindset and let it lead us toward ineffective relationships and results.
- Or . . . We can consciously engage in an alternative approach: the mutual learning mindset.

Establishing a Coaching Relationship for Great Performance

Slide: 6-32

How We Respond to Threats

- When we feel *stressed, threatened, vulnerable, embarrassed,* or otherwise *uncomfortable* . . . how do we typically respond?

- What might cause us to feel *stressed, threatened, vulnerable, embarrassed,* or *uncomfortable?*

Establishing a Coaching Relationship for Great Performance

Slide: 6-29

Establishing a Coaching Relationship for Great Performance

Slide: 6-31

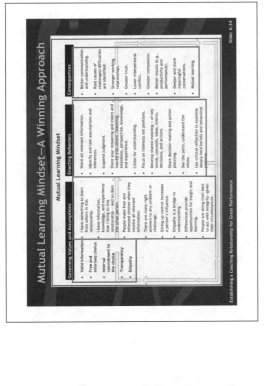

Mutual Learning Mindset—A Winning Approach

Mutual Learning Mindset

Governing Values and Assumptions	Enacting Behaviors	Consequences

Slide: 6-34

Establishing a Coaching Relationship for Great Performance

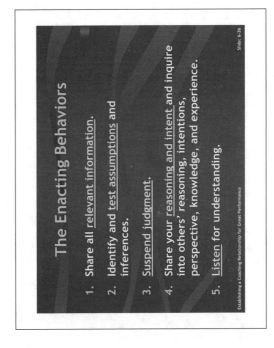

The Enacting Behaviors

1. Share all relevant information.
2. Identify and test assumptions and inferences.
3. Suspend judgment.
4. Share your reasoning and intent and inquire into others' reasoning, intentions, perspective, knowledge, and experience.
5. Listen for understanding.

Slide: 6-36

Establishing a Coaching Relationship for Great Performance

Mutual Learning Mindset

- Based on an alternative set of governing values
- Focuses on understanding and learning
- Assumes that we know and understand only a part of the puzzle
- Honors other people's perspective—*especially* when there is disagreement
- Is more likely to lead to effective relationships and positive results.

Slide: 6-33

Establishing a Coaching Relationship for Great Performance

Governing Values . . .

- Valid Information: All relevant information is shared so that everyone understands what they need to know.
- Free and Informed Choice: People make their independent decisions based on valid information, not pressure.
- Internal Commitment to Decisions: Individuals take responsibility for the decisions that they participate in.
- Transparency: Individuals feel comfortable with open, honest, and direct communication with no "hidden agendas" or undiscussables.
- Empathy: Individuals have compassion for others and differing viewpoints, and a genuine interest in understanding another's perspective.

Slide: 6-35

Establishing a Coaching Relationship for Great Performance

Reflecting on the Values and Enacting Behaviors

1. Confusion: What isn't clear? What don't you understand?

2. Transformation: Which values or behaviors are likely to *transform* your coaching interactions with others?

3. Application: How might you use or *apply* the values and behaviors in your daily coaching conversations?

Establishing a Coaching Relationship for Great Performance

Slide: 6-38

Why it's Difficult . . .

- We're socialized by our families, schools, and workplaces.
- Our surrounding culture tends to operate from a unilateral control mindset.
- It's difficult to change our underlying values and assumptions.

Establishing a Coaching Relationship for Great Performance

Slide: 6-40

The Enacting Behaviors

6. Focus on <u>interests</u>, not positions.

7. Develop <u>shared meaning</u> of key words, concepts, ideas, etc.

8. <u>Share decision making</u> and action planning.

9. See the parts, <u>understand the whole</u>.

10. Use critical reflection to examine deeply held beliefs, and behavioral patterns.

Establishing a Coaching Relationship for Great Performance

Slide: 6-37

The Difficulty of Adopting the Mutual Learning Mindset . . .

Why is it difficult to move away from the unilateral control mindset and toward one based on mutual learning?

Establishing a Coaching Relationship for Great Performance

Slide: 6-39

The Ladder of Inference

Your Actions... ...on your behalf

- Taking Action
- Developing Feelings
- Adopting Beliefs
- Forming Judgments
- Drawing Inferences
- Making Assumptions
- Adding Meaning (Interpreting)
- Paying Attention to Select Data
- Observing and Experiencing

Our beliefs and feelings affect what we pay attention to.

Avoid working with him at all cost. Use other analysts who are more reliable. Talk to management about my concerns.

Resentment. Dismissed. Miffed. Angry at promises made but not kept. Tired of having to cover for him.

Self-interest drives every aspect of Dennis' work. Lower status projects don't even appear on his radar. While he might say yes to a project, if it's not one that features his work, he won't come through on the project.

Dennis is unreliable and undependable — except when it's a high status project where he gets top billing. For him, it's all about self-promotion.

Dennis can't bother himself to work on projects where his talents aren't showcased.

Dennis obviously has other priorities—which usually involve projects that raise his status here. He works on projects that he wants to and avoids those that don't promote his talents.

Dennis doesn't consider my project a high status project. He prefers projects where he gets to shine. He doesn't respect me enough to even let me know that he wouldn't make the due date.

Dennis promised to complete his data analysis for the Miller Project by the 15th. He missed this deadline. I haven't heard a word from him.

Dennis is always on the run. His analysis is thoughtful and insightful. He is never at this desk. He missed a key deadline on one of my projects.

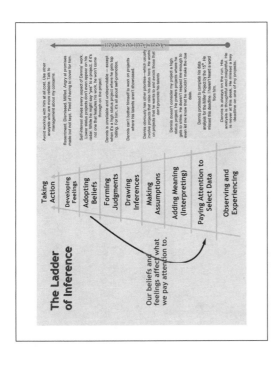

Coaching Cases

Read the case that your group has been assigned.

a) Identify the most appropriate role(s) for the coach to use in this situation.

b) Identify how a coach, using the unilateral control mindset, might act in this situation.

c) Identify how a coach, using the mutual learning mindset, might act in this situation.

Slide: 6-41

Establishing a Coaching Relationship for Great Performance

Implications of the Ladder?

1. What are the implications of the ladder for our everyday communications?

2. How can we avoid "leaping" up the ladder of inference? What actions can we take to avoid acting based only on assumptions and inferences?

3. How might we use the ladder to improve our coaching relationships with our employees?

Slide: 6-44

Establishing a Coaching Relationship for Great Performance

Why We Leap Up the Ladder

- Each of us creates a "story" to help us fill in the details of missing information.

- Our stories are informed by history, culture, misunderstandings, and perceived and real "wrongs" (or "rights"), both within and outside of our awareness.

- The stories we tell chart our *path to action*—the route we follow from observed events to the actions we take (which may or may not be grounded in reality).

- We take these "flights" up the ladder because of our *fundamental attribution error*—we tend to view others' behaviors as due to their *disposition* rather than their environment.

Slide: 6-43

Establishing a Coaching Relationship for Great Performance

Concluding Points . . .

- Performance coaching involves building relationships with employees such that they are challenged, supported, guided, and inspired to achieve great performance.

- The best coaches are thoughtful about selecting the most appropriate coaching role.

- All employee performance happens within a process—whether that process is managed or not.

Establishing a Coaching Relationship for Great Performance

Slide: 6-46

Concluding Points . . .

- When coaches use a unilateral control mindset, their ability to coach effectively and do the right thing is significantly impaired.

- If coaches instead adopt a mutual learning mindset, however, their working relationships with employees will be strengthened.

- The mutual learning mindset's governing values are transformational in nature.

- The ladder of inference is a powerful tool to slow you down, enabling you to gather more data.

Establishing a Coaching Relationship for Great Performance

Slide: 6-48

Developing Your Plan . . .

Complete Parts C and D of your personal plan for action:

- Part C: Identify specific actions you will take to develop a mutual learning mindset.

- Part D: Identify actions you can take to prevent yourself from leaping up the ladder of inference.

Establishing a Coaching Relationship for Great Performance

Slide: 6-45

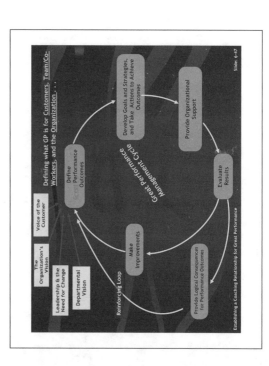

Establishing a Coaching Relationship for Great Performance

Slide: 6-47

One-Day Workshop on Performance Goal Setting

7

What's in This Chapter?

- Objectives of the one-day performance goal setting workshop
- Designing the workshop
- Workshop agenda and facilitator's guide

▲   ▲   ▲

The previous chapter presented a workshop design and offered an introduction to the key principles of performance management and the role of the manager as coach within this process. This chapter presents a workshop design focused on helping managers work with their employees to define great performance outcomes and establish measurable performance goals. Because the quality of a performance evaluation depends, in part, on the performance expectations set at the beginning of the performance period, developing goal-setting competencies is a critical first step in the process.

The workshop in the next chapter—"Diagnosing Employee Performance Problems and Developing Improvement Plans"—uses some of the participant outputs from this chapter (specifically the Performance Planning and Development Worksheet), so we recommend that you require participants to first attend this workshop. When taken together, the workshops in chapters 7 and 8 provide a foundation to assist managers with defining performance expectations, diagnosing performance problems, and developing employee performance improvement plans.

One-Day Workshop: Performance Goal Setting

Objectives

After taking part in this one-day workshop on performance goal setting, participants will be able to perform these tasks:

- Describe the purpose of setting goals and measuring performance.

- Link individual employee performance expectations to the work unit and organization's performance goals.

- Discuss the two performance accountabilities of every employee: job accountabilities and organizational accountabilities.

- Develop SMART goals.

- Describe the characteristics of effective measures and develop measures based on these characteristics.

- Apply the goal theory of motivation to increase employee commitment to performance goals.

- Develop performance goals for the people they supervise.

Materials

For the Instructor:

- Learning Activity 2: Goal Setting

- Learning Activity 7: Sharing "Aha!" Moments and Questions/Goals Review

- Learning Activity 11: The Purpose of Goal Setting

- Learning Activity 12: Defining Great Performance Outcomes

- Learning Activity 13: Performance Planning and Development—Defining Great Performance

- Learning Activity 14: Defining Performance Accountabilities

- Learning Activity 15: Performance Planning and Development—Defining Responsibilities

- Learning Activity 16: Developing SMART Goals

- Learning Activity 17: Writing SMART Goals—Case Application

- Learning Activity 18: Performance Planning and Development—Developing SMART Goals

- Learning Activity 19: Characteristics of Effective Measures

- Learning Activity 20: Developing Effective Measures—Case Application

- Learning Activity 21: Performance Planning and Development—Developing Measures of Performance

- Training Tool 1: Training Room Configuration/Layout

- Training Tool 2: Learning Goal/Objective ➔ Outcomes

- Training Tool 3: "Aha!" Sheet

- Training Tool 4: Training Program Reaction Sheet

- Training Tool 5: Selecting Group Leaders

- flipchart and marking pens

 - PowerPoint slides 7-1 through 7-35

For the Participants:

 - Handout 4: The Great Performance Management Cycle

- Handout 5: Defining Great Performance

- Handout 11: The Goal Theory of Motivation

- Handout 12: What Is Great Performance?

- Handout 13: Performance Accountabilities

- Handout 14: The Purpose and Characteristics of Effective Performance Measures

- Training Instrument 10: How Goal Setting Enables Great Performance and Applying Goal Theory

- Training Instrument 11: Defining Great Performance Application

- Training Instrument 12: Performance Planning and Development Worksheet

- Training Instrument 13: Defining Job Responsibilities

- Training Instrument 14: SMART Performance Goals

- Training Instrument 15: SMART Goals and Performance Measures Application

Using the Accompanying CD Materials

Materials for this training session are provided on the accompanying CD. Further directions and assistance in using the files can be found in the appendix, "Using the Accompanying CD Materials," at the back of the workbook.

Preparations

Before the Workshop:

1. If appropriate, meet with a representative or representatives from the executive leadership team to discuss their expectations for the Performance Goal Setting Workshop. It is especially important to do this if the organization has established a clear vision and if the leadership has defined strategic priorities that each department, work area, or individual is expected to follow.

2. Decide on your target audience for the workshop. This workshop is intended as a follow-along of the foundation session on establishing a coaching relationship. This session should precede the

workshops that are detailed in chapters 8—"Diagnosing Employee Performance Problems and Developing Improvement Plans"—and chapter 9—"Conducting the Performance Review." Although the focus of this workshop is primarily on the manager, employees would benefit equally if the workshop were modified slightly.

3. Design the program around the organization's culture, methods, and systems for performance management and goal setting. If organizational infrastructures or systems are in place for setting work area or individual goals, integrate these into your training program design. If some of these elements run counter to best practices in managing performance, then attempt to work with the leadership to change these systems to reflect a more effective way of managing performance.

4. Schedule the session and secure a training room for the workshop. If the follow-along workshop Diagnosing Employee Performance Problems and Developing Improvement Plans is planned, schedule this session at the same time.

5. Prepare training materials (handouts, training instruments, instructions, training program evaluation form, PowerPoint presentation, and supporting audio-visual materials).

6. Send a memo, letter, or email of invitation to participants, reiterating the purpose of the Performance Goal Setting Workshop and the importance of this workshop to managing employee performance and conducting performance reviews.

7. Order food and beverages as necessary.

The Day of the Workshop:

1. Arrive early at the training room.

2. Verify room setup, using **tool 1**.

3. Set up and test equipment such as flipcharts, markers, LCD projector, overhead projector, and so forth.

4. Prepare and post flipchart pages titled "Your Questions/Goals," if desired, as well as any additional flipchart pages that are detailed in the Learning Activities. You may also want to post another flipchart page highlighting key questions that you plan to address during the workshop and that relate to the objectives.

5. Place participant materials on tables.

PPT 6. Display PowerPoint **slide 7-1** as a welcome and greeting to participants as they enter the training room.

7. Greet and connect with individual participants as they enter the training room. Establish rapport as they arrive. Inquire into their department, role, time with the organization, and so forth.

Sample Agenda

8:30 a.m.   Welcome (5 minutes)

PPT   Welcome participants to the Performance Goal Setting Workshop. Introduce yourself. Display **slide 7-2**, which reveals a quote. Ask participants what the quote means to them.

Participants may offer these ideas and others:

- When you have a clear and compelling vision, obstacles and barriers to performance are less important.
- Keeping your "eye on the prize" prevents little setbacks and problems from derailing your plan.
- When you don't have a clear goal, setback and obstacles will win every time.

Reinforce any of these and related responses. Note that a major part of today's workshop is focused on the importance of getting clarity around performance goals. Let the participants know that today you'll also explore the positive consequences when the performance goals are clearly stated and the negative consequences when they aren't.

Highlight some of the key performance goal-setting questions before moving on to **learning activity 2**.

You can post these questions on a flipchart and highlight them for the group:

- How does goal setting fit into performance management?
- What role does the organization's vision play in individual performance management?
- What are SMART goals?
- How important is measurement in managing performance?
- Who develops the performance outcomes, goals, and measures for a specific position?

8:35 **Learning Activity 2: Goal Setting** (25 minutes)

Make the transition from the opening activity by suggesting that, because today's workshop focuses on goal setting, it would seem especially appropriate to start the session off with setting your own learning goals for the workshop.

Conclude the personal learning goal activity by noting that the clarity and specificity of a goal—whether it be a workshop participant's learning objective or an employee's performance objective—has a direct bearing on whether or not the goal will be attempted or achieved. Ask them to keep their personal learning goals in mind as we move through the workshop today. Encourage them to actively seek out ways to achieve their goals during the session.

Note that, similar to pursuing their own learning goals today, when managers coach others to achieve great performance, they want their performers to keep clear performance goals in mind and seek out ways to achieve these goals.

9:00 **Learning Activity 11:** The Purpose of Goal Setting (25 minutes)

Guide participants through this activity to develop an understanding of the purpose of goal setting, its importance in an overall performance management process, and the role that the coach plays in employee performance goal setting.

9:25 **Learning Activity 12: Defining Great Performance Outcomes** (45 minutes)

This activity begins with an overview of the Great Performance Management Cycle and then focuses on the first step of the cycle: defining great performance. Participants will learn how to develop great performance outcomes and then define great performance outcomes for two example positions.

10:10 Break (15 minutes)

 10:25 **Learning Activity 13: Performance Planning and Development—Defining Great Performance** (30 minutes)

This activity guides participants in completing the initial sections of a Performance Planning and Development Worksheet that they will use throughout this and future workshops.

10:55 **Learning Activity 14: Defining Performance Accountabilities** (20 minutes)

This activity introduces and guides participants to understanding the two major accountabilities of every position in every organization:

- core job responsibilities—the responsibilities for which someone within a specific job is held accountable

- organizational responsibilities—the responsibilities for which someone in the position is accountable that are common to *all* employees in the organization (for example, following work rules).

 11:15 **Learning Activity 15: Performance Planning and Development—Defining Responsibilities** (30 minutes)

 In this activity, participants continue working with their Performance Planning and Development Worksheet (**training instrument 12**), and they define the *job* and *organizational* responsibilities for the position on which they are focusing.

11:45 **Learning Activity 16: Developing SMART Goals** (15 minutes)

End the morning portion of the workshop with this brief activity, which introduces the meaning and value of having SMART goals.

Noon Lunch (60 minutes)

 1:00 p.m. **Learning Activity 7: Sharing "Aha!" Moments and Questions/Goals Review** (25 minutes)

This post-lunch activity engages participants in reflecting on the morning session and highlights key "take-aways" from the session so far. It also provides an opportunity for the group to identify which of their questions and learning objectives have already been addressed during the session.

Note: This activity is optional. If you choose to skip this activity to focus more time on approaches to goal setting or to have participants spend more time on their Performance

Planning and Development Worksheets **(training instrument 12)**, then take steps to address participant questions identified in **learning activity 2** at other times throughout the day. Discussing participant questions can occur at any time, either when a specific question seems relevant to the topic at hand or in the final integration and conclusion activity.

1:25   **Learning Activity 17: Writing SMART Goals—Case Application** (20 minutes)

In this learning activity, you ask participants to work through a number of examples by making the given performance goals into SMART performance goals.

1:45   **Learning Activity 18: Performance Planning and Development—Developing SMART Goals** (30 minutes)

This learning activity engages participants in developing SMART performance goals for their target position using the Performance Planning and Development Worksheet **(training instrument 12).**

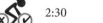

2:15   Break (15 minutes)

2:30   **Learning Activity 18: Performance Planning and Development—Developing SMART Goals,** continued (20 minutes)

2:50   **Learning Activity 19: Characteristics of Effective Measures** (20 minutes)

Transition out of the SMART goal-setting activity and into this learning activity by stating that one of the key elements of a SMART goal is measurement. This activity explores the value of measurement and some of the most important characteristics of measurement. Participants are asked to review a list of characteristics and note those that are most significant and useful to them as they consider ways to gauge the effectiveness of their performers.

3:10   **Learning Activity 20: Developing Effective Measures—Case Application** (25 minutes)

This activity is conducted prior to the final activity of the workshop, and it asks participants to work in small groups to develop effective measures for several performance examples. They are expected to apply the principles of effective measures from the previous activity when completing this exercise.

3:30   **Learning Activity 21: Performance Planning and Development—Developing Measures of Performance** (25 minutes)

This final activity engages participants in developing effective measures for great performance outcomes and the supporting job and organizational responsibility goals.

4:05   Integration and Conclusion (25 minutes)

Introduce the concluding activity by acknowledging that the participants have worked hard today at tackling the challenges at the front end of the Great Performance Management Cycle—defining outcomes and goals and the ways to measure progress.

Note that this beginning point in an employee's performance period is critical because everything that follows over the course of the performance period, leading up to and including conducting the performance review, depends on this step. The performer and the coach must both understand and agree on the great performance outcomes that the performer is about to undertake, the specific goals (both job and organizational) that must be accomplished, and how the outcomes and goals will be measured. Indicate that the purpose of today's workshop was to provide the participants with a framework for tackling this very important work.

If appropriate, review any of the remaining unanswered questions from the personal learning goals activity flipchart pages. As time permits, ask participants to answer any questions that have not yet been addressed during the workshop. Depending on the time available, you can either assign questions for the small groups to address or facilitate a large-group discussion of unanswered questions.

 Your concluding remarks should highlight these key points as you display **slides 7-33 and 7-34:**

- The Great Performance Management Cycle begins with the performer and coach working together to define great performance outcomes and goals for the position. Everything that follows within the cycle depends on clarity and agreement in this step.

- The coach is responsible for *guiding* the development of these outcomes and goals. The employee plays the primary role in this process. Some employees, however, may need more help from their coaches than others.

- We need to elevate the targets of employee performance to a level that is far beyond just getting by. Redefining performance outcomes such that employees strive toward the extraordinary and the profoundly positive is the place to start.

- Great performance is defined in terms of the organization, customers, and team or co-workers. Each employee must see the purpose of his or her individual work as achieving great things for all three audiences.

- There are five dimensions of great performance: quality, quantity, cost, timeliness, and impact on the team.

- There are two types of performance goals and accountabilities: core job responsibilities and organizational responsibilities. Managers need to ensure that employees focus on achieving great results in both areas.

- SMART goals mean that we know what our target is (specific), how to measure whether we achieve it or not (measurable), that the goal was accepted by the performer (accepted), that the goal is realistic and achievable (realistic), and that the goal is anchored to the clock—performers achieve results on time (time based).

Encourage participants to take responsibility for integrating the key lessons from the workshop into their future performance planning and goal-setting efforts. Remind participants that performance management isn't just about conducting the performance review. It must begin at the beginning—setting clear and compelling performance outcome expectations and the goals needed to achieve these expectations.

If this session is followed by the Diagnosing Employee Performance Problems and Developing Improvement Plans workshop, mention the date of this workshop and give a preview of the goals for this session. Remind participants to bring their completed Performance Planning and Development Worksheets **(training instrument 12)** to this follow-along session.

4:25   Evaluation (5 minutes)

Display **slide 7-35.** Thank the participants for attending the Performance Goal Setting Workshop and for their active involvement throughout the session.

Distribute **training tool 4** and encourage participants to leave the completed forms at their tables or a designated location.

4:30   Close

The next chapter includes an agenda and learning activities for a workshop on diagnosing performance problems, laying the groundwork for developing a performance improvement plan, and preparing for the performance review. This follow-along workshop is a natural next step in the Great Performance Management Cycle and a critical step in preparing for the face-to-face Performance Coaching Conversation and the Annual Performance Analysis and Planning Conversation.

What to Do Next

- Prepare for the one-day session.

- Compile the learning activities, handouts, training instruments, and PowerPoint slides you will use in the training.

- Decide the timing of this session in relation to the preceding one-day workshop on establishing performance coaching relationships and the follow-along workshops on diagnosing performance problems and conducting the performance review.

- Because this workshop and the workshop in chapter 8 are best offered together, review the next chapter's workshop before beginning your design for this chapter and decide on your strategy for delivering both. Note that the partially completed Performance Planning and Development Worksheet filled in by participants in chapter 7 will be used as a beginning point for the follow-along workshop of chapter 8.

PowerPoint Slides

Obstacles are those frightful things you see when you take your eyes off the goal.

— Hannah More

English playwright, novelist, educator and poet, 1745 to 1833

Our Learning Objectives . . .

- Describe the characteristics of effective measures and develop measures based on these characteristics.
- Apply goal and expectancy theory of motivation to increase employee commitment to performance goals.
- Develop performance goals for the people you supervise.

Performance Goal Setting

Slide: 7-4

Performance Goal Setting

Steps for Achieving GREAT Performance Through SMART Goals and a Clear Vision

© Russell Consulting, Inc. and American Society for Training & Development. Permission to copy only when used with *Ultimate Performance Management*.

© 2006, Photo by Jeffrey L. Russell

Our Learning Objectives . . .

- Describe the purpose of setting goals and measuring performance.
- Link individual employee performance expectations to the work unit and organization's performance goals.
- Discuss the two performance accountabilities of every employee.
- Develop SMART goals

Performance Goal Setting

Slide: 7-3

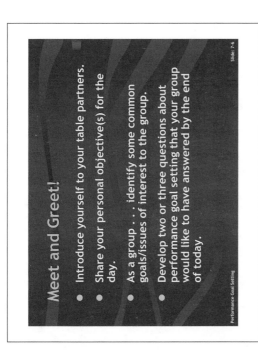

Meet and Greet!

- Introduce yourself to your table partners.
- Share your personal objective(s) for the day.
- As a group . . . identify some common goals/issues of interest to the group.
- Develop two or three questions about performance goal setting that your group would like to have answered by the end of today.

Performance Goal Setting

Slide: 7-6

The Role of Goal Setting

How does goal setting enable an employee to achieve great performance?

Performance Goal Setting

Slide: 7-8

Your Goals/Objectives . . .

What are your goals for this session?

1. What is your *learning objective*? What behavior do you want to learn/change?

2. What is the *benefit* of achieving your objective? What outcomes might you expect?

3. How much do you *value* this outcome?

Performance Goal Setting

Slide: 7-5

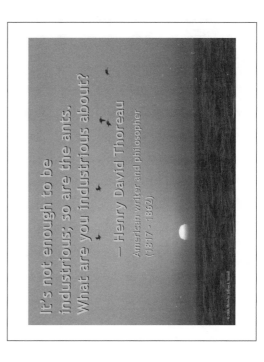

It's not enough to be industrious; so are the ants. What are you industrious about?

— Henry David Thoreau
American writer and philosopher
(1817 - 1862)

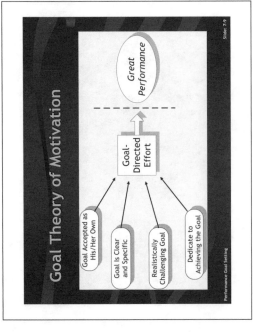

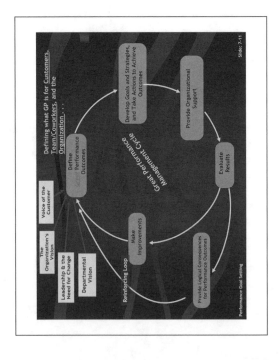

Types of Accountabilities . . .

- Core Job Responsibilities—accountabilities that relate to the broad areas in which the employee is expected to create value . . .
- Organizational Responsibilities—accountabilities that apply to <u>ALL</u> employees . . .

Performance Goal Setting

Slide: 7-18

Completing Parts B and C

For the specific <u>position</u> you are focusing on:

- Part B: Identify five to seven *job* responsibilities for this position. Complete only the <u>first</u> column.
- Part C: Identify up to three *organizational* responsibilities for this position. Complete only the <u>first</u> column.

Performance Goal Setting

Slide: 7-20

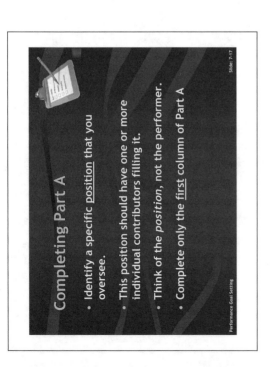

Completing Part A

- Identify a specific <u>position</u> that you oversee.
- This position should have one or more individual contributors filling it.
- Think of the *position*, not the performer.
- Complete only the <u>first</u> column of Part A

Performance Goal Setting

Slide: 7-17

Defining Accountabilities

What are some possible core job responsibilities for a . . .

- Department manager
- Retail sales associate
- Human resources generalist

Performance Goal Setting

Slide: 7-19

Slide: 7-22

Developing SMARTer Goals

As a group . . .

- Develop a SMARTer goal for the Great Performance Goal assigned to your group.
- Do <u>NOT</u> complete the "Measurement" column (this will be filled in later).
- Do identify specific actions to build greater *acceptance of any SMART goal.*

Performance Goal Setting

Slide: 7-24

Why Measure Performance?

Performance Goal Setting

Slide: 7-21

SMART Performance Goals

S – Specific

M – Measurable

A – Accepted

R – Realistic

T – Time-Based

Performance Goal Setting

Slide: 7-23

Completing Parts B and C

For the specific <u>position</u> you are focusing on:

- Part B: For each *job* responsibility, identify 2 to 4 SMART performance objectives.
- Part C: For each *organizational* responsibility, identify 1 to 3 SMART performance objectives.

Performance Goal Setting

The Purpose of Measures

- Motivate the performer to achieve great performance.
- Focus the energy of the performer on the key *drivers* of success.
- *Provide* immediate and ongoing feedback to the performer and the coach.
- Offer an early warning system to indicate that performance isn't meeting expectations.

Performance Goal Setting

Slide: 7-26

Characteristics of Good Measures

- Relevant and Important: The measure assesses outcomes that are directly relevant and critical to the overall performance outcomes.
- Easy to Understand: The measure is accessible and easy to understand by the performer, the coach, customers, and other stakeholders.
- Objective and Unbiased: The measure reflects the organization's and work area's priorities instead of those of the performer.
- Valid and Reliable: It measures what you intend to measure and generate accurate results.
- Quantitative: The measure can be observed, counted, averaged, compared, and tracked over time.

Performance Goal Setting

Slide: 7-28

If you can measure it, you can manage it, and if you can't measure it, you can't manage it.

— Lord Kelvin

Irish mathematical physicist/engineer
(1824 – 1907)

The Purpose of Measures

- Reveal a cause→effect relationship between the *behaviors* and *outcomes* resulting.
- Balance the attention and energy of the performer on an *array* of success factors not just one.
- Highlight the relationship between the performer's efforts and the longer-term priorities of the organization.

Performance Goal Setting

Slide: 7-27

Reviewing the Characteristics

On your own . . . .

- Which aren't clear? What questions do you have about any characteristic?
- Which characteristic is most important to a great measure?

In your group . . .

- Discuss your questions and most important measure characteristics.

Performance Goal Setting

Slide: 7-30

Completing Part A - Measurement

For the specific <u>position</u> you are focusing on:

- Part A: Develop one or more possible measures for each great performance dimension.

- Be prepared to share and discuss your measurements measures with your partner.

Performance Goal Setting

Slide: 7-32

Characteristics of Good Measures

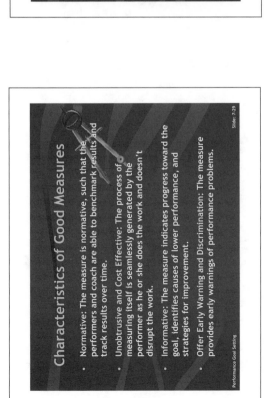

- Normative: The measure is normative, such that the performers and coach are able to benchmark results and track results over time.

- Unobtrusive and Cost Effective: The process of measuring itself is seamlessly generated by the performer as he or she does the work and doesn't disrupt the work.

- Informative: The measure indicates progress toward the goal, identifies causes of lower performance, and strategies for improvement.

- Offer Early Warning and Discrimination: The measure provides early warnings of performance problems.

Performance Goal Setting

Slide: 7-29

Developing Effective Measures

- Complete training instrument 15.

- Develop one or more effective measures for the SMART goal your group developed earlier.

- Be prepared to report out your measure or measures.

Performance Goal Setting

Slide: 7-31

Slide: 7-34

Conclusion and Integration

- There are five dimensions of great performance: *quality, quantity, cost, timeliness, and impact on the team.*

- There are two types of performance goals and accountabilities: core job responsibilities and organizational responsibilities.

- SMART goals mean that we know our target, how to measure it, that it is accepted by the performer, that it is realistic and achievable, and that it is anchored to the clock.

Performance Goal Setting

Thank You!

for being part of this coaching goal-setting program.

Best of luck in translating these lessons into results with your performers.

Please complete the evaluation form.

Slide: 7-33

Conclusion and Integration

- The Great Performance Management Cycle begins with the performer and coach working together to define Great Performance Outcomes and goals.

- The coach is responsible for *guiding the* development of these outcomes and goals. The employee plays the primary role in this process.

- We need to elevate the targets of employee performance to a level that is far beyond just getting by.

- Great performance is defined in terms of the organization, customers, and team/co-workers.

Performance Goal Setting

One-Day Workshop on Diagnosing Employee Performance Problems and Developing Improvement Plans

What's in This Chapter?

- Objectives of the one-day diagnosing employee performance problems and developing improvement plans workshop

- Ideas for designing the workshop

- Workshop agenda and facilitator's guide

In an ideal world, everything a manager as coach does to help influence and shape an employee's work effort toward great performance pays off, and wonderful things happen: The employee's performance soars, audacious targets are achieved, and customers are never disappointed. Unfortunately, none of us work in such an ideal world. In the real world that we call home, there will always be barriers, obstacles, setbacks, false starts, and missed targets. Sometimes, there will be outright failure. In our world, many things can go wrong with performance, despite the good intentions of the performer and strong support of the coach.

This chapter introduces a one-day workshop designed to guide managers to better diagnose employee performance problems, with an eye toward helping the performer get back on track. The previous two chapters presented an overview of the coaching role within the Great Performance Management (GPM) Cycle and introduced tools to aid the development of the employee's initial performance goals. The workshop we have created in this chapter builds on the same broad principles upon which the coaching relationship, the GPM Cycle, and the performance goal setting process are based: a strong partnership for performance between the employee and the coach, an employee-centered process, and the mutual learning mindset.

Because of the interdependent nature of the workshops presented in chapters 7 and 8, these workshops should be designed and delivered together. The Performance Planning and Development Worksheet completed by participants in the Setting Performance Goals workshop in chapter 7, for example, is used by participants in this chapter. We recommend, therefore, that you offer this workshop soon after the one-day workshop on setting performance goals to ensure that the ideas and concepts are fresh and that the Performance Planning and Development Worksheet completed in the goal-setting workshop remains relevant to participants.

Finally, this workshop should be offered before the Conducting Performance Coaching and Annual Performance Analysis and Planning Conversations workshop. When it's time for the coach to conduct periodic Performance Coaching Conversations or the Annual Performance Analysis and Planning Conversation, he or she should have the core knowledge, skills, and tools to facilitate a productive interaction. Using the methods and tools introduced in this workshop completes the foundation for constructing effective Performance Coaching Conversations begun in chapters 6 and 7. By working with an employee to diagnose and correct performance problems as they arise, instead of waiting until the annual review to examine why the employee's performance isn't what it should be, the employee's performance is likely to improve faster (see figure 2-3 in chapter 2) and the partnership for performance will become stronger.

One-Day Workshop: Diagnosing Employee Performance Problems and Developing Improvement Plans

Objectives

After participating in this one-day workshop on diagnosing employee performance problems and developing improvement plans, participants will be able to perform these tasks:

- Describe the two types of performance goals: *outcome* goals and *process* goals.

- Apply methods for documenting employee performance.

- Diagnose the causes of performance problems.

- Apply the 85/15 rule to explore the systemic causes of employee performance problems.

- Apply the Nine-Plus-One Performance Diagnostic Checksheet to diagnose specific employee performance problems and the manager's potential contributions to these problems.

- Apply the Cause→Effect diagram for analyzing the root causes of employee performance problems.

- Assess the performance of their employees.

- Develop positive performance improvement goals when employees are experiencing performance problems.

Materials

For the Instructor:

- Learning Activity 2: Goal Setting

- Learning Activity 7: Sharing "Aha" Moments! and Questions/Goals Review

- Learning Activity 22: The Goals of Performance Coaching

- Learning Activity 23: Strategies for Documenting Employee Performance

- Learning Activity 24: Why Things Go Wrong With Performance

- Learning Activity 25: Diagnostic Tools for Exploring the Causes of Performance Problems

- Learning Activity 26: Performance Planning and Development—Assessing Employee Performance

- Learning Activity 27: Establishing Positive Performance Improvement Goals

- Learning Activity 28: Performance Planning and Development—Developing Performance Goals

- Training Tool 1: Training Room Configuration/Layout

- Training Tool 2: Learning Goal/Objective → Outcomes

- Training Tool 3: "Aha!" Sheet

- Training Tool 4: Training Program Reaction Sheet

- Training Tool 5: Selecting Group Leaders

- flipchart and marking pens

- PowerPoint slides 8-1 through 8-40

For the Participants:

- Handout 2: The Roles of the Performance Coach

- Handout 15: The Goals of Performance Coaching

- Handout 16: Tools for Documenting Performance

- Handout 17: Using the Performance Gap to Drive Improvement

- Handout 18: Why Things Go Wrong With Performance

- Handout 19: The Components of Performance and the 85/15 Rule

- Handout 20: Nine-Plus-One Performance Diagnostic Checklist

- Handout 21: Cause→Effect Diagram

- Training Instrument 12: Performance Planning and Development Worksheet

- Training Instrument 16: Documenting Performance

- Training Instrument 17: The Causes of Performance Problems

- Training Instrument 18: Cause→Effect Diagram Application

- Training Instrument 19: Establishing Positive Performance Goals

⊙ Using the Accompanying CD

Materials for this training session are provided as electronic files on the accompanying CD. Further directions and assistance in using the files can be found in the appendix, "Using the Accompanying CD Materials," at the back of this workbook.

Preparations

Before the Workshop:

1. If appropriate, meet with a representative or representatives from the executive leadership team to discuss their expectations for the Diagnosing Employee Performance Problems and Developing Improvement Plans Workshop. For this workshop to be successful, the organization's leadership must be supportive of efforts to diagnose and address system barriers to employee performance, which may include issues involving providing sufficient resources, training, tools, equipment, and so forth. Depending on the organization, it may be critical to get this advanced support from the leadership for them to hear and address system issues that arise during the workshop.

2. Decide on your target audience for this workshop. This workshop is intended as a follow-along to the two previous workshops, on establishing a coaching relationship and setting performance goals. This session should precede the workshop detailed in chapter 9: "Conducting Performance Coaching and Annual Performance Analysis and Planning Conversations." Although the focus is primarily on the manager, employees would also benefit from this workshop if it were modified slightly.

3. Design the program around the organization's culture, methods, and systems for performance management and goal setting. If there are organizational infrastructures, systems, or tools in place to help managers diagnose and address employee performance problems, integrate these into your training program design. If some organizational practices run counter to approaches for diagnosing performance problems introduced in this workshop, then attempt to work with the leadership to change these practices and bring them more into line with this workshop's approach.

4. Schedule the session and secure a training room for the workshop. If the follow-along workshop, Conducting Performance Coaching and Annual Performance Analysis and Planning Conversations, is planned, schedule this additional workshop at the same time.

5. Prepare training materials (handouts, training instruments, instructions, training program evaluation form, PowerPoint presentation, and supporting audio-visual materials).

6. Send a memo, letter, or email of invitation to participants reiterating the purpose of the Diagnosing Employee Performance Problems and Developing Improvement Plans Workshop and the importance of this workshop to managing employee performance and conducting performance reviews. *Important:* Ask participants to bring **training instrument 12** (Performance Planning and Development Worksheet) that they have worked on in the performance goal setting workshop. They should also bring **handout 14** (The Purpose and Characteristics of Effective Performance Measures).

7. Order food and beverages as necessary.

The day of the workshop:

1. Arrive early at the training room.

2. Verify room setup, using **tool 1**.

3. Set up and test equipment such as flipcharts, markers, LCD projector, overhead projector, and so forth.

4. Prepare and post flipchart pages titled "Your Questions/Goals" if desired, and any additional flipchart pages detailed in the Learning Activities. You may also want to post another flipchart page highlighting key questions that you plan to address during the workshop and that relate to the objectives.

5. Place participant materials on tables.

PPT
6. Display PowerPoint **slide 8-1** as a welcome and greeting to participants as they enter the training room.

7. Greet and connect with individual participants as they enter the training room. Establish rapport with each. Inquire into their department, role, time with the organization, and so forth.

Sample Agenda

8:30 a.m.   Welcome (5 minutes)

Welcome participants to the Diagnosing Employee Performance Problems and Developing Improvement Plans Workshop. Introduce yourself. Display **slide 8-2**, which reveals a quote. Ask participants what the quote means to them.

Participants may offer such ideas as:

- When trying to solve a problem (falling), one needs to look at the causes instead of the result.

- Performance problems are a lot like taking an accidental fall, and just like understanding why we fell, if we want to solve performance problems, we need to examine the reasons *why* performance isn't what it should be.

Reinforce any of these and related responses. Highlight that this quote speaks to the heart of today's workshop: better understanding and diagnosing of the reasons why an employee might miss a performance target.

Highlight some of the key questions that you'll be exploring with them before moving into **learning activity 2**. You can post these questions on a flipchart and highlight them to the group:

- What is the best way to document employee performance?

- What are the most common causes of employee performance problems?

- What tools might help us diagnose the causes of performance problems?

- What is the 85/15 Rule and how does it affect employee accountability for results?

- What kinds of goals are included in a performance improvement plan and how should these goals be written to maximize their impact on the performer?

 8:35 **Learning Activity 2: Goal Setting** (25 minutes)

Introduce this learning activity to participants by noting the importance of setting their personal learning objectives for the workshop.

 9:00 **Learning Activity 22: The Goals of Performance Coaching** (30 minutes)

In this learning activity, participants review the five coaching roles introduced in the Establishing a Coaching Relationship for Great Performance Workshop from chapter 6 and learn about the two types of performance coaching goals based on these coaching roles.

Make the transition out of this activity by noting that these four goals form the foundation of all the subsequent work as the coach guides the performer toward great performance. Explain that all of the documentation, diagnosis, and improvement and development goal setting that you'll be exploring today emerges from the five roles of the coach and the four types of performance coaching goals that the coach establishes with each performer.

 9:30 **Learning Activity 23: Strategies for Documenting Employee Performance** (35 minutes)

Guide participants into this activity by asking them to identify what they are presently doing to document the performance of their employees throughout the performance period. This activity then presents some useful approaches and templates for documenting performance.

10:05 Break (15 minutes)

 10:20 **Learning Activity 24: Why Things Go Wrong With Performance** (40 minutes)

This activity begins with an exploration of the kinds of factors that may erode performance, introduces the 85/15 Rule, explores the importance of system causes of poor performance, and concludes by identifying the common causes of performance problems.

 11:00 **Learning Activity 25: Diagnostic Tools for Exploring the Causes of Performance Problems** (60 minutes)

This activity introduces the two diagnosing tools: **handout 20** (Nine-Plus-One Performance Diagnosis Checklist) and **handout 21** (Cause→Effect Diagram).

Both tools are powerful aids that participants can use for diagnosing the array of causes that lead to a given end result. This activity introduces both tools and has participants apply the Cause→Effect tool to a specific case.

Noon Lunch (60 minutes)

1:00   **Learning Activity 7: Sharing "Aha" Moments! and Questions/Goals Review** (30 minutes)

As with previous workshop designs, this post-lunch activity asks participants to reflect on the morning session and highlight key "take-aways." It also provides an opportunity for the group to identify which of their questions and learning objectives have already been addressed during the session.

 Note: This activity is optional. If you choose to skip this activity to focus more time on the diagnostic tools or having participants complete their Performance Planning and Development Worksheets (**training instrument 12**), then take steps to address participant questions identified in **learning activity 2** at other times during the day. Discussing participant

 questions can occur at any time—when a specific question seems relevant to the topic at hand or in the final summary and integration activity.

 1:30   **Learning Activity 26: Performance Planning and Development—Assessing Employee Performance** (30 minutes)

This activity involves participants in integrating previous learning activities on the types of coaching goals and the causes of performance problems into their emerging Performance Planning and Development Worksheets.

2:00   Break (15 minutes)

 2:15   **Learning Activity 26: Performance Planning and Development—Assessing Employee Performance** (continued) (25 minutes)

Participants complete this activity.

2:40   **Learning Activity 27: Establishing Positive Performance Improvement Goals** (25 minutes)

This activity introduces the idea of establishing *positive* performance goals to help focus the employee's efforts on performance improvement or development. Participants will learn the characteristics of positive performance goals and apply them to a number of performance problems.

3:05   **Learning Activity 28: Performance Planning and Development—Developing Performance Goals** (45 minutes)

This activity engages participants in developing performance improvement goals in their Performance Planning and Development Worksheet.

3:50   Integration and Conclusion (35 minutes)

Introduce the concluding activity by acknowledging the great effort of the participants toward better diagnosing areas of employee performance improvement or development. Note that understanding why things go wrong with performance and the value of looking at system causes together with the employee causes is an important first step in the performance diagnosis process.

 Highlight the tools introduced in this workshop: **handout 20** (Nine-Plus-One Performance Diagnostic Checklist), **handout 19** (Components of Performance and the 85/15 Rule),

handout 21 (Cause→Effect Diagram), and **training instrument 12** (Performance Planning and Development Worksheet). Indicate that all of these tools will be essential as participants engage in ongoing diagnosis and interactions with their performers. Note that the Performance Planning and Development Worksheet is especially useful in preparing for the periodic Performance Coaching Conversation and the Annual Performance Analysis and Planning Conversation.

Stress that none of the performance diagnostic work that participants did today or that they will do in the future should be done without the ongoing involvement of their employees. Because this is an employee-centered approach to performance management, the coach should work to position the employee to take the lead in diagnosis and performance improvement planning. Although the coach should explore these issues independently of the employee's efforts, he or she should never substitute his or her analysis and judgment for the employee's. Both perspectives are important for understanding and managing performance.

If appropriate, review any of the remaining unanswered questions from the personal learning goals activity flipchart pages. As time permits, ask participants to answer any questions that have not yet been addressed during the workshop. Depending on available time, you can either assign questions for the small groups to address or facilitate a large group discussion of unanswered questions.

Bring the session to a close by displaying **slide 8-37**. Ask participants what this quote means within the context of performance coaching. Honor responses and then offer your own perspective—especially noting that without fully appreciating and understanding the nature of the performance problem a coach is trying to address with the performer, there are an infinite number of solutions. Suggest that, in the interest of time, it makes sense to pursue the one right solution for a well-defined problem.

Your integrating remarks should highlight these key points as you display **slides 8-38 and 8-39:**

- Employee performance diagnosis and improvement planning are what a good coach does every day. When a coach sees a performance problem, there's no waiting until the scheduled quarterly "check-in" or annual review. An effective coach is actively aware of an employee's performance and stands ready to assist the employee in achieving great performance.

- Guiding employees toward great performance requires that the coach understand the key factors and forces that support or disable performance.

- Documenting employee performance by using a variety of methods and tools, including those discussed today, will be critical to ensure that their coaching and performance management decisions are based on data instead of recent events.

- The 85/15 Rule encourages managers to first look at *system* causes of performance failures before focusing on employee motivation and effort.

- The Nine-Plus-One Performance Diagnostic Checklist and the Cause→Effect Diagram are two useful tools that aid both the coach and the employee in diagnosing performance problems.

- There are four performance diagnostic states or conditions: *maintaining* performance, *improving* performance, *accepting* new responsibilities, and *growing* the job in a new direction. Both the coach and the performer use these four diagnostic states as the foundation of performance planning and development.

- When developing the employee's performance improvement plan, both the employee and the coach should focus on establishing *positive* outcome goals, then define the measures used to assess progress toward meeting the goals and the employee behaviors required to achieve them.

Encourage participants to integrate the key lessons from the workshop into their future employee performance planning and goal setting efforts. Suggest that they continue to work on the Performance Planning and Development Worksheet that they began in this workshop series.

If this workshop precedes the Conducting Performance Coaching and Annual Performance Analysis and Planning Conversations Workshop that they will be attending, highlight the dates of this workshop. Give a preview of this next workshop.

4:25   Evaluation (5 minutes)

Display **slide 8-40**. Thank the participants for attending the Diagnosing Employee Performance Problems and Developing Improvement Plans Workshop and for their active involvement throughout the session.

Distribute **training tool 4** and encourage participants to leave the completed forms at their tables or a designated location.

4:30   Close

The next chapter includes an agenda and learning activities for a workshop on Conducting Performance Coaching and Annual Performance Analysis and Planning Conversations. This next workshop integrates the key principles, tools, and methods from the workshops presented in chapters 6, 7, and 8 into a model for structuring effective face-to-face coaching conversations.

What to Do Next

- Prepare for the one-day session.

- Compile the learning activities, handouts, and PowerPoint slides you will use in the training.

- Decide the timing of this session in relation to the workshops that precede and follow this session.

PowerPoint Slides

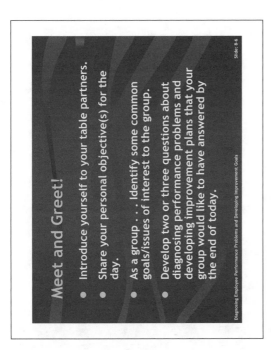

Meet and Greet!

- Introduce yourself to your table partners.
- Share your personal objective(s) for the day.
- As a group . . . Identify some common goals/issues of interest to the group.
- Develop two or three questions about diagnosing performance problems and developing improvement plans that your group would like to have answered by the end of today.

Diagnosing Employee Performance Problems and Developing Improvement Goals

Slide: 8-6

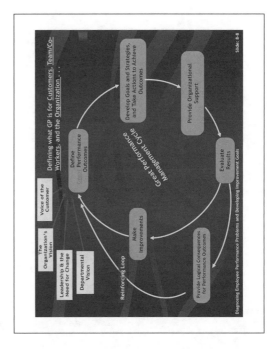

Slide: 8-8

Your Goals/Objectives . . .

What are your goals for this session?

- What is your *learning objective*? What behavior do you want to learn/change?
- What is the *benefit* of achieving your objective? What outcomes might you expect?
- How much do you *value* this outcome?

Diagnosing Employee Performance Problems and Developing Improvement Goals

Slide: 8-5

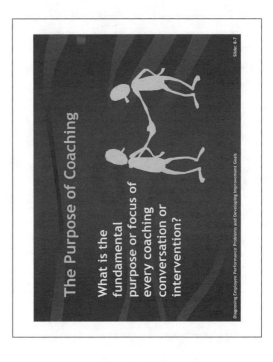

The Purpose of Coaching

What is the fundamental purpose or focus of every coaching conversation or intervention?

Diagnosing Employee Performance Problems and Developing Improvement Goals

Slide: 8-7

The Goals of Coaching

There are two types of goals that become the focus of every coaching conversation/intervention:

- Performance Coaching Outcome Goals
- Performance Coaching Process Goals

Diagnosing Employee Performance Problems and Developing Improvement Goals

Slide: 8-10

The Performance Process Goals

- Build Greater Ownership for Performance.
- Build Greater Commitment to the Job and the Organization.
- Strengthen Our Performance Partnership.
- Identify System Barriers and Challenges.

Diagnosing Employee Performance Problems and Developing Improvement Goals

Slide: 8-12

The Five Roles of Coaching

Teaching/Directing/Correcting

Motivating/Inspiring

Supporting

Developing

Problem Solving

Diagnosing Employee Performance Problems and Developing Improvement Goals

Slide: 8-9

The Performance Outcome Goals

- Maintain Performance Strengths.
- Improve Performance.
- Accept New Responsibilities.
- Grow and Develop the Job to a New Performance Level.

Diagnosing Employee Performance Problems and Developing Improvement Goals

Slide: 8-11

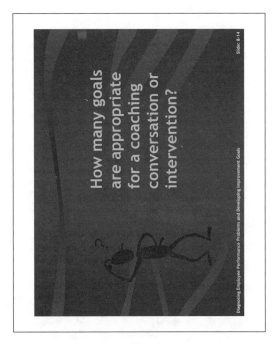

How many goals are appropriate for a coaching conversation or intervention?

Slide: 8-14

Diagnosing Employee Performance Problems and Developing Improvement Goals

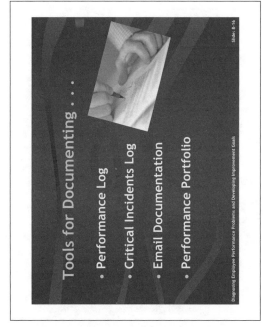

Tools for Documenting . . . .

- Performance Log
- Critical Incidents Log
- Email Documentation
- Performance Portfolio

Slide: 8-16

Diagnosing Employee Performance Problems and Developing Improvement Goals

Reactions to the Coaching Goals

- What are your general reactions to the two types of coaching goals?
- What is most useful about knowing these eight coaching goals?
- What questions do you have about any of the coaching goals?

Slide: 8-13

Diagnosing Employee Performance Problems and Developing Improvement Goals

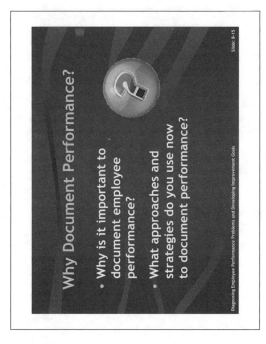

Why Document Performance?

- Why is it important to document employee performance?
- What approaches and strategies do you use now to document performance?

Slide: 8-15

Diagnosing Employee Performance Problems and Developing Improvement Goals

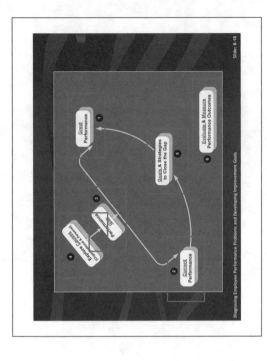

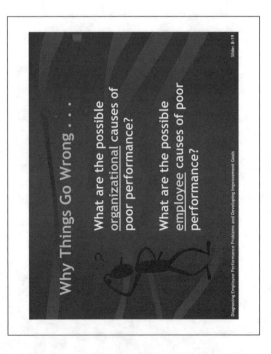

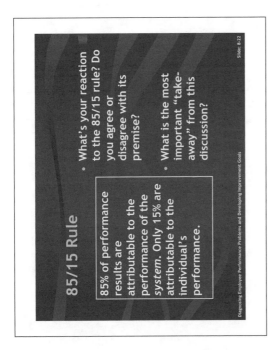

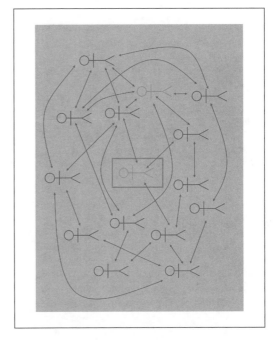

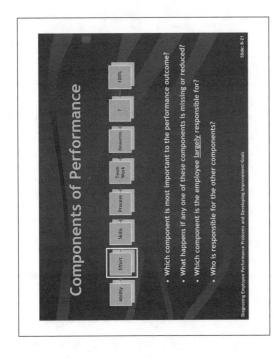

Nine-Plus-One Checklist

Review the Nine-Plus-One Checklist:

- What do you *like* about the tool?
- What *questions* do you have about the tool?
- How might you *use the tool* in preparing for a Performance Coaching Conversation?

Diagnosing Employee Performance Problems and Developing Improvement Goals

Slide: 8-26

Cause→Effect Diagram

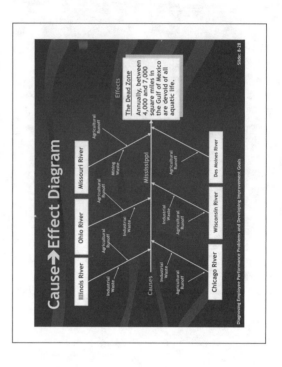

Diagnosing Employee Performance Problems and Developing Improvement Goals

Slide: 8-28

Diagnosing Performance Problems . . .

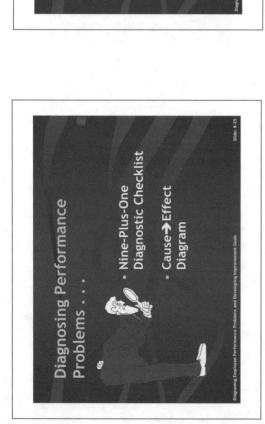

- Nine-Plus-One Diagnostic Checklist
- Cause→Effect Diagram

Diagnosing Employee Performance Problems and Developing Improvement Goals

Slide: 8-25

Cause→Effect Diagram

- Explores the relationship between the effects or performance results and the array of possible causes of these effects.
- Presents a structured brainstorming process where the coach explores how each category of causes contributes to the final effect.

Diagnosing Employee Performance Problems and Developing Improvement Goals

Slide: 8-27

Create a Cause→Effect Diagram

Effects/Outcomes

Missed Deadlines

Organizational Systems & Structures

Equipment & Tools

Policies & Procedures

Overlapping responsibilities
Hiring people without skills
Inadequate Training
Reward system encourages poor performances
Heavy workload and stress
Unresolved disagreements
Constant Change

Machine Breakdowns
Old job descriptions
Database not up to date
Old Technology

Lack of documentation
Outdated SOPs

Lacking key skills
Tends to over-promise
Expectations not always clear
Not understanding expectations
Infrequent feedback
Not available

Environment
The Employee
Supervision

Diagnosing Employee Performance Problems and Developing Improvement Goals

Slide: 8-29

Applying the Cause→Effect . . . .

As a small group . . . .

1. Select a specific performance problem that one of your employees is experiencing (no names please!).

2. Complete a Cause→Effect diagram on this employee with a performance problem.

3. Use the provided flipchart page (landscape orientation).

4. Write the "effect" to the far right, draw the "bones," and label the categories . . . Then begin exploring causes by questioning the "coach" and suggesting possible causes in each category.

Diagnosing Employee Performance Problems and Developing Improvement Goals

Slide: 8-30

The Four *Outcome* Goals

I want the performer to . . . .

- Maintain (M) performance

- Improve (I) performance

- Accept (A) new responsibilities

- Grow (G) the job to a new level

Diagnosing Employee Performance Problems and Developing Improvement Goals

Slide: 8-31

Analyzing Employee Performance

On your own . . . .

- Think of a specific employee in this role.

- Review the great performance outcomes of Part A and the Job or Organizational responsibilities and the SMART objectives listed in Parts B and C.

- Designate each outcome, responsibility area, or SMART objective with a letter designation that reflects the performance of the <u>employee</u>: M, I, A, or G.

- You have about seven minutes!

Diagnosing Employee Performance Problems and Developing Improvement Goals

Slide: 8-32

Identifying Process Goals

On your own . . . .

1. Complete Part E of the worksheet.
2. Review page three of Handout 15 and the four *process* goals.
3. Identify one or two *process* goals for the employee.
4. Identify strategies to pursue these goals.
5. You have five minutes!

Diagnosing Employee Performance Problems and Developing Improvement Goals

Slide: 8-34

Developing Improvement Goals

On your own . . . .

1. Complete one or two goals in Part F of the worksheet.
2. Focus on improvement or development areas that are the highest value/highest priority.
3. Make the goal a SMART goal.
4. Identify possible measures (using handout 14).
5. Identify specific employee behaviors that will enable the performer to achieve the goal.

Diagnosing Employee Performance Problems and Developing Improvement Goals

Slide: 8-36

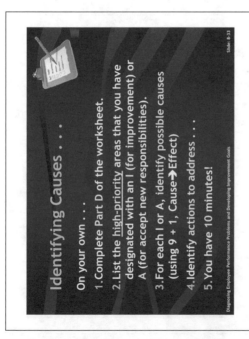

Identifying Causes . . . .

On your own . . . .

1. Complete Part D of the worksheet.
2. List the high-priority areas that you have designated with an I (for improvement) or A (for accept new responsibilities).
3. For each I or A, identify possible causes (using 9 + 1, Cause➔Effect)
4. Identify actions to address . . . .
5. You have 10 minutes!

Diagnosing Employee Performance Problems and Developing Improvement Goals

Slide: 8-33

Developing *Positive* Goals

Developing *positive* improvement goals involves (a) being behaviorally specific and (b) focusing on *increasing* behaviors and results.

She has a poor attitude.	She needs to offer _more_ ideas.
He is slow in processing claims.	He needs to process claims _more_ quickly.
She is too dependent on me.	She needs to work _more_ independently.
He is too sociable.	He needs to _increase_ his attention to completing work.

Diagnosing Employee Performance Problems and Developing Improvement Goals

Slide: 8-35

Conclusion and Integration

- Employee performance diagnosis and improvement planning is what a good coach does every day.

- Guiding employees toward Great Performance requires the coach to understand the key factors and forces that support or disable performance.

- Documenting performance using a variety to methods and tools is critical to ensure that coaching decisions are based upon data.

- The 85/15 Rule asks us to first look at *system* causes of performance failures before focusing on employee motivation and effort.

Diagnosing Employee Performance Problems and Developing Improvement Goals

Slide: 8-38

Thank You!

. . . for being part of this program on diagnosing performance problems.

Please complete the course evaluation.

Next: Conducting Coaching Conversations!

© 2008. Photo by Jeffrey Russell

An undefined problem has an infinite number of solutions.

Conclusion and Integration

- The Nine-Plus-One Performance Diagnostic Checklist and the Cause→Effect Diagram aid both the coach and the employee in diagnosing problems.

- There are four performance diagnostic states or conditions: *maintaining* performance, *improving* performance, *accepting* new responsibilities, and *growing* the job in a new direction.

- When developing improvement plans, focus on establishing *positive* improvement or development goals.

Diagnosing Employee Performance Problems and Developing Improvement Goals

Slide: 8-39

One-Day Workshop on Conducting Performance Coaching and Annual Performance Analysis and Planning Conversations

9

What's in This Chapter?

- Objectives of the one-day workshop on conducting performance coaching and annual performance analysis and planning conversations

- Ideas for designing the workshop

- Workshop agenda and facilitator's guide

▲   ▲   ▲

There's a very good chance that you bought this book just for this chapter. You've been given the job of designing a workshop on conducting performance reviews and this book seemed the perfect fit for you. If you've read chapter 2 and reviewed the workshop designs in chapters 6, 7, and 8, however, we hope that by now, you see that this book is about much more than the dreaded performance review. Our goal for the book and for this chapter is to transform your thinking—moving it away from the traditional performance appraisal model and toward an innovative employee-centered alternative.

The previous chapters have given you foundation material: the Great Performance Management Cycle, the roles of an effective coach within this cycle, the emphasis on employee ownership and responsibility for performance, the tools for setting performance objectives and diagnosing performance problems, and the mutual learning mindset. This chapter pulls all of these pieces together within the critical face-to-face Performance Coaching Conversation or Annual Performance Analysis and Planning Conversation. For beyond all of the philosophy, transformational mindsets, and tools, the actual Performance Coaching Conversation is where the real work begins. This interaction is where the employee receives feedback from the coach, performance improvement plans are developed, the employee assumes the lead role in developing these plans, and the partnership for performance between the coach and the employee is strengthened. If these Performance Coaching Conversations go well, great performance happens. If they don't go well, the performance partnership deteriorates, employee commitment to the job declines, obstacles to performance become excuses, and employee performance will likely fail.

The stakes are high. We need to build a new coaching conversation skill set in our managers that enables them to see the significant benefits of a meaningful dialogue with their direct reports. We need to help them view the Performance Coaching Conversation and the Annual Performance Analysis and Planning Conversation as a simple, straight-forward, and even an exciting process that they and their direct reports will see as essential for their mutual success. Our goal with the Performance Coaching Conversation and the Annual Performance Analysis and Planning Conversation is to introduce a process that both the employee and the coach will look forward to conducting on a regular basis. Rather than a review that takes place once or twice a year, the Performance Coaching Conversation becomes a routine conversation between the coach and the employee. Instead of focusing on appraisal and judgment of past performance, our reconceived coaching conversation focuses on improving performance for the future. The process is no longer orchestrated and driven by the manager; our coaching conversation is employee-centered—a process where the employee takes the lead in analyzing performance and developing improvement plans.

The more formal annual or semi-annual "review" still takes place, but the official forms are filled out following the Annual Performance Analysis and Planning Conversation. This annual process—which could also be semi-annual, depending on the expectations of the organization—is built on the same employee-centered foundation of the more frequent Performance Coaching Conversation. In fact, as you will see in the supporting materials for the workshop design featured in this chapter, little is different between these two conversations. The basic structure of each conversation is precisely the same. The Annual Performance Analysis and Planning Conversation adds a few extra steps—mostly related to completing the necessary performance review forms and exploring performance goals for the next performance period.

This chapter introduces the Performance Coaching Conversation and the Annual Performance Analysis and Planning Conversation in a one-day workshop design that leads managers in a different approach to the traditional performance appraisal review. The previous two chapters introduced tools to aid in the development of performance objectives, analyze employee performance, explore the root causes of performance problems, and develop performance improvement plans. The workshop in this chapter integrates all of the previous work done within the partnership for performance and builds skills in the manager for constructing a meaningful coaching conversation.

Because of the developmental nature of the workshops in chapters 6 through 9, the workshops should be offered in sequence, with each workshop building on the work of the preceding one. Also, all workshop designs in chapters 6 through 8 build toward the integrating workshop in this chapter. The Performance Planning and Development Worksheet (**training instrument 12**), completed by participants in both the Performance Goal Setting Workshop and Diagnosing Employee Performance Problems and Developing Improvement Plans Workshop, will be used in this chapter as well.

We recommend, therefore, that you offer this workshop soon after the one-day workshop on diagnosing performance problems and developing improvement plans. This will help ensure that participants will begin implementing their routine coaching conversations rather than waiting for the annual review. Our goal is to get managers to transform the way they interact with their direct reports and to strengthen their performance partnerships; therefore, we need to put a new, transformational process in their hands: the Performance Coaching Conversation and the Annual Performance Analysis and Planning Conversation.

One-Day Workshop: Conducting Performance Coaching and Annual Performance Analysis and Planning Conversations

Objectives

As a result of participating in this one-day workshop on conducting Performance Coaching Conversations and Annual Performance Analysis and Planning Conversations, participants will be able to perform these tasks:

- Describe the purpose of the traditional performance review and of the transformational Performance Coaching Conversation alternative.

- Describe why the traditional performance review tends to be counterproductive and discourages rather than encourages great employee performance.

- Identify some common rating errors in the traditional review and identify strategies to overcome these rating errors.

- Identify the hazards that occur when the coach and employee use a unilateral control mindset as compared to the opportunities that ensue when both use a mutual learning mindset.

- Practice the mutual learning mindset and the governing values, assumptions, and behaviors that constitute this mindset.

- Conduct the employee-centered Performance Coaching Conversations and Annual Performance Analysis and Planning Conversations.

Materials

For the Instructor:

- Learning Activity 2: Goal Setting

- Learning Activity 29: The Performance Management Quiz

- Learning Activity 30: Performance Reviews From the Dark and Light Sides

- Learning Activity 31: Common Errors of the Traditional Review

- Learning Activity 32: The Purposes of Performance Reviews

- Learning Activity 33: The Great Performance Management Cycle and the Performance Coaching Conversation

- Learning Activity 34: Active Listening and the Values, Assumptions, and Behaviors of the Mutual Learning Mindset

- Learning Activity 35: The Performance Coaching and Annual Performance Analysis and Planning Conversations

- Learning Activity 36: The Performance Coaching Conversation—Behavioral Modeling

- Learning Activity 37: Practicing the Performance Coaching Conversation—Participant Role Plays

- Learning Activity 38: The Organization's Expectations and Obligations for Documenting Performance Conversations

- Training Tool 1: Training Room Configuration/Layout

- Training Tool 2: Learning Goal/Objective ➔ Outcomes

- Training Tool 3: "Aha!" Sheet

- Training Tool 4: Training Program Reaction Sheet

- Training Tool 5: Selecting Group Leaders

- flipchart and marking pens

- PowerPoint slides 9-1 through 9-40

For the participants:

- Handout 4: The Great Performance Management Cycle (optional, as participants received this handout in a previous learning activity)

- Handout 8: Unilateral Control and Mutual Learning Mindsets (optional, as participants are likely to have received this handout in earlier workshops)

- Handout 9: Values and Behaviors for Mutual Learning (optional, as participants are likely to have received this handout in earlier workshops)

- Handout 16: Tools for Documenting Performance (optional, as participants received this handout in a previous learning activity)

- Handout 22: Actions for Reducing Rating Errors

- Handout 23: The Purposes of Performance Reviews

- Handout 24: Reframing the Traditional Review

- Handout 25: Unbundling the Process

- Handout 26: Whole Body Listening

- Handout 27: The Four Skills of Active Listening

- Handout 28: The Performance Coaching Conversation

- Handout 29: Evolutionary vs. Revolutionary Performance Management

- Training Instrument 20: Performance Management Quiz

- Training Instrument 21: Performance Reviews From the Dark and Light Sides

- Training Instrument 22: Common Errors in Performance Reviews

- Training Instrument 23: Actions to Reduce Errors in Performance Reviews

- Training Instrument 24: Identifying the Purposes of Performance Reviews

- Training Instrument 25: Active Listening Application

Using the Accompanying CD Materials

Materials for this training session are provided either in this workbook or as electronic files on the associated CD. Further directions and assistance in using the files can be found in the appendix, "Using the Accompanying CD Materials," at the back of the workbook.

Preparations

Before the Workshop:

1. If appropriate, meet with a representative or representatives from the executive leadership team to discuss their expectations for the Performance Coaching and Annual Performance Analysis and Planning Conversations Workshop. For this workshop to be successful, the organization's leadership must not only support the idea of their managers conducting routine performance coaching conversations, but they should also model these practices in their own actions as leaders. If possible, get the members of the leadership team to attend this session together with their managers—or run a special session for the leadership team. Either way, the organization's leadership should be on board with this approach and then demonstrate it in their actions.

2. Decide on your target audience for the workshop. This workshop is intended as a follow-along to the previous three workshops on establishing a coaching relationship, setting performance objectives, and diagnosing performance problems and developing improvement plans. Although the focus is primarily on the manager, employees would benefit equally if the workshop were modified slightly.

3. Design the program with the organization's culture, methods, and systems for performance management and providing performance feedback and reviews in mind. If some organizational practices run counter to approaches to the Performance Coaching Conversation and the Annual Performance Analysis and Planning Conversation approaches introduced in this workshop, then attempt to work with the leadership to bring these practices more into line with the approach introduced in this book.

4. Schedule the session and secure a training room for the workshop.

5. Prepare training materials (handouts, training instruments, instructions, training program evaluation form, PowerPoint presentation, and supporting audio-visual materials).

6. Send a memo, letter, or email of invitation to participants reiterating the purpose of the Conducting Performance Coaching and Annual Performance Analysis and Planning Conversations Workshop and the importance of this workshop to managing employee performance and building employee ownership of their success. Ask participants to bring **training instrument 12** (Performance Planning and Development Worksheet), which they worked on in previous sessions.

7. Order food and beverages as necessary.

The Day of the Workshop:

1. Arrive early at the training room.

 2. Verify room setup, using **tool 1**.

3. Set up and test equipment such as flipcharts, markers, LCD projector, overhead projector, and so forth.

4. Prepare and post flipchart pages titled "Your Questions/Goals" if desired, as well as any additional flipchart pages detailed in the Learning Activities. You may also want to post another flipchart page highlighting key questions that you plan to address during the workshop and that relate to the objectives.

 5. Place participant materials on tables. Ensure that a copy of **training instrument 20** (the Performance Management Quiz) is placed in front of each participant's chair and on top of all other materials.

 6. Display PowerPoint **slide 9-1** as a welcome and greeting to participants as they enter the training room.

7. Greet and connect with individual participants as they enter the training room. Establish rapport with each, as they arrive. Inquire into their department, role, time with the organization, and so forth.

8. Guide participants to their seats and encourage them to complete the Performance Management Quiz that you have placed in front of their chairs.

Sample Agenda

8:30 a.m. Welcome (5 minutes)

 Welcome participants to Conducting Performance Coaching and Annual Performance Analysis and Planning Conversations Workshop. Introduce yourself. Ask them to complete the Performance Management Quiz (**training instrument 20**) as you begin the day.

 Display **slide 9-2**, which reveals a quote from W. Edwards Deming. Ask participants for their reactions.

Participants may offer reactions such as:

- What did Deming have against performance reviews?

- Then why do we have to do them?

- Sounds as though they more counterproductive than useful.

- Is there a way to make the review more effective?

- Why do they create these kinds of effects on people and performance?

Respond by suggesting that Deming was critical of performance reviews and performance ratings because they focused on judging or evaluating someone's past performance rather than on improving it. He also expressed concerns with rating systems, which were imprecise and incomplete, and the fact that it was often difficult to sort out an individual's contribution to performance from the performance of the larger system.

Inform the participants that today's task is to build an alternative approach to performance reviews—what we call the Performance Coaching Conversation and the Annual Performance Analysis and Planning Conversation—that avoids many of the problems that Deming identified, all the while building employee commitment to achieving great performance for the organization.

Highlight some of the key questions that you'll be exploring with them before moving into **learning activity 2**. Some of the questions you can post on a flipchart and highlight to the group include:

- What is the purpose of the performance review?
- What are some common problems with the traditional performance appraisal?
- How can we create a meaningful employee-centered review process?
- How often should the Performance Coaching Conversation occur?
- How often should the Annual Performance Analysis and Planning Conversation occur?

 8:35 **Learning Activity 2: Goal Setting** (25 minutes)

Introduce this learning activity by noting the importance of participants setting personal learning objectives for the workshop. This activity also identifies key questions that the participants would like to answer in the workshop.

 8:50 **Learning Activity 29: The Performance Management Quiz** (10 minutes)

Guide participants through each of the questions on this quiz. This activity asks participants as a large group to identify what they believe to be the correct answers.

 9:00 **Learning Activity 30: Performance Reviews From the Dark and Light Sides** (20 minutes)

This activity asks participants to think of a particularly bad performance review they experienced and a particularly positive one. Based on their individual experiences, the participants will offer some suggestions to enhance and strengthen performance reviews, which will be reinforced in subsequent learning activities.

 9:20 **Learning Activity 31: Common Errors of Traditional Reviews** (25 minutes)

This brief activity identifies some of the most common errors of traditional performance reviews and asks participants to develop ways to reduce these errors in the review process.

 9:45 **Learning Activity 32: The Purposes of Performance Reviews** (35 minutes)

This activity asks participants to identify the multiple purposes of the performance review and ends with you highlighting what should be the core purpose of the alternative Performance Coaching Conversation and the Annual Performance Analysis and Planning Conversation.

10:20   Break (15 minutes)

 10:35   **Learning Activity 33: The Great Performance Management Cycle and the Performance Coaching Conversation** (10 minutes)

In this activity, you offer a quick review of the Great Performance Management Cycle (introduced in chapter 6) and briefly identify the role of both the Performance Coaching Conversation and the Annual Performance Analysis and Planning Conversation within the cycle.

10:45   **Learning Activity 34: Active Listening and the Values, Assumptions, and Behaviors of the Mutual Learning Mindset** (45 minutes)

Transition participants from the previous activity. Note the role that the mutual learning mindset and active listening play within the Great Performance Management Cycle and during the Performance Coaching Conversation and the Annual Performance Analysis and Planning Conversation.

This learning activity reconnects participants with the mutual learning mindset, highlights four active listening skills, and has participants practice active listening within the mutual learning mindset.

Noon   Lunch (60 minutes)

1:00   **Learning Activity 35: The Performance Coaching Conversation and the Annual Performance Analysis and Planning Conversation** (40 minutes)

This activity introduces the model for conducting the Performance Coaching Conversation and the Annual Performance Analysis and Planning Conversation. Participants will review the conversation model, identify and answer questions about the model, and be encouraged to modify the model to suit their particular approach and personality.

1:40   **Learning Activity 36: The Performance Coaching Conversation—Behavioral Modeling** (35 minutes)

In this activity, you will use behavioral modeling to demonstrate the Performance Coaching Conversation, active listening, and the governing values, assumptions, and behaviors of the mutual learning mindset. Participants will observe, comment on, and offer questions about the model-in-practice.

2:05   Break (15 minutes)

 2:20   **Learning Activity 37: Practicing the Performance Coaching Conversation—Participant Role Plays** (50 minutes)

This learning activity engages participants in practicing the Performance Coaching Conversation and applying it to one of their performance partnerships. Participants will pair up with another person from the group, role play the performance coaching situation described in the Performance Planning and Development Worksheet (**training instrument 12**), debrief, and then switch roles.

The activity ends with a final question and answer period to refine participant understanding and application of the Performance Coaching Conversation model.

3:10   **Learning Activity 38: The Organization's Expectations and Obligations for Documenting Performance Conversations** (40 minutes)

In this activity you will highlight your organization's expectations for documenting the Annual Performance Analysis and Planning Conversation. You will distribute and review the forms that must be completed following the annual performance conversations. You will also highlight key dates when completed forms are due to human resources.

4:00   Integration and Conclusion (25 minutes)

Introduce the concluding activity by highlighting the major accomplishments of the day. The participants have learned

- the purpose of performance reviews within the larger framework of the Great Performance Management Cycle

- why traditional performance reviews are counterproductive

- an employee-centered alternative: the Performance Coaching Conversation model that is based on the mutual learning mindset.

Ask people to refer to their Performance Review Quiz (**training instrument 20**) as you display **slides 9-35 and 9-36** and elicit their responses to each of the questions on the quiz. Celebrate the participants choosing the right answers based on the insights and lessons of the day.

If appropriate, review any of the remaining unanswered questions from the personal learning goals activity flipchart pages. As time permits, ask participants to answer any questions that have not yet been addressed during the workshop. Depending on available time, you can either assign questions for the small groups to address or facilitate a large-group discussion of unanswered questions.

Your concluding remarks should highlight these key points as you display **slides 9-37 and 9-38:**

- The traditional performance review deserves the bad reputation that it has—because it is based on the unilateral control mindset.

- The employee-centered Performance Coaching Conversation and Annual Performance Analysis and Planning Conversation offer an innovative alternative that is based on the mutual learning mindset.

- Many of the errors in the traditional performance review are eliminated or significantly reduced by the frequency and focus of the Performance Coaching Conversation and the Annual Performance Analysis and Planning Conversation approach.

- Reiterate the organization's formal process for documenting the Annual Performance Analysis and Planning Conversation.

Encourage participants to integrate the key lessons from the workshop into their future Performance Coaching Conversations and Annual Performance Analysis and Planning Conversations.

 Conclude by displaying **slide 9-39**. Note that Lao Tzu, Chinese poet and philosopher, suggests that the best leaders aren't in front and "leading the charge"; instead, they are quiet, leading from behind, enabling others to say "Amazing, we did it all by ourselves!"

4:25   Evaluation (5 minutes)

 Display **slide 9-40**. Thank the participants for attending the Conducting Performance Coaching and Annual Performance Analysis and Planning Conversations Workshop and for their active involvement throughout the session.

 Distribute **tool 4** and encourage participants to leave the completed forms at their tables or a designated location.

4:30   Close

The next chapter includes an agenda and learning activities for a half-day workshop for employees on the Great Performance Management Cycle, their role and responsibilities throughout the cycle, and the Performance Coaching Conversation and the Annual Performance Analysis and Planning Conversation. This next workshop takes steps to build employee ownership of performance and increases their knowledge of and comfort with the new Performance Coaching Conversation process.

What to Do Next

- Prepare for the one-day session.

- Compile the learning activities, handouts, and PowerPoint slides you will use in the training.

- Decide the timing of this session in relation to the workshops that precede it.

PowerPoint Slides

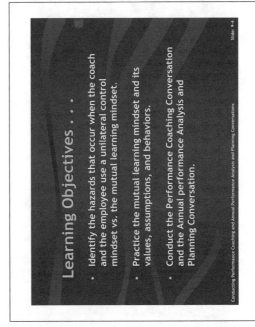

Meet and Greet!

- Introduce yourself to your table partners
- Share your personal objective(s) for the day
- As a group . . . identify some common goals/issues of interest to the group
- Develop two or three questions about performance reviews and coaching conversations that your group would like to have answered by the end of today.

Conducting Performance Coaching and Annual Performance Analysis and Planning Conversations

Slide: 9-6

Performance Management Quiz

6. The best way to kick off a performance coaching conversation is to . . .

7. Star performers don't generally benefit from performance reviews . . .

8. What percentage of time should the employee and coach talk . . .

9. The halo/horn effect in performance reviews means that a coach needs to be aware of . . .

10. The four skills of active listening include . . .

Conducting Performance Coaching and Annual Performance Analysis and Planning Conversations

Slide: 9-8

Your Goals/Objectives . . .

What are your goals for this session?

- What is your *learning objective?* What behavior do you want to learn/change?
- What is the *benefit* of achieving your objective? What outcomes might you expect?
- How much do you *value* this outcome?

Conducting Performance Coaching and Annual Performance Analysis and Planning Conversations

Slide: 9-5

Performance Management Quiz

1. Coaching conversations/reviews should be conducted . . .

2. One way to deal with the recency effect in performance reviews is to . . .

3. The purpose of the Performance Coaching Conversation and the Annual Performance Analysis and Planning Conversation is to . . .

4. The purpose of the coach is to . . .

5. The problem with most traditional performance reviews, is that . . .

Conducting Performance Coaching and Annual Performance Analysis and Planning Conversations

Slide: 9-7

Slide: 9-10

Common Rater Errors . . . .

1. Rater Characteristics
2. Relationship between the Coach and Employee
3. Recency Effect
4. Halo/Horn Effect
5. Timing Errors
6. Restriction in the Rating Scale
7. Contrast Effect

Conducting Performance Coaching and Annual Performance Analysis and Planning Conversations

---

Slide: 9-12

Tools for Documenting . . . .

- Performance Log
- Critical Incidents Log
- Email Documentation
- Performance Portfolio

Conducting Performance Coaching and Annual Performance Analysis and Planning Conversations

---

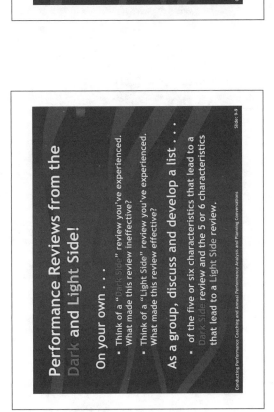

Slide: 9-9

Performance Reviews from the Dark and Light Side!

On your own . . . .

- Think of a "Dark Side" review you've experienced. What made this review ineffective?
- Think of a "Light Side" review you've experienced. What made this review effective?

As a group, discuss and develop a list . . . .

- of the five or six characteristics that lead to a Dark Side review and the 5 or 6 characteristics that lead to a Light Side review.

Conducting Performance Coaching and Annual Performance Analysis and Planning Conversations

---

Slide: 9-11

Actions to Reduce Rater Errors

As a small group, identify . . . .

Coach Actions . . .

- How might the coach reduce rater errors?
- What actions can the coach take before and during a performance review to reduce these sources of error?
- How will the coach ensure equity/fairness in his/her assessments?

Employee Actions . . . .

- What can an employee do to help you reduce rating errors (and ensure the accuracy of the performance assessment process)?

Conducting Performance Coaching and Annual Performance Analysis and Planning Conversations

Purpose/Importance of PR

In your small group . . . .

- For your assigned individual/group, identify the purpose the performance review fulfills for this individual or group and identify its value and importance to this individual or group's interests and needs.

Conducting Performance Coaching and Annual Performance Analysis and Planning Conversations

Slide: 9-14

The Core Purposes of Reviews

Individual Performer, Supervisor, and Coach

- Align employee contributions with the needs/goals of the team, department, and organization.
- Explore the employee's potential future contributions to the team, department, and organization.
- Celebrate and reward great performance outcomes.
- Provide negative consequences when warranted.
- Identify performance goals for the next period.

Conducting Performance Coaching and Annual Performance Analysis and Planning Conversations

Slide: 9-16

What is the purpose of the performance review?

The Core Purposes of Reviews

Individual Performer, Supervisor, and Coach

- Provide employee feedback on performance.
- Identify barriers to performance.
- Develop improvement plans.
- Enhance employee commitment to the job, team, and organization.
- Identify performer's support needs.
- Identify the employee's training, development, and career goals.

Conducting Performance Coaching and Annual Performance Analysis and Planning Conversations

Slide: 9-15

The Core Purposes of Reviews

Team/Work Unit, Department, and Organization

- Ensure objective, data-based assessments of employee performance.
- Equitably distribute pay adjustments based on performance.
- Identify high potentials for future development.
- Flag problem performers for tracking and follow-up.
- Ensure quality outcomes from employee effort.

Conducting Performance Coaching and Annual Performance Analysis and Planning Conversations

Slide: 9-18

Unbundling the Process

- Critical Incident Coaching Conversation: Addressing specific performance problems when they arise; exploring and addressing causes.
- Performance Coaching Conversation and Annual Performance Analysis and Planning Conversation: Facilitating employee commitment to great performance and the organization; developing growth and improvement plans.
- Performance Review: Completing the official assessment forms and rating the employee, documenting performance issues, and determining pay and other HR outcomes.

Conducting Performance Coaching and Annual Performance Analysis and Planning Conversations

Slide: 9-20

The Core Purposes of Reviews

Team/Work Unit, Department, and Organization

- Value the employee's contribution to the team/work unit effort.
- Identify training and development goals for the overall team, work unit, department, and organization.
- Align individual's efforts with the needs/goals of the team, department, and organization.

Conducting Performance Coaching and Annual Performance Analysis and Planning Conversations

Slide: 9-17

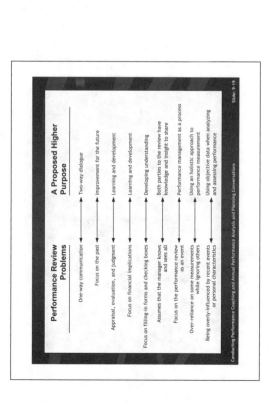

Performance Review Problems	A Proposed Higher Purpose
One-way communication	Two-way dialogue
Focus on the past	Improvement for the future
Appraisal, evaluation, and judgment	Learning and development
Focus on financial implications	Learning and development
Focus on filling-in forms and checking boxes	Developing understanding
Assumes that the manager knows and sees all	Both parties to the review have knowledge and insight to share
Focus on the performance review as an event	Performance management as a process
Over-reliance on some measurements while ignoring others	Using an holistic approach to performance measurement
Being overly-influenced by recent events or personal characteristics	Using objective data when analyzing and assessing performance

Conducting Performance Coaching and Annual Performance Analysis and Planning Conversations

Slide: 9-19

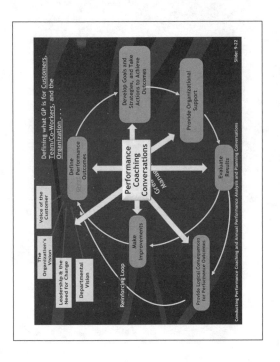

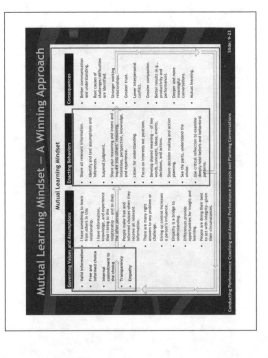

Active Listening Skills

- Drawing Out
- Clarifying
- Reflecting
- Paraphrasing

Conducting Performance Coaching and Annual Performance Analysis and Planning Conversations

Slide: 9-25

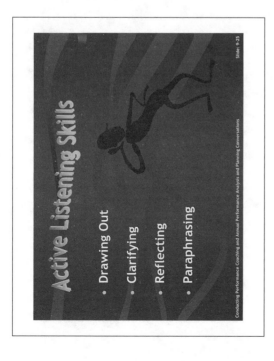

Practicing Active Listening

- Get into groups of three
- Three rounds: each will take turns as speaker, listener, and observer
- Read Training Instrument 26 for information about your role
- Speaker: Select something that's important to you now!
- Listener: Don't try to solve the problem!
- Observer: Be prepared to give feedback.

Conducting Performance Coaching and Annual Performance Analysis and Planning Conversations

Slide: 9-26

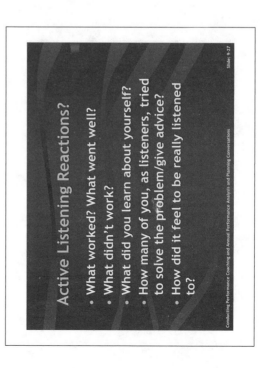

Active Listening Reactions?

- What worked? What went well?
- What didn't work?
- What did you learn about yourself?
- How many of you, as listeners, tried to solve the problem/give advice?
- How did it feel to be really listened to?

Conducting Performance Coaching and Annual Performance Analysis and Planning Conversations

Slide: 9-27

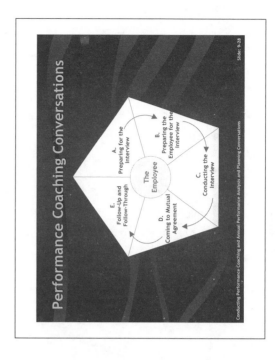

Performance Coaching Conversations

A. Preparing for the Interview

B. Preparing the Employee for the Interview

C. Conducting the Interview

D. Coming to Mutual Agreement

E. Follow-Up and Follow-Through

The Employee

Conducting Performance Coaching and Annual Performance Analysis and Planning Conversations

Slide: 9-28

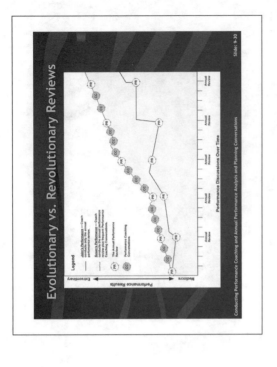

Slide: 9-30

Evolutionary vs. Revolutionary Reviews

Conducting Performance Coaching and Annual Performance Analysis and Planning Conversations

Slide: 9-32

Debriefing Your Role Play

Coach . . .
- What went well with the process?
- What didn't go as well?
- Where did you get stuck?
- What would you do differently?

Employee . . .
- Provide feedback on what worked about the conversation and what didn't work.

Conducting Performance Coaching and Annual Performance Analysis and Planning Conversations

Slide: 9-29

Reactions to the Conversation

- What do you LIKE about the Performance Coaching Conversation process?
- What isn't clear? What's confusing?
- What questions do you have about the process?
- How might you customize or modify the process to better fit your own approach and practice?

Conducting Performance Coaching and Annual Performance Analysis and Planning Conversations

Slide: 9-31

Coaching Conversation Role Play

- Note the flow of the conversation.
- What are you hearing that works or doesn't work for your own approach?
- How are mistakes handled?
- At key points, what would you do or say that's different from what the coach says or does?

Conducting Performance Coaching and Annual Performance Analysis and Planning Conversations

Slides related to your organization's performance review process

Slide: 9-34

Conducting Performance Coaching and Annual Performance Analysis and Planning Conversations

Performance Management Quiz

6. The best way to kick off a Performance Coaching Conversation is to . . . C

7. Star performers don't generally benefit from performance reviews . . . NO

8. What percentage of time should the employee and coach talk . . . D or E

9. The halo/horn effect in performance reviews means that a coach needs to be aware of . . . E

10. The four skills of active listening include . . . A

Slide: 9-36

Conducting Performance Coaching and Annual Performance Analysis and Planning Conversations

Quality is impossible if people are afraid to tell the truth.

— W. Edwards Deming

U.S. Quality leader (1900 – 1993)

Performance Management Quiz

1. Coaching conversations/reviews should be conducted . . . C

2. One way to deal with the recency effect in performance reviews is to . . . A

3. The purpose of the Performance Coaching Conversation and the Annual Performance Analysis and Planning Conversation is to . . . E

4. The purpose of the coach is to . . . E

5. The problem with most traditional performance reviews, is that . . . E

Slide: 9-35

Conducting Performance Coaching and Annual Performance Analysis and Planning Conversations

Concluding Thoughts . . . .

- Many of the errors in the traditional performance review are eliminated or significantly reduced by the frequency and focus of the Performance Coaching Conversation and the Annual Performance Analysis and Planning Conversation approach.

- (Notes on the organization's performance review process.)

Conducting Performance Coaching and Annual Performance Analysis and Planning Conversations

Slide: 9-38

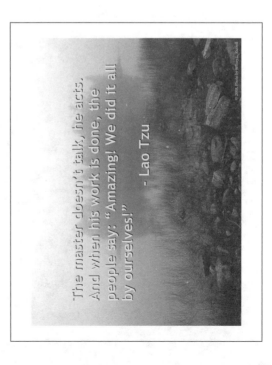

Thank You!

. . . for being part of this coaching conversations skills development program.

Please complete the course evaluation!

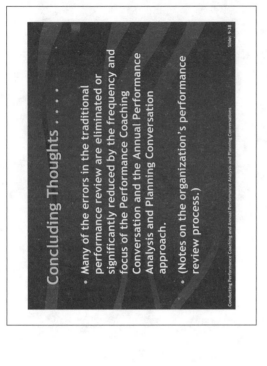

Concluding Thoughts . . . .

- The traditional performance review deserves its bad reputation because it is based on the unilateral control mindset.

- The Performance Coaching Conversation and the Annual Performance Analysis and Planning Conversation offer an innovative alternative that is based in the mutual learning mindset.

Conducting Performance Coaching and Annual Performance Analysis and Planning Conversations

Slide: 9-37

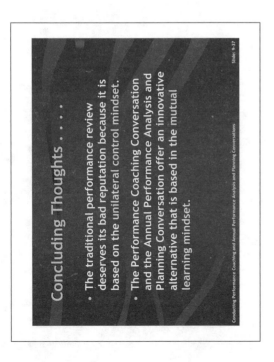

"The master doesn't talk, he acts,
And when his work is done, the people say: "Amazing! We did it all by ourselves!"

– Lao Tzu

Half-Day Workshop on the Employee's Role Within the Partnership for Performance and Performance Coaching Conversations

10

What's in This Chapter?

- Objectives of the half-day workshop on the employee's role within the partnership for performance and the Performance Coaching Conversation

- Ideas for designing the workshop

- Workshop agenda and facilitator's guide.

▲　　▲　　▲

Most of the workshops in this book have targeted their skill-building efforts on your organization's managers and supervisors. Because they are charged with the responsibility of overseeing the work of others, it is natural that we have focused this book on strengthening their managerial skills in this area. As we have said all along, however, a truly effective performance management system involves a partnership between the manager acting as a coach and the frontline employee. We made the case early on that a well-defined performance management system is employee-centered and that the coach plays a facilitative role to ensure that employee ownership and self-management occur. To enable frontline employees to fulfill these roles, we need to help them better understand their active role within this process and then begin building the skills of self-management.

This chapter introduces a half-day workshop designed to help frontline employees understand their role within the Great Performance Management Cycle, their role and responsibilities throughout the cycle, the importance of bringing a mutual learning mindset to the process, and their role within the Performance Coaching Conversation and the Annual Performance Analysis and Planning Conversation. The driving purpose of this workshop is to build employee ownership of their role within the process and to develop their skills so they can meaningfully participate in Performance Coaching Conversations.

This employee workshop is a stand-alone workshop that can be offered at any time in relation to the workshop series for managers and supervisors. Although all of the workshops in this book can easily accommodate participation by both managers and their direct reports—something we actively encourage—this workshop is focused exclusively on frontline employees.

Note: In the "What to Do Next?" section at the end of this chapter, we encourage you to consider increasing the length of this workshop to a full day. If you decide to expand the length of this workshop to include the three additional learning activities, you are likely to achieve greater understanding of the mutual learning mindset in your employees. Employees will also learn how to apply a new tool—the ladder of inference—and have a chance to practice active listening within the context of their Performance Coaching Conversations.

Half-Day Workshop: The Employee's Role Within the Partnership for Performance and Performance Coaching Conversations

Objectives

After participating in this half-day workshop on the employee's role within the partnership for performance and the Performance Coaching Conversations, participants will be able to perform these tasks:

- Describe the Great Performance Management Cycle and their role within the cycle.

- Apply the mutual learning mindset to their role within the Great Performance Management Cycle.

- Actively participate in Performance Coaching Conversations and the Annual Performance Analysis and Planning Conversation.

- Describe the organization's formal processes and timeframes for documenting performance.

Materials

For the instructor:

- Learning Activity 5: The Great Performance Management Cycle

- Learning Activity 8: Unilateral Control and Mutual Learning Mindsets—Two Approaches to Managing Relationships With Others

- Learning Activity 32: The Purposes of Performance Reviews

- Learning Activity 35: The Performance Coaching Conversation and the Annual Performance Analysis and Planning Conversation

- Learning Activity 38: The Organization's Expectations and Obligations for Documenting Performance Conversations

- Training Tool 1: Training Room Configuration/Layout

- Training Tool 3: "Aha!" Sheet

- Training Tool 4: Training Program Reaction Sheet

- Training Tool 5: Selecting Group Leaders

- flipchart and marking pens
- PowerPoint slides 10-1 through 10-36

For the participants:

- Handout 3: The Dynamic Nature of the Coaching Relationship
- Handout 4: The Great Performance Management Cycle
- Handout 5: Defining Great Performance
- Handout 6: Actions for Encouraging Employee Ownership
- Handout 7: The Role of the Coach in Shaping Great Performance
- Handout 8: Unilateral Control and Mutual Learning Mindsets
- Handout 9: Values and Behaviors for Mutual Learning
- Handout 23: The Purposes of Performance Reviews
- Handout 24: Reframing the Traditional Review
- Handout 25: Unbundling the Process
- Handout 28: The Performance Coaching Conversation
- Handout 29: Evolutionary vs. Revolutionary Performance Management

- Training Instrument 5: What Enables Great Performance?
- Training Instrument 6: Building Employee Ownership for Great Performance
- Training Instrument 7: A Personal Plan for Action
- Training Instrument 8: Responding to Threat and Embarrassment
- Training Instrument 24: Identifying the Purposes of Performance Reviews

Using the Accompanying CD

Materials for this training session are provided either in this workbook or as electronic files on the accompanying CD. Further directions and assistance in using the files can be found in the appendix, "Using the Accompanying CD Materials," at the back of this workbook.

Preparations

Before the Workshop:

1. If appropriate, meet with a representative or representatives from the executive leadership team to discuss their expectations for The Employee's Role Within the Partnership for Performance and

Performance Coaching Conversations Workshop. For this workshop to be successful, the organization's leadership must support efforts to build employee ownership of this process instead of expecting that performance management and feedback to be the sole purview of managers and supervisors. The leadership will better appreciate this perspective if they have actively participated in the other workshops included in this book.

2. Decide on your target audience for the workshop. This workshop is designed to focus on building employee ownership for their role within the Great Performance Management Cycle, as well as within the Performance Coaching Conversation and the Annual Performance Analysis and Planning Conversation. Managers and supervisors are encouraged to attend this session, just as employees are encouraged to attend all the other workshops included in this book.

3. Design the program around the organization's culture, methods, and systems for performance management and setting objectives. If there are organizational infrastructures, systems, tools, or processes that help build employee ownership for their performance, integrate these into your training program design. If some organizational practices run counter to employee involvement in performance management, then attempt to work with the leadership to change these practices to bring them more in line with this workshop's approach.

4. Schedule the session and secure a training room for the workshop. Consider the sequencing of this workshop amidst the entire array of workshops that are more geared for managers. The employee skills for self-management are just as important as the manager's coaching skills. Ensure that this workshop is scheduled before or soon after the Performance Coaching and Annual Performance Analysis and Planning Conversations workshop to help build a shared vocabulary and toolset in both managers and their direct reports.

5. Prepare training materials (handouts, training instruments, instructions, training program evaluation form, PowerPoint presentation, and supporting audio-visual materials).

6. Send a memo, letter, or email of invitation to participants reiterating the purpose of The Employee's Role Within the Partnership for Performance and Performance Coaching Conversations Workshop and the importance of this workshop to employee ownership of their performance and understanding of their role within the Great Performance Management Cycle, as well as the Performance Coaching Conversation and Annual Performance Analysis and Planning Conversation.

7. Order food and beverages as necessary.

The Day of the Workshop:

1. Arrive early at the training room.

2. Verify room setup, using **tool 1**.

3. Set up and test equipment such as flipcharts, markers, LCD projector, overhead projector, and so forth.

4. Prepare and post flipchart pages titled "Your Questions/Goals" if desired, as well as any additional flipchart pages that are detailed in the Learning Activities. You may also want to post another flipchart page highlighting key questions that you plan to address during the workshop and that relate to the objectives.

5. Place participant materials on tables.

 6. Display PowerPoint **slide 10-1** as a welcome and greeting to participants as they enter the training room.

7. Greet and connect with individual participants as they enter the training room. Establish rapport, and inquire into their department, role, time with the organization, and so forth.

Sample Agenda

8:30 a.m.   Welcome (5 minutes)

Welcome participants to The Employee's Role Within the Partnership for Performance and Performance Coaching Conversations Workshop. Introduce yourself. Display **slide 10-2**, which reveals a quote by Herbert Agar. Ask participants what the quote means to them—especially in the context of performance management.

Participants may offer these ideas and others:

- People don't like hearing bad news, although it may be news that they *need* to hear.

- Managers and their direct reports need to find ways to engage in meaningful dialogue around performance issues.

- It's difficult to improve performance without people talking honestly to one another.

Reinforce any of these and related responses. Make the point that the focus of today's workshop is on creating working relationships between managers and employees, such that they can speak openly and honestly to each other.

Highlight some of the key questions that you'll be exploring with them during the workshop. You can post these questions on a flipchart and highlight them for the group:

- Who is responsible for managing performance?

- What role does the manager as coach play within the performance management cycle?

- What role does the employee play within this cycle?

- How can managers and employees adopt a learning framework throughout the performance management process?

- What role should both the manager and the employee take within the Performance Coaching Conversation and the Annual Performance Analysis and Planning Conversation?

 8:35   **Learning Activity 5: The Great Performance Management Cycle** (60 minutes)

This activity introduces the Great Performance Management Cycle and guides participants in exploring the role of the coach and of the employee throughout this cycle.

The purpose of this activity is to help provide employees a larger framework for understanding the factors that contribute to achieving great performance.

9:30   **Learning Activity 8: Unilateral Control and Mutual Learning Mindsets—Two Approaches to Managing Relationships With Others** (25 minutes)

This activity introduces the underlying values, assumptions, and enacting behaviors of the mutual learning mindset. Participants will ask and answer questions about these values, assumptions, and behaviors.

This activity, when used within this workshop, should be modified to fit the timeframe for the half-day program. To reduce the time of this activity by half, it is recommended that the content is covered and handouts are distributed but that small-group discussions are eliminated. If this workshop is expanded to a full day, then the full activity should be used.

The key take-away from this activity is the importance of assuming a learning mindset within a process that often produces the opposite.

10:00   Break (15 minutes)

10:15   **Learning Activity 32: The Purposes of the Performance Review** (30 minutes)

This activity asks participants to identify the multiple purposes of the performance review and ends with you highlighting the core purpose of the alternative Performance Coaching Conversation and the Annual Performance Analysis and Planning Conversation.

10:45   **Learning Activity 35: The Performance Coaching and Annual Performance Analysis and Planning Conversations** (35 minutes)

This activity introduces the model for conducting the Performance Coaching Conversation and the Annual Performance Analysis and Planning Conversation. Participants will review the conversation model and identify and answer questions about the model.

11:20   **Learning Activity 38: The Organization's Expectations and Obligations for Documenting Performance** (30 minutes)

In this activity—slightly abbreviated from the version presented in chapter 9—you will highlight your organization's expectations for documenting the Annual Performance Analysis and Planning Conversation. You will distribute and review the forms that must be completed following the annual performance conversations and highlight key dates when completed forms are due to human resources.

11:50   Integration, Conclusion, and Evaluation (10 minutes)

Introduce the concluding activity by reiterating that the organization has moved away from the traditional performance review process and toward a process that strengthens the working relationship between employees and their managers and increases the frequency of communications around performance.

Distribute **training tool 4** and ask participants to complete the course evaluation as you offer some concluding remarks. Encourage participants to leave the completed forms at their tables or a designated location.

Your concluding remarks should highlight these key points as you display **slide 10-34:**

- Achieving great performance results from a strong performance partnership between the employee and the coach, with the coach playing a supporting role.

- When both the employee and the manager assume a mutual learning mindset within the performance management process, communication and understanding are enhanced and great performance is more likely.

- The more often the employee and manager meet to discuss performance using the Performance Coaching Conversation approach, the stronger their relationship will be, the earlier problems are identified and addressed, and the faster the employee's performance improves.

- The main purpose of the performance review is to maximize communication with an aim at improved performance. The "form" should never get in the way of this communication and understanding.

Encourage participants to integrate the lessons from the workshop into their future interactions with their manager—especially in relation to managing their performance.

Reinforce the importance of the employee's role in managing his or her own performance and the value of bringing a mutual learning mindset into all working relationships.

End the session by displaying **slide 10-35** with a quote from Lao Tzu, the Taoist poet and philosopher. Suggest that the best coaches enable people to say, "Amazing! We did it all by ourselves!"

12:00   Close. Display **slide 10-36**, reminding participants to fill out the evaluation form.

◆ What to Do Next

- Prepare for the half-day session.

- Consider expanding this workshop to a full day by adding learning activities that support the core learning objectives for this workshop. These learning activities would work well to expand this workshop to a full day: expanding **learning activity 8** to the full 50 minutes, **learning activity 10, learning activity 11, learning activity 22**, and **learning activity 38**.

- Compile the learning activities, handouts, and PowerPoint slides you will use in the training.

- Decide the timing of this session in relation to the manager-oriented workshops that may precede or follow this session.

PowerPoint Slides

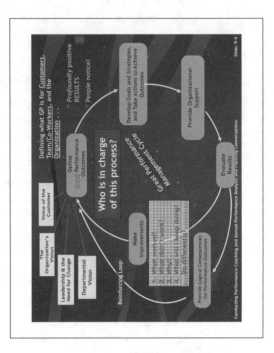

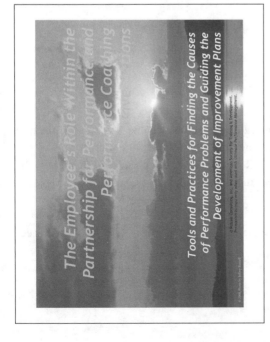

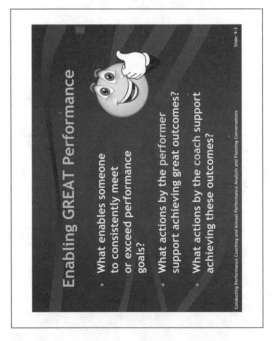

❶ Define Great Performance

Transforming Role of Employee . . .
- Talk to customers.
- Interview co-workers and coach.
- Become a strategic thinker.
- Be a change agent.
- Reflect on past results.
- Be a critical thinker.
- Develop a vision of GREAT success.
- Ask great questions . . .

Transforming Role of Coach . . . .
- Set the expectation that the employee is responsible.
- Demonstrate GREAT performance as a coach.
- Translate the vision.
- Communicate the value of the employee's work.
- Challenge status quo thinking.
- Ask great questions, inquire, show curiosity . . .

Conducting Performance Coaching and Annual Performance Analysis and Planning Conversations

Slide: 9-6

❸ Provide Resources and Support

Transforming Role of Employee . . .
- Identify what he or she needs to achieve GP goals/outcomes.
- Anticipate barriers and roadblocks.
- Recognize the organization's resource limitations.
- Ask for help.
- Be resourceful and innovative.

Transforming Role of Coach . . .
- Ask "What do you need from me/organization to accomplish GP?"
- Listen.
- Offer ideas to enable great performance.
- Identify useful resources.
- Follow through on commitments.
- Be available.
- Periodically check in . . . .

Conducting Performance Coaching and Annual Performance Analysis and Planning Conversations

Slide: 9-8

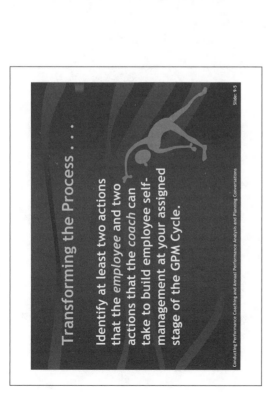

Transforming the Process . . . .

Identify at least two actions that the *employee* and two actions that the *coach* can take to build employee self-management at your assigned stage of the GPM Cycle.

Conducting Performance Coaching and Annual Performance Analysis and Planning Conversations

Slide: 9-5

❷ Develop GP Goals/Strategies

Transforming Role of Employee . . .
- Identify the "gap."
- Identify how to close the gap.
- Identify high leverage.
- Self-assess needed skills and knowledge.
- Reflect on past strategies and results.
- Be a critical thinker.
- Develop a plan/strategy.

Transforming Role of Coach . . . .
- Ask about the gap . . .
- Assess employee strengths, improvement areas . . . .
- Do "root cause" analysis of past performance.
- Ask great questions . . .
- Listen.
- Inquire.
- Challenge.
- What ideas do you have . . .

Conducting Performance Coaching and Annual Performance Analysis and Planning Conversations

Slide: 9-7

⑤ Make Improvements

Transforming Role of Employee . . .

- Reflect on past results.
- Be a critical thinker.
- Focus on cause, not blame.
- Explore system issues.
- Ask great questions . . .

Transforming Role of Coach . . .

- Ask questions to generate reflection.
- Listen.
- Inquire and challenge.
- Focus on cause, not blame.
- Explore system issues.
- Be receptive to receiving feedback.

Conducting Performance Coaching and Annual Performance Analysis and Planning Conversations

Slide: 9-10

How We Respond to Threats

- When we feel *stressed, threatened, vulnerable, embarrassed,* or otherwise *uncomfortable . . .* how do we typically respond?

- What might cause us to feel *stressed, threatened, vulnerable, embarrassed,* or *uncomfortable?*

Conducting Performance Coaching and Annual Performance Analysis and Planning Conversations

Slide: 9-12

④ Evaluate Performance

Transforming Role of Employee . . .

- Take the lead . . .
- Determine the frequency.
- Make assessment part of the work process.
- Use valid GP measures.
- Talk to customers, co-workers, and coach.
- Focus on trends, not incidents . . .

Transforming Role of Coach . . .

- Establish the expectation that the employee is responsible . . .
- Share expectations regarding frequency.
- Model the process . . .
- Keep in touch.
- Observe.
- Inquire.
- Ask great questions . . .

Conducting Performance Coaching and Annual Performance Analysis and Planning Conversations

Slide: 9-9

⑥ Provide Logical Consequences

Transforming Role of Employee . . .

- Be clear about what is important to you.
- Identify intrinsic rewards.
- Tell the coach.
- Negotiate customized rewards.
- Recognize resource limitations.

Transforming Role of Coach . . .

- Find out what the employee values.
- Follow through.
- Be consistent.
- Let people know that performance DOES matter (and reward accordingly).
- Don't promise what you can't deliver.

Conducting Performance Coaching and Annual Performance Analysis and Planning Conversations

Slide: 9-11

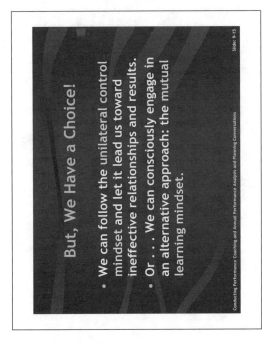

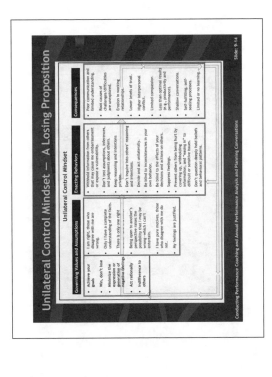

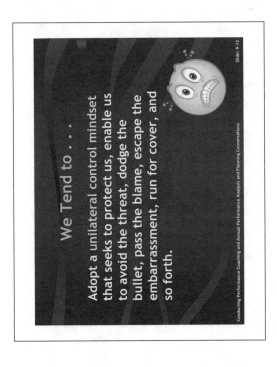

Governing Values . . .

- Valid Information: All relevant information is shared so that everyone understands what they need to know.
- Free and Informed Choice: People make their independent decisions based on valid information, not pressure.
- Internal Commitment to Decisions: Individuals take responsibility for the decisions that they participate in.
- Transparency: Individuals feel comfortable with open, honest, and direct communication with no "hidden agendas" or undiscussables.
- Empathy: Individuals have compassion for others and differing viewpoints and a genuine interest in understanding another's perspective.

Conducting Performance Coaching and Annual Performance Analysis and Planning Conversations
Slide: 9-18

The Enacting Behaviors

- Focus on interests, not positions.
- Develop shared meaning of key words, concepts, ideas, etc.
- Share decision making and action planning.
- See the parts, understand the whole.
- Use critical reflection to examine deeply held beliefs and behavioral patterns.

Conducting Performance Coaching and Annual Performance Analysis and Planning Conversations
Slide: 9-20

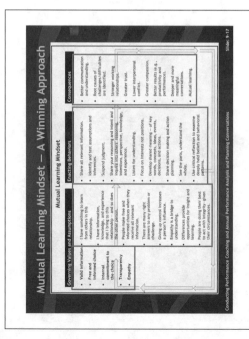

Mutual Learning Mindset – A Winning Approach

Slide: 9-17

Conducting Performance Coaching and Annual Performance Analysis and Planning Conversations

The Enacting Behaviors

- Share all relevant information.
- Identify and test assumptions and inferences.
- Suspend judgment.
- Share your reasoning and intent and inquire into others' reasoning, intentions, perspective, knowledge, and experience.
- Listen for understanding.

Conducting Performance Coaching and Annual Performance Analysis and Planning Conversations
Slide: 9-19

Purpose/Importance of PR

In your small group . . . .

- For your assigned individual/group, identify the purpose the performance review fulfills for this individual or group and identify its value and importance to this individual or group's interests and needs.

Conducting Performance Coaching and Annual Performance Analysis and Planning Conversations

Slide: 9-22

The Core Purposes of Reviews

Individual Performer, Supervisor, and Coach

- Align employee contributions with the needs/goals of the team, department, and organization.
- Explore the employee's potential future contributions to the team, department, and organization.
- Celebrate and reward great performance outcomes.
- Provide negative consequences when warranted.
- Identify performance goals for the next period.

Conducting Performance Coaching and Annual Performance Analysis and Planning Conversations

Slide: 9-24

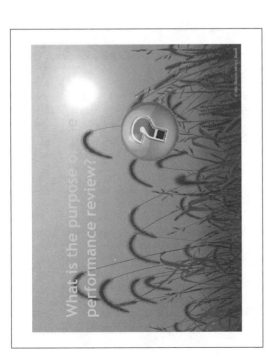

The Core Purposes of Reviews

Individual Performer, Supervisor, and Coach

- Provide employee feedback on performance.
- Identify barriers to performance.
- Develop improvement plans.
- Enhance employee commitment to the job, team, and organization.
- Identify performer's support needs
- Identify the employee's training, development, and career goals.

Conducting Performance Coaching and Annual Performance Analysis and Planning Conversations

Slide: 9-23

The Core Purposes of Reviews

Team/Work Unit, Department, and Organization

- Value the employee's contribution to the team/work unit effort.
- Identify training and development goals for the overall team, work unit, department, and organization.
- Align individual's efforts with the needs/goals of the team, department, and organization.

Conducting Performance Coaching and Annual Performance Analysis and Planning Conversations

Slide: 9-25

The Core Purposes of Reviews

Team/Work Unit, Department, and Organization

- Ensure objective, data-based assessments of employee performance.
- Equitably distribute pay adjustments based on performance.
- Identify high potentials for future development.
- Flag problem performers for tracking and follow-up.
- Ensure quality outcomes from employee effort.

Conducting Performance Coaching and Annual Performance Analysis and Planning Conversations

Slide: 9-26

A Proposed Higher Purpose

Performance Review Problems	A Proposed Higher Purpose
One-way communication	Two-way dialogue
Focus on the past	Improvement for the future
Appraisal, evaluation, and judgment	Learning and development
Focus on financial implications	Learning and development
Focus on filling-in forms and checking boxes	Developing understanding
Assumes that the manager knows and sees all	Both parties to the review have knowledge and insight to share
Focus on the performance review as an event	Performance management as a process
Over-reliance on some measurements while ignoring others	Using an holistic approach to performance measurement
Being overly-influenced by recent events or personal characteristics	Using objective data when analyzing and assessing performance

Conducting Performance Coaching and Annual Performance Analysis and Planning Conversations

Slide: 9-27

Unbundling the Process

- Critical Incident Coaching Conversation: addressing specific performance problems when they arise; exploring and addressing causes
- Performance Coaching Conversation and the Annual Performance Analysis and Planning Conversation: facilitating employee commitment to great performance and the organization; developing growth and improvement plans
- Performance Review: completing the official assessment forms and rating the employee, documenting performance issues, and determining pay and other HR outcomes.

Conducting Performance Coaching and Annual Performance Analysis and Planning Conversations

Slide: 9-28

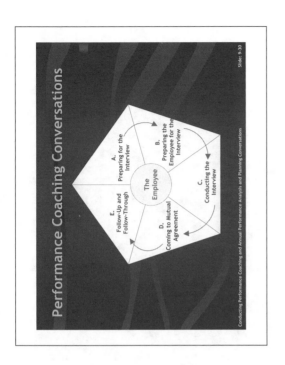

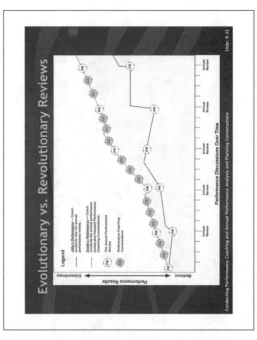

Concluding Thoughts . . .

- Achieving great performance results from a strong partnership.
- When both the employee and the manager assume a mutual 'learning mindset' great performance is more likely.
- The more frequent the Performance Coaching Conversation, the faster the employee's performance improves.
- The performance review "form" should never get in the way of communication and understanding.

Conducting Performance Coaching and Annual Performance Analysis and Planning Conversations

Slide: 9-34

Thank You!

. . . for being part of this performance coaching skills development program.

Please complete the workshop evaluation!

Slides related to your organization's performance review process

Conducting Performance Coaching and Annual Performance Analysis and Planning Conversations

Slide: 9-33

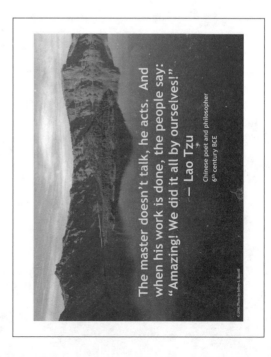

The master doesn't talk, he acts. And when his work is done, the people say: "Amazing! We did it all by ourselves!"

— Lao Tzu

Chinese poet and philosopher
6th century BCE

Appendix A: Using the Accompanying CD Materials

Using the Compact Disc—General

Contents of the Compact Disc

You will find the handouts and other tools referenced throughout this workbook on the accompanying CD. To access any of these files, insert the CD and click on the appropriate file name:

- Handout [number].pdf

- Training Instrument [number].pdf

- Training Tool [number].pdf

- Learning Activity [number].pdf

- [Title of PowerPoint slide].ppt

The PowerPoint presentation slides that accompany each of the suggested workshops in chapters 6 through 10 are located on the CD as .ppt files. Each slide is numbered according to the order in which it appears in the chapters. You can access individual slides by opening the PowerPoint presentations for the specific workshop (chapter) of interest.

Computer Requirements

All of the files can be used on a variety of computer platforms.

To read or print the .pdf files on the CD, Adobe Acrobat Reader software must be installed on your system. This program can be downloaded free of cost from the Adobe website, www.adobe.com.

To use or adapt the contents of the PowerPoint presentation files on the CD, Microsoft PowerPoint software must be installed on your system. If you want to view the PowerPoint documents, you must have an appropriate viewer installed on your system. Microsoft provides downloads of various viewers free of charge on its website, www.microsoft.com.

Printing from the CD

To print the materials for your workshops, follow these steps:

1. Insert the CD into your computer. Your computer should automatically open up a Windows Explorer window that displays a list of all files on the CD.

2. Locate the handout, tool, instrument, learning activity, or PowerPoint file you are looking for and double click on the file to open it. If the file you are opening is in .pdf format, the document will open using Adobe Acrobat software. If the file you are opening uses the .ppt format, the document will open in Microsoft PowerPoint.

3. Print the page or pages of the document(s) that you need for the learning activity and workshop.

4. You can print the presentation slides directly from the CD using Microsoft PowerPoint. Just open the .ppt files and print as many copies as you need. You can also make handouts of the presentations by printing 2, 4, or 6 slides per page. These slides will be in color, with design elements embedded. PowerPoint also permits you to print these in grayscale or black-and-white representations. Many trainers who use personal computers to project their presentations bring along viewgraphs, just in case there are glitches in the system.

PowerPoint Presentations

Adapting the PowerPoint Slides

You can modify or otherwise customize the slides by opening and editing them in the appropriate application. You must, however, retain the denotation of the original source of the material; it is illegal to pass it off as your own work. You may indicate that a document was adapted from this workbook, written and copyrighted by Jeffrey and Linda Russell and the American Society for Training & Development, and published by ASTD. The files will open as "Read Only," so before you adapt them, save them onto your hard drive under a different filename.

Showing the PowerPoint Slides

The following PowerPoint presentations are included on the CD:

(Chapter 6) *Establishing a Coaching Relationship for Great Performance*

(Chapter 7) *Performance Goal Setting*

(Chapter 8) *Diagnosing Employee Performance Problems and Developing Improvement Plans*

(Chapter 9) *Conducting Performance Coaching and Annual Performance Analysis and Planning Conversations*

(Chapter 10) *The Employee's Role Within the Partnership for Performance and Performance Coaching Conversations*

Table A-1. Navigating Through a PowerPoint Presentation

KEY	POWERPOINT "SHOW" ACTION
Space bar *or* Enter *or* Mouse click	Advance through custom animations embedded in the presentation.
Backspace	Back up to the last projected element of the presentation.
Escape	Abort the presentation.
B or b B or b (repeat)	Blank the screen to black. Resume the presentation.
W or w W or w (repeat)	Blank the screen to white. Resume the presentation.

The presentation is in .ppt format, which means that it automatically shows full screen when you double click on its filename. You can also open Microsoft PowerPoint and launch it from there.

Use the space bar, the enter key, or mouse clicks to advance through a presentation. Press the backspace key to back up. Use the escape key to exit a presentation. If you want to blank the screen to black as the group discusses a point, press the B key. Press it again to restore the show. If you want to blank the screen to a white background, do the same with the W key. Table A-1 summarizes these instructions.

We strongly recommend that trainers practice presentations before they use them in training situations. You should be confident that you can cogently expand on the points featured in the presentations and discuss the methods for working through them. If you want to engage your training participants fully (rather than worry about how to show the next slide), become familiar with this simple technology before you need to use it. A good practice is to insert notes into the Speaker's Notes feature of the PowerPoint program, print them out, and have them in front of you when you present the slides.

Learning Activities

This section refers to the learning activities identified in the training designs found in chapters 6 through 10. Each learning activity includes this information:

- **Objectives**. The objectives for each learning activity identify how the activity will help benefit workshop participants. The learning objectives are the primary cognitive, affective, or behavioral outcomes that the activity is attempting to achieve for participants.

- **Materials**. Included in the list of materials is everything the trainer will need to successfully conduct that learning activity. A master copy of each handout or tool appears at the end of the activity or can be printed from the appropriate .pdf file on the accompanying CD. For most activities, it is recommended that handouts be customized to fit the needs of the organization.

- **Time**. An estimate is given for the amount of time needed to complete the learning activity. This time includes introducing the activity, the activity itself, and debriefing and transitioning to the next learning activity.

- **Preparations**. This section offers brief instructions on what the trainer should do in advance of the activity. Possible advance work includes copying materials, defining a situation or case, preparing flipchart pages, or arranging the training room to accommodate special needs for the activity.

- **Instructions**. We provide step-by-step instructions for guiding participants through the activity. Key points you should make, likely reactions or answers from participants, and suggested responses to participant questions are included here. Variations on the activity process are also included in these instructions.

- **Debriefing**. The debriefing section guides you in helping participants integrate the activity into their learning. By offering key summary points, posing integrating or synthesizing questions to participants, or guiding participant action planning, you can significantly strengthen learning and transition learners to the next activity.

The activities included on the CD are

- Learning Activity 1: What Is a Coach?

- Learning Activity 2: Goal Setting

- Learning Activity 3: Performance Coaching and the Roles of the Coach

- Learning Activity 4: Coaching Cases—Using the Right Coaching Role

- Learning Activity 5: The Great Performance Management Cycle

- Learning Activity 6: Personal Action Planning

- Learning Activity 7: Sharing "Aha!" Moments and Questions/Goals Review

- Learning Activity 8: Unilateral Control and Mutual Learning Mindsets—Two Approaches to Managing Relationships With Others

- Learning Activity 9: Case Studies—Unilateral Control vs. Mutual Learning

- Learning Activity 10: The Ladder of Inference

- Learning Activity 11: The Purpose of Goal Setting

- Learning Activity 12: Defining Great Performance Outcomes

- Learning Activity 13: Performance Planning and Development—Defining Great Performance

- Learning Activity 14: Defining Performance Accountabilities
- Learning Activity 15: Performance Planning and Development—Defining Responsibilities
- Learning Activity 16: Developing SMART Goals
- Learning Activity 17: Writing SMART Goals—Case Application
- Learning Activity 18: Performance Planning and Development—Developing SMART Goals
- Learning Activity 19: Characteristics of Effective Measures
- Learning Activity 20: Developing Effective Measures—Case Application
- Learning Activity 21: Performance Planning and Development—Developing Measures of Performance
- Learning Activity 22: The Goals of Performance Coaching
- Learning Activity 23: Strategies for Documenting Employee Performance
- Learning Activity 24: Why Things Go Wrong With Performance
- Learning Activity 25: Diagnostic Tools for Exploring the Causes of Performance Problems
- Learning Activity 26: Performance Planning and Development—Assessing Employee Performance
- Learning Activity 27: Establishing Positive Performance Improvement Goals
- Learning Activity 28: Performance Planning and Development—Developing Performance Goals
- Learning Activity 29: The Performance Management Quiz
- Learning Activity 30: Performance Reviews From the Dark and Light Sides
- Learning Activity 31: Common Errors of Traditional Reviews
- Learning Activity 32: The Purposes of Performance Reviews
- Learning Activity 33: The Great Performance Management Cycle and the Performance Coaching Conversation
- Learning Activity 34: Active Listening and the Values, Assumptions, and Behaviors of the Mutual Learning Mindset
- Learning Activity 35: The Performance Coaching Conversation and the Annual Performance Analysis and Planning Conversation
- Learning Activity 36: The Performance Coaching Conversation—Behavior Modeling
- Learning Activity 37: Practicing the Performance Coaching Conversation—Participant Role Plays
- Learning Activity 38: The Organization's Expectations and Obligations for Documenting Performance Conversations

Training Tools

This workbook offers five training tools to help you create an environment that supports learning. Although the use of any of these tools is optional, we believe that effective trainers use tools like these to facilitate learning.

Training Tool 1: Training Room Configuration/Layout

Training room layout and configuration play a critical role in facilitating learning. The way you organize participants' seating influences their focus during the session (toward the trainer or fellow participants, or both) and helps set expectations for interaction or involvement. This tool offers a training room configuration that the authors have found to be most conducive to learning.

Training Tool 2: Learning Goal/Objective → Outcomes

Having participants set specific learning goals and objectives for your workshops is an essential step that focuses their energy and attention on achieving meaningful results. Research into both goal setting and the Expectancy Theory of Motivation suggests that people will have more commitment to achieving a goal (in this case, a learning objective) if they are involved in developing that goal for themselves. Further, the Expectancy Theory of Motivation (see Vroom [1964] and Porter and Lawler [1968] in For Further Reading) suggests that motivation to achieve a goal is enhanced by a combination of three questions: (1) If I try to achieve a specific goal, will I be successful? (2) If I am successful in achieving the goal, what are the outcomes I am likely to receive? (3) How important are these outcomes?

This participant goal-setting worksheet attempts to increase participant motivation to learn by asking them to (a) identify a specific goal for themselves, (b) identify the rewards or outcomes they are likely to realize if they achieve that learning objective, and (c) identify how important these rewards or outcomes are to them. These three questions help focus the participants' attention on learning, which will help to increase the likelihood of realizing a reward or outcome that is highly valued.

Training Tool 3: "Aha!" Sheet

The "Aha!" Sheet is a simple tool to help focus the learning of participants. During the training day, participants are immersed in a wide variety of new ideas, models, methods, and strategies. Some of these ideas will easily stick and become part of the participant's new consciousness. Others, however—no matter how useful or relevant—can too easily be lost as the learner attempts to integrate new knowledge and skills into practice. By encouraging participants to use the "Aha!" Sheet to recognize and record significant learning moments, ideas, methods, and strategies—in their own words—they are more likely to retain their learning. The "Aha!" Sheet also serves as an after-the-training memory jogger that reminds participants of key learning points from the session.

Training Tool 4: Training Program Reaction Sheet

Evaluating the effectiveness of your training program provides you with an opportunity both to measure the impact that the training has had on participant learning and behavior as well as organizational results and to give you ideas for improving or enhancing the workshop for future sessions.

Many variations on training program design are available, and you are encouraged to review the training evaluation literature and resources to develop your own evaluation or use what others have developed. In the book *The Winning Trainer* (1996), Julius Eitington offers a wide variety of training evaluation tools, emphasizing those that actively involve the participants. Included in the chapter "Using Participative Methods to Evaluate Training" are both quantitative methods (the reaction sheet) to group processes and post-training follow-up learning and behavioral change assessments.

One other useful resource is *ASTD Trainer's Toolkit: More Evaluation Instruments* (Stadius, 1999). This book offers a variety of training evaluation forms used by organizations throughout the United States and includes articles from *T+D* magazine.

ASTD's "Learning Outcomes Report" (available for download by ASTD members in .pdf format in the Research section of the ASTD website) is published annually and highlights the results of efforts to measure organizational investments in education and training. The report includes multiple training evaluation forms (reaction sheets and follow-up assessments) that were used in the research and are available to the training community. Interested organizations can also participate in ASTD's ongoing research on this topic by becoming part of the annual study of learning outcomes.

In this tool, we offer one format for evaluation of your training program and its learning outcomes as well as a set of questions that you may find useful.

Training Tool 5: Selecting Group Leaders

When you ask participants to "discuss this in your small groups," it is useful to have the group select a discussion or group leader. Leaders help focus the energy of the group and help create some accountability to the assigned task. Encouraging the rotation of leadership among the group members to distribute participation and responsibility is also a good idea. This tool offers some ideas for selecting and rotating group leaders.

Training Instruments

Training instruments include specific tools, checklists, and assessments that are used before, during, and following the training seminars. These training instruments are provided on the CD:

- Training Instrument 1: What Is a Coach?
- Training Instrument 2: Responsibilities of the Performance Coach
- Training Instrument 3: Selecting the Best Coaching Roles
- Training Instrument 4: Which Coaching Role Is Best?

- Training Instrument 5: What Enables Great Performance?
- Training Instrument 6: Building Employee Ownership for Great Performance
- Training Instrument 7: A Personal Plan for Action
- Training Instrument 8: Responding to Threat or Embarrassment
- Training Instrument 9: Mutual Learning and Coaching Cases
- Training Instrument 10: How Goal Setting Enables Great Performance and Applying Goal Theory
- Training Instrument 11: Defining Great Performance Application
- Training Instrument 12: Performance Planning and Development Worksheet
- Training Instrument 13: Defining Job Responsibilities
- Training Instrument 14: SMART Performance Goals
- Training Instrument 15: SMART Goals and Performance Measures Application
- Training Instrument 16: Documenting Performance
- Training Instrument 17: The Causes of Performance Problems
- Training Instrument 18: Cause→Effect Diagram Application
- Training Instrument 19: Establishing Positive Performance Goals
- Training Instrument 20: Performance Management Quiz
- Training Instrument 21: Performance Reviews From the Dark and Light Sides
- Training Instrument 22: Common Errors in Performance Reviews
- Training Instrument 23: Actions to Reduce Errors in Performance Reviews
- Training Instrument 24: Identifying the Purposes of Performance Reviews
- Training Instrument 25: Active Listening Application

Handouts

Handouts are provided for participants to support learning both during and after the training. The handouts provided on the CD include

- Handout 1: The Definition of a Coach
- Handout 2: The Roles of the Performance Coach
- Handout 3: The Dynamic Nature of the Coaching Relationship
- Handout 4: The Great Performance Management Cycle
- Handout 5: Defining Great Performance
- Handout 6: Actions for Encouraging Employee Ownership

- Handout 7: The Role of the Coach in Shaping Great Performance
- Handout 8: Unilateral Control and Mutual Learning Mindsets
- Handout 9: Values and Behaviors for Mutual Learning
- Handout 10: The Ladder of Inference
- Handout 11: Goal Theory of Motivation
- Handout 12: What Is Great Performance?
- Handout 13: Performance Accountabilities
- Handout 14: The Purpose and Characteristics of Effective Performance Measures
- Handout 15: The Goals of Performance Coaching
- Handout 16: Tools for Documenting Performance
- Handout 17: Using the Performance Gap to Drive Improvement
- Handout 18: Why Things Go Wrong With Performance
- Handout 19: The Components of Performance and the 85/15 Rule
- Handout 20: Nine-Plus-One Performance Diagnostic Checklist
- Handout 21: Cause➔Effect Diagram
- Handout 22: Actions for Reducing Rating Errors
- Handout 23: The Purposes of Performance Reviews
- Handout 24: Reframing the Traditional Review
- Handout 25: Unbundling the Process
- Handout 26: Whole Body Listening
- Handout 27: The Four Skills of Active Listening
- Handout 28: The Performance Coaching Conversation
- Handout 29: Evolutionary vs. Revolutionary Performance Management

Tips for Trainers

Designing and delivering a high-quality training program involves blending the suggested workshop agendas, handouts, training tools, and PowerPoint slides with your own insights, experience, and knowledge. You also need a solid grounding in the broader topic of performance management and performance reviews. We strongly encourage you to read and then reread chapter 2 to gain a comfort level with our recommended approach to performance management and our transformational employee-centered Performance Coaching Conversation.

You will also need to become deeply familiar with your organization's performance management culture, methodology, and practice. Performance reviews often have mixed responses in most organizations, so you should gain a clear understanding of how the process is perceived in yours. The assessment work that you did in chapter 3 should give you the insights and knowledge you need. Take a long look at the data you uncovered and then begin planning your workshops by weaving together the various strands that reflect the best practices as well as the practical realities of your organization.

The sample workshop agendas, handouts, and training instruments and tools should be the jumping off place for your own design. They can never be a substitute for your own experience or style. Become familiar enough with each workshop design so you can tell your own stories, offer your own examples, and use recent organizational events to help you ground the material in people's immediate experience. Participants need to see that the workshop design reflects what is real for them. You can increase the likelihood of this happening by investing up-front design time that puts the organization's stamp on the workshop.

You must also consider the issue of timing. The time to kick off your workshops on performance management, coaching, and performance reviews is at the *beginning* of the performance period rather than at the end. Although your organization's leaders might ask for performance review training because the time for annual reviews is fast approaching, you may instead want to suggest that the leaders step back from the pressing deadline and think about their larger objectives in performance management. You can then make the argument that starting with performance coaching and goal setting is preferred to how to conduct the review. You may choose to go forward with some performance review workshops, but design them in such a fashion that you set the stage for a more systematic approach in the new performance year. These are only a few examples of how you can adjust your workshops according to what you learn from your needs assessment and where your organization is within the performance management cycle. The most important thing to do is slow down and define the needs and expectations of key players—and then design the best array of organization development and training to meet these needs.

Finally, as you begin to construct your own workshop designs for whatever training you decide to offer, stay flexible. The estimated timeframes for each learning activity can and should be changed according to what you learn in your needs assessment, the goals for the session, your own personal style, the examples and cases you introduce, the stories you have to share, the personality of the organization or group, and where your executive leadership team wants you to focus.

You will find that your training designs will continue to improve as your confidence and competence in delivering your workshops increase and you receive positive and constructive feedback from participants. Don't expect to get it 100 percent right the first time out. Reflect on what worked and what didn't (based on feedback and your own intuition) and then make the appropriate adjustments. As with good problem solving and decision making, the process of designing a training program involves combining discipline with your own instincts and experience.

We are confident that the training programs that emerge from this dynamic process will hit their mark. Your participants will learn some things that are entirely new to them, your organization will begin to shift its practices to reflect what you are teaching, and your own learning as an human resource development professional will continue.

Appendix B: Handouts

Handout 1. The Definition of a Coach

ORIGIN OF THE WORD . . .

Coach is derived from the Hungarian word for a carriage that carried people between Budapest and Vienna:
Kocsi czeker (car of Kocs; Oxford English Dictionary).
In 1849, students at British universities began using "coach" as a slang term for "someone who carries you through an examination or challenge."

Notes:

....

....

....

....

....

....

....

....

....

....

AN EFFECTIVE COACH . . .

- guides, facilitates, and supports a person toward realizing his or her potential
- helps another person overcome challenges to achieve his or her goals by enabling the person to achieve his or her best
- enables a person to achieve a level of accomplishment that wouldn't have been possible without the coaches' guidance, prodding, and encouragement

Notes:

....

....

....

....

....

....

....

....

....

Handout 2. The Roles of the Performance Coach

- ❑ **Directing:** Providing direction, instruction, and correction to the performer and facilitating the performer's acquisition of basic job competencies. The primary focus of this role is to direct the performer toward achieving the desired outcomes.
- ❑ **Motivating/Inspiring:** Helping the performer become self-motivated and inspired by the work itself and the opportunities for success. The primary focus of this role is to help the performer discover what he or she finds rewarding about the work and its outcomes.
- ❑ **Supporting:** Providing organizational, professional, and emotional support to the performer to build his or her self-confidence. The primary focus of this role is to help the performer gain confidence in his or her abilities.
- ❑ **Developing:** Challenging the performer to learn, grow, take risks, change, and leap out of his or her performance "comfort zone." The primary focus of this role is to push the performer to the next level of performance by setting a higher bar and challenging the performer's self-defined limits.
- ❑ **Problem Solving:** Guiding the performer in discovering solutions to complex problems by posing provocative questions and challenges to the performer's usual way of thinking. The primary focus of this role is to help the performer master the art of problem solving, root-cause analysis, and paradoxical thinking.

Notes:

....

....

....

....

....

....

....

....

....

....

....

....

....

....

....

....

Handout 3.   The Dynamic Nature of the Coaching Relationship

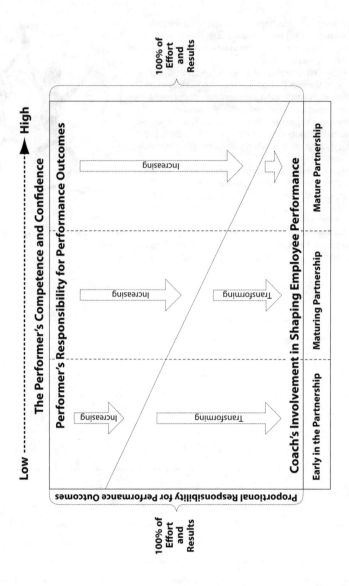

Handout 4. The Great Performance Management Cycle

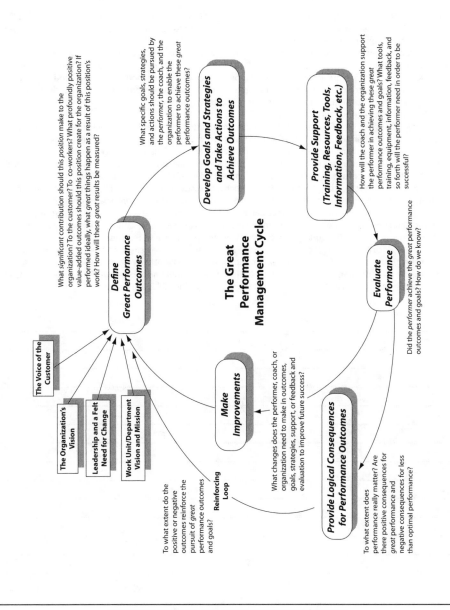

Handout 5. Defining Great Performance

Great performance within the Great Performance Management Cycle means more than "business as usual" or "just getting the job done." Defining great performance involves reaching toward new and compelling outcomes that lie above and far beyond normal expectations.

Great performance is the profoundly positive result that happens when people perform at their best. When people combine maximum talent with maximum effort and a burning desire to achieve something significant, great performance outcomes are achieved. With great performance, everyone notices and everybody wins.

Great performance outcomes are usually defined in terms of the profoundly positive results that the position creates for the company or organization, for customers, and for co-workers.

Here are some great performance outcomes:

- *Mortgage Loan Officer:* The officer creates value through strong customer partnerships. Through these relationships, customers feel heard and respected. The officer anticipates customer questions and communicates complex financial information in clear and understandable ways. The officer anticipates additional financial needs of the customer and proactively suggests other bank products and services that may ease the customer's financial anxieties. Customers feel that their financial information is dealt with sensitively and confidentially. Co-workers also feel listened to and respected and are comfortable approaching the officer with questions and customer problems. Overall, the bank benefits from the loyalty and commitment customers leverage toward the bank as a result of their enduring partnership with the officer.
- *Manager:* The department manager creates profoundly positive outcomes for the department's customers by anticipating, listening to, and proactively responding to emerging customer needs. Customers know they can approach the manager at any time when quality, productivity, or timeliness problems arise. The manager continually seeks out ways to exceed customer expectations through routine dialogue sessions where emerging issues are explored and the partnership is strengthened. The manager's team members' needs are anticipated and anxieties are addressed through routine one-on-one conversations that strengthen the performance partnership. The organization benefits from the manager's strategic insight on future trends and strategies for maximizing value and reducing costs.

Notes:

_____

_____

_____

_____

_____

_____

_____

_____

_____

_____

_____

_____

_____

Handout 6.   Actions for Encouraging Employee Ownership

1. DEFINE GREAT PERFORMANCE (GP) OUTCOMES	
Employee actions for ownership and self-management:	**Coach** actions to encourage employee ownership and self-management:
❏ Talk to customers. ❏ Interview co-workers and coach. ❏ Become a strategic thinker. ❏ Be a change agent. ❏ Reflect on past results. ❏ Be a critical thinker. ❏ Develop a vision of *great* success. ❏ Ask questions, inquire, be curious, etc.	❏ Set the expectation that the employee is responsible for performance. ❏ Demonstrate *great* performance as a coach. ❏ Translate the vision into meaning. ❏ Communicate the value of the employee's work. ❏ Challenge status quo thinking. ❏ Ask great questions, inquire, show curiosity, etc.
2. DEVELOP GOALS AND STRATEGIES TO ACHIEVE GP	
Employee actions for ownership and self-management:	**Coach** actions to encourage employee ownership and self-management:
❏ Identify the gap between "current" and "desired" performance. ❏ Identify ways to close the gap. ❏ Identify areas of "high leverage"—where a small effort will lead to the greatest gain or improvement. ❏ Self-assess needed skills and knowledge. ❏ Reflect on past strategies and results. ❏ Be a critical thinker. ❏ Develop a plan or strategy.	❏ Ask about the gap between current and desired performance. ❏ Know where the employee is strong and where he or she needs to improve and identify strategies for closing the gap. ❏ Do root-cause analysis of past performance results. ❏ Listen. ❏ Inquire. ❏ Challenge. ❏ Ask: "What ideas do you have for . . . ?"
3. PROVIDE ORGANIZATIONAL SUPPORT	
Employee actions for ownership and self-management:	**Coach** actions to encourage employee ownership and self-management:
❏ Identify what is needed to achieve GP goals or outcomes. ❏ Anticipate barriers and roadblocks. ❏ Recognize the organization's resource limitations. ❏ Ask for help when needed. ❏ Be resourceful and innovative.	❏ Ask: "What do you need from me or the organization to accomplish GP outcomes and goals?" ❏ Listen. ❏ Offer ideas to enable great performance. ❏ Identify useful resources. ❏ Follow through on commitments. ❏ Be available when needed. ❏ Check in periodically.

continued on next page

Handout 6. Actions for Encouraging Employee Ownership, *continued*

4. EVALUATE PERFORMANCE RESULTS	
Employee actions for ownership and self-management:	**Coach** actions to encourage employee ownership and self-management:
❏ Take the lead—don't wait for the coach to ask you. ❏ Determine the frequency of assessment: How often would be most useful to you to achieve GP outcomes and goals? ❏ Make assessment part of the work process. ❏ Use valid measures that directly assess great performance outcomes. ❏ Talk to customers, co-workers, and coach. ❏ Focus on trends, not incidents.	❏ Establish the expectation that the *employee* takes the lead in this process. ❏ Share expectations regarding frequency, and negotiate. ❏ Model the process: Ask the right questions to generate critical reflection by the performer. ❏ Keep in touch; be available. ❏ Observe. ❏ Inquire.
5. MAKE IMPROVEMENTS	
Employee actions for ownership and self-management:	**Coach** actions to encourage employee ownership and self-management:
❏ Reflect on past results. ❏ Be a critical thinker: (a) What worked? (b) What didn't? (c) Why? (d) What should I keep doing, and what should I change? ❏ Focus on cause, not blame. ❏ Explore system issues.	❏ Ask questions to generate critical reflection. ❏ Listen. ❏ Inquire and challenge. ❏ Focus on cause, not blame. ❏ Explore system issues and causes. ❏ Be receptive to receiving feedback from the performer.
6. PROVIDE LOGICAL CONSEQUENCES TO RESULTS ACHIEVED	
Employee actions for ownership and self-management:	**Coach** actions to encourage ownership and employee self-management:
❏ Be clear about what is important, what is motivating, and what drives job commitment. ❏ Identify intrinsic rewards—rewards generated by the work itself and from within (e.g., sense of accomplishment, achieving a personal best, more meaningful work, and so forth). ❏ Tell the coach what's important to you (what motivates you to do good work). ❏ Negotiate customized rewards. ❏ Recognize the organization's resource limitations.	❏ Find out what the employee values. ❏ Follow through and deliver on promised rewards. ❏ Be consistent. ❏ Let people know that performance *does* matter (and reward accordingly). ❏ Don't promise what you can't deliver.

Handout 7. The Role of the Coach in Shaping Great Performance

At the Beginning . . . and Ongoing

1. Define and describe your vision for the organization or unit's future and the values that will enable it to achieve this goal.
2. Discover what the employee seeks to accomplish or achieve through his or her work. What does he or she aspire to in work and life? How does this personal aspiration connect with the organization's vision?
3. Discuss and define—in writing—specific great performance *outcome* expectations that describe results from the employee's successful job performance.
4. Discuss and define—in writing—specific performance *process* expectations (if any) that describe *how* the work is to be done.
5. Discuss the employee's needs for learning and develop a learning or training plan that helps achieve the great performance outcomes that you both will support.
6. Discover what the employee values. Identify and discuss the rewards you will provide for successful performance: "What specific benefits and rewards will the employee receive for great performance?"

Throughout the Employee's Experience

7. Encourage open, two-way communication. Be available. Have an "open door" to ensure the employee knows that questions and ideas are encouraged.
8. Vary your coaching role to reflect the characteristics of the performer, the task, and the work environment.
9. Provide ongoing direction and support to the employee.
10. Observe the employee performing the work. Are the great performance outcomes being achieved?

At Regular Intervals

11. Give frequent, timely, and constructive feedback to correct errors and improve quality. Encourage the employee's critical reflection and learning.
12. Follow through on the commitments you have made to provide the employee with resources, training, mentoring, feedback, and so forth.
13. Expect results and reward great performance when it happens.
14. Meet at least quarterly to discuss what's going well, what's *not* going well, and what changes need to occur (from both the employee's and your perspectives).

Handout 8.   Unilateral Control and Mutual Learning Mindsets

Unilateral Control Mindset

Governing Values and Assumptions	Enacting Behaviors	Consequences
• Achieve your goals	• Withhold information from others that may cause me embarrassment or expose a vulnerability	• Poor communication and limited understanding
• Win, don't lose	• Don't test assumptions, inferences, and judgments about others	• Root causes of challenges/difficulties are unexplored
• Minimize the expression or generation of negative feelings	• Keep reasoning and intentions private	• Erosion in working relationships
• I am right, those who disagree with me are wrong	• Don't inquire into others' reasoning and intentions	• Lower levels of trust
• Only I have a complete understanding of the facts	• Decide and act unilaterally	• Higher interpersonal conflict
• There is only one right answer–and it is mine	• Be blind to inconsistencies in your reasoning and behavior	• Limited compassion
• Being open to another's perspective raises the possibility that I may be wrong–which I can't entertain	• Be blind to the effects of your decisions and actions on others	• Less than optimal results (e.g., productivity and performance)
• Act rationally	• Suppress feelings	• Shallow conversations
• Be indifferent to others	• Prevent others from being hurt by covering up, withholding information, and "easing-into" difficult or sensitive issues	• Self-fulfilling, self-sealing processes
• I have pure motives; those who disagree with me do not	• Don't question deeply held beliefs and behavioral patterns	• Limited or no learning
• My feelings are justified		

© 2009, Russell Consulting, Inc.

continued on next page

Handout 8. Unilateral Control and Mutual Learning Mindsets, *continued*

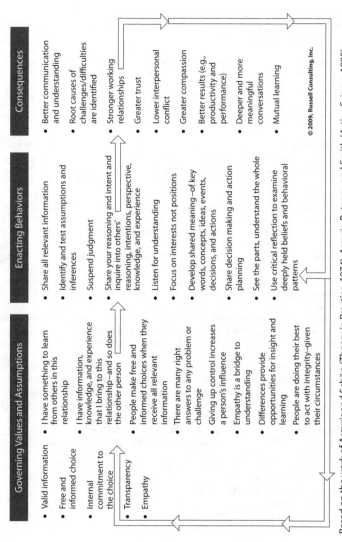

Mutual Learning Mindset

Governing Values and Assumptions	Enacting Behaviors	Consequences
Valid information	• Share all relevant information	• Better communication and understanding
Free and informed choice	• Identify and test assumptions and inferences	• Root causes of challenges/difficulties are identified
Internal commitment to the choice	• Suspend judgment	• Stronger working relationships
Transparency	• Share your reasoning and intent and inquire into others' reasoning, intentions, perspective, knowledge, and experience	• Greater trust
Empathy	• Listen for understanding	• Lower interpersonal conflict
• I have something to learn from others in this relationship	• Focus on interests not positions	• Greater compassion
• I have information, knowledge, and experience that I bring to this relationship—and so does the other person	• Develop shared meaning—of key words, concepts, ideas, events, decisions, and actions	• Better results (e.g., productivity and performance)
• People make free and informed choices when they receive all relevant information	• Share decision making and action planning	• Deeper and more meaningful conversations
• There are many right answers to any problem or challenge	• See the parts, understand the whole	• Mutual learning
• Giving up control increases a person's influence	• Use critical reflection to examine deeply held beliefs and behavioral patterns	
• Empathy is a bridge to understanding		
• Differences provide opportunities for insight and learning		
• People are doing their best to act with integrity—given their circumstances		

© 2009, Russell Consulting, Inc.

Based on the work of Argyris and Schön (Theory in Practice, 1974); Argyris, Putnam, and Smith (*Action Science*, 1985); Schwarz (*The Skilled Facilitator*, 2002); and Gerard and Ellinor (*Dialogue at Work*, Pegasus Communications, 2001)

Handout 9. Values and Behaviors for Mutual Learning

GOVERNING VALUES

- **Valid Information:** All relevant information is shared, so everyone understands what he or she needs to know to make a . . .
- **Free and Informed Choice:** People make their independent decisions based on valid information, not on pressure, which enables them to have . . .
- **Internal Commitment to Decisions:** Individuals take responsibility for the decisions they participate in, based on . . .
- **Transparency:** Individuals feel comfortable with open, honest, and direct communication with no "hidden agendas" or "undiscussables," which is best done with . . .
- **Empathy:** Individuals have compassion for others with differing viewpoints and have a genuine interest in understanding another person's perspective.

ENACTING BEHAVIORS

- **Share all relevant information.** People can only make informed choices or decisions when they have all the information they need. Consequently, we're required to actively participate in dialogue with each other to share what we're thinking and what we know. Sharing all relevant information also involves saying "I don't have an opinion" or "I don't have anything to add to the discussion," rather than remaining silent (and causing people to *wonder* if we are sharing all relevant information).
- **Identify and test assumptions and inferences.** When you observe others making statements, taking actions, or making decisions, don't speculate on their intentions or motivations. This enacting behavior first involves you in *identifying* when you are making an assumption or inference, then testing the assumption or inference directly by asking the other person for more information.
- **Suspend judgment.** In our normal conversations, we tend to make quick value judgments about what others have said or done. We view others' statements or actions as good, bad, right, wrong, foolish, bold, brutish, bullying, caring, and so forth, often without hard data behind our conclusions. With the mutual learning mindset, we test our assumptions and suspend our judgments about others. By suspending judgments, we put enough distance between our judgments and ourselves to free us from having to act upon or be influenced by them.
- **Share your reasoning and intent and inquire into others' reasoning, intentions, perspective, knowledge, and experience.** This enacting behavior enables others to see how you reached the conclusions and judgments you did and to then explore areas of your reasoning where they reasoned differently. When you explain to others *why* you think the way you do about something or why you made the statement you did, they are better able to understand the basis for your words, actions, and purpose or reasons for doing something. The second half of this behavior involves actively *inquiring* into others' reasoning, intent, perspective, and so forth. When you genuinely inquire into others' reasoning and intentions, you are better able to understand and appreciate what lies behind their words and actions. Mutual learning naturally evolves from the rich dialogue that emerges from this sharing of reasoning and intentions and with it an appreciation of divergent experience and backgrounds.
- **Listen for understanding.** The mutual learning mindset depends on the skill of reflective listening, with a focus on understanding and appreciating another's perspective. Reflective listening involves paying attention to what lies behind the words of others and then "mirroring" and paraphrasing what is learned back to the speaker in a way that demonstrates your understanding. Reflective listening enables the speaker to confirm or disconfirm what you heard, leading to a deeper understanding of what the other was saying or thinking.
- **Focus on interests, not positions.** Rather than focusing on positions, which we tend to defend and hold, focus on better understanding, sharing your *interests* and exploring the interests of others. Our interests reflect the underlying needs and desires we have in a given situation. When we focus on *interests*, it is far easier to find a solution. When, however, we focus on *positions*, we tend to *defend* and protect these positions, which profoundly limits understanding, agreement, and learning.
- **Develop shared meaning of key words, concepts, ideas, events, decisions, and actions.** Creating a shared meaning and understanding of specific dates, times, places, and key words ensures that relevant information is available to all and enables people to make free and informed decisions and choices. When we have a shared understanding of key events

continued on next page

Handout 9. Values and Behaviors for Mutual Learning , *continued*

and decisions, we are more able to have an informed discussion on the issues before us. When we agree on the meaning of key terms (e.g., quality, learning, consensus, conflict, opportunity, and so forth), we work from a shared understanding of the word or idea instead of drawing different meanings of these words and continuing in different directions.

- ***Share decision making and action planning.*** When we act unilaterally, we attempt to impose "our way" on others. Mutual learning involves working *with* others to jointly decide what will happen and how to implement the decision. Rather than imposing our way of thinking, then, we share our own ideas about next steps (and our reasoning behind them) and then invite others to share their thoughts (and their supporting reasoning). Based on this *valid information*, we can then make informed choices about what to do next.
- ***See the parts, understand the whole.*** By gathering all valid information in a given situation, we can appreciate the pieces of the puzzle and make an informed choice about what to do next. Mutual learning, however, moves participants beyond the parts and allows them to see the larger context and the fabric of the whole. People are moved to make decisions and take action in their lives based on the pieces *and* the whole. By understanding the whole instead of just looking at the parts, we can begin to appreciate why people do what they do. The larger context of their lives is as much responsible for their decisions and actions as a specific event or circumstance. When we see things holistically, we tend to be more empathetic and understanding toward others and, therefore, more open to their experiences, perspectives, insights, and so forth.
- ***Use critical reflection to examine deeply held beliefs and behavioral patterns.*** Critical reflection is the capacity to think deliberately about something in such a way that our underlying beliefs are open to challenge and change. Socrates once said that "an unexamined life is not worth living." He challenges us to critically examine our deeply held beliefs and behavioral patterns so that we are aware of their power and role in our life and are then able to entertain and explore alternative beliefs and behaviors that may be more facilitative of understanding and learning.

Handout 10.   The Ladder of Inference

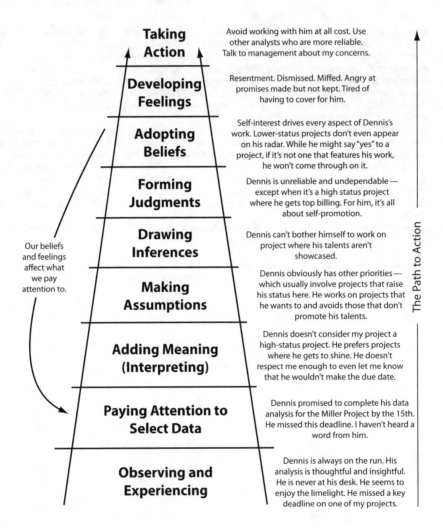

Taking Action — Avoid working with him at all cost. Use other analysts who are more reliable. Talk to management about my concerns.

Developing Feelings — Resentment. Dismissed. Miffed. Angry at promises made but not kept. Tired of having to cover for him.

Adopting Beliefs — Self-interest drives every aspect of Dennis's work. Lower-status projects don't even appear on his radar. While he might say "yes" to a project, if it's not one that features his work, he won't come through on it.

Forming Judgments — Dennis is unreliable and undependable — except when it's a high status project where he gets top billing. For him, it's all about self-promotion.

Drawing Inferences — Dennis can't bother himself to work on project where his talents aren't showcased.

Making Assumptions — Dennis obviously has other priorities — which usually involve projects that raise his status here. He works on projects that he wants to and avoids those that don't promote his talents.

Adding Meaning (Interpreting) — Dennis doesn't consider my project a high-status project. He prefers projects where he gets to shine. He doesn't respect me enough to even let me know that he wouldn't make the due date.

Paying Attention to Select Data — Dennis promised to complete his data analysis for the Miller Project by the 15th. He missed this deadline. I haven't heard a word from him.

Observing and Experiencing — Dennis is always on the run. His analysis is thoughtful and insightful. He is never at his desk. He seems to enjoy the limelight. He missed a key deadline on one of my projects.

Our beliefs and feelings affect what we pay attention to.

The Path to Action

Handout 11. Goal Theory of Motivation

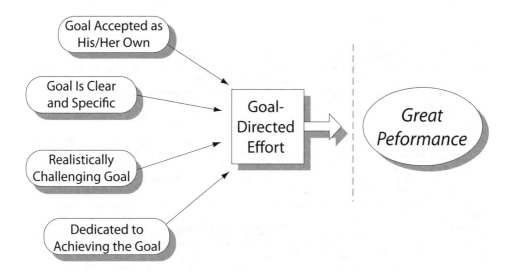

Handout 12. What Is Great Performance?

"Great performance outcomes" describes the broad, profoundly positive outcomes that result from an employee's best work, as defined by customers (internal and external), the organization's vision, the leader's vision, and the department or work area's vision. When an employee's work is done (at the end of the month, quarter, or year, depending on the "cycle time" for performance), great performance is the expected accomplishments and achievements.

Great performance outcomes . . .

- are profoundly better than mediocre (just getting by), acceptable, or even good performance outcomes.
- push individuals far beyond incremental improvement or accomplishments. They urge people to break the boundaries of past experience and quality. *What profound result occurs because of the work I do?*
- answer the question: *What value or significant outcome do I want to create for my* **customers** (C), *my* **team**/*co-workers* (T), *and the* **organization** *overall* (O)?
- focus on the *strategic end result* that occurs through an employee's work rather than on daily *operational* behaviors and actions.

The great performance categories that performance goals might address include expectations concerning: *quality, quantity, cost, timeliness,* and *impact on the work of others (team).* Within each category, the outcomes should be identified as geared toward customers (C), team/co-workers (T), or the organization overall (O).

Because employees are closest to the customer, they are in the best position to understand and define great performance in each of these areas.

PERFORMANCE DIMENSION	GREAT PERFORMANCE EXAMPLE
Quality	• *My customers will be* delighted *as a result of the value I add to our service. I will continuously exceed their expectations for the "goodness" and quality of the services I provide.* (C) • *Each customer will leave with a smile on his or her face because the service I provided exceeded their expectations.* (C) • *I will anticipate my customers' needs and issues in such a way as to help them solve future problems, not just current ones.* (C)
Quantity	• *I will manage and maintain our materials supply system such that teams on the assembly line (my customers) will have the* exact *number of parts and raw materials to build their product—with no stockpiling of parts.* (O)
Cost	• *Our operating costs will be maintained* below *our operating costs for last year.* (O)
Timeliness	• *The board of directors will receive key customer service information every quarter such that they are able to make strategic decisions regarding product development, design, and quality improvement.* (O) • *I will consistently beat estimated delivery dates promised to my customers.* (C)
Impact on Team	• *Other members on my team will receive information on product quality from me in such a way that they are able to make improvements in their work.* (T) • *I will anticipate the information needs of my co-workers and proactively provide this information in such a way that enables them to make informed and timely decisions.* (T)

Notes:

....

....

....

Handout 13. Performance Accountabilities

CORE JOB RESPONSIBILITIES

The essential job responsibilities or functions are the *broad* areas in which the person doing a specific job creates valued outcomes for the customer, his or her co-workers, and the company. Within each essential job responsibility, numerous tasks may need to be performed.

A typical job will have *four* to *seven* essential job responsibilities or functions. Here are some examples, for a variety of different jobs:

- develops positive relationships with the customer
- prepares an annual operating budget for the company
- manages the company's payroll
- interviews and hires candidates to fill vacant positions
- analyzes customer feedback and prepares reports for service teams
- oversees customer service quality and process improvement.

ORGANIZATIONAL RESPONSIBILITIES

A position's organizational responsibilities involve accountabilities that apply to *all* employees. These accountabilities relate to each employee's responsibilities for building community, relating well to customers, sharing information, contributing to another's success, and so forth. Here are some examples:

- shares information with co-workers
- works collaboratively with others
- builds positive relationships with customers/partners
- follows the company's work rules
- represents the company in a positive and professional way.

Handout 14. The Purpose and Characteristics of Effective Performance Measures

A performance measure is an indicator or gauge that points to an issue, condition, or outcome that is essential to achieving the overall performance target. Its purpose is to show you how well the performer and the performance management system are working. If there is a problem with performance, an effective measure raises an early warning flag and can subsequently help the performer and the coach identify what actions need to be taken to address it. Measures are as varied as the types of performance outcomes they are seeking to measure and monitor.

The purpose of performance measures is to

- **motivate** and inspire the performer to achieve *great* performance
- **focus** the energy of the performer on the key *drivers* of success—the behaviors and actions that contribute most to goal attainment
- provide immediate and ongoing **feedback** to the performer and his or her coach on the progress the individual is making toward achieving the performance objectives
- offer an **early warning** system to alert the performer and his or her coach that performance results aren't meeting expectations
- reveal a **cause→effect relationship** between the *behaviors* of the individual performer and the *outcomes* resulting from these behaviors
- **balance** the attention and energy of the performer on an *array* of success factors, not just one (for example, using multiple measures that encourage both greater numbers of customer interactions *and* ensure the quality of these interactions)
- highlight the relationship between the performer's efforts and the overarching and **longer-term priorities** and strategies of the organization.

CHARACTERISTICS OF EFFECTIVE MEASURES

The ideal measures of employee performance have the following characteristics:

- **Relevant and Important**—An effective measure assesses outcomes that are directly relevant and critical to the overall performance outcomes of the individual performer, his or her work area, and the larger organization.
- **Easy to Understand**—The measure is accessible and easy to understand by the performer, coach, customers, and other stakeholders who may be invested in the performance success of the performer. The measure is intuitively and transparently obvious as a common-sense indicator of performance results.
- **Objective and Unbiased**—The measure reflects the organization and work area's priorities as opposed to the personal priorities of an individual performer.
- **Valid and Reliable**—The performance measure actually measures what you intend to measure, and the measurement should generate accurate and consistent results over time.
- **Quantitative**—The measure is something that can actually be observed, counted, averaged, compared, and tracked over time. While qualitative data can help identify ideas or strategies for improvement, numbers are the best measures of performance progress.
- **Normative**—The measure is normative, such that the performer and coach are able to benchmark the performer's results and then track these results over time and compare them to the results of other employees who do similar work.
- **Unobtrusive and Cost Effective**—The process of measuring is seamlessly generated by the performer as he or she does the work instead of as an after-the-fact data-gathering process done by the performer, the coach, or others. It is unobtrusive in that gathering the data doesn't interrupt or disrupt the work of the performer, coach, or others, and cost effective in that the process of measuring should simply involve gathering data that is already being generated by the performer or the system as the work is being done.
- **Informative**—The measure indicates progress toward the goal, helps generate/identify possible causes of lower performance, and identifies possible strategies for improving the systems and work processes for reaching the goal.
- **Offers Early Warning and Is Discriminating**—The measure provides early warnings of performance problems and is able to identify small yet meaningful changes in performance. Detecting small changes early on can, in turn, enable corrections to be made before problems escalate and major performance milestones or goals are missed.

Handout 15. The Goals of Performance Coaching

The fundamental purpose of performance coaching is moving the employee's performance to a new level. To achieve this overarching goal, the coach selects the most appropriate coaching role (from **handout 2**) and approaches the coaching opportunity by asking a key question:

> *As a result of this performance coaching conversation, what do I hope the employee will do? What is my goal for this conversation and what goal do I want the employee to set for him- or herself as a result?*

There are two types of performance coaching goals: *outcome goals* and *process goals*.

PERFORMANCE COACHING *OUTCOME* GOALS

1. ***Maintain Performance Strengths (M).*** I want the employee to continue performing at his or her current level of performance effectiveness in a given area or overall. I'd like to see the employee remain committed and motivated to this level of job performance. Given recent resource reductions or increases in workload for the employee, what do I want the employee to keep doing in spite of these reductions or workload increases?

   > **Questions to Explore**: *What is the employee doing right? What is going well with the employee's performance? What should the employee keep doing? What is the significant positive value that this employee's performance brings to the organization? Which of the five coaching roles is most appropriate to help the employee achieve these goals?*

   Notes:

2. ***Improve Performance (I).*** I want the employee to improve his or her performance overall or in specific areas where performance is falling short of expectations. I'd like to see the employee *increase* his or her commitment to meeting or exceeding performance expectations. I want to see performance data indicate an improvement overall or in specific performance dimensions.

   > **Questions to Explore**: *What isn't going well or being done right? What isn't working? What data suggest that performance isn't what it should be? Why is improvement in this area necessary? What are the likely causes of the performance decline? What must be done to correct the problem? What can I do to assist the employee with improving in this area? What are my expectations for the future? What are the consequences for the organization and for the employee if difficulties continue in this area? Which of the five coaching roles is most appropriate to help the employee achieve these goals?*

   Notes:

3. ***Accept New Responsibilities (A).*** I want the employee to accept new responsibilities or duties that reflect new and emerging issues, priorities, or goals for our department, the organization as a whole, or specifically for his or her job. I'd like the employee to accept these new duties, responsibilities, and directions with ownership, commitment, and motivation.

continued on next page

Handout 15.   The Goals of Performance Coaching, *continued*

> **Questions to Explore**: *What changes are occurring both in- and outside the organization that have a likely impact on the performance of this position? What specific changes should the employee prepare for and respond to? How different from past performance are the new responsibilities being added? To what extent do the new responsibilities change the job scope and authority—and therefore have an impact on compensation and other HR issues? What will the employee have to learn to be successful in this new performance area? What new behaviors and actions will the employee have to learn and demonstrate to fulfill these new responsibilities? How can I, and others, help the employee succeed in this new area? How much of a transition time should I grant the employee to learn the new responsibilities before I hold him or her accountable for results? Which of the five coaching roles is most appropriate to help the employee achieve these goals?*

Notes:

4. ***Grow and Move the Job to a New Level (G).*** I want the employee to enhance his or her value to the organization by moving his or her performance to a new level. I'd like the employee to take the initiative by growing the job and enhancing the level of performance outcomes. I want the employee to build on his or her existing performance levels.

> **Questions to Explore:** *Does the employee take the lead in suggesting ways to enhance his or her performance? How could this employee enhance his or her overall performance or one or more specific performance dimensions? How can I, as a coach, enable the performer move his or her performance to the next level? Which of the five coaching roles is most appropriate to help the employee grow or enhance his or her performance outcomes?*

Notes:

Performance Coaching *Process* Goals

1. ***Build Greater Ownership for Performance.*** I want the employee to take greater responsibility and ownership for his or her own success. I want to increase the employee's capacities to self-manage his or her own performance.
2. ***Build Greater Commitment to the Job and the Organization.*** I want the employee to strengthen his or her commitment to the work that he or she is doing and to the organization as a whole. I want to see greater initiatives by the employee that display a desire to improve and grow in his or her job and to improve and grow the organization.
3. ***Strengthen Our Performance Partnership.*** I want to see our coaching partnership become stronger and more effective. I want to see both the employee and myself making active investments in building our working relationship. I want to see more honest communication, greater levels of trust and respect, and a growing confidence in our performance partnership.
4. ***Identify System Barriers and Challenges.*** I want to better understand barriers to the employee's performance that may be caused by my own actions or inactions or to other factors within the larger performance management system that may be negatively affecting the employee's performance. I want to know what I need to do differently to support the employee's performance improvement, growth, and development. When performance problems arise, I want to be better able to separate out the employee's individual effort from potential system causes of things gone wrong.

Notes:

Handout 16.   Tools for Documenting Performance

❑ *Performance Log.* An informal record kept by the coach of significant examples of an employee's accomplishments, behaviors, failures, successes, milestones, setbacks, awards, and so forth. If used, the performance log must record *positive* performance as well as performance *problems* and should be maintained for all of the coaches' direct reports (not just for those experiencing problems).

❑ *Critical Incidents Log.* The critical incidents log approaches documentation similarly to the performance log. The critical incidents log, like the performance log, documents *positive* performance as well as *problems* in performance. The critical incidents log, however, includes much greater detail than the performance log. If used, critical incident logs should be maintained for *all* employees. Critical incidents logs typically include this information:

- date, time, location
- description of the event
- names of others who observed the behavior (if appropriate)
- consequences of the employee's actions and behaviors
- what the coach discussed with the performer at the time
- previous discussions, if any, about the incident
- specific improvement expected or existing behavior encouraged
- consequences that were identified if improvement didn't occur and follow-up dates that were set
- employee's reaction to the incident, the coaching conversation or intervention, and expectations resulting from conversation.

❑ *Email Documentation.* This approach involves the coach sending an email to the performer that documents significant examples of the employee's behaviors, accomplishments, failures, successes, and so forth. As with the other forms of performance documentation, the coach sends emails to document positive performance as well as performance problems or improvement areas. The coach may also choose to send emails to him- or herself, documenting key conversations, results, agreements and commitments made, and so forth, as a critical "note to myself." Email folders can be created within Outlook or other email managers to preserve and organize these documentary notes.

❑ *Performance Portfolio.* The performance portfolio is a folder maintained by both the performer and the coach that contains tangible evidence of specific performance accomplishments and outcomes. The portfolio may contain copies of reports, awards, and commendations. Photographs of key events that celebrate or recognize employee contributions and copies of letters or emails from key stakeholders or customers can also be included in the portfolio. The portfolio is maintained to provide documentary evidence of goals achieved, milestones reached, commendations received, and so forth.

Handout 17. Using the Performance Gap to Drive Improvement

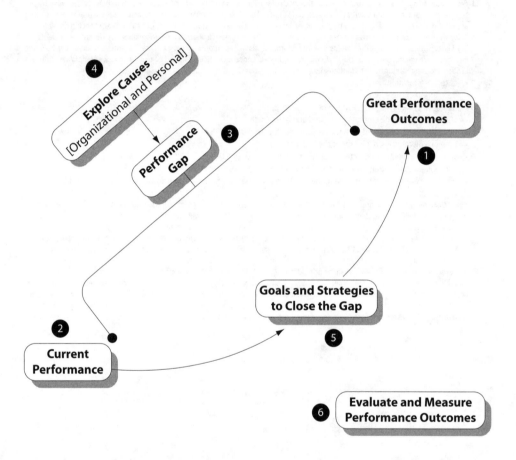

Handout 18. Why Things Go Wrong With Performance

ORGANIZATIONAL CAUSES

- unclear or confusing direction or expectations
- lack of feedback on performance
- lack of skill and knowledge training and development
- poor communication—about expectations, direction, purpose, and so forth
- conflict with coworkers
- inadequate tools and resources
- workload pressures and workload stress
- fear of failure
- few rewards
- no consequences (good or bad) for good or bad performance
- poor match between job and person
- failure to accommodate special needs when appropriate.

PERSONAL ORIGINS

- lack of desire or motivation to succeed
- personal or emotional problems interfering with performance
- inability to work well with others
- resistance to change—rigid and inflexible
- lack of self-discipline—unable or unwilling to translate ideas into action
- poor organizational skills—disorganized.

Handout 19. The Components of Performance and the 85/15 Rule

Ability + Effort + Skills + Process + Team Work + Resources + ? = 100%

Handout 20. Nine-Plus-One Performance Diagnostic Checklist

❏ 1. **Have you made performance expectations clear?** Does the employee know <u>what</u> he or she is expected to do? If necessary, have you defined *how* work is to be done?

(*Note:* For most jobs, the *what* is far more important than the *how.*)

❏ 2. **Does the employee know that his or her performance isn't what it should be?** Do you let the employee know when he or she isn't meeting job expectations?

❏ 3. **Have you set performance goals that are challenging but realistic?** Is the workload reasonable? Are you punishing your best performers by giving them most of the challenging work? Do the goals stretch the employee's capabilities in the right way?

❏ 4. **Does the employee have the skills, knowledge, and ability to do the job? Has he or she received the necessary training?** Has the job changed such that new skills and knowledge are required? Has the job out-grown him or her?

❏ 5. **Have you provided the employee access to the tools, equipment, financial resources, people, and information resources that he or she needs to get the job done?** Does the employee know where to access these resources?

❏ 6. **Are the working relationships between the employee and his or her co-workers positive and cooperative?** Or, instead, are there conflicts between the employee and other workers? Is he or she potentially the target of unfair treatment, discrimination, or harassment by others? Are people withholding information from him or her?

❏ 7. **Does the employee know that he or she can seek you out to clarify job duties, ask for direction and support, problem solve, or identify ways to improve job performance?** Or are you just too busy to "touch base," share issues, and discuss concerns?

❏ 8. **Have you consistently provided clear and positive rewards to the employee and other workers when performance standards are met or exceeded?** Do you consistently withdraw positive rewards from those who fail to meet expectations? Do you make it clear that performance *does* matter to you?

❏ 9. **Does the employee have a physical, mental, or emotional disability that might limit his or her ability to do the job?** Does the employee hold back from certain tasks? Do you see patterns in his or her work behaviors that suggest limited physical or mental capacities?

Plus One

❏ Does the employee exhibit any behaviors that suggest that he or she is experiencing a personal problem, lacks desire or motivation, demonstrates inflexibility in working with others, exhibits resistance to change, or has a difficult time accepting orders from others?

Handout 21. Cause→Effect Diagram

WHAT IS THE CAUSE→EFFECT DIAGRAM?

The Cause→Effect Diagram helps you understand the possible *causes* or origins of a specific *effect* or outcome. The diagram (also called a "fishbone diagram," because it has the look of a fish skeleton) explores these possible causes from four to six (and sometimes more) major dimensions or directions—with the causes springing from each dimension contributing to the final outcome or effect in some way. **When to Use:** when you want to understand the range of possible causes of a specific outcome.

HOW TO DEVELOP AND USE THE DIAGRAM

1. Define the "effect" or outcome that you want to better understand and solve. Write this outcome in the effect box to the far right of the diagram.
2. Identify the major cause categories and draw them in the diagram. Some common categories include systems and structures, policies and procedures, equipment and tools, resources, people, environment, and measurement. Any category may be appropriate, however, based on the organization, the environment, and the nature of the issue.
3. With the major cause categories in mind, brainstorm all the possible causes that lead to or contribute to the effect. You can brainstorm a general list of potential causes and then assign each cause to one or more of the cause categories or dimensions, or you can focus on one cause dimension at a time and fill in the diagram accordingly. For each cause, draw a line out from the cause category line and then label the end of this new line with the cause.
4. For each individual cause (now assigned to a category on the diagram), ask the following questions: "Why does this happen?" "What causes *this* cause?" The purpose of step four is to discover the underlying cause of each cause. Write the causes of each cause on the original cause's line (creating a mini-fishbone diagram for each cause).
5. Review the completed diagram. Look for patterns and relationships between individual causes and cause categories. *Are there some causes that appear repeatedly? Which cause category suggests the greatest need for improvement or change? Is more data needed to verify the effects or document the possible causes?*
6. The purpose of the Cause→Effect Diagram is to uncover a theory of the underlying causes and their patterns. The next steps in the problem-solving process are to document the causes and begin to develop a plan that addresses these major causes.

OUTCOMES

A completed Cause→Effect Diagram gives you a clearer picture of the complexity of the problem you are trying to solve and shows you areas for high-leverage impact on the effect or outcome. The result can help focus your energy on the major cause categories, allowing you to make adjustments or improvements in many areas.

Handout 22. Actions for Reducing Rating Errors

A Few Actions the *Coach* can Take to Reduce Rating Errors:

- Have employees rate themselves.
- Conduct performance coaching conversations more frequently.
- Discuss performance issues as they occur rather than waiting until the review to bring them up.
- Ensure that all performance dimensions are reviewed, not just select high-profile or high-impact areas.
- Work at relationship building with the performer long before the review occurs.
- Have clear performance standards and evaluate the performer against these standards rather than compare him or her to other performers.
- Use objective measures of performance—measures that are not influenced by the coach's interpretation or bias.
- To avoid both the recency and halo/horn effects, document performance throughout the year and discuss each performance incident with the performer at the time of the documentation.
- Maintain a portfolio folder that holds examples of the employee's work over the performance period.

A Few Actions the *Performer* can Take to Reduce Rating Errors:

- Rate him- or herself.
- Identify performance issues as they arise to ensure that the coach is aware of them.
- Ask for more frequent coaching conversations.
- Document his or her own performance in formal ways, such as by maintaining a portfolio of performance results throughout the year.
- Develop performance measures in concert with the coach.
- Develop a strong working relationship with the coach, such that there is open, honest, and frequent communication.

Handout 23. The Purposes of Performance Reviews

PURPOSES OF REVIEWS FOR THE EMPLOYEE AND COACH

- Provide employee feedback on performance.
- Identify barriers to performance.
- Develop improvement plans.
- Enhance employee commitment to his or her job, team, and organization.
- Identify the employee's training, development, and career goals.
- Align employee contributions with the needs and goals of the team, department, and organization.
- Explore the employee's potential future contributions to the team, department, and organization.
- Celebrate and reward great performance outcomes.
- Provide negative consequences when warranted.
- Identify performance goals for the next performance period.

PURPOSES OF REVIEWS FOR THE TEAM, DEPARTMENT, AND ORGANIZATION

- Value the employee's contribution to the team or work unit effort.
- Identify training and development goals for the overall team, work unit, department, and organization.
- Align individual's efforts with the needs/goals of the team, department and organization.
- Ensure objective, data-based assessments of employee performance.
- Equitably distribute pay adjustments based on performance.
- Identify high potentials for future development.
- Flag problem performers for tracking and follow-up.
- Ensure quality outcomes from employee effort.

Handout 24. Reframing the Traditional Review

PERFORMANCE REVIEW PROBLEMS		A PROPOSED HIGHER PURPOSE
One-way communication	→	Two-way dialogue
Focus on the past	→	Improvement for the future
Appraisal, evaluation, and judgment	→	Learning and development
Focus on financial implications	→	Learning and development
Focus on filling in forms and checking boxes	→	Developing understanding
Assumes that the manager knows and sees all	→	Both parties to the review have knowledge and insight to share
Focus on the performance review as an event	→	Performance management as a process
Over-reliance on some measurements while ignoring others	→	Using a holistic approach to performance measurement
Being overly influenced by recent events or personal characteristics	→	Using objective data when analyzing and assessing performance

Handout 25. Unbundling the Process

The performance management and performance review process is strengthened when the various goals and desired outcomes of the process are "unbundled" and dealt with via separate methods. The first method involves a Performance Coaching Conversation in response to a specific performance problem. The second method involves the Performance Coaching Conversation and the Annual Performance Analysis and Planning Conversation. These conversations are the foundation of an effective process focused on guiding an employee toward *great* performance. The third method is the formal performance review process. This process plays an important follow-along role that translates the results from coaching conversations into employee and organizational outcomes.

- *Critical Incident Coaching Conversation.* This informal conversation occurs as soon as possible after a specific employee performance problem. The focus of this conversation is on providing timely feedback to the performer on the incident, clarifying or redefining performance expectations, exploring causes of the incident, and discussing corrective actions that the employee might take. The coach uses the Mutual Learning Mindset to explore the employee's point of view of what just occurred, its causes, and possible actions by the employee and the coach to bring performance results back into alignment with expectations. These critical incident coaching conversations are subsequently discussed in the more formal Performance Coaching Conversations and the Annual Performance Analysis and Planning Conversation.

  Primary Purpose: Addressing specific employee performance issues in a timely fashion and utilizing a mutual learning mindset to explore causation and identify positive actions to improve performance.

- *Performance Coaching Conversation and the Annual Performance Analysis and Planning Conversation.* The (very frequent) Performance Coaching Conversation and the Annual Performance Analysis and Planning Conversation are geared toward the goal of maximizing employee performance, facilitating employee commitment to his or her job and organization, creating performance improvement plans, creating growth and development plans, and identifying employee support requirements and system barriers to performance.

  Both the Performance Coaching Conversation and the Annual Performance Analysis and Planning Conversation are focused on building a strong performance partnership through open and frequent communication between the coach and the performer. This is an employee-centered process where the employee is expected to take the lead in exploring avenues toward achieving great performance.

  Depending on the organization's policy or the characteristics of a given position, the coach may decide to hold the Annual Performance Analysis and Planning Conversation more than once a year.

  Primary Purpose: Enhancing employee movement toward great performance and strengthening the performance partnership.

- *Formal Performance Review.* The formal performance review occurs at least one day *after* the Annual Performance Analysis and Planning Conversation. In this follow-along, the official performance review forms are completed by the coach. If the form includes formal ratings for each performance dimension and a final evaluation rating the employee's work, the coach completes these ratings. These ratings may be used for determining annual performance-based pay adjustments, promotions, and other administrative and human resources outcomes. As appropriate, the formal review documents employee performance issues, performance improvement plans, and any consequences discussed with the employee at the time of the review.

  The performance review form should reflect the substantive results from the Annual Performance Analysis and Planning Conversation but should not be discussed during this annual conversation.

  Primary Purpose: Documenting employee performance and translating employee performance into individual and organizational outcomes.

Handout 26. Whole Body Listening

When using the mutual learning mindset, active listening within Performance Coaching Conversations means paying attention to more than what the other person is saying—it means surfacing and exploring the assumptions, reasoning, and intent of the other person. This always involves going beyond the words the other person uses to discover and understand the speaker's underlying perspectives, reasonings, intentions, and emotions. When you actively listen, you hold back your own need to inform, persuade, or express yourself and, instead, move into dialogue that is focused on understanding.

Your goal in active listening is to help the other person express what he or she thinks, feels, and needs; surface the other person's underlying assumptions, judgments, reasoning, and intentions; demonstrate that you understand the other person's perspective; and enable the emergence of true dialogue between you and the other person that is based on understanding.

To listen actively, follow these tips:

- Stop talking . . .
- Pay attention with your *whole* body—Show your interest with your eyes, hands, posture, and so forth. Shift your physical focus *toward* the other person.
- Maintain good eye contact—listen with your eyes; observe everything.
- Stop thinking about what you will say next and instead focus on discovering the meaning, reasoning, intentions, assumptions, and so forth, behind the other person's perspective.
- Listen for the deeper meaning behind the message.
- Seek out the *unknowns*: What does the person know about this situation or concern that you don't know?
- Don't make assumptions about what you are hearing, or that you have correctly understood something. A key enacting behavior in the mutual learning mindset, not making assumptions requires you to identify and test out the assumptions you are making with the speaker.
- Suspend judgment. An enacting behavior in the mutual learning mindset, suspending judgment allows your brain to consider alternative interpretations of what you are hearing.
- Listen for understanding. Another enacting behavior of the mutual learning mindset, this encourages you to seek confirmation from the speaker that what you have heard matches what the speaker intended.
- State your concerns only *after* you have heard and expressed understanding of the other person's concerns and needs.

Handout 27. The Four Skills of Active Listening

Active listening with the mutual learning mindset involves a variety of skills to first surface, then clarify, and finally verify the listener's understanding of what the speaker has said. The goal of active listening is to focus the listener's energy on extracting meaning from the conversation so that the speaker's perspective is heard clearly and objectively, and that this meaning is not affected by the listener's assumptions, inferences, interpretations, or judgments.

DRAWING OUT . . .

Drawing out involves asking open-ended questions to explore what the speaker hasn't told you and to mine for additional *facts, assumptions, reasonings, intentions,* and *feelings.*

Examples:
- *How do you feel about that?* (feelings)
- *Can you tell me exactly what happened?* (facts)
- *Tell me more about . . .*
- *Could you tell me more about what led you to that conclusion? I'd like to better understand your reasoning.*
- *What were/are your intentions in this situation? What were/are you hoping to accomplish?*
- *About your last concern, why do you think it happened that way?*
- *How have you thought of handling that?*
- *I'm not sure I understand your main concern, could you tell me more about . . .*

If the person talks mostly about feelings, ask "fact" questions. If the speaker talks mostly about "facts," explore "feelings." Drawing out what he or she *doesn't* say can deepen your understanding. It's also useful to ask questions about the nonverbal cues you observe or hear. In using drawing out with the mutual learning mindset, your goal is to gather valid information that will enable you to make a free and informed choice (as appropriate) in how to respond to the other person's situation or request.

CLARIFYING . . .

Clarifying questions in the mutual learning mindset involves asking open-ended questions to remove ambiguity or confusion in your own mind regarding what you have heard and to improve clarity of meaning. It is possible that the speaker is saying one thing but means something else. Clarifying helps clear up the confusion and definitions or meaning of ideas.

Examples:
- *I'm not sure I understand, earlier you indicated a willingness to move forward but I am now hearing some reluctance. Did I get something confused? Could you give me some more information so that I'm clear?*
- *I'm not sure I heard what you said earlier. Could you clarify when this happened?*
- *I'd like to understand what you just said, but I am confused about one thing . . .*
- *You indicated that you wanted more feedback from me—but also said that you wanted more independence. Could you help me understand what you're asking for from me?*

continued on next page

Handout 27. The Four Skills of Active Listening, *continued*

REFLECTING . . .

The reflecting skill in the mutual learning mindset involves "mirroring" or reflecting back to the speaker what you observe or hear in the words and actions expressed by the speaker. Reflecting essentially involves holding a mirror up to the other person and then describing what you are hearing or seeing. In its most powerful form, reflecting involves more about what you *see* than what you *hear*, because they may be different. Reflecting gives you the opportunity to check out this "mixed" message from the speaker. This skill allows you to honor, validate, and confirm what you *see* or sense in the other person and raise a question when what you *see* or *observe* is inconsistent with what you *hear* (the speaker's gestures, facial expressions, and so forth, seem to run contrary to the words that he or she is using). You always end reflecting with: *Did I hear you correctly? Did I get it right?*

Examples:
- *You're saying that you're not interested in taking on this project? Did I hear you correctly?*
- *You said that you wanted to work more closely with Steve, but I sensed some hesitation in your voice. Do you have reservations about working with Steve—or have I misunderstood what I thought was a hesitation in your voice? Am I missing something?*
- *So my understanding is that you wanted to move forward with the project? Is that right?*

PARAPHRASING . . .

This skill involves summarizing for the speaker what you understand based on what you have heard and seen. In summarizing, you take what the speaker has said to you together with what you have observed and offer a statement that reduces what the speaker has said or done down to a few bullet points. As with reflecting, you always end paraphrasing with: *Did I hear you correctly? Is that what you were trying to say? Have I correctly summarized what you were trying to say?* This allows the speaker to *correct* any misunderstandings and enables you to verify whether or not you heard and interpreted the speaker's intentions and meaning accurately.

Examples:
- *Let me summarize what I think I heard you say . . . . Did I understand correctly?*
- *So your main concerns were . . . . Is that right? Did I miss anything?*
- *So let me summarize what I've understood from what you've said . . . . Is that what you were trying to say? Did I hear you correctly?*
- *You stated that you weren't interested in the project and you also expressed some anger about the way the decisions on project assignments were made. Did I capture all of what you said and were feeling?*

> *Note: Paraphrasing* is most useful when the speaker has stated relatively clearly and fully what he or she is thinking or feeling about something. There are times, however, when thoughts and feelings are not expressed clearly or fully. Even though you may have heard the person accurately, you haven't necessarily understood what the speaker means—or you may sense what the speaker is trying to say, but he or she can't find the right words. If this occurs, it might be necessary to *clarify* what has been said or *draw out* the speaker further. *Reflecting* is most useful when you want to validate or affirm what you see or sense in the other person and when you are receiving *mixed* messages. If and when this happens, go back and use *clarifying* skills to better understand what the person is thinking and feeling.

Handout 28. The Performance Coaching Conversation

The Performance Coaching Conversation and the Annual Performance Analysis and Planning Conversation should be conducted within a larger process that involves *ongoing* conversations throughout the employee's performance cycle. Within this process, the coach has worked with the performer at the beginning of the performance cycle to help define "great performance" and then has guided him or her in identifying specific actions that he or she will take to achieve great performance. The coach has engaged the performer in identifying actions that the coach and others will take to support the employee's great performance results. The Annual Performance Analysis and Planning Conversation is a special integrating conversation that brings together all previous discussions and interactions between the coach and the performer and is intended to be the basis for future performance planning as well as the final assessment that becomes part of the employee's formal performance review document.

A. Preparing Yourself for the Performance Coaching Conversation

This phase ensures that you have prepared yourself mentally for the performance discussion with the employee to whom you are giving feedback.

1. Review the job description to verify its accuracy. Ensure that it describes great performance outcomes. Consult with HR if changes are warranted. Be prepared to make adjustments and revisions as appropriate.

2. If this is one of the frequent Performance Coaching Conversations between you and your direct report, review the performer's job description and complete as much of the Performance Planning and Development Worksheet as necessary. Alternatively, you may want to retrieve the most recent worksheet that you used to prepare you for a previous conversation. Consult the employee's performance portfolio and other documentation of performance. Clearly identify both your *outcome* and *process* goals for this conversation.

3. If this is the Annual Performance Analysis and Planning Conversation that feeds into the formal performance review form and process, do your homework. Consult the employee's performance portfolio and other documentation of performance. Complete the Performance Planning and Development Worksheet, clearly defining your objectives for and desired outcomes of the process. Identify the performance measures you are using to assess the employee's performance in each responsibility area. Based on your assessment of the employee's performance, complete a preliminary or draft version of the official performance review form. Clearly identify performance areas where you need more data from the employee and note any assumptions and inferences you may be making as you do your preliminary assessment.

4. For performance that is *going well,* ensure that the worksheet identifies actions that *you,* the *organization* and the *employee* can take to reinforce and sustain the positive performance.

5. For performance that is *not going well,* ensure that the worksheet identifies potential causes of the performance problems. Identify *organizational* and *employee-centered* reasons why performance may not be what it should and possible ideas and actions (by the employee, by you, and by the organization) for addressing the causes.

6. Ensure that you establish *realistic goals* for the coaching conversation. What are the most important goals or outcomes that you hope to accomplish during this conversation?

7. Anticipate the employee's *potential behavioral reactions* and plan your response.

B. Preparing the Employee for the Conversation

This phase prepares the employee for either the Performance Coaching Conversation or the Annual Performance Analysis and Planning Conversation. Ask the employee to review his or her (a) overall job description, (b) core job duties and organizational responsibilities, and (c) performance portfolio. Encourage the employee to talk to his or her peers and customers to gather their perspectives on his or her performance as part of preparing for the conversation. Ask the employee to consider the following questions in advance of the coaching conversation. The intent of these questions is to encourage critical reflection and help build employee ownership and accountability for performance outcomes.

- **What is going well with your job?** This question can include variations such as: What part of the job is working? What are some of the good things that are happening in each of your job responsibility areas? What recent accomplishments are you especially proud of? What about your job do you feel good about?

continued on next page

Handout 28.   The Performance Coaching Conversation, *continued*

- ***What is not going well with your job?*** This question can include these variations: What about the job isn't working as well as you'd like? What problems or difficulties in any of your job responsibility areas have you experienced lately?
- ***Why is your job going well and why isn't it going well? What is enabling you to meet your performance goals? What factors support achieving your performance results?*** If you are experiencing performance challenges, what might be the *causes* of these things not going well?
- ***What changes or improvements could you make in how you do your job to help improve what is not going well?*** This question can include variations such as: What could you do to address the causes of things not going well that would improve your future performance outcomes and goals?
- ***How might I (as your supervisor) help you to be more successful in your job?*** This question can include variations such as: What can I do more or less of to enable you to achieve your performance goals?
- ***What do you see as performance areas where there may be a need for new responsibilities or where performance could be moved up to a new level?*** This question invites the employee to identify new responsibilities or growth areas that are driven by the organization's strategic goals, new customer expectations, new technological capacities, and so forth. This encourages him or her to look forward strategically for new ways to serve the organization and its customers.
- ***For the Annual Performance Analysis and Planning Conversation.*** How would you assess your overall performance and your performance for each of your job and organizational responsibilities? For each responsibility area, to what extent are you exceeding, meeting, or failing to meet your performance goals? What measures are you using to gauge your performance in each area? What factors are supporting or limiting your success in each of these areas?
- ***For the Annual Performance Analysis and Planning Conversation.*** What are your long-term professional development and career goals? Where do you see yourself five years from now? What's most important to you in your work? What would you most like to accomplish in your work here?

Develop a one-page version of these questions in advance of each Performance Coaching Conversation, and give the employee a copy. In addition, give the employee a copy of his or her job description to ensure that he or she is focusing on published expectations for the position. For the Annual Performance Analysis and Planning Conversation, you may also wish to provide the employee with a blank performance review form if appropriate.

C. Conducting the Coaching Conversation

Your goal in conducting the Performance Coaching Conversation is to better understand the employee's perceptions of his or her work. Follow this sequence closely:

1. ***Welcome the employee to the conversation.*** Set the tone for the rest of the session. Begin by reiterating the reason for the conversation, your goals for the session, and the reasoning behind your desire to have him or her share the performance self-assessment before you share your assessment.

   You might start out with language such as:

   "As I mentioned to you the other day, I'm planning to have more frequent coaching conversations with everyone who reports to me. These discussions will help me better understand everybody's concerns, needs, and issues. It also gives me a chance to clarify my own thoughts and expectations. As you recall, several days ago I asked you to think about a number of questions in preparation for today's conversation (or Annual Performance Analysis and Planning Conversation).

   "My intention in asking you to think about these questions was to encourage you to do a self-assessment of your own performance and some critical reflection on your past work, as well as to get you to start thinking about things both you and I could do to support your performance in the future.

   "My preference would be to have you start things off—because I'd like to hear your own perspectives and insights about your performance—and then I'll add my comments and thoughts when you're done. Does that sound okay to you?

   "So, to begin, I'd like to hear your thoughts about what is *going well* in your job . . . ."

2. ***Explore what's going well and why it's going well.*** Ask the employee to highlight his or her strengths—what's "going well" with his or her performance. Use active listening skills and ask clarifying questions to improve your understanding of what he or she has said. Ask for more information and explore the reasoning behind the employee's conclusions.

continued on next page

Handout 28. The Performance Coaching Conversation, *continued*

3. ***Present your "going well" thoughts.*** After the employee is finished with a self-assessment of his or her strengths, discuss your thoughts and observations. Link your observations concerning his or her behavior and performance with the self-assessment whenever possible. Identify additional areas that were not mentioned where possible. Explain the data and reasoning behind your statements. Acknowledge the employee's contributions and positive results. Explore actions that both you and the employee can take to maintain performance outcomes in these areas.

4. ***Explore areas for improvement and the causes of performance difficulties.*** Transition from the discussion of what's going well by indicating that achieving great performance involves exploring areas for improvement and identifying what the employee can do to move toward his or her goal. Ask the employee first to discuss areas for improvement (what isn't going well) in his or her job overall and in specific performance dimensions, then to share his or her ideas for possible *causes* of performance problems in these areas. Use active listening to gather valid information, explore the employee's reasoning, and verify your understanding of what was said.

5. ***Present your "improvement desired" thoughts.*** Following the employee's ideas, present your own thoughts and observations, linking (as much as possible) what he or she stated with the improvement areas that you have observed for his or her performance overall and for each responsibility area. Share the data behind your observations and explain your reasoning. Identify additional performance areas for improvement using specific examples, data, incidents, and so forth. Identify any assumptions you are making and ask the employee for alternative interpretations of these assumptions. Use constructive feedback and focus on specific, observable, and measurable performance outcomes and behaviors rather than on abstract terms such as commitment, attitude, dedication, and so forth.

6. ***Seek acknowledgment of performance problems and discuss consequences.*** If improvement in specific performance behaviors or outcomes is part of your goal, get the employee to acknowledge that a change in behaviors or performance outcomes is desired. If he or she does not agree that there is a problem with performance or that a change in behavior is necessary, have the employee state—in his or her own words—the *consequences* of *not* changing his or her behavior or outcomes. Explain the reasoning behind your request as this: By thinking through these consequences him- or herself, the employee might better appreciate their meaning and impact.

7. ***Discuss employee's ideas for future action.*** Once you both agree that one or more improvements in performance are warranted, ask the employee if he or she understands what the goal is in this performance area and to identify possible actions that, given the identified causes, he or she could take to address the performance issue and move his or her performance closer to the desired outcome. If appropriate, assist the employee in defining and refining the performance goal and identifying ways to measure success. Follow his or her ideas for action with your own. Link your recommendations with his or her ideas as much as possible. Explain the reasoning and intentions behind your suggested actions.

8. ***Discuss your support for improvement actions.*** Ask the employee to identify ways that you can be most helpful in supporting his or her efforts to achieve the performance goals. Follow his or her ideas with your own. Link your comments with the employee's ideas as much as possible. Explain the reasoning and intentions behind your ideas for additional support for his or her efforts.

9. ***Explore employee ideas for new responsibilities and areas of growing performance to a new level.*** Invite the employee to share his or her ideas about new directions and responsibilities for his or her position, as well as areas where he or she might grow and develop the job to a new level to better respond to the organization's requirements for the future. Gather more information by asking the employee to clarify any of these new areas that aren't clear to you. Test out any assumptions you are making about these ideas. Inquire into the reasoning behind his suggested new responsibility areas. Add your own ideas regarding new responsibilities, behaviors, and outcomes that may be required of the employee in the future and your ideas as to where the employee could move performance to a new level. Explain your reasoning and the intentions behind your own suggestions.

D. Coming to Mutual Agreement

As the coaching conversation winds down, bring the ideas you've discussed together by having each of you summarize what you each have committed to do to support the employee's current performance, improve performance, accept new responsibilities, or move performance to higher levels.

continued on next page

Handout 28. The Performance Coaching Conversation, *continued*

1. ***Summarize key next steps.*** Ask the employee to summarize his or her understanding of the conclusions and actions that you have both agreed to as a result of this coaching conversation. Reinforce the understandings and expectations that agree with yours and seek clarification if and when you have a different understanding of what's been agreed to. Identify additional areas where understanding is still needed, if appropriate, and verify his or her understanding of them.
2. ***Reiterate mutual agreement.*** End the conversation with a clear reiteration of the mutual agreement that both of you have achieved. Summarize the actions each of you have committed to take to improve, enhance, and sustain high levels of performance for the future. Ensure that you summarize what specifically you will each do differently or keep doing to enable great performance. Summarize key areas where you will provide appropriate assistance and support.
3. ***If this is the Annual Performance Analysis and Planning Conversation,*** indicate that you will be finalizing any official performance appraisal or review forms based on today's discussion and that you want to schedule another meeting to discuss your final performance rating. Indicate that the conversation today has been helpful, that it has filled in your understanding of the employee's performance, and that your final assessment will reflect what you learned in this discussion and what each of you have agreed to do for the future.
4. ***Offer employee assistance if warranted.*** If you have discussed long-standing performance problems the employee is experiencing and you suspect that there may be a *personal* problem behind these performance issues, *do not* state your suspicions, but instead indicate that *if* the performance problems discussed today are a result of personal problems, the organization's Employee Assistance Program (EAP) may be helpful. Note that EAP provides free and confidential assistance upon request. Explain that your reason for offering EAP is based on your desire to support the employee being successful in his or her job.
5. ***Determine the next Performance Coaching Conversation.*** Establish a follow-along schedule for future Performance Coaching Conversations to discuss the employee's performance progress and provide additional support if needed.
6. ***Conclusion.*** End the interview with appreciation for the employee's performance and his or her commitment to performance improvement. Reiterate how helpful today's conversation has been in helping you understand how best to support his or her future performance.

E. Follow-up and Monitor Performance Progress

After your conversation, make sure you take the following actions:

1. Summarize the key conclusions and actions agreed to during the coaching conversation in an email or memo and send this to the employee, inviting him or her to talk with you if he or she has a different understanding of the results from your conversation or to offer additional understandings.
2. If this is the Annual Performance Analysis and Planning Conversation, complete and finalize official performance appraisal forms based on insights gained during your coaching interview and schedule the follow-up meeting with him or her to present your final performance ratings.
3. If this is the Annual Performance Analysis and Planning Conversation, schedule a follow-along Performance Coaching Conversations with the employee at which time you will finalize, based on the annual conversation, the great performance and annual goals for the new performance year.
4. Follow-through in providing or supporting the training, information, equipment, and other organizational support that you said you would provide.
5. Observe the employee in action and reinforce positive behaviors and outcomes.
6. Continue tracking performance outcomes, gathering performance data, and documenting results in performance logs and the employee's performance portfolio.
7. Reward *any* degree of performance improvement. Reinforce all positive behaviors and outcomes—as long as they are moving the employee toward his or her performance goals.
8. Conduct ongoing Performance Coaching Conversations as needed to discuss the employee's progress, identify new performance expectations and directions, renegotiate performance goals, and so forth, as required because of new issues, changes, priorities, initiatives, and performance challenges.

Handout 29. Evolutionary vs. Revolutionary Performance Management

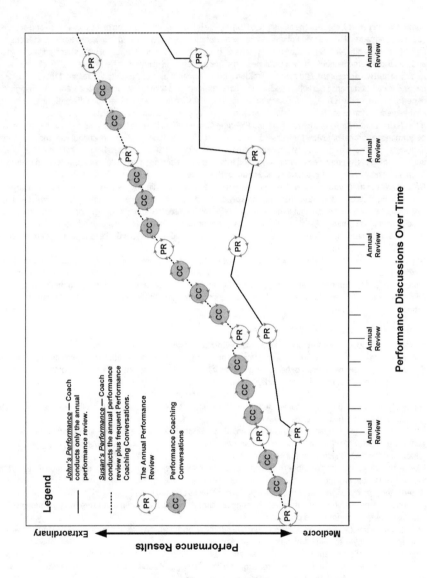

Appendix C: Training Instruments

Training Instrument 1. What Is a Coach?

On your own . . . and with your partner:
- Think of the most successful coach you've ever known.
- Consider the ***characteristics*** of this person. What qualities and attributes did this person have that made him or her an effective coach for you? What did he or she ***do*** to make you think of him or her as an effective coach?
- Tell your partner a story that gives a good example of how this coach influenced your life in a positive way.
- Listen to your partner's story. What coaching characteristics and behaviors do you hear in the story?

As a table group:
- Identify the common qualities, attributes, and behaviors of the coaches in our lives. List these common characteristics in the space below.
- What roles or titles did our effective coaches have in our lives (for example, teacher, boss, mentor, parent, and so forth)?

CHARACTERISTICS, ATTRIBUTES, AND BEHAVIORS OF AN EFFECTIVE COACH . . .

Common titles held or roles played by coaches in our lives:

Training Instrument 2. Responsibilities of the Performance Coach

1. Guide and _____ a person toward achieving his or her potential.

2. Encourage his or her personal and professional _____.

3. Increase an employee's long-term _____ to the organization.

4. Assess an employee's _____ and _____ levels.

5. Guide the employee in discovering and assist the employee in fully applying his or her _____ and skills in the workplace.

6. Guide the employee in discovering and addressing his or her performance _____ and vulnerabilities.

7. Guide the employee in exploring the root _____ of performance problems.

8. Recognize—and celebrate—employee _____ and _____.

9. _____ the performer to push beyond their comfort zone.

10. Facilitate employee _____-management.

Notes:

Training Instrument 3. Selecting the Best Coaching Roles

Consider the following factors concerning the **task(s)**, **work environment**, and **performer** when deciding on the best mix of coaching roles. Place an X on the dotted line for each task, environment, or person's characteristic. Then, place an X on the dotted line for each of the five coaching roles that best describes the performer's observed behaviors.

CHARACTERISTICS OF THE <u>TASK</u> OR TASKS BEING PERFORMED

Nature of the Task(s):	Complex ◄-----------------------------►	Simple
Desired Outcome(s):	Fuzzy/Unclear ◄-----------------------------►	Clear
Consequences of Failure:	Significant ◄-----------------------------►	Insignificant
Time Available:	Very Little ◄-----------------------------►	Ample

CHARACTERISTICS OF THE PERFORMANCE <u>ENVIRONMENT</u>

Environment:	Rapidly Changing ◄-----------------------------►	Stable
Decision Making:	Centralized ◄-----------------------------►	Distributed
Resource Availability:	Limited ◄-----------------------------►	Sufficient
Accountability Culture:	No Performance Accountability ◄-----------------------------►	People Are Held Accountable

CHARACTERISTICS OF THE <u>PERSON</u> YOU ARE COACHING

Competence Level:	Very Low ◄-----------------------------►	Very High
Self-Confidence Level:	Very Low ◄-----------------------------►	Very High
Workload/Workload Stress:	Excessive ◄-----------------------------►	Manageable
Temperament/Attitude:	Why Try? ◄-----------------------------►	I Can Do It!
Willingness to Take Risks:	Low ◄-----------------------------►	High
Achieves Great Performance:	Rarely ◄-----------------------------►	Almost Always

ASSESSING THE BEST <u>COACHING ROLES</u> TO USE FOR THIS TASK/SITUATION/PERSON

Placing an × on the Continuum Notes the Need for This Role

Coaching Role	The Performer . . .	Needs <u>More</u> of This Role Needs <u>Less</u> of This Role	The Performer . . .
Directing/Correcting	Needs hands-on direction/ guidance and correction.	◄-------------------------------►	Needs little direction and guidance. Very self-directed and self-correcting.
Motivating/Inspiring	Lacks interests in or energy for the job; no initiative.	◄-------------------------------►	Brings energy and enthusiasm to the task. Self-starter.
Supporting	Lacks self-confidence. Seems unsure of self.	◄-------------------------------►	Displays confidence and self-assurance.
Developing	Displays comfort with status quo. Good but not great performer.	◄-------------------------------►	Is always challenging his or her past performance levels. An active learner and experimenter.
Problem Solving	Appears unable to solve challenging problems. No learning from mistakes/errors.	◄-------------------------------►	Looks for root causes of problems/errors; is skilled at systems thinking and looking outside the box.

Training Instrument 4. Which Coaching Role Is Best?

For the case or cases your group has been assigned, identify the *primary* and *secondary* coaching role or roles that are most appropriate for the person or situation.

- **Reluctant Roy**—Roy has worked for you for the past five months and has generally been a good worker. He knows how to do the job, has never complained about the work, and has even helped train some of the newer workers. Lately, however, you've seen him slow down. He shows no enthusiasm for his tasks and occasionally grumbles to other employees about this "rat-hole" of a workplace. Which coaching role(s) is/are best? Why?

- **Misfit Mary**—Although Mary has worked a series of different jobs within the company over the past several years, she has never really settled comfortably into any of her positions. In a recent restructuring, Mary ended up in your department. It became readily apparent that although she seemed to have right skills and knowledge to do her job, she seemed to lack many of the basic workplace skills (such as punctuality and attendance) that you generally take for granted in people. Given recent belt tightening in the company, if you were to terminate her, there's a good chance you wouldn't be able to hire a replacement. You need to make this work out. Which coaching role(s) is/are best? Why?

- **Over-Dependent Bob**—Bob is starting his seventh year with your company and is one of your more experienced and capable workers. His problem, however, is that he tends to shy away from complex and challenging projects. When he is given a challenging project, he regularly runs to you for help with each major step of a task. Even though you believe, based on his past work, that he has the knowledge and skills to do the job right, he seems to depend on you for everything. He seems unwilling to take risks. Which coaching role(s) is/are best? Why?

- **Steve the Follower**—Although Steve has worked with you for two years, he still seems intimidated by any complex task with lots of things to consider in the decision making and implementation stages. He has made it clear that he much prefers assisting other people rather than assuming a leadership role. He is always the last to volunteer for a new task and, if you ask him to stretch himself in a new assignment, is quick to let you know that he isn't skilled enough to handle the work. Which coaching role(s) is/are best? Why?

- **Sidetracked Sally**—Sally has more knowledge than most of your other workers combined. Unfortunately, you find it hard to work with her because she appears bored and uninterested in the work most of the time. She approaches most of her work with obvious reluctance. You give her the most complex work on the team, but she still lacks motivation or enthusiasm. Despite her own tepid performance, other workers occasionally seek her out for advice when you're not around. Which coaching role(s) is/are best? Why?

Training Instrument 5. What Enables Great Performance?

What enables a performer to *consistently meet or exceed* his or her performance goals?

....

....

....

....

....

....

What actions by the *employee* enable great performance outcomes?

....

....

....

....

....

....

What actions by the *coach* enable great performance outcomes?

....

....

....

....

Training Instrument 6. Building Employee Ownership for Great Performance

As a group, identify specific actions that the performer and the coach can each take to build greater ownership of great performance for your assigned step of the GPM Cycle.

The GPM Cycle	Actions That the Employee/Performer Can Take	Actions That the Coach Can Take
❶ Define Great Performance Outcomes		
❷ Develop Great Performance Goals, Strategies, and Actions		
❸ Provide Resources and Support		
❹ Evaluate Performance		
❺ Make Changes or Improvements		
❻ Provide Logical Consequences		

Training Instrument 7. A Personal Plan for Action

A. THE ROLE OF THE PERFORMANCE COACH

Identify key insights, "ahas!" and "take-aways" from the exploration of the importance of the performance coach, the five roles that the coach uses to bring out the best in others, and diagnosing when to use each coaching role:

....

....

....

....

....

....

B. COACHING ACTIONS FOR BUILDING GREATER EMPLOYEE OWNERSHIP

Specific actions that I can take to encourage those who report to me to take greater ownership of their performance and to see that they create their own success:

1. ....

   ....

2. ....

   ....

3. ....

   ....

4. ....

   ....

5. ....

   ....

C. DEVELOPING AND SUSTAINING A MUTUAL LEARNING MINDSET

Specific actions that I can take to develop and consistently demonstrate a mutual learning mindset in my coaching interactions with others:

1. ....

   ....

2. ....

   ....

continued on next page

Training Instrument 7.   A Personal Plan for Action, *continued*

3. ....
....

4. ....
....

5. ....
....

D. ACTIONS TO PREVENT MY LEAPING UP THE LADDER OF INFERENCE

Specific actions that I can take to integrate the ladder of inference into my thoughts and actions as a coach and the steps I will take to prevent "leaping" up the ladder:

1. ....
....

2. ....
....

3. ....
....

4. ....
....

5. ....
....

Training Instrument 8. Responding to Threat or Embarrassment

HOW PEOPLE RESPOND WHEN THREATENED OR EMBARRASSED

How do people typically respond when they are threatened, feel vulnerable, are embarrassed, or are otherwise uncomfortable when interacting with others?

....
....
....
....
....
....
....

THE CAUSES OF THREAT OR EMBARRASSMENT TO THE COACH

What might cause a coach to feel threatened, vulnerable, embarrassed, or otherwise uncomfortable during interactions with others, including with those whom the coach is coaching?

....
....
....
....
....
....
....

Notes:

Training Instrument 9. Mutual Learning and Coaching Cases

For the case or cases your group has been assigned, identify how a coach using the unilateral control mindset would respond and then identify how a coach using the mutual learning mindset would respond. Be prepared to report your two sets of strategies to the full group.

1. **Case Number One**—Steve has been a skilled welder on your team for the past several years. In the past, he has demonstrated that he is able to do the job and do it well, but, in recent months, you have seen a decline in his quality and productivity. You've chatted with him informally about his performance issues and his response was irritation and stating that he felt that you were picking on him. Recently you've called him out on several safety problems: not returning his welding tools to their proper location after use and failing to consistently wear his steel-tipped boots. A few of his co-workers—friends of his—have approached you with information that he has been talking about quitting his job because it's just a dead end.

   Which coaching role or roles are appropriate for the coach to use in this situation?

   A coach using the unilateral control mindset would likely . . .

   A coach using the mutual learning mindset would instead . . .

2. **Case Number Two**—Janice has just joined your information technology team as an IT technician. In this role, she is on the front line for providing technology troubleshooting and support for other employees in your company. The IT technician role requires good diagnostic skills and a deep knowledge of both hardware and software application. Most important, however, it requires solid relationship management skills—specifically managing relationships with those asking for tech support. You have observed Janice on the phone and on a few site visits and it's clear that she has the diagnostic skills and knowledge of the hardware and software she has been asked to support. You also observed her interacting with a few customers and, although you perceived that she could improve a bit by building a rapport with a customer, you felt that she was on the right path. Recently, however, you've received complaints from a few department managers suggesting that she doesn't spend enough time understanding the customer's problem.

   Which coaching role or roles are appropriate for the coach to use in this situation?

   A coach using the unilateral control mindset would likely . . .

   A coach using the mutual learning mindset would instead . . .

continued on next page

Training Instrument 9. Mutual Learning and Coaching Cases, *continued*

3. **Case Number Three**—Steve is one of your most senior purchasing agents. His expertise at sorting through purchasing options and finding the best deals has saved the company thousands of dollars over the years. When it comes to his working relationship with his co-workers, however, there is much to be desired. He tends to be abrupt with others and intolerant of differing opinions. Although these conflicts don't surface very often, whenever the team is asked to explore new purchasing procedures, software, or methods, Steve is the first to offer his opinion and quickly dismiss others' opinions. Steve tends to prefer working solo, which isn't a problem most of the time. However, when he needs to collaborate with another member of the team or one of the younger purchasing agents asks him for direction, he makes it very clear that he doesn't want to be disturbed or bothered with others.

Which coaching role or roles are appropriate for the coach to use in this situation?

A coach using the unilateral control mindset would likely . . .

A coach using the mutual learning mindset would instead . . .

Training Instrument 10.   How Goal Setting Enables Great Performance and Applying Goal Theory

1. THE ROLE OF GOAL SETTING IN ENABLING GREAT PERFORMANCE

How does setting clear and challenging goals enable great performance in employees? What is it about setting a goal that moves an employee toward great performance?

....

....

....

....

....

....

2. APPLYING GOAL THEORY TO THE COACHING ROLE

What are the implications of goal theory on how a coach should guide the goal-setting process? What might a coach need to do within the goal-setting process to take full advantage of goal theory as a motivational tool?

....

....

....

....

....

....

Notes:

Training Instrument 11. Defining Great Performance Application

For each position, identify whether the GP outcome is focused on the **organization** overall (O), **customers** (C), or the **team**/co-workers (T).

Great Performance for Office Manager

PERFORMANCE DIMENSION	GREAT PERFORMANCE FOR AN OFFICE MANAGER
Quality:	
Quantity:	
Cost:	
Timeliness:	
Impact on Team:	

Great Performance for Sales Associate

PERFORMANCE DIMENSION	GREAT PERFORMANCE FOR A SALES ASSOCIATE
Quality:	
Quantity:	
Cost:	
Timeliness:	
Impact on Team:	

continued on next page

Training Instrument 11. Defining Great Performance Application, *continued*

For each position, identify whether the GP Outcome is focused on the **organization** overall (O), **customers** (C), or the **team**/co-workers (T).

Great Performance for Company Accountant/Comptroller

PERFORMANCE DIMENSION	GREAT PERFORMANCE FOR AN ACCOUNTANT/COMPTROLLER
Quality:	
Quantity:	
Cost:	
Timeliness:	
Impact on Team:	

Great Performance for IT Tech Support Specialist

PERFORMANCE DIMENSION	GREAT PERFORMANCE FOR AN IT TECH SUPPORT SPECIALIST
Quality:	
Quantity:	
Cost:	
Timeliness:	
Impact on Team:	

Training Instrument 12. Performance Planning and Development Worksheet

Position: _____   Employee: _____   Date: _____

A. GREAT PERFORMANCE OUTCOMES–POSITION

❶ *What is GREAT performance for this position?* What GREAT performance outcomes represent the *target* for the employee's positive contributions? Develop GP outcomes for each performance dimension and then designate the target of each contribution as to the **organization (O)**, **customers (C)**, or **team**/co-workers (**T**). ❷ How will the performer and coach know that great performance is achieved within each performance dimension? Identify specific measures of success. ❸ For the **employee**, identify whether each great performance outcome is an area where the employee should **maintain (M)** performance, **improve (I)** performance, **accept (A)** new responsibilities, or **grow (G)** or enhance in this role by moving it to a higher level of performance.

DIMENSIONS	❶ GREAT PERFORMANCE OUTCOME [Identify each outcome's target as an O, C, or T]	❷ MEASURING GREAT PERFORMANCE	❸ M, I, A, OR G?
Quality:			
Quantity:			
Cost:			
Timeliness:			
Impact on Team:			

continued on next page

Training Instrument 12. Performance Planning and Development Worksheet, *continued*

B. Essential Job Functions--Position and Employee

❶ *Describe the essential job functions for this* **position.** Identify five to seven major job categories of the position's work by describing the key areas where this position contributes to great performance. Examples: develop a positive relationship with the customer, develop an annual budget, manage the work of others, and so forth. ❷ For each job function, develop two to four SMART performance goals for this position. ❸ For the ***employee***, identify whether each overall job function or specific SMART goal is an area where the employee should **maintain (M)** performance, **improve (I)** performance, **accept (A)** new responsibilities, or **grow (G)** or enhance in this job function by moving it to a higher level of performance.

❶ Essential Job Functions	❷ SMART Performance Goals	❸ M, I, A or G?
1.		
2.		
3.		
4.		
5.		
6.		
7.		

continued on next page

Training Instrument 12.   Performance Planning and Development Worksheet, *continued*

C. ORGANIZATIONAL RESPONSIBILITIES–POSITION AND EMPLOYEE

❶ *Describe the organizational responsibilities for this* **position.** Identify two to three responsibilities that are expected of every employee. Examples: follow work rules, display teamwork, attendance, courtesy toward customers, and respect for company equipment and property. ❷ For each organizational responsibility, identify two to four SMART performance goals for this position. ❸ For the ***employee***, identify whether each organizational responsibility or specific SMART goal is an area where the employee should **maintain (M)** performance, **improve (I)** performance, **accept (A)** new responsibilities, or **grow (G)** or enhance in this organizational responsibility by moving it to a higher level of performance.

❶ ORGANIZATIONAL RESPONSIBILITIES	❷ SMART PERFORMANCE GOALS	❸ M, I, A OR G?
1.		
2.		
3.		

D. IDENTIFYING POTENTIAL CAUSES LIMITING IMPROVEMENT OR FUTURE DEVELOPMENT

Review Sections A, B, and C and focus on those **high-value/high-priority** *GP expectations, job/organizational respon-sibilities, and SMART goals where the employee needs to* **improve** *performance,* **accept** *new responsibilities, or* Grow *performance to a new level.* ❶ List these high-value/high-priority areas in the first column below. ❷ For each area, identify the causes that may be limiting the employee's performance in this area today or may limit future performance. Use **handout 20**, Nine-Plus-One Performance Diagnostic Checklist, and **handout 21**, Cause→Effect Diagram, to identify possible employee and system causes. ❸ Identify what can be done (by the employee, coach, team members, and others) to improve or enable performance in each area.

❶ AREA FOR IMPROVEMENT OR DEVELOPMENT (FROM B AND C)	❷ CAUSES LIMITING CURRENT OR FUTURE PERFORMANCE	❸ ACTIONS TO TAKE TO ADDRESS THESE LIMITATIONS

continued on next page

Training Instrument 12. Performance Planning and Development Worksheet, *continued*

❶ Area for Improvement or Development (from B and C)	❷ Causes Limiting Current or Future Performance	❸ Actions to Take to Address These Limitations

E. Identifying Process Goals for the Performance Coaching Conversation

What *process* goals do you have for the upcoming Performance Coaching Conversation with this employee? Do you want to **build ownership for performance**, **build greater commitment to the job/organization**, **strengthen the performance partnership**, or **identify system barriers and challenges**? ❶ Identify your performance coaching process goals and ❷ your strategy for addressing each goal during your coaching conversation with the employee.

❶ Process Goals	❷ Strategy for Addressing This Goal in the Coaching Conversation

continued on next page

Training Instrument 12. Performance Planning and Development Worksheet, *continued*

F. Developing Performance Improvement or Growth Outcome Goals

Develop performance-improvement or development-outcome goals for the employee. Identify the ***highest-value/highest-priority*** performance or responsibility areas from parts A and B where you want the employee to maintain current performance or to improve most, or where he or she should accept new responsibilities or grow in the job, and identify the top four or five maintain, improve, accept, or growth goals. For each goal, identify the ❶ *positive* behavior or outcome for the employee, ❷ how the employee and coach might measure success, and ❸ specific behaviors and actions that the employee will engage in that, when practiced, are likely to move the employee's performance closer to the goal.

1. ❶ Positive Behavior or Outcome Goal	❷ Performance Measure

❸ Specific employee ***behaviors*** that will enable the performance goal to be achieved:

a. ....

b. ....

c. ....

d. ....

2. ❶ Positive Behavior or Outcome Goal	❷ Performance Measure

❸ Specific employee ***behaviors*** that will enable the performance goal to be achieved:

a. ....

b. ....

c. ....

d. ....

continued on next page

Training Instrument 12. Performance Planning and Development Worksheet, *continued*

3. ❶ Positive Behavior or Outcome Goal	❷ Performance Measure

❸ Specific employee ***behaviors*** that will enable the performance goal to be achieved:

a. ....

b. ....

c. ....

d. ....

4. ❶ Positive Behavior or Outcome Goal	❷ Performance Measure

❸ Specific employee ***behaviors*** that will enable the performance goal to be achieved:

a. ....

b. ....

c. ....

d. ....

5. ❶ Positive Behavior or Outcome Goal	❷ Performance Measure

continued on next page

Training Instrument 12. Performance Planning and Development Worksheet, *continued*

❸ Specific employee *behaviors* that will enable the performance goal to be achieved:

a. ....

b. ....

c. ....

d. ....

G. Supporting Employee Performance

What specific actions might the coach and others take that support or enable the employee to achieve his or her performance improvement or growth goals? What guidance, training, tools, equipment, information, and so forth, could the coach make available to enable the employee to be successful?

Coaching/Supervisory/Organizational Actions to Support Great Employee Performance

❶

❷

❸

H. Preparing for the Performance Coaching Conversation

What actions will the coach take in advance to prepare for the Performance Coaching Conversation? What performance analysis, root cause exploration, or data collection should be done in advance of the coaching conversation? What feedback, information, or upper management support does the coach need in advance of the conversation? What questions will the employee be asked to consider prior to the session? Review the employee's performance log and performance portfolio for documentation on performance results.

....

....

....

....

....

....

....

....

....

....

Training Instrument 13. Defining Job Responsibilities

JOB RESPONSIBILITIES FOR *DEPARTMENT MANAGER*

The specific job responsibilities for a department manager might include:
- *Managing the department's budget*

-
-
-
-
-
-

JOB RESPONSIBILITIES FOR *RETAIL SALES ASSOCIATE*

The specific job responsibilities for a retail sales associate might include:
- *Stock and restock merchandise*

-
-
-
-
-
-

JOB RESPONSIBILITIES FOR *HUMAN RESOURCE GENERALIST*

The specific job responsibilities for a human resource generalist might include:
- *Ensure that all job descriptions for assigned classes of jobs are accurate*

-
-
-
-
-
-

Training Instrument 14.   SMART Performance Goals

SMART performance goals and objectives provide clarity, specificity, measurability, and employee commitment to the performer's effort.

S — ....

....

....

M — ....

....

....

A — ....

....

....

R — ....

....

....

T — ....

....

....

Training Instrument 15.   SMART Goals and Performance Measures Application

PERFORMANCE GOAL	A SMARTer PERFORMANCE GOAL . . .	AN EFFECTIVE MEASURE OF THIS SMART GOAL
1. Sustain strong customer relationships.	• Achieve an overall customer satisfaction rating of 8.0 on the 10-point satisfaction scale by July 1st.	• Employee uses three-question "postcard" on-the-spot surveys for every fifth customer using a 10-point scale.
2. Strengthen partnerships with key suppliers.		
3. Reduce operational costs.		
4. Align department goals with the organization's strategic priorities.		
5. Share critical information and collaborate with others.		

All Groups: Actions to Ensure That a Goal Is "Accepted":

Training Instrument 16. Documenting Performance

WHY DOCUMENT EMPLOYEE PERFORMANCE?
Why might it be important for a coach to document the performance of an employee?

....

....

....

....

....

....

....

HOW DO YOU DOCUMENT PERFORMANCE NOW?
What tools and strategies do you currently use to document the performance of an employee now?

....

....

....

....

....

....

....

....

Training Instrument 17. The Causes of Performance Problems

WHAT ORGANIZATIONAL FACTORS CAUSE PERFORMANCE PROBLEMS?

What actions or inactions by the organization, coach, team members, and so forth could contribute to less than optimal performance results for an employee?

....

....

....

....

....

....

....

WHAT ARE THE POSSIBLE EMPLOYEE CAUSES OF PERFORMANCE PROBLEMS?

What employee actions, inactions, behaviors, characteristics, and so forth could contribute to less than optimal performance results in the employee's work?

....

....

....

....

....

....

....

Training Instrument 18. Cause → Effect Diagram Application

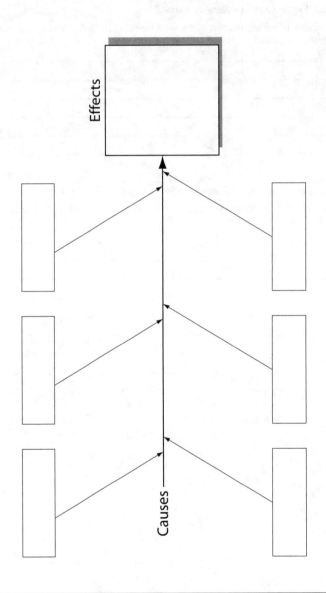

Training Instrument 19. Establishing Positive Performance Goals

Negatively Stated Goal	→	Positively Stated Improvement Goal
She has a poor attitude.	→	She needs to offer <u>more</u> ideas for improving her work.
He is slow in processing claims.	→	He needs to process claims <u>more</u> quickly.
She is too dependent on me.	→	She needs to work <u>more</u> independently. She needs to make <u>more</u> of her own decisions.
He is too sociable with others.	→	He needs to <u>increase</u> attention to completing his own work.
1. She misses too many deadlines.	→	
2. He never answers the phone politely.	→	
3. She is rude to customers.	→	
4. He doesn't communicate with co-workers.	→	
5. She rarely tries to solve work problems on her own.	→	
6. He doesn't take an active role in our team meetings.	→	
7. She needs to be less prickly when dealing with our suppliers.	→	
8. He doesn't seem to appreciate the importance of quality.	→	
9. She is too much of a "lone wolf."	→	

Training Instrument 20. Performance Management Quiz

Review the following statements and questions and identify the *best* answer from among the response options.

1. Performance Coaching Conversations should be conducted

    a. once a year, according to the organization's policy
    b. once each quarter, using the annual calendar
    c. formally at least once a year and informally as often as needed, based on performance
    d. whenever the employee requests feedback on performance
    e. as infrequently as possible (to lessen the pain all round).

2. One way to deal with the *recency* effect in performance reviews is to

    a. document performance events as they happen throughout the year
    b. ask the employee to update you whenever he or she achieves a performance goal
    c. gather data on other performers for comparison purposes
    d. schedule performance conversations when people are less busy and are able to reflect back on the entire performance period
    e. a and c only.

3. The purpose of the Performance Coaching Conversation and the Annual Performance Analysis and Planning Conversation is to

    a. discuss problems with the employee's performance
    b. guide the employee's future work performance
    c. increase employee commitment to his or her work
    d. clarify job duties and expectations, review past performance, and discuss future performance expectations
    e. all of the above.

4. The purpose of a *performance coach* is to

    a. challenge the performer to move to the next level
    b. diagnose the causes of the employee's performance problems
    c. take the lead in identifying ways to improve the employee's performance
    d. all of the above
    e. a and b only.

5. The problem with most traditional performance reviews is that

    a. the focus of the review is on past performance vs. a future orientation
    b. it tends to be a one-way affair
    c. they don't occur frequently enough to catch and correct problems early
    d. there is often too much focus on which rating the employee will receive
    e. all of the above.

continued on next page

Training Instrument 20. Performance Management Quiz, *continued*

6. The best way to kick off a performance coaching conversation is to

   a. first, identify the employee's performance strengths and then shift to areas for improvement
   b. praise the employee for his or her contributions over the past year
   c. ask the employee to present his or her analysis of his or her performance
   d. "ease into" the conversation by setting the proper tone by discussing noncontroversial things first.
   e. a and b.

7. Star performers generally don't benefit much from performance coaching or performance reviews.　　　True　　　False

8. What is the desired percentage of time that both the coach and employee should talk during the Performance Coaching Conversations?

   a. Coach talks 100% and employee listens.
   b. Coach talks 90% and employee talks 10%.
   c. Coach talks 70% and employee talks 30%.
   d. Coach talks 30% and employee talks 70%.
   e. Coach talks 10% and employee talks 90%.
   f. Coach listens and the employee talks 100%.

9. The *halo/horn* effect in performance reviews means that a coach needs to be aware of

   a. evaluating all employees against the same performance standard
   b. paying attention to an employee's success in one performance dimension while ignoring problems with others
   c. focusing too much on performance results at the expense of *how* the employee works with others
   d. discounting an employee's performance successes because of a performance problem in one important area
   e. B and D.

10. The four skills of active listening are

   a. drawing out, clarifying, reflecting, and paraphrasing
   b. positive regard, pure inquiry, reflecting, and clarifying
   c. using the whole body, drawing out, reflecting, honoring
   d. drawing out, inquiring, mirroring, summarizing.

Training Instrument 21. Performance Reviews From the Dark and Light Sides

PERFORMANCE REVIEWS FROM THE DARK SIDE

Think about a performance review that you either received or gave that you perceived to be ineffective and counterproductive and that may even have led to an erosion in the working relationship between the coach and the performer.

What factors or characteristics regarding how and when this review "from the Dark Side" was done contributed to this failure? Make a list of the things done wrong or not at all . . .

....

....

....

....

....

....

....

....

....

....

....

PERFORMANCE REVIEWS FROM THE LIGHT SIDE

Reflect on a performance review that you either received or gave that you perceived was very effective and productive, and which led to an improvement in the working relationship between the coach and the performer.

What factors or characteristics regarding how and when this review "from the Light Side" was done contributed to this success? Make a list of the things done right . . .

....

....

....

....

....

....

....

....

....

....

....

Training Instrument 22. Common Errors in Performance Reviews

Please fill in the blanks as the facilitator guides you through the common errors in performance reviews.

1. .... **Characteristics:** Experience and knowledge level of the "rater" or coach, as well as the coach's direct knowledge of the performer's work and outcomes.

2. **Relationship Between the** .... **and Employee:** The quality of their communication and the level of trust, mutual respect, and understanding between the coach and the employee influence the accuracy of the assessment. In addition, the coach's personal beliefs, values, and prejudices can distort his or her objective perspective of the performer.

3. .... **Effect:** Recent events or incidents tend to influence the coach's assessment of the employee's performance (for example, a missed deadline a week before the review will affect the results more than a letter of commendation from a customer six months earlier).

4. **Halo/**.. **Effect:** The tendency of a coach to perceive a person as, overall, good or bad based on one or two characteristics, which tends to affect the rater's perceptions of the employee's performance (for example, the coach rates a performer as an overall poor performer based on a single incident or characteristic [horn effect] or, on the other hand, the coach might overlook poor performance if the coach sees the performer perform very well in one area [halo effect]).

5. .... **Errors:** The length of time between a performance incident and the rating of an employee's performance is likely to affect the *accuracy* of the assessment.

6. **Restriction in the** .... **Scale:** When the coach assesses everyone too severely, too leniently, or only those clustered near the center of a rating scale.

7. .... **Effect:** When the coach rates a performer based on how his or her performance compares to other performers rather than on how the performer meets set standards and established performance objectives.

Training Instrument 23. Actions to Reduce Errors in Performance Reviews

ACTIONS THE *COACH* CAN TAKE TO REDUCE RATING ERRORS . . . .

How might the coach reduce rater errors?
What actions can the coach take before and during a performance review to reduce these sources of error?
How will the coach ensure equity and fairness in his or her assessments?

....

....

....

....

....

....

....

....

....

....

ACTIONS THE *PERFORMER* CAN TAKE TO REDUCE RATING ERRORS . . . .

What can an employee do to help the coach reduce rating errors (and ensure the accuracy of the performance assessment process)?

....

....

....

....

....

....

....

....

....

....

....

Training Instrument 24. Identifying the Purposes of Performance Reviews

What is the purpose of a performance review? What is the role and function of the performance review for each of the following stakeholders? *Note:* for most of these stakeholders, there are *multiple* objectives or functions.

INDIVIDUAL/GROUP	PURPOSE/VALUE/IMPORTANCE What is the specific purpose, benefit, value, and importance of the review to this individual/group?
Employee	
Supervisor/Coach	
Team, Work Unit, or Department	
Organization as a Whole	

Training Instrument 25. Active Listening Application

SPEAKER'S ROLE

Purpose: To experience being listened to. To practice the skills of clear thinking and communicating ideas. To share your thoughts or feelings about something important to you.

Instructions: Choose a topic from the list below. Make sure that you select a topic that you care about, that is unresolved for you, and is one that you are currently dealing with.

- a challenging or difficult coworker or employee
- a decision you need to make
- an "upper management" decision that is making things difficult for you
- a project that isn't going the way that it should be go
- something about your work that you find frustrating
- some new development in your job that you're very excited about
- any other topic that meets these criteria.

LISTENER'S ROLE

Purpose: To practice the use of whole body active listening with a mutual learning mindset. To demonstrate your ability to focus all of your energy on another person to extract meaning from what the person is saying. To demonstrate understanding.

Instructions: Use whole body active listening and the mutual learning mindset to "tune into" the concerns, ideas, reasonings, intentions, motivations, feelings, and so forth of the speaker. Use all *four* active listening skills:

- Use *drawing out* to explore new territory.
- Use *clarifying* to remove confusion or contradiction.
- Use *reflecting* to "mirror" the ideas, thoughts, and feelings you hear or see.
- Use *paraphrasing* to demonstrate your clear understanding of what you are hearing or seeing.

Use the *paraphrasing* or *reflecting* skills at least four to five times to practice communicating back to the speaker that you understand what he or she is saying or feeling.

Important: Avoid *solving* the problem, giving advice, or offering your own opinion.

Finish the listening session with a summary *paraphrasing* to demonstrate your understanding.

OBSERVER'S ROLE

Purpose: To give feedback on your observation of the listener regarding his or her listening skills. To develop your own skills as an observer or listener—striving to understand meaning through observation alone.

Instructions: Use the observer's worksheet below to record your observation notes. Use a ✓ for every instance of a desired active listening behavior. Identify where the listener could most improve. Note expressions of a *mutual learning mindset*.

continued on next page

Training Instrument 25. Active Listening Application, *continued*

ACTIVE LISTENING SKILL	OBSERVATION NOTES: FREQUENCY (✓), EFFECTIVENESS, AND SUGGESTIONS FOR IMPROVEMENT.
Whole Body Listening	To what extent did the listener shift his or her body toward the speaker and use his or her eyes, posture, and focus to demonstrate attention? ....
Clarifying and Drawing Out	To what extent did the listener draw out and clarify reasoning, intentions, motivations, facts, feelings, and so forth from the speaker? ....
Reflecting and Paraphrasing	To what extent did the listener reflect back what was heard or seen and ask "Did I hear or understand or see correctly? Did I get it right?" ....
MLM Enacting Behaviors	To what extent did the listener demonstrate the enacting behaviors of the *mutual learning mindset*? ....

When the discussion ends:

1. Ask the *Listener*:
   - (a) How did you feel about your use of the listening skills? What did you do well? What was comfortable or awkward?
   - (b) Did you try to use the enacting behaviors of the *MLM*?
   - (c) What would you do *differently* to improve your listening skills?

2. Ask the *Speaker*:
   - (a) What did the listener do that *helped* you say what you wanted to say? How was it helpful?
   - (b) What did the listener do that made it more difficult to get your point across? How or why was it more difficult?

3. Give your own feedback to the listener.

Appendix D: Training Tools

Training Tool 1. Training Room Configuration/Layout

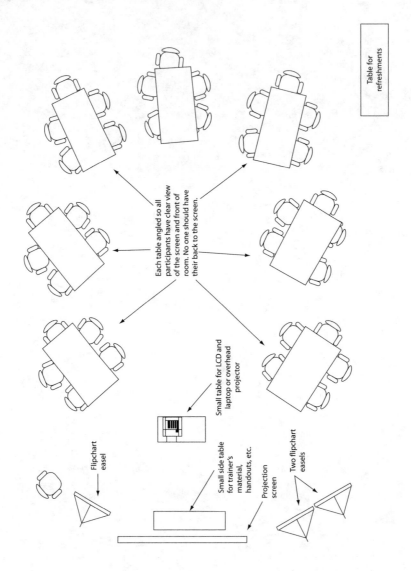

Table for refreshments

Each table angled so all participants have clear view of the screen and front of room. No one should have their back to the screen.

Small table for LCD and laptop or overhead projector

Flipchart easel

Small side table for trainer's material, handouts, etc.

Projection screen

Two flipchart easels

Training Tool 2. Learning Goal/Objective → Outcomes

1. *Learning Objective:* What do I want to learn or what behavior do I want to change as a result of this course?

....

....

....

....

....

....

To what degree do I believe that this program will help me achieve this objective?

	❑	❑	❑	❑	❑	❑	
Not at All	1	2	3	4	5	6	**Quite a Bit**

2. *Outcomes From Achieving My Learning Objective:* What are the potential rewards/outcomes that I expect to get if I achieve my objective?

....

....

....

....

....

....

To what degree do I believe that achieving my objective will bring this outcome about?

	❑	❑	❑	❑	❑	❑	
Not at All	1	2	3	4	5	6	**Quite a Bit**

3. *Value of This Reward:* How valuable is this reward? To what degree do I value this outcome or reward?

	❑	❑	❑	❑	❑	❑	
Not at All	1	2	3	4	5	6	**Quite a Bit**

Training Tool 3. "Aha!" Sheet

Aha *!*

Topic: _____

Jot down the most significant insights, perspectives, and practical ideas that you pick up from this seminar. These **Ahas!** are the ideas, tools, methods, and approaches that you are most likely to remember and put into practice when you return to work.

Identify the ideas that will help you transfer your learning from this session to your workplace.

1. ....
....
....

2. ....
....
....

3. ....
....
....

4. ....
....
....

5. ....
....
....

6. ....
....
....

7. ....
....
....

8. ....
....
....

9. ....
....
....

Training Tool 4. Training Program Reaction Sheet

Workshop Title: _____

Date: _____   **Instructor**: _____

Use the following scale when rating each of the following dimensions of this training program

Strongly Disagree	Disagree	Slightly Disagree	Slightly Agree	Agree	*Strongly Agree*
1	2	3	4	5	6

Logistics/Administrative Issues

1. The training room was arranged such that it facilitated my learning.	
2. The training room temperature was comfortable throughout the session.	

Workshop Content

3. I had the knowledge and/or skills required to effectively participate in this workshop.	
4. The workshop's learning objectives were clearly defined.	
5. This workshop was timely and relevant—it covered an issue with which I am currently dealing.	
6. This workshop provided practical and useful knowledge and skills that are immediately applicable to my job.	
7. This workshop provided me with new information, ideas, methods, and techniques.	
8. This workshop helped me achieve my personal learning objectives for this topic/issue.	

Workshop Design

9. The participant materials (handouts, workbooks, cases, etc.) were useful throughout the workshop.	
10. This workshop was delivered in an effective way for me to learn this topic.	
11. I had enough time to understand, learn, and integrate the workshop materials.	
12. The workshop content was logically organized.	
13. There was a good mix of teaching methods, formats, and audiovisuals that enabled me to learn the course content.	

continued on next page

Training Tool 4. Training Program Reaction Sheet, *continued*

TRAINER/WORKSHOP INSTRUCTOR

	Strongly Disagree	Disagree	Slightly Disagree	Slightly Agree	Agree	**Strongly Agree**
	1	2	3	4	5	6

14. The instructor was knowledgeable in the workshop subject.	
15. The instructor was organized and prepared.	
16. The instructor established a good learning environment.	
17. The instructor was open to participants' questions and issues and was willing to adjust the program to meet participants' needs.	
18. The instructor generated active discussion and involvement by participants.	
19. Overall, I was satisfied with the instructor.	

OVERALL ASSESSMENT

20. Overall, the pace of this workshop was (circle one):

TOO FAST | TOO SLOW | JUST RIGHT

21. This workshop (circle one):

Did not meet my expectations | Met my expectations | Exceeded my expectations

22. My overall evaluation of this workshop is (check one box):

| **Very Poor** | 1 ❑ | 2 ❑ | 3 ❑ | 4 ❑ | 5 ❑ | 6 ❑ | 7 ❑ | 8 ❑ | 9 ❑ | 10 ❑ | *Excellent* |

COMMENTS

23. What I found **most helpful** from this workshop was . . .
24. **Ideas for improving/strengthening** this workshop include . . .

Your Name: ....

> **Why *Your Name*?** To enable the facilitator to follow-up with you if your comments or improvement suggestions require clarification and to enable the facilitator to better understand and respond to your issue/concern. However, you may omit your name if you would like to.

Training Tool 5. Selecting Group Leaders

Small group discussions during a workshop are an effective way to enhance participation and understanding of the content being delivered. The productive efforts of these discussions are enhanced when the group selects a leader to help focus the energy of the group, keep the group on track, and create accountability for the assigned task.

Here are some ideas for selecting and rotating group leaders:

- the person with the first—or last—birthday of the year, or closest to July 4th, or closest to the current date
- the person with the most distinctive middle name
- the person who had the farthest or shortest distance to travel from his or her home to attend this workshop
- the person with the shortest or longest hair
- the person to the right or left of the last discussion leader
- the most or least senior person in terms of years with the organization
- the person with the most unusual hobby
- the person with the longest or shortest job title.

Appendix E: Learning Activities

Learning Activity 1. What Is a Coach?

OBJECTIVES

The objectives of this learning activity are to
- explore participant perceptions of the role of a coach
- have participants share personal stories about an effective coach in their life
- clarify the origins and definition of the word "coach" and discuss the implications of the term in the workplace.

MATERIALS

The materials needed for this activity are

- Training Instrument 1: What Is a Coach?

- Handout 1: The Definition of a Coach

- Training Tool 5: Selecting Group Leaders

- flipchart and marking pens

- PowerPoint slides 6-2 to 6-7.

TIME

30 minutes

PREPARATIONS

- Prior to this learning activity, ensure that each participant has a copy of the training instruments and handouts.
- Have a prepared flipchart page as detailed in the activity as well as flipchart markers.

INSTRUCTIONS

1. Display **slide 6-2** as you ask participants to respond to the question "What does it mean to be a coach?" Draw participants out with their ideas. Without agreeing or disagreeing with any of the definitions offered, indicate that you'd like the group to define what a coach is by sharing examples of coaches in their own lives.

2. Display **slide 6-3** as you distribute **training instrument 1**. Point out the instructions at the top of the page. Ask participants to initially work by themselves to think of someone in their life whom they might call a coach who had a significant effect on them at the time and perhaps even now. Ask them to think of a specific event in their relationship with their coach that captures the essence of the coaches' relationship with them.

3. Ask individuals to find a partner at their table or the next table with whom they will share this story about the coach in their lives. Once everyone has a partner for this exercise, direct them to spend the next eight minutes sharing their respective stories (about four minutes each). Ask them to pay particular attention to the characteristics, attributes, and behaviors that their partner's coach brought to the relationship.

4. After about eight minutes, call time and then direct each of the table groups to share key insights about the characteristics, attributes, and behaviors of the effective coaches people described in their stories. Display **slide 6-4** as you invite the small groups to spend the next 10 minutes identifying and discussing the common characteristics, attributes, and behaviors, and then filling in the two columns on **training instrument 1**. If desired, guide the table groups in selecting a leader for this discussion by using one of the suggested methods outlined in training tool 5.

5. After about 10 minutes, reconvene the large group. Ask participants to share some of the characteristics, attributes, and behaviors of the coaches in their lives—what enabled those people to be effective coaches. Record some of

continued on next page

Learning Activity 1. What Is a Coach?, *continued*

their responses on a flipchart page. Some of the shared characteristics and behaviors might include listened well, caring, empathetic, challenged me, offered a helping hand, didn't make it easy for me, told me what I needed to hear instead of what I wanted to hear, encouraged me, helped me see the bigger picture, accepted nothing less than my best, picked me up when I fell, honored my feelings and anxieties, pushed me, helped me see the world as it is instead of the way I wanted it to be, and so forth.

6. Ask the large group to describe some of the roles that these coaches played in their lives. Some of the roles that people might offer include: teacher, pastor/priest/rabbi/imam, parent, athletic coach, neighbor, and so forth. You may want to add some additional titles such as voice, drama, or music coach, or perhaps even a birthing coach (the latter title, you might add with a smile, certainly involves bringing the best out in others!).

7. Invite participants to bring all of this together in a definition of a coach—in answer to the first question at the beginning of this activity. Ask the group: What, exactly, does a coach do?

8. PPT Ask participants to turn to page two of **training instrument 1** as you display **slide 6-5** and explain that the word "coach" comes from the Hungarian term for a special carriage that was used for carrying people between Budapest and Vienna. Note that the term was later adapted by British students as a slang term for someone who helped "carry them" successfully through an examination or challenge.

9. PPT Conclude the activity by displaying **slide 6-6**, distributing **handout 1**, and referring to the definition of coach on the handout. Emphasize that an effective coach helps others overcome challenges to achieve their goals by enabling them to achieve their best. Transition from this definition to the focus of today's workshop on building a strong and effective performance coaching relationship between managers and their direct reports. Note that regardless of the kinds of coaches they thought of when they told their personal stories, most all of the characteristics, attributes, and behaviors that they identified also apply to their role as a performance coach for the members of their teams.

10. PPT Display **slide 6-7** and offer the final word on the role of a coach from none other than Nanny McPhee. Mention that Nanny McPhee is a character from the popular movie of the same name. Explain that Nanny McPhee was summoned by a distraught father to deal with his unruly children. Nanny McPhee skillfully guided all of the children into becoming responsible people, helping their overwhelmed father to solve a variety of family problems, and, over time, making her presence less and less needed by the children and the family.

Debriefing

- Coaching involves a coach who cares very deeply about the welfare and success of another person.
- Coaches come in many forms and play a number of different roles in our lives.
- An effective coach uses a wide variety of behaviors to challenge, support, encourage, enable, guide, and shape the thoughts and actions of the person being coached.
- The aim of the coach is—to quote Nanny McPhee—to be there when needed, even if not wanted, but also to know when it's time for the person being coached to step out on his or her own.
- Suggest that in today's workshop we'll explore the role of the performance coach in the workplace, a role that involves many of the same characteristics and behaviors that we've explored in this activity.

Learning Activity 2. Goal Setting

OBJECTIVES

The objectives of this learning activity are to
- build camaraderie and community among participants
- identify their personal learning objectives for the workshop
- discuss shared learning goals and objectives with other participants
- identify key questions to answer during the workshop.

MATERIALS

The materials needed for this activity are

- Training Tool 2: Goal Setting Worksheet

- Training Tool 3: Aha! Sheet
- flipchart and marking pens
- **PPT** PowerPoint slides 6-8 to 6-10, 7-3 to 7-6, 8-3 to 8-6, or 9-3 to 9-6, as appropriate to the workshop.

TIME

🕐 25 minutes

PREPARATIONS

- Prior to this learning activity, ensure that each participant has a copy of training tools 2 and 3.
- Prepare a single flipchart page that is entitled "Your Questions/Goals."

INSTRUCTIONS

1. **PPT** Review the specific goals for the session with **slides 6-8, 7-3 and 7-4, 8-3 and 8-4**, or **9-3 and 9-4**, according to which workshop you are facilitating.
2. **PPT** Distribute **tool 2** and, as you display **slides 6-9, 7-5, 8-5, or 9-5** (depending on the workshop), ask participants to identify
   - their objective for the workshop and how likely it is that they will realize this objective through this session
   - what's in it for them if they achieve their objective and how likely it is that reward will materialize
   - how important this positive benefit or reward is to them.
3. **PPT** After a couple of minutes, display **slides 6-10, 7-6, 8-6, or 9-6**, and ask participants to work in their small group to (a) meet and greet (not included in 6-10 because this is the second activity of the session); (b) share their personal objectives (the first of the questions on the Goal Setting Worksheet); and (c) identify, as a group, two or three questions about performance coaching, performance management, or performance reviews (based on which workshop is being conducted) that the group would like to address during the workshop. Give the small groups approximately seven minutes for this activity.
4. Have the groups report their questions and record them on the prepared flipchart page. Post the page or pages in a prominent location in the room. Highlight the importance of the participants taking responsibility for their own learning by exploring the answers to these questions as you work through the content of the workshop. Note that one of your goals for this workshop is to link the issues and tools explored today with the questions that the group has identified. Indicate that anyone at any time can call out a question that seems appropriate given the topic being discussed. Indicate as well that time may be set aside right after lunch and toward the end of the day to highlight and answer specific questions.
5. Distribute **tool 3**. Encourage them to be active participants in their own learning by using the "Aha!" Sheet to record the key learning moments and insights that will be most useful to them beyond the session. Note that one thing we know about adult learning is that we tend to learn and remember things that we make our own. By jotting

continued on next page

Learning Activity 2. Goal Setting, *continued*

down insights that they learn from their table partners, from others in the room, or from you as the facilitator, they make these insights their own.

6. Note the schedule for breaks and lunch and the locations of restrooms, telephones, and refreshments. Remind them to turn off their cell phones as a courtesy to others.

Debriefing

After the group has identified its goals and questions for the session and you have recorded these on the flipchart, conclude this activity by emphasizing that whether or not learning occurs in this session depends on the extent to which they actively seek out new insights, learning, and tools, and the extent to which they find the answers to their questions.

Learning Activity 3. Performance Coaching and the Roles of the Coach

OBJECTIVES

The objectives of this learning activity are to
- describe the characteristics of effective coaches
- identify when performance coaching is appropriate
- describe the five coaching roles
- apply a methodology for selecting the right coaching role.

MATERIALS

The materials needed for this activity are
- Handout 2: The Roles of the Performance Coach
- Handout 3: The Dynamic Nature of the Coaching Relationship
-   Training Instrument 2: Responsibilities of the Performance Coach
- Training Instrument 3: Selecting the Best Coaching Roles
- PPT PowerPoint slides 6-11 through 6-16.

TIME

30 minutes

PREPARATIONS

- Be familiar with the discussions and outcomes from learning activity 1 with its focus on defining coaching and the role of a coach in general.
- Prior to this learning activity, ensure that you have copies of the handouts and training instruments for each participant.

INSTRUCTIONS

1. PPT Begin this activity by bridging from the previous activity on the definition of a coach. Display **slide 6-11** as you emphasize the point that coaching is a relationship, not an event. Within that framework, then, every interaction between a manager and his or her employee provides the manager with a coaching opportunity. Note that by focusing on the relationship instead of specific events, the role a coach plays toward maximizing a performer's contribution is significantly enhanced.

2. PPT Distribute and refer to **training instrument 2** as you display **slides 6-12 and 6-13** on the responsibilities of effective coaches. As you begin revealing each of the 10 responsibilities of the performance coach, ensure that you make references to the group's earlier discussion of the fundamental role and characteristics of a coach.

3. In summary, emphasize that the key responsibility of the performance coach is to develop a deep understanding of the person he or she is coaching and then, based upon that understanding, adjust his or her actions to guide the employee toward achieving his or her greatest potential and achieving maximum positive impact on the organization.

4. PPT As you display **slide 6-14**, distribute **handout 2** on the five coaching roles. Indicate that the broad responsibilities outlined in training instrument 2 translate into the five coaching roles outlined on handout 2. Briefly summarize each as you gradually reveal the five roles. Ask participants if they have any questions on these five coaching roles.

5. PPT As you display **slide 6-15** and distribute **handout 3** on the evolving and dynamic relationship between the coach and the performer, note that as the performer increases in competence and confidence, the involvement of the coach transforms from a high level of involvement to a relatively low level of involvement. Indicate, however, that even a low involvement strategy requires the coach to be thoughtful about which role he or she brings to the coaching relationship.

continued on next page

Learning Activity 3. Performance Coaching and the Roles of the Coach, *continued*

6. 🖉 PPT Distribute **training instrument 3** as you display a graphic of the instrument in **slide 6-16**. Note that this instrument is designed to offer the participants some insight into how to select the coaching role or mix of roles that best responds to the person they are coaching, given the tasks being performed within the work environment. As time permits, walk participants through an example on **slide 6-15**, finishing up with a final blend of the five coaching roles (all revealed on **slide 6-15**).

DEBRIEFING

At the end of this activity, make these final comments:
- Coaching is more about the relationship than an event.
- As the performer's competence and confidence grows, this relationship changes—especially with regard to the degree and nature of the coach's involvement with the performer.
- There are five different roles of the performance coach: Each role is appropriate at different times and in different degrees, based on such factors as the characteristics of the performer, the work environment, and the performer's work.

Learning Activity 4. Coaching Cases—Using the Right Coaching Role

OBJECTIVES

The objective of this learning activity is to
- apply insights from the previous activity to specific coaching situations.

MATERIALS

The materials needed for this activity are
- Handout 2: The Five Roles of the Performance Coach

- Training Instrument 3: Selecting the Best Coaching Roles

- Training Instrument 4: Which Coaching Roles Are Best?
- flipchart and marking pens if desired
- **PPT** PowerPoint slides 6-17 through 6-18.

TIME

30 minutes

PREPARATIONS

- Handout 2 and training instrument 3 should have already been distributed in learning activity 3.
- Training instrument 4 should be ready for distribution.

INSTRUCTIONS

1. Let the participants know that it is now time for them to apply their knowledge about the dynamic nature of the coaching relationship and the five potential roles of the coach to a specific situation.
2. **PPT** Display **slide 6-17** as you distribute **training instrument 4**. Assign one or two of the coaching cases (depending on the number of table groups and the time allotted for the activity) to each table group. Ask them to refer to **handout 2** and **training instrument 3** as they read their assigned case and then determine which coaching role or mix of roles they would recommend based on the case's details. You may wish to assign an individual case to two or more table groups to not only ensure that all cases are discussed but also to explore different perspectives and recommendations that the groups may generate.
3. Suggest to the groups that many of these cases may well involve the coach playing multiple roles. If this is the case, direct them to indicate in their response to the case the relative priority of the roles—the order in which their suggested roles should be utilized by the coach.
4. Give the small groups five to eight minutes to read and discuss their case(s) and to identify which coaching role or roles they would recommend—and why. Indicate that they should designate someone to be prepared to report out the answers for their group.
5. After the times is up, invite each table group to report their suggested coaching strategy to the large group.
6. As each table group reports their suggested coaching role or roles, probe for the reasons why they chose the primary and secondary roles. If multiple groups tackled the same case, compare and contrast the groups' recommendations and rationales. Acknowledge that to identify the best coaching role or roles, the groups may have had to make some assumptions. Indicate that, in the real world, they will be expected to make fewer assumptions and instead to base their coaching strategy on available data regarding the performer, task, and work environment.
7. **PPT** Display **slide 6-18** and, after each case is discussed, reveal the suggested primary and secondary coaching roles. Note that there are many alternative views in these cases and that an argument could be made for roles different from the "answers" on slide 6-18.

continued on next page

Learning Activity 4. Coaching Cases—Using the Right Coaching Role, *continued*

DEBRIEFING

Conclude the discussion of the coaching cases and the importance of matching the role to the performer, task, and work environment:

- Choosing the best coaching strategy involves gathering real data on the performer who is being coached, the task or tasks that this performer is expected to complete, and the surrounding work environment.
- Encourage participants to exercise the full array of coaching roles instead of over-relying on the role that they find most comfortable.
- Suggest that they use **training instrument 3** to help them sort out the characteristics of the performer, task, and environment to enable them to select the right array of coaching roles.

Learning Activity 5. The Great Performance Management Cycle

OBJECTIVES

The objectives of this learning activity are to
- identify the factors that enable great employee performance outcomes
- describe the Great Performance Management (GPM) Cycle as the foundation of effective performance management
- explore the concept of great performance outcomes as the focus for employee effort
- identify the actions that a coach can take to facilitate employee ownership of the GPM Cycle.

MATERIALS

The materials needed for this activity are
- Handout 3: The Dynamic Nature of the Coaching Relationship
- Handout 4: The Great Performance Management Cycle
- Handout 5: Defining Great Performance
- Handout 6: Actions by Employees and Coaches that Facilitate Great Performance
- Handout 7: The Role of the Coach in Shaping Great Performance
- Training Instrument 5: What Enables Great Performance?
- Training Instrument 6: Building Employee Ownership of Great Performance
- Training Instrument 7: Personal Plan for Action
- Training Tool 5: Selecting Group Leaders
- PPT PowerPoint slides 6-19 through 6-27 or 10-3 through 10-11
- flipchart pages and markers.

TIME

60 minutes

PREPARATIONS

- Handouts 4 through 7 and training instruments 5 and 6 should be ready for distribution.
- Prepare two flipchart pages. One flipchart page should be titled "Enablers of Great Performance." The second flipchart page will have two headings at the top with a line drawn vertically down the center of the page. The left-hand column should be titled "Employee Actions" and the right-hand column should be titled "Coach Actions."

INSTRUCTIONS

1. Transition into this learning activity by highlighting key lessons from earlier in the workshop: the meaning of the word coach as bringing out the best in others; the dynamic nature of the coaching relationship; the five roles of the coach; and the importance of finding the best coaching role by assessing the performer, the task, and the environment. Indicate that our next task involves bringing this coaching relationship into the performance management process. Note that, in this lesson, they will learn about the Great Performance Management Cycle and the roles that the performer and the coach play within that cycle.
2. Distribute **training instrument 5** as you display **slide 6-19** or **10-3**. Ask the table groups to take the next eight minutes or so to identify the factors that enable great performance in general and then to identify actions that both the performer and the coach can take to enable great performance. Ask each group to select someone to facilitate the discussion. *Note:* For ideas to help the groups select a discussion leader, refer to **training tool 5**.
3. After about eight minutes, reconvene the large group and facilitate a discussion of the three questions on **training instrument 5**. As the groups report their answers to the first question, record the responses on the prepared flipchart page entitled "Enablers of Great Performance." After the first question has been recorded, move to the

continued on next page

Learning Activity 5. The Great Performance Management Cycle, *continued*

second question, exploring the actions of the performer contributing to great performance. Record the groups' responses in the left-hand column entitled "Employee Actions." Once you have recorded all of the answers to the second question, move on to the third question and record the groups' answers in the right-hand column entitled "Coach Actions."

4. Once you have completed both of the flipchart pages, ask the large group to identify some key actions that seemed to surface as critically important to great performance. Reinforce what you hear from the group whenever possible and call attention to several of the actions that you believe are especially important.

5. Make the point that all performance—great or otherwise—occurs within a larger framework or process that directs and reinforces the work of both employees and their coaches. Highlight any of the actions listed on the flipchart that represents steps within this process. This might include establishing clear goals, developing measures of success, evaluating performance, providing training, and so forth.

6. **PPT** Transition into an introduction to the Great Performance Management Cycle by displaying **slide 6-20** or **10-4** and distributing **handout 4**. Lead participants through the GPM Cycle, following the suggested animation sequence on the slide. Offer a high-level overview of the key steps within the GPM Cycle first, starting with "define great performance" and ending with the "logical consequences for performance outcomes" reinforcing loop. As you walk participants through the cycle, emphasize that all of the steps in this process occur naturally, but the key difference between great performance and just getting by is that the great performance outcomes process is actively managed to ensure its success.

7. **PPT** After completing the broad overview of the cycle and the steps within it, return to the top: define great performance outcomes. Note that because everything that an employee does is based on this first step in the process, it is important that we spend a bit more time understanding what great performance means in this context. Gradually reveal additional information about the define great performance outcomes step on **slide 6-20** or **10-4** as you explain that great performance is defined as performance outcomes that are profoundly positive value-added results that the performer creates for the company or organization, for customers, and for co-workers.

8. Indicate that great performance is always defined for a position instead of an individual performer. Emphasize that when defining what great performance looks like for a position, it is important to think of the position rather than the person who is currently holding the position or who previously held the position. Ask participants why focusing on the position instead of the person is important. Agree with any participant who answers by saying that great performance for a position shouldn't be limited by who happens to be holding the job now or who recently held the job. Emphasize that when we think of great performance we need to focus on the profoundly positive outcomes that we'd like to see, rather than be limited by the known capacities, limitations, performance problems, and so forth, of the person occupying the job at present.

9. Note that great performance goes far beyond just doing the job. It involves reaching toward a new level of outcomes that are beyond normal expectations. When great performance outcomes are achieved, everybody notices and everybody wins. Distribute **handout 5** and present two examples of great performance to help participants appreciate the concept:

   - **Mortgage Loan Officer**—The officer creates value through strong customer partnerships. Through these partnerships, customers feel listened to and respected. The officer anticipates customer questions and communicates complex financial information in clear and understandable ways. The officer anticipates additional financial needs of the customer and proactively suggests other bank products and services that may ease the customer's financial anxieties. Customers feel that their financial information is dealt with sensitively and confidentially. Co-workers also feel listened to and respected and are comfortable approaching the officer with questions and customer problems. Overall, the bank benefits from the loyalty and commitment customers feel for the bank as a result of their partnership with the officer.

   - **Manager**—The department manager creates profoundly positive outcomes for the department's customers by anticipating, listening to, and proactively responding to emerging customer needs. Customers feel they can approach the manager at any time when quality, productivity, or timeliness problems arise. The manager continually seeks out ways to exceed customer expectations through routine dialogue sessions where emerging issues are explored and the

continued on next page

Learning Activity 5. The Great Performance Management Cycle, *continued*

partnership is strengthened. The manager's team members' needs are anticipated and anxieties are addressed through routine one-on-one conversations that strengthen the performance partnership. The organization benefits from the manager's strategic insight on future trends and strategies for maximizing value and reducing costs.

10. [PPT] Ask the large group: How is great performance is defined? Where do the ideas for framing great performance come from? Solicit ideas from the group in answer to these questions, honoring and expanding upon those offered, then advance the animation on **slide 6-20 or 10-4** to reveal the four broad sources for identifying great performance:

   • **The Voice of the Customer**—Note that customers know what great performance looks like. Understanding the definition of great performance always begins with understanding the profoundly positive outcomes that the customer wants to experience as a result of interacting with the performer and organization.

   • **The Organization's Vision**—The organization's vision describes the key results or outcomes that it wants to create in the world, for its customers, and for itself. The vision provides an important context within which the great performance outcomes for an individual position should be defined.

   • **Leadership and a Felt Need for Change**—Above and beyond what customers may want and what the vision may ask for from a position, an individual leader may have his or her own set of great expectations for how a position needs to change to bring the greatest value to customers, co-workers, and the organization or company as a whole.

   • **Work Unit or Department Vision and Mission**—The final source for defining great performance are the expectations established by the specific vision and mission for the work area or department. Although likely echoing elements of the customers' voice, the organization's vision, and even the leader's ideas for change, the work unit vision and mission can add important context and direction to an individual position's contribution to customers, co-workers, and the organization overall.

11. After concluding your summary of the sources for defining great performance expectations, direct participants' attention to the "make improvements" step within the GPM Cycle. Ask: What, specifically, is being improved? Honor all responses offered, making an effort to link each response to your own answer to this question. The ideal answer is that the improvements made at this step can include many things, including refining great performance outcomes, changing the goals and strategies to achieve these outcomes, adjusting the support provided to the performer, and even revising the methods and processes for evaluating results.

12. Next, ask: How might a performer know what to improve? Again, honor all responses offered. Note that this is the step in the GPM Cycle where learning occurs and that learning is driven by four key questions. These questions are asked following the "evaluate performance" step and lead to identifying what improvements need to be made. These four questions are

   • What worked? What went well with performance?

   • What didn't work? What didn't go well?

   • Why did things go well or not go well?

   • What should the performer keep doing and what should the performer change based upon the previous answers?

13. Note that these four questions represent the foundation of an effective performance evaluation process that will drive all performance toward great performance. State that a variation of these four questions lies at the heart of the Performance Coaching Conversation, which they will learn more about in future workshops.

14. [PPT] Conclude the overview of the GPM Cycle by revealing the last animated text on **slide 6-20 or 10-4** and asking the group "Who is responsible for this process?" Some participants will say the coach or manager is responsible, some might say that it's the performer who is responsible, still others might suggest that both are responsible. Offer your final comments on this question by suggesting that it is indeed a shared responsibility between the coach and the performer—but that, in the final analysis, the performer is responsible for his or her own performance. Although the coach always fulfills a critical facilitative role within this cycle, the performer is the one who does the work and achieves or doesn't achieve the great performance outcomes defined within the process. Refer to **handout 3** from learning activity 3 to reinforce the idea that, as the partnership between the coach and the performer matures, the employee's responsibility for achieving results gradually increases to the point where the performer is largely self-directed and -managed.

continued on next page

Learning Activity 5. The Great Performance Management Cycle, *continued*

15. [PPT] Suggest that a key challenge for the coach, then, is to move the performer toward taking full responsibility for his or her performance. Display **slide 6-21 or 10-5** as you distribute **training instrument 6**. Assign each of the six steps of the GPM Cycle to one or more small groups. Give the groups about eight minutes to identify specific actions that both the performer and coach can take to facilitate employee ownership of the GPM Cycle.

16. [PPT] After about eight minutes, reconvene the larger group and facilitate a sharing from each group for their respective step of the GPM Cycle. After hearing from one or more groups for each step of the GPM Cycle, display **slides 6-22 through 6-27 or 10-6 through 10-11**, which offer some suggested actions for both the performer and the coach. After displaying slide 6-22 or 10-6, indicate that you will be sharing these "answers" in a summary handout at the conclusion of the exercise.

17. [PPT] At the conclusion of the small group reports and the sharing of **slides 6-22 through 6-27 or 10-6 through 10-11**, distribute **handout 6**, which lists the answers from the slides. Emphasize that a coach intervenes within the GPM Cycle and within his or her partnership with the employee according to the most appropriate coaching role (from learning activity 3) and with behaviors appropriate to the current step within the GPM Cycle.

18. Finally, distribute **handout 7** to participants, indicating that this handout provides a simple summary of the key actions that a coach might take throughout the GPM Cycle.

DEBRIEFING

In your concluding remarks for this learning activity, summarize the following key points:

- All performance happens within a larger framework called the Great Performance Management Cycle.
- Great performance outcomes are defined at the beginning of the GPM Cycle and represent the foundation and target for the employee's work.
- The employee is responsible for his or her own performance and success. Although the coach plays a facilitative and supporting role (based on the five coaching roles discussed in learning activity 3), in the end the employee is the one who does the work and achieves (or does not achieve) the desired results.
- The coach intervenes within the GPM Cycle based on the most appropriate coaching role and requirements of the GPM Cycle step.

Learning Activity 6. Personal Action Planning

OBJECTIVES

The objectives of this learning activity are to
- have participants integrate and apply learned key lessons and skills to their own situation
- share and refine their personal development based on feedback from another participant.

MATERIALS

The materials needed for this activity are
- Training Instrument 7: Personal Plan for Action

- PPT PowerPoint slides 6-28 or 6-45.

TIME

🕐 20 minutes

PREPARATIONS

- Training instrument 7 should be ready for distribution.

INSTRUCTIONS

1. PPT Distribute **training instrument 7** as you display either **slide 6-28 or 6-45**. Indicate to the participants that it's time for them to begin building their personal action plan for strengthening their coaching skills and partnerships for performance.
2. PPT **If completing Parts A and B of the plan:** Display **slide 6-28** and give participants about eight minutes to complete parts A and B of their action plan.
   - **Part A** asks them to identify key lessons and insights from the earlier discussion of the role of the coach, the five coaching roles, and the importance of diagnosing and determining the most appropriate coaching role to use with those they manage.
   - **Part B** asks them to identify specific actions they can take to build greater employee ownership of the Great Performance Management Cycle.
2. After about eight minutes, ask participants to partner up with someone at their table or the next table and share their action plans with one another. Encourage people to especially focus on part B. Ask them to revise their action plans based on the feedback and ideas that they receive from their partners. Give participants about 10 minutes for sharing their plans.
4. PPT If completing Parts C and D of the plan: Display **slide 6-45** and ask participants to turn to their personal action plan (**training instrument 7**) and complete parts C and D. Note that these last two parts of the plan ask them to apply key insights from the mutual learning mindset and ladder of inference to their situation.
5. Give participants about eight minutes to complete their plans.
   - **Part C** asks them to identify specific actions they will take to develop a mutual learning mindset in their interactions with others—and especially in their role as a performance coach.
   - **Part D** asks to them to identify actions they can take to prevent themselves from leaping up the ladder of inference as a performance coach and in their daily interactions with others.
6. After about eight minutes, ask participants to partner up with someone at their table or the next table and share their action plans with one another. Encourage people to especially focus on part D. Ask them to revise their action plans based on the feedback and ideas that they receive from their partners. Give participants about six minutes for sharing their plans.

DEBRIEFING

Offer the following summary comments:
- Translating the lessons from the coaching relationship and the GPM Cycle depends on participants integrating key insights and actions into a personal plan.

Learning Activity 7. Sharing "Aha!" Moments and Questions/Goals Review

OBJECTIVES

The objectives of this learning activity are to
- identify key insights, lessons, and "take-aways" from the workshop so far
- involve participants in answering specific questions that they identified at the beginning of the day.

MATERIALS

The materials needed for this activity are
- flipchart pages highlighting the key questions for the workshop identified in learning activity 2
- flipchart and marking pens.

TIME

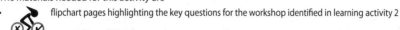 25 minutes

PREPARATIONS

- During the morning break and over the lunch hour, review the set of questions and learning objectives the group identified at the start of the day. Identify any that from your perspective have been addressed either directly or indirectly over the course of the morning session.
- Put a check mark in front of or circle the number of questions or learning objectives that have been answered in the previous activities. You will reference these highlighted items and ask participants to formally answer them during this activity.

INSTRUCTIONS

1. Welcome the group back from lunch. Ask them to turn to their table partners and take about three minutes to quickly share some of the key insights, discoveries, and Ahas! that were uncovered in the morning session. Lightheartedly, encourage those who have blank "Aha!" Sheets to "steal" Ahas! from others at their table. Ask the participants to be ready to report to the larger group one or two significant Ahas!
2. After about three minutes, invite the groups to share a few of their most significant Ahas! Reinforce the Ahas! offered by commenting on each, acknowledging the importance of each insight to the session's topic.
3. Shift the group's attention to the flipchart page or pages listing the group's questions and learning objectives identified at the beginning of the workshop. Call attention to those questions or objectives that you have checked or circled and note that you think the group may be ready, based on the morning's session, to answer these. Invite anyone from the larger group to offer his or her ideas for each highlighted question or learning objective.
4. Alternatively, and as time permits, you may want to select specific questions or learning objectives and assign each to a different small group. Give each group three to five minutes to develop an answer to their assigned question based on the morning's content as well as insights from their own experience.
5. After three to five minutes, ask each group to report its answers. Reinforce what the groups have offered and add additional suggestions or ideas as appropriate. As the groups report, check off the questions that have been answered.
6. Call attention to the remaining questions. If time is available, ask if any of these remaining questions can be answered at this time. For all remaining unanswered questions, encourage participants to look for answers to or ideas about these questions in the second half of the workshop.

DEBRIEFING

Offer the following summary comments:
- Acknowledge the group's ability to synthesize the morning's workshop materials and apply them skillfully to their learning objectives and questions.
- Ask participants to keep the remaining unanswered questions in mind throughout the rest of the workshop to see if they can answer them. Indicate that these remaining questions will be examined at the very end of today's workshop.

Learning Activity 8. Unilateral Control and Mutual Learning Mindsets—Two Approaches to Managing Relationships With Others

OBJECTIVES

The objectives of this learning activity are to
- introduce two approaches for managing our interpersonal relationships and particularly the coaching relationship with performers
- enable participants to see the importance of moving away from their "default" unilateral control mindset and toward a more constructive and facilitative mutual learning mindset.

MATERIALS

The materials needed for this activity are
- Handout 8: Unilateral Control and Mutual Learning Mindsets—Ineffective and Effective Approaches and Strategies for Engaging Others
- Handout 9: Governing Values and Enacting Behaviors for Mutual Learning
- Training Instrument 8: Responding to Threat and Embarrassment

- flipchart and marking pens, if desired
- PPT PowerPoint slides 6-29 through 6-40 or 10-12 through 10-20.

TIME

50 minutes

PREPARATIONS

- In advance of this activity, it is important to gain a deep familiarity with the governing values and enacting behaviors of the mutual learning mindset. Within this activity you will lead participants through each of these values and behaviors. This process works best when you have concrete examples of what these values mean and what they look like. Part of your preparations for this activity should therefore involve identifying specific examples from your organization—or your own professional experience—for how these values and behaviors actually work in the real world.
- The handouts 8 and 9 should be ready for distribution.

INSTRUCTIONS

1. Display **slide 6-29 or 10-12** and distribute **training instrument 8** as you ask people to work in their small groups to answer the two questions on the slide and in the handout. Give the groups about five minutes to discuss these two questions.
2. After about five minutes, reconvene the large group and call for a general reporting out of *how* people respond to stress, threat, vulnerability, and embarrassment and *why* a coach might feel stressed, threatened, vulnerable, embarrassed, or otherwise uncomfortable in a coaching relationship. If you wish, you may choose to record the groups' answers on two prepared flipchart pages.
3. For the first question, you might hear some of the following descriptions of *how* people respond to stress, threat, vulnerability, or embarrassment:
   - withdraw into themselves
   - attack the other person
   - decide to get even later
   - move into a defensive posture
   - rationalize and justify their own behavior
   - blame the other person for their bad intentions
   - feel sorry for themselves
   - assume the worst about the other person and his or her intentions
   - withhold information that could cause further embarrassment
   - play the victim
   - run for cover.
4. For the second question regarding why a coach might feel stressed threatened, vulnerable, or embarrassed when coaching others, you may hear such answers as:
   - not being liked by the person being coached
   - not knowing everything

continued on next page

Learning Activity 8. Unilateral Control and Mutual Learning Mindsets—Two Approaches to Managing Relationships With Others, *continued*

- being wrong
- having someone challenge the coach's authority
- making a mistake
- feeling attacked
- being disrespected
- being found out as less than perfect
- not having a solution to a problem
- lacking self-confidence
- intimidation by others
- feeling wronged.

5. **PPT** Acknowledge the responses given. Note that when people feel stressed, threatened, or vulnerable or face embarrassment, they tend to behave in very consistent ways—ways that give them the illusion that their behaviors actually protect them. Display **slide 6-30 or 10-13** as you make the statement that most of us adopt a unilateral control mindset that insulates us from people and information that we find disconcerting and uncomfortable.

6. **PPT** Distribute **handout 8** as you display **slide 6-31 or 10-14** and state that research from the renowned organizational psychologist Chris Argyris and others (see chapter 2 for additional references) indicates that most people adopt the protective shield of the unilateral control mindset. Introduce this mindset by clicking through the slide, moving from left to right, first highlighting the governing values and assumptions of this way of relating to others when embarrassed or threatened and then highlighting the *enacting behaviors* and negative *consequences*.

7. Point out that the arrows within the diagram that move across the mindset elements suggest that the values influence the assumptions, which in turn influence the behaviors, leading to the set of negative consequences. State that the resulting behaviors, in turn, feed back into and reinforce the values, assumptions, and behaviors, leading to *more* counterproductive outcomes and continuing the cycle. Note that this is what we call a "downward spiral"—an ever negative process that leads to increasingly negative outcomes.

8. **PPT** Suggest to participants that there is another way—it's not all "doom and gloom." Indicate that many thoughtful people are able to respond differently if they *think* differently. Display **slide 6-32 or 10-15**, noting that we all have a choice. We can mindlessly follow the unilateral control mindset and its counterproductive strategies and results, or we can consciously adopt a different mindset, one that is based upon mutual learning. Display slide **6-33 or 10-16**, and click through the bullet points on this page. Note that the mutual learning mindset is informed by a very different set of values and assumptions and therefore leads to a different set of outcomes.

9. **PPT** Direct participants to the second page of **handout 8** as you display **slide 6-34 or 10-17**. As you did with the unilateral control mindset, click through the bullet points. Indicate that we will be digging deeper into the governing values and assumptions and the resulting enacting behaviors in a few minutes.

10. Highlight in summary that the values, assumptions, and enacting behaviors of the mutual learning mindset lead to a profoundly different set of consequences—all of them positive. Call attention to several of these as you finish your high-level overview of this mindset. Also note that, as with the unilateral control mindset, the consequences that result from this approach feed back into and reinforce the more productive values, assumptions, and behaviors. Here the process becomes an "upward spiral," leading to increasingly improved communication and understanding and a significantly stronger relationship based upon trust and respect.

11. **PPT** Distribute **handout 9** as you display **slides 6-35 through 6-37** or **10-18 through 10-20** and shift the participants' attention to the details of the values and behaviors of the mutual learning mindset. Highlight each of the governing values and enacting behaviors. Whenever possible, give specific organizational or personal examples of how each value or enacting behavior might play itself out in interpersonal relationships. Take your time with this review and answer questions that may arise as you move through these three slides.

Note: If this activity is being conducted with the half-day workshop for employees, then the activity ends at this point.

continued on next page

Learning Activity 8. Unilateral Control and Mutual Learning Mindsets—Two Approaches to Managing Relationships With Others, *continued*

12. **PPT** Display **slide 6-38** and ask participants to discuss among themselves the three questions on the slide. Invite them to work together over the next eight minutes or so to resolve any values or behaviors that are confusing or not clear; to identify the values or behaviors that are most transformational to their coaching role; and finally to identify ways to, as a coaches, integrate and apply the values and behaviors of the mutual learning mindset in their daily interactions.

13. After about eight minutes, reconvene the group and guide the reporting of the participants' answers. Address any remaining areas of confusion or ambiguity by providing additional examples or restating the value or behavior in different ways. Invite the groups to share which values and behaviors are transformational and why. Finally ask the groups to identify specific ways to integrate and apply the values and behaviors to their coaching relationships.

14. **PPT** End this activity with **slide 6-39**, asking why it is difficult to shift away from the unilateral control mindset and toward the mutual learning mindset. Solicit participant suggestions about why it's difficult to leave the unilateral control mindset and embrace a different approach. Some of the responses you might hear are
    - It's what we know.
    - There often aren't good alternatives out there.
    - My boss operates this way—it's the only way to survive.
    - It takes too much energy!
    - We don't have the skills.
    - We don't have the time to do it right.
    - The mutual learning model seems too "touchy feely."

15. **PPT** Acknowledge some of the reasons people have offered as you display **slide 6-40** and summarize by suggesting that most of us are raised with and surrounded by this approach (in our schools, families, and workplaces). Our surrounding culture tends to follow the unilateral control approach, and it is difficult to change our underlying "program"—the set of values and assumptions upon which our own behaviors are based.

16. **Optional as time permits:** If you have time available within this activity, ask participants to work in their groups to identify three specific actions a coach could take to cultivate a mutual learning mindset and move away from the unilateral control mindset. After the small group discussion, draw out specific actions or strategies that coaches could use to integrate the mutual learning mindset into their daily coaching behaviors. Record these on a flipchart page if time permits.

DEBRIEFING

Make the following summary comments for this activity:
- State that when faced with stressful, threatening, embarrassing, or psychologically vulnerable situations, people tend to move into a defensive posture and use the unilateral control mindset.
- Reiterate that people always have a choice in how they respond to these stressors and that, when people are thoughtful and reflective, they can choose a healthier response pattern. This mutual learning mindset, if integrated into how we think about ourselves and others, can transform uncomfortable situations into learning opportunities.
- Note that adopting the mutual learning mindset and using it consistently won't be easy. People tend to use the unilateral control mindset because they have been socialized by their families, at school, and in their workplaces to use this approach to human interactions.
- Suggest that despite the misunderstandings, false assumptions, and erroneous judgments that spiral out of the unilateral control mindset—and the resulting conflict, frustration, discord, and unhappiness it creates—we continue using this counterproductive approach. This is because most people remain unaware of an alternative, such as the mutual learning mindset, and because their surrounding culture tends to operate from a unilateral control perspective.
- Finally, note that changing from a unilateral control mindset to a mutual learning mindset involves changing the underlying set of values and assumptions that structure how we engage the world. Changing our behaviors is relatively easy; changing the underlying values *causing* these behaviors is far more difficult.

Learning Activity 9. Case Studies—Unilateral Control vs. Mutual Learning

OBJECTIVES

The objectives of this learning activity are to
- enable participants to apply the lessons from the unilateral control and mutual learning mindsets to a variety of coaching situations
- help participants identify how the mutual learning mindset might demonstrate itself in coaching situations.

MATERIALS

The materials needed for this activity are
- Training Instrument 9: Mutual Learning and Coaching Cases

- `PPT` PowerPoint Slide 6-41

- flipchart paper and markers, if desired.

TIME

🕐 30 minutes

PREPARATIONS
- Training instrument 9 should be ready to be distributed.
- Review the three cases in training instrument 9 and identify, in advance, the best coaching role(s) as well as some possible behaviors and actions of both the unilateral control mindset and the mutual learning mindset that you can share with the group.

INSTRUCTIONS
1. Begin this follow-along activity to learning activity 8 by suggesting that it is important to examine how a performance coach using the unilateral control mindset might approach a typical coaching challenge and how a coach using the mutual learning mindset should approach the same challenge.
2. `PPT` Display **slide 6-41** as you distribute **training instrument 9**. Assign one of the three cases to each of the participant table groups. Ask each group to review the coaching challenge and then to (a) note the coaching role called for in this situation (from learning activity 3), (b) identify how a coach using the unilateral control mindset might deal with this situation, and (c) identify how a coach following the mutual learning mindset might deal with this situation. Encourage the participants to identify specific behaviors and actions that both the unilateral control and mutual learning coaches would use to deal with this challenge. Verify that the instructions are clear and then give the groups 10 minutes to complete this activity.
3. After about 10 minutes, reconvene the group and then facilitate a discussion of each of the three cases. Invite one group to go first, addressing each of the three questions on the slide and instrument.
4. First, explore the most appropriate coaching role or roles that the coach should use and why. Ask other groups that have been assigned the same case to share their thoughts on the appropriate coaching role. Offer your insights on the best role or set of roles.
5. Working with the same case, next invite a different group to identify specific behaviors that a coach might exhibit if the coach was using the unilateral control mindset. Invite other groups that also discussed this case to share their thoughts. Offer your own insights on behaviors that a unilateral control coach might exhibit, borrowing heavily from handout 9.
6. Before moving to the mutual learning mindset behaviors, ask the group why you had them identify unilateral control behaviors when, in reality, these are behaviors that they *shouldn't* be bringing into their coaching relationships. Solicit answers from the group and then offer your response: By making an effort to identify unilateral control behaviors, coaches might learn to recognize these behaviors in their own actions!

continued on next page

Learning Activity 9. Case Studies—Unilateral Control vs. Mutual Learning, *continued*

7. Continuing with the same case, invite another group to share the behaviors they have identified that a mutual learning coach might use in this situation. Ask other groups to share their ideas of how a mutual learning coach might approach this challenge. Offer your own insights on behaviors that a mutual learning coach might exhibit.
8. Repeat this process for each of the remaining two coaching cases.

DEBRIEFING

Conclude this activity by
- Highlighting the importance of a performance coach bringing the mutual learning mindset into his or her everyday coaching interactions. Suggest that it might be helpful if the coach first identifies what a unilateral control approach might look like—and then identifies how a mutual learning approach can be used.
- Noting that the effective performance coach makes an assessment of the most appropriate of the five coaching roles and then consciously explores how to bring a mutual learning mindset into his or her coaching relationship with the performer.
- Reminding participants that the key challenge for the performance coach using the mutual learning mindset is working consciously to change the underlying values and assumptions that, in turn, drive his or her behaviors. When the underlying "program" is changed, then the coach will find the mutual learning mindset as easy to use as the unilateral control mindset might have once been for him or her.

Learning Activity 10. The Ladder of Inference

OBJECTIVES

The objectives of this learning activity are to
- introduce participants to a powerful tool that will help them stay in a mutual learning mindset
- guide participants in applying the ladder of inference to future coaching situations.

MATERIALS

The materials needed for this activity are
- Handout 10: The Ladder of Inference
- **PPT** PowerPoint slides 6-42 through 6-44
- flipchart pages and markers.

TIME

30 minutes

PREPARATIONS

- Handout 10 should be ready for distribution.
- Prepare a flipchart page entitled "Actions to Avoid Leaping up the Ladder."

INSTRUCTIONS

1. **PPT** Tell participants that there is a very useful tool to help a coach stay in the mutual learning mindset instead of falling back on old counterproductive unilateral control behaviors. Distribute **handout 10** as you display **slide 6-42** and introduce the ladder of inference.
2. Credit that much of the initial development of this tool was done by the same Chris Argyris who brought us the underlying framework for the mutual learning mindset that we have explored at some depth today. Note that two of the enacting behaviors of the mutual learning mindset involve identifying and testing the assumptions that we make about others and then suspending judgment to prevent us from drawing conclusions and taking actions based on flawed assumptions and reasoning.
3. Indicate that the ladder of inference stands firmly on the ground. Use a laser pointer to highlight the base of the ladder as you click to reveal "Observation and Experience." Note that the foundation upon which the ladder rests is the world of direct information and knowledge. Suggest that what happens at this level is what each of us directly observes, sees, feels, and so forth. At this level, what happens here is best captured by a camcorder recording precisely what each person says and does. This is the level of observation with no filtering or interpretation.
4. **PPT** Click on **slide 6-42** again to bring up the next animation, describing a series of observed facts about Dennis. Refer to the handout as you read out the facts about Dennis. Click again and indicate, when the words "Path to Action" are revealed, that over the course of the next few minutes you will chart the path that the observer in this situation takes from the facts about Dennis to the eventual actions that are taken in relation to Dennis.
5. **PPT** Click on **slide 6-42** again to bring up the first rung of the ladder labeled "Paying Attention to Select Data." Suggest to the group that our brains are bombarded with an overwhelming amount of data and that, to make sense of the world, we tend to filter and sift through the data and focus on the data points that matter most to us. Ask people to identify, from the observation level description about Dennis, which data might interest us the most? If people say "missed my deadline," agree with this and then make your point by saying that we tend to focus on this flagged data point as the beginning of our journey up the ladder. Click on the slide again and reveal the details we decide to pay attention to at the right of the slide.
6. **PPT** Click on **slide 6-42** again and note that the next rung up the ladder, "Adding Meaning (Interpreting)" involves us asking ourselves: *Now what's behind Dennis missing this important deadline.* Note that our brains abhor a vacuum,

continued on next page

Learning Activity 10. The Ladder of Inference, *continued*

so we try to make sense of the situation. Click again on the slide and note that, in this case, we make sense of the situation by interpreting Dennis' behavior as lacking respect for his work.

7. `PPT` Click on **slide 6-42** again to reveal the next rung up the ladder titled "Making Assumptions," then clicking again to highlight the assumption that I am making about *why* Dennis missed the deadline. Again note that our brains work this way because we need to explain things to ourselves, making sense of the situation so that we can then respond accordingly.

8. Click to reveal "Drawing Inferences" and click again to display the inference we make based on our assumptions.

9. Click to reveal the next rung, "Forming Judgments," and click again to display the judgment we are making based on our assumptions and inferences. Note that as we move up the ladder, the story becomes ever stronger and mutually reinforcing. Let the participants know that you'll discuss this fact a bit later.

10. Reveal "Adopting Beliefs" and its accompanying statements about our new belief about Dennis and continue on through the balance of the rungs of the ladder. Note how we are now forming an emotional response to this problem with Dennis, which, in turn, causes us to move toward a set of actions and behaviors that are informed not only by our assumptions, inferences, and judgments, but also by how we *feel* about being so abused by Dennis.

11. Finish up the story of Dennis by saying that this process is made even more counterproductive by the reinforcing loop that causes our beliefs and feelings about the other person to, in turn, influence what we pay attention to. Ask participants to identify how this self-reinforcing loop may work in Dennis' situation. Encourage correct responses or add your own interpretation: When our beliefs and feelings are strongly fixed in our minds, they cause us to see what we want to see and ignore things that don't agree with our mental model of the way this person behaves. As an example, if Dennis were to suddenly come through for us on a project, we might say to ourselves: *What is he after from me? What is he trying to get me to do?* And, when Dennis disappoints us again (confirming our beliefs and feelings) then we say to ourselves: *See! There he goes again! Just as I predicted!*

12. Ask participants: Do you see this ladder operating in your life? How many times each week do you leap up the ladder? Acknowledge participant responses and suggest that leaping up the ladder of inference is so natural for us that it happens dozens of times a day for most of us. State that despite knowing how the ladder works, you find yourself leaping up the ladder many times a day. Ask participants *why* we tend to leap up the ladder of inference.

13. `PPT` Acknowledge participant responses to this question and then display **slide 6-43**. Gradually reveal the points on this page, noting that it is natural to leap up the ladder. Our brains need answers, and, if we don't have data, we tend to make assumptions about what could be true or draw inferences from what we know to fill in details about the things we don't know.

14. `PPT` Display **slide 6-44** as you ask participants to work in their groups to answer the three questions on this slide as they review and reflect upon handout 10. Give the groups about four minutes to discuss their answers.

15. After about four minutes, reconvene the group and lead a discussion of the answers to these questions. Respond to participant ideas for the implications for our everyday communications and their suggestions for ways to avoid leaping up the ladder. Add your own thoughts on the second question—emphasizing the importance of slowing down, gathering more data, asking more questions, and actually talking to the other person (in this case Dennis). Note the importance of returning to the "ground" upon which the ladder rests.

16. Turn to the final question related to how a coach might use the ladder to improve his or her coaching relationships. Acknowledge the answers given by the participants and add your own. Emphasize that coaches can use the ladder of inference to slow down their thought process and suspend their judgment when trying to analyze and understand why an employee's performance isn't what the coach thinks it should be. The ladder is a powerful tool that reminds us to gather more data and ask more questions—before we make assumptions, inferences, and judgments about others.

17. Finally, make the point that, in our situation with Dennis, he may indeed be an arrogant jerk. He may, in fact, be in it for himself and you may be right in viewing his actions as intentional. When people—in this case Dennis—continue to present data to us that suggests something isn't right (such as repeatedly missing project deadlines), their actions may indeed be based upon bad intentions. Even when people consistently act in ways that undermine or disappoint us,

continued on next page

Learning Activity 10. The Ladder of Inference, *continued*

however, we need to gather still more data: *Have I always been clear in my communications and expectations with Dennis? Does Dennis have too much on his plate and does he actually have the ability to say "no" to me or others about due dates? How might Dennis view my own behavior? Might his apparent unwillingness to meet my deadlines have anything to do with the way in which I behave, treat him, give direction, demand accountability, and so forth?*

Debriefing

Conclude this activity by
- highlighting the value of the ladder of inference in helping the coach to focus on what is known instead of making assumptions and inferences
- encouraging participants to use the ladder to slow down their path to action to ensure that it is informed by data instead of assumptions and inferences
- asking participants to integrate the ladder of inference into their daily routine interactions with those people whom they are coaching.

Learning Activity 11. The Purpose of Goal Setting

OBJECTIVES

The objectives of this learning activity are to
- identify the role that goal setting plays within the performance management process
- guide participants in identifying how using goal theory within goal setting enhances employee motivation and job commitment.

MATERIALS

The materials needed for this activity are
- ☐ Handout 11: Goal Theory of Motivation

- ✎ Training Instrument 10: How Goal Setting Enables Great Performance and Applying Goal Theory

- [PPT] PowerPoint slides 7-7 through 7-10

- flipchart pages and markers.

TIME

⏱ 25 minutes

PREPARATIONS

- Training instruments 10 and handout 11 should be ready for distribution.
- Prepare two flipchart pages entitled "How Goal Setting Enables Great Performance" and "How Goal Theory Guides Coaching."

INSTRUCTIONS

1. [PPT] Introduce the activity by displaying **slide 7-7**, which contains a quote by Henry David Thoreau. Ask participants what Thoreau was getting at. What is the meaning of his words within the context of performance management? Acknowledge and validate comments offered and suggest your own interpretation: It's not enough that we're working hard. Hard labor toward the wrong goal is misdirected and results in considerable amounts of wasted energy. Argue that Thoreau contends that we need to be clear in the *purpose* and direction of our work, which is why goal setting is so important to performance management. Everything begins and ends with such clarity of purpose and direction.

2. [PPT] Display **slide 7-8** and distribute instrument 10 as you ask participants to work in their small groups to identify how goal setting enables performers to achieve great performance. Give the groups about four minutes for their discussion.

3. After about four minutes, reconvene the group and solicit their responses on how goal setting enables performers to achieve great performance. Record the groups' responses on the prepared flipchart page. Some of the responses you hear may include
   - Goals tell performers what's important and what they need to focus on.
   - Goals provide a mechanism for the employee and the coach to evaluate the employee's performance.
   - Goals challenge the performer to reach higher and further.
   - Goals provide a clear link between the work of the individual and the work of the team, department, and organization.
   - Goals provide a reason to celebrate once they've been achieved.
   - Goals can provide internal motivation for the employee.

4. Highlight the groups' suggestions and add your own thoughts as to the value and role that goals play in moving toward great performance.

5. [PPT] ☐ Display **slide 7-9** as you distribute **handout 11**. Summarize the key elements of goal theory and why it matters within the GPM Cycle. Make the following points:
   - When a goal is *accepted* by the person accomplishing a task, this person is more likely to be committed to achieving the goal.

continued on next page

Learning Activity 11. The Purpose of Goal Setting, *continued*

- Understandably, the more *specific* and *clear* a goal is, the greater likelihood that the person performing the task will be able to hit the target.
- A goal that is realistically challenging tends to produce a higher level of effort than one that is perceived as easy. Ask the group what "realistically challenging" means. Indicate that to be most effective a goal needs to be a *stretch* goal, although not so much of a stretch that the person doesn't feel as if he or she could accomplish the goal.
- Finally, the more that the performer is internally committed to achieving a goal, the more likely he or she will find a way to accomplish it.
- When all four of these characteristics combine, the result is a higher level of goal-directed effort, hopefully leading toward higher performance.

6. ✏ PPT Ask people to return to their small groups and respond to the second question on **training instrument 10** as you display **slide 7-10**: *What are the implications of goal theory on how a coach should guide the goal setting process? What might a coach need to do within the goal setting process to take full advantage of goal theory as a motivation tool?* Give the small groups about four minutes to discuss this question and generate some answers.

7. After about four minutes, ask the groups to report their implications and ideas for applying goal theory within the GPM Cycle and in the coaching role. As time permits, record the groups' ideas and suggestions on the prepared flipchart page. Some ideas people might offer include
- Involve employees in setting their own performance goals.
- Work at establishing *challenging* performance goals that stretch the employee's capabilities but that they still see as attainable.
- Ensure clarity of the goal so there is no confusion in direction or effort.
- Prevent the employee from setting goals that are unrealistically challenging.

DEBRIEFING

Concluding this activity:
- Emphasize that goals play a critically important role within the GPM Cycle and that the coach must take steps to ensure that the goals are clear and realistically challenging for the performer.
- Goal theory presents a useful model for ensuring that the performance goals that are set lead to goal-directed behavior by the performer.
- The core elements of goal theory are ensuring that the goal is *accepted* by the performer as his or her own goal, that it is *clear* and *specific*, that it is *realistically challenging*, and that the performer is *committed* to trying to reach the goal.

Learning Activity 12. Defining Great Performance Outcomes

OBJECTIVES

The objectives of this learning activity are to
- review the Great Performance Management Cycle and identify the importance of defining great performance within this cycle
- identify the characteristics of great performance outcomes
- enable participants to define and develop great performance outcomes.

MATERIALS

The materials needed for this activity are
- Handout 4: The Great Performance Management Cycle
- Handout 5: Defining Great Performance
- Handout 12: What Is Great Performance?
- Training Instrument 11: Defining Great Performance Application
- PPT PowerPoint slides 7-11 through 7-15
- flipchart pages and markers.

TIME

45 minutes

PREPARATIONS

- If participants have already taken part in learning activity 5, then they will already have received handouts 4 and 5—two handouts referred to in this activity. Ask participants to bring handouts 4 and 5 to the Goal Setting workshop. If participants have not done learning activity 5, then these two handouts should be ready for distribution.
- Review training instrument 11 in advance of the activity and develop your own set of possible great performance outcomes for each job title and its related performance dimensions.
- As an alternative to using training instrument 11, you may want to substitute real job titles from your organization and create an instrument that follows the same format as training instrument 11. Doing so enables a real-world application and may lead to some insights regarding the job titles and their great performance outcomes as perceived by participants. If you elect this option, you will need to modify slide 7-15 to reflect these organization-specific job titles.
- Prepare flipchart pages as outlined in the activity.

INSTRUCTIONS

1. PPT Begin the activity by displaying **slide 7-11**, and distributing or asking participants to locate **handout 4**. Present a quick overview of the GPM Cycle to refamiliarize participants with this important model for guiding an employee toward great performance. Focus particular attention on the top of the cycle—great performance—and its role in providing a compelling direction and purpose to an employee's efforts.
2. PPT Display **slide 7-12** and distribute **handouts 5 and 12** as you highlight key characteristics of great performance outcomes. Suggest that great performance pushes the coach and the performer to consider the profoundly positive outcomes that the performer filling a position should aspire to.
3. PPT Display **slide 7-13** as you note that great performance outcomes are understood in terms of quality, quantity, cost, timeliness, and impact on others. Point out the example for a generic position and how each of these dimensions translates into specific outcomes for customers, the organization, and his or her co-workers or team.
4. PPT Display **slide 7-14** as you ask participants to read the example in **handout 12** and, as they read, to note any questions that they have about great performance for this position and the different performance dimensions.

continued on next page

Learning Activity 12. Defining Great Performance Outcomes, *continued*

Give participants about three minutes to work by themselves in reviewing **handout 12**. After about three minutes, ask the small groups to share their reactions to and questions about defining great performance with each other. Give the groups about five minutes for this discussion.

5. After about five minutes, solicit reactions and questions from the group. When a question is asked, inquire as to whether anyone else in the room might have some thoughts about this question. Once others have answered or tried to answer each question, offer your own thoughts about the questions asked.

6. Distribute **training instrument 11** and display **slide 7-15** as you assign one of the four job titles to each of the small groups. Encourage the groups to review the great performance example in **handout 12** as they define the five great performance dimensions for their job title. Ask them to think audaciously and boldly—pushing the conventional expectations for their assigned job title to the highest level of performance. Give the groups about eight minutes for this activity. Ask them to work quickly to fill in as many of the great performance dimensions as possible in the time they have.

7. After about eight minutes, invite each group to share their definition of great performance for their assigned job title. Encourage individuals to take notes on **training instrument 11** for any title that their group did not focus on. If more than one group worked on the same job title, encourage a free-flowing compare-and-contrast discussion between the two or more groups. When appropriate, add your own thoughts on what great performance might look like for each of these four job titles.

DEBRIEFING

Concluding this activity:

- Stress that defining great performance is the first and most important step of the GPM Cycle.
- Great performance is the profoundly positive outcome that both the coach and the performer hope that the performer achieves as a result of his or her efforts.
- Great performance is defined in terms of quality, quantity, cost, timeliness, and impact on the team.

Learning Activity 13. Performance Planning and Development—Defining Great Performance

OBJECTIVES

The objectives of this learning activity are to
- enable participants to develop great performance outcomes for one of their direct reports
- give feedback to participants on the clarity of their great performance outcomes for one of their direct reports.

MATERIALS

The materials needed for this activity are
- ⬜ Handout 12: What Is Great Performance?

- 🔗 Training Instrument 11: Defining Great Performance

- Training Instrument 12: Performance Planning and Development Worksheet
- PPT PowerPoint slide 7-16 and 7-17.

TIME

🕐 30 minutes

PREPARATIONS

- Ensure that all participants have copies of handout 12 from learning activity 12.
- Two copies of training instrument 12 should be ready for distribution to each participant.
- Participants should also have their completed copies of training instrument 11 from learning activity 12.

INSTRUCTIONS

1. This activity should typically follow learning activity 12, where participants first discuss the concept of great performance outcomes and where they practice developing great performance outcomes for a generic position.
2. 🔗 Distribute two copies of **training instrument 12** to each participant. Tell the participants that this worksheet is intended to be helpful for them as they coach their performers. Note that although they are working alone today in completing this form, the best practice is for the coach to work with each of his or her employees to jointly fill in the worksheet. Indicate that, consistent with our goal of encouraging employee self-management and ownership of this process, coaches should use the mutual learning mindset to work collaboratively with their performers to jointly complete the worksheet. The purpose of this worksheet is to define great performance outcomes and identify improvement or development strategies to move the performer toward these outcomes. Emphasize that both the coach and the employee must work together to fully define the expectations for the employee's position and role within the organization. Indicate that you have given the participants two copies of training instrument 12. State that they will be working with one copy in today's workshop and that the other copy is for their use in the future when working with other performers.
3. PPT 🔗 Display **slide 7-16**. Present a quick overview of the key elements of **training instrument 12**, noting that they will only be working on parts A, B, and C in today's workshop. State that the other sections of this instrument will be completed in future workshops.
4. Indicate to the participants that it is now time for them to think about the great performance outcome expectations for one of the positions that they oversee. This position may have one person or several people fulfilling this role. To help them make their choice, encourage participants to select a position in which at least one employee may be experiencing some performance problems. Note that while the focus of this workshop is on goal setting, not performance improvement, it may be helpful to think through their great performance outcome expectations for a position that may be challenging one or more of their employees.
5. PPT 🔗 Display **slide 7-17** as you ask participants to complete part A of the Performance Planning and Development Worksheet **(training instrument 12)** by identifying this position's title and then thinking of the profoundly positive great performance outcomes that this position, when it is performed optimally, would ideally create for the organization, the position's customers, and the team or co-workers. Direct the participants to think of these three outcome targets for each of the great performance outcome dimensions of quality, quantity, cost, timeliness, and impact on the team. For ideas

continued on next page

Learning Activity 13. Performance Planning and Development—Defining Great Performance, *continued*

    when completing part A, encourage them to refer to **handout 12** or to their responses on **training instrument 11** from learning activity 12.

6. Tell them not to fill in the "measurement" column on the far right. Indicate that this column will be filled in later in today's workshop.

7. Before participants begin this exercise, encourage them to focus on the position instead of on a specific individual who may currently be fulfilling this role as they complete part A of the worksheet. Ask the larger group why it might be important that they not think of someone currently in this job as they identify great performance outcomes. As much as possible, agree with any participant answers you receive and then note that the major reason they should identify great performance for a specific position without thinking of the incumbent is that it's important not to allow their thinking to be limited by the current performer's abilities or limitations. Indicate that their objective for completing part A is to think of the *position,* not a person, as they describe the profoundly positive, value-added outcomes or contributions that, in an ideal world, this position would create. If an example is needed to explain this issue, note that if they were to think of a specific person currently filling a position—Harry, for example—their thinking might be constrained by the belief that Harry is simply incapable of achieving these results. As a consequence, their belief about Harry's abilities may, in turn, influence the expansiveness of the great performance outcomes that they could define for this less-than-optimal performer.

8. Give participants about 10 minutes to complete this activity on their own. Indicate that if individuals have questions about how to do this to call you over and you'll try to help. Walk around the room as people work on this activity. Offer assistance and direction to those who look confused or frustrated.

9. After about 10 minutes, ask people to partner up with someone at their table or the next table to share their newly minted great performance outcome definition for the position they selected. Encourage them to choose as a partner someone who either knows the position well and who could enrich or add to their perspective—or to choose a partner who doesn't know the position at all, but who could ask probing questions to push their thinking deeper. Their partner should provide feedback and suggestions to improve the clarity, specificity, expansiveness, and so forth, of their great performance outcome definitions in each of the great performance dimensions.

10. Give people about four minutes each to share their great performance expectations—for a total of about eight minutes. Provide a time check after four minutes, encouraging people to balance out talking about each other's definitions.

11. After about eight minutes, call the attention of participants back to the larger group. Ask participants how the activity went, what they found most difficult, what questions they have about defining great performance for a position, and so forth. If people express frustration or confusion, try to respond to the issue raised by providing additional examples, clarifying the process, or offering to assist them following the workshop. As time permits, you may want to ask one or two participants to share examples of how they defined great performance for the position that they chose.

12. Inquire into how many of the job descriptions of the employees in their work area incorporate some version of the great performance outcomes that we have been discussing. Celebrate those participants who say that great performance outcomes are defined in the job descriptions in their area. Encourage the other participants to work with human resources to begin updating the job descriptions of their employees to reflect the new great performance outcomes that they will soon be developing for each position.

13. Conclude this activity by noting that today you are having them define and develop, on their own, the great performance outcomes and goals for a specific position. Normally, acting as a coach, they would be working collaboratively with their employees to develop these outcomes and the set of goals to help accomplish them. Today's workshop will build essential knowledge and skills to enable them to then work with individual employees to mutually define these great performance outcomes and goals.

DEBRIEFING

Concluding this activity:
- Note that great performance can only be achieved if individual performers have a clear idea of what is expected of them.
- Indicate that the Performance Planning and Development Worksheet (training instrument 12) that they have begun completing will be an important tool that they will use beyond today's workshop to prepare them for the Performance Coaching and Annual Performance Analysis and Planning Conversations that they will soon be having with their direct reports.

Learning Activity 14. Defining Performance Accountabilities

OBJECTIVES

The objectives of this learning activity are to
- identify the two performance accountabilities that become the focus for performance coaching conversations
- practice defining performance accountabilities for a specific position.

MATERIALS

The materials needed for this activity are
- 📄 Handout 13: Performance Accountabilities

- ✏️ Training Instrument 13: Defining Performance Accountabilities

- PPT PowerPoint slides 7-18 through 7-19

- flipchart pages and markers.

TIME

🕐 20 minutes

PREPARATIONS

- Handout 13 and training instrument 13 should be ready for distribution.
- Prepare three flipchart pages entitled "Department Manager," "Retail Sales Associate," and "HR Generalist."

INSTRUCTIONS

1. PPT 📄 Begin the activity by making the point that the great performance outcomes for every position are achieved through two sets of accountabilities. Display **slide 7-18** and distribute **handout 13** while noting that these two accountabilities are the *core job responsibilities*, which are specific to every position, and the more broadly defined *organizational responsibilities*, which should apply to *all* positions within an organization or department, regardless of the job responsibilities.

2. Note that, for the core job responsibilities, the goal is to define five to seven broad areas in which the person holding this position would be expected to perform and, in doing so, would move that person toward the great performance outcomes defined earlier in the process.

3. 📄 Suggest that each of these five to seven job responsibilities would be accomplished by the performer through an assortment of behaviors and activities. Point out, for example, that accomplishing the job responsibility "develops positive relationships with the customer" on **handout 13** would involve the employee pursuing a variety of actions, strategies, and behaviors to enable him or her to fulfill this job responsibility.

4. Emphasize that a position's organizational responsibilities encompass an array of employee accountabilities that touch upon being a good member of the community. Suggest that these include such accountabilities as relating well to all customers (internal and external), sharing information, contributing to others' success, and so forth.

5. Ask participants why organizational responsibilities are important to great performance for an individual contributor. The hoped-for response is that even if employees fulfill their *job* responsibilities, if they fail to achieve their *organizational* responsibilities, they are likely to create problems for the organization, the customer, or the team. State that if an employee isn't a good member of the community, overall performance is destined to decline and great performance won't be achieved.

6. As time permits, give an example of an employee who performed his or her *job* responsibilities very well but didn't get along with co-workers, didn't share information, or expressed little interest in meeting the needs of external customers. Emphasize that, in this case, the employee's manager appropriately held the employee accountable for these *organizational* responsibilities and subsequently disciplined him or her.

continued on next page

Learning Activity 14. Defining Performance Accountabilities, *continued*

7. **PPT** Distribute **training instrument 13** as you display **slide 7-19**. Indicate that, for the next several minutes, you'd like each table group to identity three or four possible core job responsibilities for one of these three positions. Assign a position title to each table group. Encourage the groups to think of *broad* job responsibilities for their assigned position—such as "builds strong customer partnerships"—rather than identifying individual behaviors—such as "greets the customer in a friendly and welcoming voice." Give the groups about three to four minutes for this activity.

8. After about three or four minutes, reconvene the large group and ask for example job responsibilities for each of the three positions. Record the groups' answers on the prepared flipchart pages. Comment on the responsibilities given, point out any answers that may be more *behaviors* and *actions* instead of broad responsibilities. Offer your own examples as necessary to enable participants to feel comfortable with this important step.

9. Ask participants why it might be useful to work through this step of defining job responsibilities *without* first reviewing the formal job description. Agree with participants who state that defining job responsibilities before looking at the job description offers the opportunity to define a job as it should be instead of being limited to what the job description currently says. Emphasize the importance of working closely with human resources to revise the current job description to reflect these new insights about great performance and job responsibilities.

10. Ask for questions about defining job responsibilities and provide clarification of the process and additional examples if warranted.

DEBRIEFING

Concluding this activity:

- Stress that achieving great performance depends on an individual contributor understanding and working to accomplish two accountabilities: job responsibilities and organizational responsibilities.
- Note that when an employee is performing his or her *job* responsibilities well but failing to fulfill his or her *organizational* responsibilities, a performance improvement plan needs to be developed and a Performance Coaching Conversation needs to occur.
- Note that, as with defining great performance outcomes, the formal job description for a position should be updated to reflect their latest thinking about how a specific job contributes value to the organization, customers, and co-workers. The job description should be revised to include both the *job* responsibilities and the *organizational* responsibilities. Because performance conversations, annual performance planning, pay level, discipline, and so forth, are all anchored to the job description, encourage participants to work with the HR department to ensure that the description is accurate.

Learning Activity 15. Performance Planning and Development—Defining Responsibilities

OBJECTIVES

The objective of this learning activity is to
* enable participants to develop *job* and *organizational* responsibilities for a specific position that they oversee.

MATERIALS

The materials needed for this activity are
* Handout 13: Performance Accountabilities

* Training Instrument 12: Performance Planning and Development Worksheet

* Training Instrument 13: Defining Job Responsibilities
* PPT PowerPoint slide 7-20.

TIME

30 minutes

PREPARATIONS

* All participants should have a partially completed training instrument 12 from learning activity 13 as well as handout 13 and training instrument 13 from learning activity 14.

INSTRUCTIONS

1. PPT Indicate that it's again time to work on the Performance Planning and Development Worksheet. Display **slide 7-20** and ask participants to complete parts B and C of **training instrument 12**. Note that, in these two parts of their plan, you are asking them to identify the core *job* and *organizational* responsibilities for the position for which they identified the great performance outcomes in part A.
2. Suggest that both the job and organizational responsibilities collectively define this position's accountabilities and that someone who performs these responsibilities well will tend to move toward achieving great performance. Encourage participants to use the examples from **handout 13** as well as those they identified in their small group discussions on **training instrument 13** from learning activity 14 as they complete the first columns only in parts B and C on their worksheet. Give people about eight minutes to identify these job and organizational responsibilities.
3. After about eight minutes, ask participants to reconnect with their partner from the earlier personal planning activity and share their list of job and organizational responsibilities for the position. As with the previous planning and development activity, encourage them to give each other feedback on the clarity, specificity, and expansiveness of the two responsibility areas. Ask them to revise their planning and development worksheet based on the feedback and ideas that they receive from their partner. Give participants about 10 minutes for sharing, discussing, and revising their individual action plans. Call out a time check after about five minutes to ensure that both partners have an equal opportunity to receive feedback on their work.
4. After about 10 minutes, call participants back to the larger group. Ask participants how the activity went, what they found most difficult, what questions they have about job and organizational responsibilities, and so forth. If people express frustration or confusion, try to respond to the issue raised by providing additional examples, clarifying the process, or offering to assist them following the workshop. As time permits, you may want to ask one or two participants to share examples of job or organizational responsibilities that they defined for their position.
5. Note that managers should use a similar process for defining specific job and organizational responsibilities for every position they oversee. Suggest that most job descriptions today do a good job of capturing job responsibilities, but may not fully capture organizational responsibilities. Encourage participants to compare the job and organizational responsibilities that they define for each position to what the official job description says for these positions.

continued on next page

Learning Activity 15. Performance Planning and Development—Defining Responsibilities, *continued*

6. Again emphasize that if there is a difference between what they and the performer define as job and organizational responsibilities for a position and what is included in the official description for that position, they should work with human resources to first discuss the implications of adding these responsibilities and then amend the job description if possible.

Debriefing

Concluding this activity:

- Stress the importance of defining *job* and *organizational* responsibilities for each position that participants oversee.
- Note that the performance planning and development that they have done up to this point today lays a solid foundation for the next steps of the process: developing SMART goals and developing measures to gauge the performer's success at achieving great performance.

Learning Activity 16. Developing SMART Goals

OBJECTIVES

The objective of this learning activity is to
- involve participants in applying the lessons from the previous activity to developing SMART goals for various performance problems.

MATERIALS

The materials needed for this activity are
- 🔗 Training Instrument 14: SMART Goals

- PPT PowerPoint slide 7-21.

TIME

🕐 15 minutes

PREPARATIONS

- Training instrument 14 should be ready for distribution.

INSTRUCTIONS

1. Introduce the activity by first acknowledging that in previous learning activities you focused on defining great performance and identifying job and organizational responsibilities for a specific position. Suggest that the next critical step in performance planning and development is to translate these job and organizational responsibilities into goals that are actionable by the performer.
2. State that for these responsibilities to be actionable, the performance goals need to be SMART. Note that a SMART goal is one that has specific characteristics.
3. PPT 🔗 Display **slide 7-21** as you distribute **training instrument 14**. Walk the large group through each of the SMART letters—providing the following details:
   - **S** stands for *specific*. For a goal to be most effective, it must be clear, focused, and well defined. Vague or ambiguously worded goals can lead to misdirected efforts and performance failures when the performer's definition of the goal doesn't match the manager's definition.
   - **M** stands for *measurable*. A goal is measurable to the extent to which both the performer and the coach will know if and when the performance goal is attained—or not. A lack of measurement leaves room for interpretation and argument as to whether a goal was attained or not.
   - **A** stands for *accepted*. There are multiple definitions of the SMART acronym out in the public domain. Some suggest that the A represents achievable. Acknowledge that achievable is important, but that it is actually addressed with the R in the SMART acronym. Indicate that, in our version of SMART, the A represents the degree to which performers accept the goal as their own instead of one that might be imposed upon them. The more accepted a goal is, the more likely performers will be committed to accomplishing the goal. As time permits, you can reference goal theory introduced in learning activity 11.
   - **R** stands for *realistic*. When a goal is perceived by performers as realistic, they believe that they have the capability to accomplish the goal. Why does this matter? If people don't believe that they'll achieve a goal, their commitment to achieving it will be dampened. Note that the challenge in goal setting (as was discussed in learning activity 11) is to set a challenging goal that stretches performers beyond their comfort zones—but not so challenging that they feel overwhelmed and defeated by the goal.
   - **T** stands for *time based* or *time bound*. Goals are most powerful when there is a specific target date that the performer is expected to meet. If the goal is something that the performer is expected to perform "some day," he or she will be less focused on moving forward on that goal. Note that without date-specified goals, other work, priorities, and interruptions will tend to push the "some day" goal into the background.

continued on next page

Learning Activity 16. Developing SMART Goals, *continued*

4. Ask participants if they have questions about any of these characteristics. Answer these questions and provide examples to help participants better understand how each of the SMART characteristics contribute to results.
5. Indicate that in the next learning activity they will have a chance to practice developing SMARTer performance goals.

DEBRIEFING

Concluding this activity:
- Stress that SMART performance goals help focus and guide the work of performers.
- SMART goals are clear, measurable, realistically challenging, accepted by the performer, and anchored to the clock or calendar.
- The absence of SMART goals leads to confusion, frustration, and performance disappointment—all of which are avoidable with a little time spent at the beginning of the performance cycle.

Learning Activity 17. Writing SMART Goals—Case Application

OBJECTIVES

The objective of this learning activity is to
- enable participants to develop SMART performance goals.

MATERIALS

The materials needed for this activity are
- Training Instrument 14: SMART Performance Goals

- Training Instrument 15: SMART Goals and Performance Measures Application
- [PPT] PowerPoint slide 7-22

- flipchart pages and markers.

TIME

20 minutes

PREPARATIONS

- Review training instrument 15. Develop your own answers for the SMARTer goal column for each of the five great performance outcomes or goals.
- Participants should already have training instrument 14 from learning activity 16.
- Prepare flipchart page entitled "Enhancing Employee Acceptance."

INSTRUCTIONS

1. Transition from learning activity 16 by indicating that it's time to see if they can use the insights from the SMART goals activity and apply them to some typical job responsibility areas.
2. [PPT] Display **slide 7-22** and distribute **training instrument 15**. Note that the instrument provides a possible SMARTer version for the first performance goal. Ask the large group for another SMART goal for this example. Honor suggestions offered, enhancing or refining the examples given to ensure that the SMART characteristics are present.
3. Acknowledge that it's difficult to create SMART goals with the *accepted* written into the goal itself. Suggest that this characteristic of a SMART goal is addressed more by how the goal is written and who writes it instead of integrating it into the goal itself. Refer participants to **training instrument 14** for the meaning of the SMART acronym.
4. Assign one of the remaining four performance goals to each table group. Indicate that you'd like them to spend the next five minutes working in their table groups to develop a SMARTer version of their assigned performance goal. Tell them that they are free to invent what is necessary to meet the SMART test.
5. Ask the participants *not* to complete the "Measurement" column to the right of the SMARTer Performance Goal column. Tell them that you will be filling this column in later in the workshop.
6. Call attention to the "All Groups" statement near the bottom of the page. Ask all of the groups to identify specific actions for making any performance goal accepted by the performer in addition to their assigned goal. Give the table groups about four minutes for this exercise.
7. After about four minutes, reconvene the large group and facilitate reporting of their SMART examples. Honor what you are able to in their responses. Offer your own ideas and suggestions for improving the SMARTness of any answer when warranted.
8. Lead a discussion about ways to enhance acceptance of any performance goal. Record these on the prepared flipchart page.

DEBRIEFING

Conclude this activity by
- emphasizing again that SMART goals are clear, measurable, accepted by the performer, realistically challenging, and anchored to the clock or calendar.

Learning Activity 18. Performance Planning and Development—Developing SMART Goals

OBJECTIVES

The objective of this learning activity is to
- guide participants in developing SMART goals for their target position's *job* and *organizational* responsibilities.

MATERIALS

The materials needed for this activity are
- Training Instrument 12: Performance Planning and Development Worksheet

- Training Instrument 15: SMART Goals and Performance Measures Application
- PPT PowerPoint slide 7-23.

TIME

50 minutes

PREPARATIONS
- All participants should have a partially completed training instrument 12 from learning activities 13 and 15, training instrument 14 from learning activity 16, and training instrument 15 from learning activity 17.

INSTRUCTIONS
1. Following the development of example SMART goals in learning activities 16 and 17, tell the participants that it's time to practice their new SMART goal development skills on their own target position. Ask them to have **training instrument 14** on hand.
2. PPT Display **slide 7-23** to again return to their Performance Planning and Development Worksheet **(training instrument 12)**, this time completing the middle "SMART Performance Goals" column for parts B and C. Note that in these parts of the worksheet they should develop one to five SMART performance goals for each of the position's core job responsibilities.
3. Acknowledge that, in reality, there may be a dozen SMART goals for each core job responsibility. Note, however, that in the interest of time and due to the space limitations of the worksheet, you want them to focus on developing only two to four SMART goals for part B and one to three SMART goals for part C. Suggest that doing so will help them become more comfortable with developing well defined goals, enabling them to develop SMART goals in collaboration with their employees in the future.
4. Encourage participants to refer to the examples that the group developed in **training instrument 15** when working on their SMART goals. Give participants about 20 minutes to complete the SMART goals columns for parts B and C on **training instrument 12**.
5. After about 20 minutes, ask participants to again reconnect with their partner from the previous learning activities and share their SMART goals. Again, encourage the partners to give each other specific and constructive feedback on the clarity, specificity, measurability, and so forth, of their SMART performance goals. Give participants about 15 minutes for sharing and refining their SMART goals.
6. When the time is up, call participants back to the larger group. Ask them how the activity went, what they found most difficult, and what questions they have about SMART goal development. As with previous personal planning segments, if people express frustration or confusion, try to respond to the issues and questions raised by providing additional examples, clarifying the process, or offering to assist them following the workshop. As time permits, you may want to ask one or two participants to share examples of SMART goals that they developed.
7. Reiterate to the participants that, due to time and space constraints, they were asked to focus on developing a more limited number of SMART goals for the position's job and organizational responsibility areas. Tell them that all of the job

continued on next page

Learning Activity 18. Performance Planning and Development—Developing SMART Goals, *continued*

and organizational dimensions should be more fully defined in collaboration with the performer to ensure that each accountability area comprises SMART performance goals.

DEBRIEFING

Concluding this activity:

- Acknowledge that developing SMART performance goals can be challenging—but that, in fact, is the point. Suggest that if performance coaches are not clear about what they expect from their performers, then it will be even more difficult for the performer to know if and when he or she has accomplished the goal.
- Suggest that by developing SMART performance goals, the performer starts off on the right foot and both the performer and the coach will know what to focus on during performance coaching conversations.
- Emphasize that the coach should use the mutual learning mindset when developing SMART goals—and that these goals should be developed jointly with the performer. Because we want the employee to take the lead in the GPM Cycle, the most important role for the coach in the goal-setting process is to ask questions of the performer that provoke him or her to thinking differently, even expansively, about the job.

Learning Activity 19. Characteristics of Effective Measures

OBJECTIVES

The objectives of this learning activity are to
- define the purpose of measurement in relation to goal setting and performance management
- identify the characteristics of measures that make them most effective.

MATERIALS

The materials needed for this activity are
- Handout 14: The Purpose and Characteristics of Effective Performance Measures

- Training Instrument 15: SMART Goals and Performance Measures Application

- PPT PowerPoint slides 7-24 through 7-30

- flipchart pages and markers.

TIME

20 minutes

PREPARATIONS

- Review handout 14 carefully and develop a comfort level with the purpose and characteristics of effective measures. Develop one or more examples for each of the seven purposes and nine characteristics.
- Handout 14 should be ready for distribution.
- Participants should have a partially completed training instrument 15 from learning activity 17.

INSTRUCTIONS

1. PPT Display **slide 7-24** and ask: *Why measure performance?* Encourage the group to offer their ideas about why it is important to measure actual performance results.
2. PPT Display **slide 7-25** and present the quote by Irish mathematical physicist and engineer Lord Kelvin: "If you can measure it, you can manage it, and if you can't measure it, you can't manage it." Suggest that Kelvin spoke to the critical nature of measurement as being central to your ability to manage something.
3. PPT Display **slides 7-26 and 7-27** as you distribute **handout 14**. Walk participants through the seven purposes of measurement within the Great Performance Management Cycle.
4. PPT Display **slides 7-28 and 7-29** and refer to page two of **handout 14**, again walking participants through the eight characteristics of effective measures.
5. PPT Display **slide 7-30** and ask participants to review the list of eight characteristics of effective measures on their own, note any characteristics that aren't clear, and identify the one or two characteristics that are the most important characteristics for contributing to great performance from their perspective. Ask participants to take about three minutes to read page two and note their questions and their most important characteristic.
6. PPT After about three minutes, refer to **slide 7-30** and ask the groups to discuss their questions, sort out confusing characteristics, and identify and discuss the most important characteristics. Give the group three to four minutes, as time permits, to discuss these issues.
7. When the time is up, reconvene the large group and call for sharing of areas of confusion; questions about the characteristics; and, finally, the characteristics that are the most important in helping achieve great performance.

DEBRIEFING

Bring the activity to a close by making the following point:
- Effective measurement is critical to achieving great performance. The clearer and more robust the measures, the more they will provide both the performer and the coach an effective way to gauge whether or not the employee is on the right path and creating the desired great performance outcomes.

Learning Activity 20. Developing Effective Measures—Case Application

OBJECTIVES

The objective of this learning activity is to
- have participants apply insights from learning activity 19 on the characteristics of effective measures to a specific performance goal.

MATERIALS

The materials needed for this activity are
- Training Instrument 15: SMART Goals and Performance Measures Application
- PPT PowerPoint slide 7-31
- flipchart pages and markers, if desired.

TIME

25 minutes

PREPARATIONS

- Each participant should have their partially completed training instrument 15 from learning activity 17.
- Anticipate and prepare an array of possible measures for each of the performance goals on training instrument 15.

INSTRUCTIONS

1. Introduce the activity by suggesting to participants that it's time to take their insights from learning activity 19 and apply their skills to developing some effective measures.
2. Ask participants to locate **training instrument 15** from learning activity 17. Display **slide 7-31** and direct their attention to the far right column labeled "An Effective Measure of This SMART Goal." Note that earlier you had asked them to keep this column blank. State that they should work in their table groups for the next seven minutes to develop an effective way to measure the SMARTer performance goal that their group had defined in learning activity 17. Encourage them to use page two of **handout 14** to ensure that the measure they create is an effective one.
3. After about seven minutes, reconvene the large group and invite each of the small groups to share their effective measures. Honor earnest attempts and, when appropriate, suggest ways to enhance or strengthen their measures.
4. Ask if participants have any remaining questions or issues about developing effective measures. Encourage other participants to answer any questions that arise and offer your own thoughts as appropriate.

DEBRIEFING

Concluding the activity:
- Emphasize that measurement is central to moving an employee toward great performance. Note that this activity lays the groundwork for what they will do next: develop effective measures for their target position's great performance outcomes as well as supporting job and organizational responsibilities.

Learning Activity 21. Performance Planning and Development—Developing Measures of Performance

OBJECTIVES

The objective of this learning activity is to
- have participants apply their insights from the measurement learning activity to their own target position.

MATERIALS

The materials needed for this activity are
- Training Instrument 12: Performance Planning and Development Worksheet

- **PPT** PowerPoint slide 7-32

- flipchart pages and markers, if desired.

TIME

🕐 25 minutes

PREPARATIONS

- Each participant should have the partially completed training instrument 12 from previous learning activities.

INSTRUCTIONS

1. **PPT** Transition out of the previous activity by indicating that it is time for the participants to apply the lessons of measurement to the position that they have been developing throughout the day. Display **slide 7-32** and ask participants to return to **training instrument 12** and complete the "Measuring Great Performance" column in part A of their worksheet.
2. Tell them that this part of the worksheet focuses on developing effective measures for the great performance outcomes that they identified earlier. Indicate that our goal for this activity is to focus on identifying two or three broad performance measures of the employee's overall performance instead of zeroing in on the details.
3. Give participants about eight minutes to identify one or two ways to measure the great performance outcomes for each of the performance dimensions. Encourage them to call you over if they have questions or are struggling with their situation.
4. After about eight minutes, call time and again ask them to find their partner from earlier and spend the next 10 minutes (five minutes each) sharing and giving feedback on each others' measures. Encourage the partners to provide feedback on the extent to which the measures developed have the characteristics of effective measures discussed earlier and summarized on handout 14.
5. Indicate that they should make revisions and corrections to their measures based on the feedback they are getting. Provide a time check at about the five minute mark to make sure that each participant has time to discuss their measures.
6. After about 10 minutes, reconvene the larger group. Ask them how the activity went, what they found most difficult, and what questions they have about performance measure development. As with previous personal planning segments, if people express frustration or confusion, try to respond to the issue raised by providing additional examples, clarifying the process, or offering to assist them following the workshop. As time permits, you may want to ask one or two participants to share examples of the great performance outcome measures that they developed.
7. Conclude the activity by noting that you have only focused on measuring the overall great performance outcomes for a specific position. Indicate that they may need to work with a given employee, depending on the person who is filling this position, to develop specific performance measures for many if not all of the job functions that they identified in parts B and C of this worksheet. Note that, as discussed earlier today, their task as a coach is to work collaboratively with employees to develop these performance measures rather than doing it for them. Remind them that filling in this worksheet is the shared responsibility of the coach and the performer working together and agreeing on the key performance outcomes and goals and the ways to measure progress toward achieving them.
8. Tell participants that the remaining pages of this worksheet will be completed in the follow-along workshop on diagnosing performance problems and developing improvement plans.

continued on next page

Learning Activity 21. Performance Planning and Development—Developing Measures of Performance, *continued*

DEBRIEFING

Wrap up the activity by making the following points:
- Developing effective measures of performance is essential to manage performance. Repeat the quote from Lord Kelvin: "If you can't measure it, you can't manage it!"
- The mutual learning mindset and goal theory encourage coaches to define these measures *with* the performer rather than *for* the performer. Because our goal is employee self-management—including self-correction when performance slips off track—involving the employee in developing these key metrics is essential.

Learning Activity 22. The Goals of Performance Coaching

OBJECTIVES

The objectives of this learning activity are to
- remind participants of the role of diagnosing performance challenges within the framework of the Great Performance Management Cycle
- review the five roles of an effective coach
- introduce the eight goals of performance coaching, which serve as the focus of all coaching conversations and interventions.

MATERIALS

The materials needed for this activity are

- ☐ Handout 2: The Roles of the Performance Coach

- Handout 4: The *Great* Performance Management Cycle
- Handout 15: The Goals of Performance Coaching
- **PPT** PowerPoint slides 8-7 through 8-14

- flipchart pages and markers, if desired.

TIME

⏱ 30 minutes

PREPARATIONS

- Handout 15 should be ready for distribution.
- If participants attended the Establishing a Coaching Relationship for Great Performance Workshop or the Performance Coaching Workshop, they already have handouts 2 and 4. Request that participants use these previously distributed handouts or bring additional copies as desired.

INSTRUCTIONS

1. **PPT** Introduce this activity by displaying **slide 8-7** and asking: *What is the fundamental purpose or focus of every performance coaching conversation or intervention?* Facilitate a brief large group discussion of this question and then provide a summary conclusion to the question by noting that the fundamental purpose of every coaching conversation is to move the performer toward some goal. Note that sometimes this goal is performance improvement, other times this goal might simply be sustaining current levels of performance. Regardless of the type of goal, however, every coaching conversation and intervention is anchored to a specific performance goal that the coach is attempting to accomplish with the employee.
2. **PPT** ☐ Display **slide 8-8** and, if desired, refer to **handout 4**, reminding participants that all performance coaching goals are addressed within the Great Performance Management Cycle. Remind participants that the employee is primarily responsible for moving through this cycle. The aim for performance coaching is to target coaching goals for the performer within this process.
3. **PPT** ☐ Display **slide 8-9** and, if desired, refer to **handout 2**, noting that the goals of every coaching conversation or intervention are also anchored to one or more of the five coaching roles. Suggest that they will see how some of these five roles translate into specific coaching goals as we move into exploring these goals.
4. ☐ **PPT** Distribute **handout 15** as you display **slide 8-10** and explain that there are two types of performance coaching goals: *outcome* goals relate to specific results that they want the employee to maintain or achieve and *process* goals relate more to the relationship between the performer and his or her job, organization, and coach.
5. **PPT** Display **slides 8-11 and 8-12** as you walk through a high level overview of the four outcome goals and the four process goals. Once you have completed the overview, ask participants to read the details about these eight kinds

continued on next page

Learning Activity 22. The Goals of Performance Coaching, *continued*

of coaching goals and to make take note of any questions they have about them. Give them about five minutes to read through the details of the eight goals.

6. **PPT** After about five minutes, display **slide 8-13** and ask participants to work in their table groups to share their general reactions to the types of goals and to try and answer each other's questions about these goals.

7. After about five minutes, reconvene the large group and ask for general reactions to the types of goals, what they found most helpful about these goals, and what questions they still have about these coaching goals. Honor and reinforce key insights and, for remaining questions, invite other participants in the room to answer what they can.

8. **PPT** Display **slide 8-14** as you ask the large group: *How many goals are appropriate for a coaching conversation or intervention?* Honor the ideas participants suggest and add that all eight goals may be part of a given coaching conversation. Suggest that every coaching conversation will have at least two goals: an *outcome* goal of some sort (improvement, maintaining, development, and so forth) and a *process* goal that's focused on relationships.

DEBRIEFING

Offer these concluding remarks at the end of the activity:

- Every coaching conversation or coaching intervention must be anchored back to a performance goal. A coach should never initiate a coaching conversation or intervention without being clear what this goal is.
- There are two kinds of performance coaching goals: *outcome* goals, which relate to the performance results, and *process* goals, which relate to the relationship between the performer and his or her work, organization, and coach.
- Most coaching conversations involve more than one goal at a time. The coach may want the performer to maintain specific performance dimension levels and improve in other areas while also building greater employee commitment to the job and strengthening the coaching relationship.

Learning Activity 23. Strategies for Documenting Employee Performance

OBJECTIVES

The objectives of this learning activity are to
- highlight the advantages of documenting employee performance
- identify specific methods for documenting employee performance.

MATERIALS

The materials needed for this activity are
- a packet of 3x5 index cards sufficient for three cards per table group
- Handout 16: Tools for Documenting Performance
- Training Instrument 16: Documenting Performance
- PPT PowerPoint slides 8-15 through 8-17
- flipchart pages and markers.

TIME

 35 minutes

PREPARATIONS

- Handout 16 and training instrument 16 should be ready for distribution.
- Prepare two flipchart pages entitled "Why Document Performance" and "Your Documentation Tools."

INSTRUCTIONS

1. **PPT** Display **slide 8-15** as you distribute **training instrument 16**. Ask participants to work in their table groups to answer the two questions on the slide and training instrument 16. Give the groups about three or four minutes for this brief small group discussion.
2. After about three or four minutes, reconvene the group and facilitate a discussion of the two questions. For the first question, record participant responses on the appropriate flipchart. Summarize participant ideas about the importance of documenting performance, highlighting points that are especially important. Reinforce the responses and add your own reasons:
   - to remind ourselves of actual performance results as we prepare for a coaching conversation
   - to ensure that we focus on the full array of performance results instead of only those that happened more recently (the recency effect) or that loom large in our minds
   - to give us insights into performance patterns and potential causes of performance problems.
3. Suggest that it is important to document performance because our memories are imperfect and can be unduly influenced by things outside of our consciousness.
4. Shift your focus to the second question and record participant responses about their current approaches, tools, and strategies for documenting performance. Honor the ideas offered and celebrate creative strategies and tools. Note that to the extent that these approaches and tools work, they have accomplished their primary task: ensuring that we consider the full array of performance data when we prepare for a coaching conversation.
5. **PPT** Distribute **handout 16** as you display **slide 8-16**. Briefly review each of the four tools for documenting performance. Display **slide 8-17** and ask participants to develop two or three questions about the four tools and then to write each of these questions on separate 3 × 5 index cards. Give the groups about four minutes for this exercise.
6. After about four minutes, reconvene the large group and ask a representative from each group to distribute their two or three questions to different table groups. Once all index cards are distributed, ask the groups to spend the next five minutes answering the questions that they have been given.

continued on next page

Learning Activity 23. Strategies for Documenting Employee Performance, *continued*

7. After about five minutes, ask each group to read one of their questions and their group's response to the question. After each group's answer, reinforce or add your own thoughts to the answer. Move to the next group's question and answer and repeat the process until all questions have been asked and answered.

8. Before concluding this activity, emphasize the following important points:
   - The coach documents the facts. Both good and bad incidents and results are recorded and the coach discusses each incident and result with the performer at the time of the occurrence.
   - The coach documents objectively based upon data. Adding interpretation or judging the intentions or motivations of the performer has no place here—doing this can seriously erode the level of trust in the coaching relationship and may compromise the coach's perceived objectivity. This compromised objectivity may, in turn, undermine efforts to terminate an employee or undercut legal defense of disciplinary actions.
   - The process used by the coach for documenting performance must be open and transparent. Everything that is documented by the coach should be freely shared with the performer at the time of the entry and any time following the entry. There is no place for secrets or for writing things that the coach wouldn't feel comfortable sharing with the performer at any time.

DEBRIEFING

Wrap up the activity by making the following points:
- The mutual learning mindset encourages us to create a transparent process for documenting performance. This means that every note we make in the performance log reflects an incident, event, or outcome that we have already discussed with the employee. If our actions are informed by the mutual learning mindset, then our emails to ourselves or entries in the performance log are never surprises to the employee when we bring them up them during Performance Coaching Conversations, they are just reminders to both of us about things that we previously discussed.
- Documenting performance is central to performance management and is critical to the coach's preparation for the coaching conversation.
- The purpose of documentation is to ensure that all essential aspects of an employee's performance are considered when preparing for a coaching conversation.
- Whatever tools and processes a coach uses to document performance, he or she must ensure that both positive and negative incidents and results are recorded.
- Everything that a coach documents should be discussed with the performer at the time of documentation and freely shared with the employee upon request.
- Though the coach's methods for documenting incidents or performance are not necessarily part of the employee's personnel file, most of the documentary methods are subject to legal discovery. All the more reason to keep the documentation objective and fact-based and to discuss the incident or performance with the employee at the time.

Learning Activity 24. Why Things Go Wrong With Performance

OBJECTIVES

The objectives of this learning activity are to
- identify the multiple reasons an employee's performance may sometimes not live up to expectations
- introduce participants to the 85/15 Rule as a way to understand performance within a larger context
- describe the key components of performance and the responsibility of both the performer and the coach in managing these components.

MATERIALS

The materials needed for this activity are
- Handout 17: Using the Performance Gap to Drive Improvement
- Handout 18: Why Things Go Wrong With Performance
- Handout 19: The Components of Performance and the 85/15 Rule
- Training Instrument 17: Why Things Go Wrong With Performance
- PPT PowerPoint slides 8-18 through 8-24
- flipchart pages and markers.

TIME

🕐 40 minutes

PREPARATIONS

- Handouts 17, 18, and 19 and training instrument 17 should be ready for distribution.
- Each table group should have a flipchart easel with paper and markers that it will use in the problem solving process.
- Two prepared flipchart pages entitled "Organizational Causes" and "Employee Causes."

INSTRUCTIONS

1. PPT Display **slide 8-18** as you distribute **handout 17**. Click through the steps of analyzing performance and developing improvement plans. State that the process begins with actual performance being compared to great performance, resulting in a performance "gap." Emphasize that understanding and addressing this performance gap is what drives performance improvement. Suggest that the first step after identifying the performance gap (overall or for a specific performance dimension) is to identify potential causes. Once causes are identified, the goals and strategies that are developed work to close the gap by addressing those causes. The final step is then reassessing whether actual performance meets expectations and beginning the process over again.

2. PPT Display **slide 8-19** as you distribute **training instrument 17**. Ask the table groups to discuss the two questions on the slide and instrument and to agree upon, from their perspectives, the top four or five organizational reasons and the top four or five employee reasons why an employee's performance might be less than optimal. Give the groups about five minutes to discuss the two questions and generate their reasons.

3. 🔵 After about five minutes, reconvene the large group and have the small groups report in a round-robin fashion, with each group giving one item from their list for organizational causes. Once the organizational list is complete, move to the list of employee causes—again using a round-robin reporting system until all ideas are listed.

4. Invite participants to react to the two lists. Ask: *What are the implications of these two lists regarding how they might respond to an employee's performance problems?* Encourage a discussion of the value of considering both sources as reasons why an employee's performance doesn't match expectations.

5. PPT Display **slide 8-20**. Click through each of the points on the organizational side of the slide, providing examples for each and expanding upon what each means in terms of a barrier to employee performance. As you click through

continued on next page

Learning Activity 24. Why Things Go Wrong With Performance, *continued*

the slide, indicate that very shortly you will distribute a handout that summarizes what is on this slide, but for the moment you want them to pay attention to each of these potential causes.

6. When you come to the organizational cause "Conflict with co-workers," ask the group: *Why is this an organizational cause instead of an employee cause?* Honor responses given and add your perspective: the organization has a duty to maintain a healthy and productive work environment. If disruptive conflict between employees isn't addressed quickly and effectively, then the consequence can be that individual performance declines. Though an individual employee may be the cause of a conflict that disrupts the work of others, it's up to the organization to deal with the conflict before it negatively affects performance.

7. Once you have clicked through the organizational list, shift to the right-hand side of the slide and display the list of employee causes. As you move through the list, again give examples of each, expanding upon the specific cause. Distribute **handout 18**, and ask for comments and additional questions from the group about any of these causes.

8. PPT Distribute **handout 19** as you display **slide 8-21**. Indicate that employee performance is a result of all of the boxes lined up in this graphic, with the final box being the net performance result. Note that in the example on this slide and on their handout, the box at the far right indicates 100 percent—meaning the employee's performance precisely met expectations. Indicate that the final box represents the employee's performance results and that it is conceivable that a given employee could actually exceed expectations—in which case the number would be greater than 100 percent—or the employee could fall short, perhaps considerably short, of expectations—in which case the number would be less than 100 percent.

9. PPT Begin revealing the four questions on **slide 8-21** and, after each question, ask the group for their thoughts.

   • *Which component is most important to the performance outcome?* A number of participants might say "Effort." When you hear the word effort, click to see the Effort box highlighted. Acknowledge that most of the time people identify effort as the biggest contributor.

   • *What happens if any one of these components is missing or reduced?* Again, solicit participant ideas, but don't comment on any suggestions made.

   • *Which component is the employee* largely *responsible for?* Solicit comments, but don't comment. A number of participants will say "Effort."

   • *Who is responsible for the other components?* Again solicit comments.

10. After you have revealed all of the questions on the slide and solicited comments from the group, offer the following summary statement:

    "Employee performance, as we have learned from the GPM Cycle, is a partnership between the individual contributor and the larger organization—including the coach and other members of the performer's team or work area. When we look at the components of performance on handout 19 and on slide 8-21 within this partnership perspective, then the responsibility for each of these components is shared between the performer and others. Even for the Effort component, where the employee is the one who independently brings motivation and commitment to the job, the organization plays a role in influencing whether the employee actually chooses to bring effort to the job.

    "Though the organization is responsible for skills and ability (we hired and trained the employee), even here there is a shared responsibility. The employee must let us know what skill and knowledge development needs he or she has and then take responsibility for acquiring these skills and understanding these knowledge areas.

    "The key take-away for you from this exercise, I hope, is that getting to 100 percent or better in that final performance box requires all cylinders firing at close to full capacity. If any one component is missing or reduced in its influence, then performance is likely to suffer. Many performers are able to creatively work around such barriers, but the extra effort and frustrations this might require could be avoided if the missing or eroded component were directly addressed early on."

11. PPT Ask for reactions to your summary comments and remarks. Respond to comments and questions before displaying **slide 8-22**, highlighting the 85/15 Rule. Call attention to the box at the bottom of **handout 19**.

continued on next page

Learning Activity 24. Why Things Go Wrong With Performance, *continued*

12. **PPT** Ask participants to read the 85/15 Rule on their own and, after two minutes, ask them to discuss their reactions to the rule by displaying the two questions on **slide 8-22**. Give the groups about three minutes to react to and discuss the 85/15 Rule and the two questions on the slide.

13. After about three minutes, solicit participant reactions to the two questions. Encourage participants who disagree with it to offer their reasoning. Encourage those who agree to offer their reasoning for why it sounds true to them.

14. Acknowledge that the 85/15 Rule can be challenging to fully embrace. State that the 85/15 Rule has its origins in the quality improvement movement in the 1980s and 1990s. It was popularized by such quality leaders as W. Edward Deming, who argued that we can't truly measure the performance of the individual until we factor out the underlying system influences that either support or erode performance.

15. Suggest that it's possible to find middle ground on this rule. First, indicate that even the 85/15 Rule holds the person fully accountable for their contribution to the performance problem. If someone isn't achieving their performance goals, they are still at least 15 percent responsible for the outcomes and therefore can be held accountable for them.

16. Encourage those who don't agree with the percentages (they argue that it lets people off the hook) to at least accept the premise that when performance isn't as expected, the first place we need to look is at the system rather than the individual. Suggest that too often when an employee hits a rough spot, we focus on their effort first rather than looking at the larger system within which the person is performing. Encourage participants to look at the system first, eliminate the system as the source of the problem, and then turn to focus on the individual's effort and contribution.

17. Indicate that they can choose any percentage they want 80/20, 75/25, 70/30 . . . even 55/45 as long as the balance tips toward examining the system causes first and then turning to what the employee is doing or not doing that could lead to reduced performance outcomes.

18. **PPT** Display **slide 8-23**. Suggest that this is one free "Aha!" for the day and this principle is key to the effectiveness of a coach. Indicate that when things go wrong, the coach *must* focus on understanding *cause* instead of focusing on blame. Indicate that they will learn some additional tools for staying focused on cause in the next learning activity.

19. **PPT** End this activity with **slide 8-24**. The first click brings up an individual contributor. Suggest to participants that they won't be able to "fix" the performer in the middle without—click again to reveal the relationships and connections—understanding the context of the individual's working environment and relationships.

DEBRIEFING

Finish this learning activity by highlighting the following points:

- Diagnosing performance problems first involves being open to and examining the array of possible causes of the problem and then exploring solutions and performance improvement plans.

- There are two main sources of most performance problems: those caused by the *organization* and those caused by the *employee*.

- The 85/15 Rule simply encourages us to look at the system first before turning our attention to the employee. In most cases, the performance results that we see are a function of both the employee and the system working well together—or not. Diagnosing the origins of such problems is the first step to finding a cure.

- When the coach focuses on cause, this important shift in perspective puts the employee in a new light, having been acknowledged within the larger fabric of the forces driving or limiting employee performance.

Learning Activity 25. Diagnostic Tools for Exploring the Causes of Performance Problems

OBJECTIVES

The objectives of this learning activity are to
- introduce two diagnostic tools that participants can use to aid their exploration of the causes underlying performance problems
- guide participants in integrating and applying both tools to specific performance problems.

MATERIALS

The materials needed for this activity are
- 📄 Handout 20: Nine-Plus-One Performance Diagnostic Checklist
- Handout 21: Cause→Effect Diagram
- Training Instrument 18: Cause→Effect Diagram Application
- PPT PowerPoint slides 8-25 through 8-30
- Each table group will need one flipchart page and markers. They will place the page either on their table or on the wall near their table. Because the flipchart page should be positioned in landscape format when used by the group, it is better to give each group a single page that they can work with on their table or taped to the wall instead of working on a flipchart easel, which holds the page in the less desirable portrait orientation.

TIME

🕐 60 minutes

PREPARATIONS

- Handouts 20 and 21 and training instrument 18 should be ready to distribute.

INSTRUCTIONS

1. PPT Display **slide 8-25**. Transition into this activity by stating that effective coaches need a number of tools in their toolkits to help them explore the causes of performance problems thoughtfully and objectively. Suggest that though there are a number of tools that coaches can use, two tools they will learn more about and apply today are the Nine-Plus-One Performance Diagnostic Checklist and the Cause→Effect Diagram.
2. Acknowledge that some of them may be familiar with the Cause→Effect Diagram as its use was popularized as a tool for quality and productivity improvement. Indicate that this tool is also known as a Fishbone Diagram because it presents a structure like the bones of a fish. Tell the group that they will use this tool to help in diagnosing a specific performance problem.
3. 📄 PPT Distribute **handout 20** as you display **slide 8-26**. Ask participants to read the Nine-Plus-One Diagnostic Checklist and to reflect on the three questions on the slide. Give participants about three or four minutes to review handout 20.
4. 📄 PPT After about three or four minutes, ask participants to discuss their reactions to **handout 20** and their answers to the questions on **slide 8-25** in their table group. Give the groups about four minutes to discuss their reactions: identify what they like about the tool, answer each others' questions, and identify how they might use the checklist in preparing for a performance coaching conversation.
5. After about four minutes, reconvene the group and lead a discussion about the checklist. Ask what they like most about the tool and if they have any remaining questions about the checklist. If questions arise, invite other participants to respond to the questions. Finally, ask participants how they might use the checklist to prepare for a performance coaching conversation. Honor suggestions that participants offer and add this final comment:

"If and when one of your employees is experiencing a problem with performance, use this tool to make sure that you have done all you can to enable the employee to succeed. If you can honestly say 'yes' to all of the first eight questions and you've made provisions to address the ninth, then you can approach the coaching session with confidence that you've done your best."

continued on next page

Learning Activity 25. Diagnostic Tools for Exploring the Causes of Performance Problems, *continued*

6. Encourage participants to keep this checklist in an accessible location and to review it when performance problems surface. State that the purpose of the checklist is to slow down their thought process, encourage them to withhold their judgment about the cause of the performance problems, and help them approach the performance coaching conversation after some critical reflection.

7. PPT Display **slide 8-27** as you distribute **handout 21** and **training instrument 18**. Identify that the purpose of the diagram is to explore the relationship between the effects or performance results and the array of possible causes of these effects. This tool presents a structured brainstorming process where the coach explores how each category of causes contributes to the final end result: the employee's performance.

8. Transition to the next slide by indicating that for the next half-hour or so, the participants will learn how to use this diagramming technique to analyze employee performance problems. Indicate that you'll walk them through two examples and then they'll develop a diagram for a specific performance problem example from their small group.

9. PPT Display **slide 8-28**. Indicate to participants that, in the Gulf of Mexico, there is an area between 4,000 and 7,000 square miles that is completely devoid of marine life. Ask participants if they can guess where the dead zone might be located in the Gulf. Next, tell them that the dead zone is located beginning where the Mississippi River empties into the Gulf. Tell participants that the dead zone is the effect of a whole host of causes. Ask them: *If you were a marine biologist, where would you go to find the causes of the dead zone?* Agree with the responses, noting that you would have to go "up river" to identify the origins of the problem.

10. PPT Reference **slide 8-28**, pointing out that the Mississippi River is the main channel leading to the "effect" and that each of the "branches" (ribs in the fishbone diagram) represents the major tributaries of the Mississippi: the Ohio, the Missouri, the Illinois, the Wisconsin, and so forth. Click through the text on this slide, noting that each river or branch makes its own contributions to the "mix" in the Mississippi River, leading to the final result in the dead zone. When revealing and discussing the assigned "causes" for each river, note that these examples are our guesses and likely represent only a few of the potential pollutants in any of these rivers. [If participants express interest in this issue, indicate that research into the causes seems to suggest that the biggest contributors to the dead zone are excess nutrients, such as nitrogen and phosphorus, mostly from rivers that run through agricultural states of Iowa, Illinois, Indiana, Ohio, and southern Minnesota.]

11. PPT Transition away from this natural example by suggesting that, in the workplace, each of the tributaries or ribs is labeled more conventionally. Display **slide 8-29** and demonstrate how each of the ribs is labeled with a different organizational dimension. Note that the participants can define these dimensions similarly or follow the instructions on **handout 21**.

12. PPT Click through **slide 8-29** as you present an example diagram. Highlight the "Effect" (missed deadlines) and then ask the group: *How might Policies and Procedures contribute to missed deadlines?* Click to display the two possible causes for this factor. Then highlight all of the other possible causes for all of the other "bones" of the diagram. Acknowledge that these are very general examples of causes. Suggest that, for their own diagram, they will need to get far more specific in order for the diagram to be most helpful. Ask participants if they have any questions about how to develop and use the diagram as a brainstorming tool for diagnosing potential causes.

13. PPT Indicate that it's now time for them to work in their small groups to apply the Cause→Effect diagram to a specific performance situation that one member of their group is currently dealing with. Display **slide 8-30** and ask the groups to spend the next 15 minutes exploring the potential causes of one performance problem.

14. Instruct them to briefly discuss and then decide which employee performance problem they want to explore. Emphasize that they are not to identify the employee by name but to just list the less than optimal performance outcomes (the "effect"), to label the different "bones" or categories of causes, and then begin by focusing on one cause category at a time.

15. Tell them that they are to use the flipchart page at or near their table and that they should work with the flipchart in landscape orientation to allow a full documentation of the likely performance causes. Give the groups about three minutes to select their example performance situation and then direct them to begin creating their Cause→Effect Diagram. Indicate that if any group is struggling, they should call you over. As the tables begin their work, wander

continued on next page

Learning Activity 25. Diagnostic Tools for Exploring the Causes of Performance Problems, *continued*

around the room, checking in with each group, providing direction and assistance as necessary. At about the 10-minute mark, tell the group that they have about five minutes remaining to sketch out the beginnings of a Cause→Effect Diagram for their selected situation.

16. After about 15 minutes, call the groups' attention back to the front of the room and move into a debriefing of the tool. Ask the groups to report what worked, what didn't work, what they found easy, and what they found frustrating. Encourage the groups to share their reactions, insights, and frustrations with the tool.

17. Ask for volunteers to present a brief summary of the key causes of the performance effects that their group focused on. Caution participants again not to use names as they share what they discovered.

18. Ask participants what step should follow the use of this tool. Honor responses and then indicate the Cause→Effect Diagram is a structured brainstorming tool to help them identify some causes leading to the undesirable performance effect. Suggest that the tool should give them some ideas to explore at a deeper level, on their own or in their performance coaching conversation, with the employee in question. Emphasize that the tool, up to this point, is made up of their *assumptions* and *inferences*. Indicate that these assumptions and inferences may be wrong, so it is important to use the tool as a beginning point for their inquiry into causes rather than the end point.

19. As you draw the activity to a close, ask if participants have any remaining questions about the tool. Answer the questions directly or encourage others to do so. Offer your insights and responses to help participants see the benefits of the tool. Acknowledge that building the diagram for the first time can be confusing, but that if they stick with it, they will find it a powerful tool for uncovering possible causes of almost any problem or effect that they want to solve.

Debriefing

Conclude the activity by making the following points:

- The Nine-Plus-One Diagnostic Checklist offers a simple list of possible system causes of performance failures. By walking through this checklist before your performance coaching conversation, you can help develop an effective line of inquiry for your coaching interaction.
- The Cause→Effect Diagram doesn't tell you what *is* the cause. It suggests what the cause or causes might be. The next step for the coach is to take the insights from the diagramming process and begin verifying and validating the assumptions and inferences that went into creating the diagram.
- Both of these tools offer a method for focusing on *cause* instead of blame. By helping them stay focused on exploring causes of a performance problem, these two tools reinforce the mutual learning mindset and its governing values and enacting behaviors that were explored in the Developing a Coaching Relationship Workshop.

Learning Activity 26. Performance Planning and Development—Assessing Employee Performance

OBJECTIVES

The objective of this learning activity is to
- enable participants to identify the coaching goals for a coaching conversation.

MATERIALS

The materials needed for this activity are
- ☐ Handout 15: The Goals of Performance Coaching

- Training Instrument 12: Performance Planning and Development Worksheet

- `PPT` PowerPoint slides 8-31 and 8-34

- flipchart pages and markers, if desired.

TIME

🕐 55 minutes

PREPARATIONS

- Participants should already have a partially completed training instrument 12 from previous learning activities.

INSTRUCTIONS

1. Transition into this activity by indicating that the next task involves analyzing the performance outcomes and behaviors of one of their employees—the one that they have been focusing on as they completed training instrument 12, the Performance Planning and Development Worksheet, in the workshop on goal setting.
2. State that this activity is based on insights gained from learning activity 22, in which they learned about the eight performance coaching goals, and learning activity 25, in which they learned methods for identifying possible causes of performance problems.
3. Ask participants to locate **training instrument 12**—the Performance Planning and Development Worksheet— and **handout 15** on the goals of performance coaching.
4. Highlight the first three parts of this worksheet that they completed at the Setting Performance Goals Workshop. Indicate that in completing Part A earlier they identified the Great Performance Outcomes for a specific position that they managed and how they might measure whether these outcomes are achieved. At this point you may want to remind them of the importance of framing a position's core purpose as achieving great performance rather than just getting the job done.
5. Tell them that in Parts B and C they have already identified the core job and organizational responsibilities for this position and developed an array of SMART goals for many of these responsibilities.
6. Indicate that when they completed the first three parts of the worksheet, they were asked not to think of a specific person but of the *position* that this person held. Tell them that, in this activity, their focus shifts to one person on their team who is currently filling this position.
7. Ask them to think of a specific individual who, from their perspective, is failing to meet all or some of the Great Performance Outcomes or the job and organizational responsibilities that they identified in Parts A, B, and C of the worksheet. State that this person may be struggling in his or her role, falling short of expectations, or not achieving the performance outcomes that he or she seems capable of. Note that, in any of these cases, the individual is not performing at a level that is desired or that reflects what you think he or she fully is able to achieve.
8. Remind participants of learning activity 22 (the first learning activity of the Diagnosing Performance Problems and Developing Improvement Plans workshop), in which they learned about the four *outcome* goals and the four *process* goals for performance coaching. Indicate that in this activity they will use **training instrument 12** to identify some initial performance coaching goals for the employee who is failing to meet expectations.

continued on next page

Learning Activity 26. Performance Planning and Development—Assessing Employee Performance, *continued*

9. PPT Refer participants to the list of the four coaching outcome goals on **handout 15**. Display **slide 8-31** and note the letter designation for each of these four outcome goals: **M** for maintaining strength, **I** for improving performance, **A** for accepting a new responsibility, and **G** for growing or moving the job to a higher performance level. Indicate that the four process goals on page three of **handout 15** will be addressed later in this exercise and that they should ignore these process goals for now.

10. PPT Display **slide 8-32** as you ask participants to think of this employee's work and then to apply the M, I, A, or G designation to each of the Great Performance Outcome dimensions in Part A as well as for each job or organizational responsibility area overall or specific SMART performance goals from Parts B and C. Tell them that if they haven't developed SMART performance goals for a dimension in the first column of Parts B and C, they should simply identify an entire job or organizational responsibility area as an M, I, A, or G. Indicate that if they have developed one or more SMART goals for a dimension, however, they should identify each SMART goal with an M, I, A, or G. Give participants about seven minutes to complete this M, I, A, and G designation exercise.

11. PPT After about seven minutes, display **slide 8-33** and ask participants to shift their focus to Part D of their worksheet. Give a brief overview of this section. Indicate that over the next 10 minutes they should identify the high-value or high-priority Great Performance Outcome dimensions, job or organizational responsibility dimensions, or SMART goals from Parts A, B, and C that they designated with an I, A, or G. Tell them to list these high-value or high-priority I, A, or G areas in the first column of Part D. Encourage them to write only a couple of words or a phrase to capture the improvement area.

12. Add that you also want them to complete the middle and right-hand columns in Part D for each performance area they have listed in the first column. Encourage them to refer to the Nine-Plus-One Performance Diagnostic Checklist and the Cause→Effect Diagram to identify possible causes limiting the employee's current or future performance. Ask them to identify specific actions that they, the employee, or others in the organization could take to address the current or future barriers to employee performance in each improvement area. Give the participants 10 minutes for this activity and provide a time-check about five minutes into the process.

13. After about 10 minutes, ask participants to partner up with someone at their table or the next table to share their employee performance diagnosis, the potential causes posing a limitation to current or future performance, and their ideas for addressing these causes. Encourage them to choose as a partner someone who either knows the employee well and could enrich or add to their perspective or someone who doesn't know the employee's performance but who could ask probing questions to push their thinking deeper. Their partner should provide feedback and suggestions to improve the accuracy of the I, A, or G designations, the clarity of the potential causes that may be limiting performance, and the specificity of the actions to address the causes. Give people 10 minutes for this "pairing and sharing" exercise. Provide a time-check after about five minutes.

14. After about 10 minutes, call the participants back to the larger group. Ask them how the activity went, what they found most helpful or difficult, whether it was useful to have another person's perspective on the employee's performance, and so forth. If people express frustration or confusion, try to respond to the issue raised by providing additional examples, clarifying the process, or offering to assist them following the workshop. As time permits, you may want to ask one or two participants to share examples of an I or A area, what underlying causes might be limiting current or future performance, and possible actions that the employee or the manager could take.

15. PPT Shift participants' attention to Part E of **training instrument 12** as you display **slide 8-34**. Ask them to spend the next five minutes reflecting on the four coaching process goals for their upcoming performance coaching conversation. Ask them to identify one or two process goals that they would like the employee to achieve as a result of their face-to-face interaction with the employee and to also identify their strategy for addressing these goals during the coaching conversation.

16. After about five minutes, ask the large group if they have any questions about this step of the process. Indicate that the goals of their performance coaching conversations must include both *outcome* goals—specifically goals for improvement, growth, or development—and *process* goals—goals that strengthen the employee's engagement with his or her job, organization, and relationship with the coach or that identify system barriers to performance.

continued on next page

Learning Activity 26. Performance Planning and Development—Assessing Employee Performance, *continued*

17. Conclude this activity by highlighting the importance of developing specific outcome and process goals for the coaching relationship. In this activity, they identified where they will eventually focus their improvement or development efforts during the Performance Coaching Conversation. Stress that any performance areas identified with an M—an indication of an area of performance strength that the employee should *maintain*—also needs to be highlighted and celebrated during the Performance Coaching Conversation. Indicate that these performance strengths should never be taken for granted and that they will be raised during the coaching conversation to reinforce what's working and to ensure that both the employee and the coach take steps to maintain performance in these areas.

18. State that what the participants learn about their employees and their performance during this performance analysis will be integrated into the next steps in the performance planning process as well as during the Performance Coaching Conversation and the Annual Performance Analysis and Planning Conversation.

DEBRIEFING

Conclude the activity by making the following points:

- Effective performance planning begins with identifying areas for improvement or development and identifying barriers to performance in these areas. These form the foundations for developing specific *outcome* goals for the performance coaching conversation.
- Equally important for a coach is to identify and develop *process* goals as part of the performance planning process to ensure that key relationships are strengthened or that system barriers to performance are identified.
- Defining and focusing the coaches' efforts on a few high priority areas is the starting point. Developing specific positive performance or improvement goals is the next step in the process—and the focus of the next learning activity.

Learning Activity 27. Establishing Positive Performance Improvement Goals

OBJECTIVES

The objectives of this learning activity are to
- introduce a positive approach to setting performance improvement goals
- enable participants to apply this positive approach to specific performance improvement goal examples.

MATERIALS

The materials needed for this activity are
- Training Instrument 19: Establishing Positive Performance Goals Application

- PPT PowerPoint slide 8-35

- flipchart pages and markers, if desired.

TIME

25 minutes

PREPARATIONS

- Training instrument 19 should be ready for distribution.
- Review training instrument 19 and develop some possible behaviorally specific, positively stated improvement goals. You may use your own examples following the reporting phase of this activity.

INSTRUCTIONS

1. Begin by indicating that in the previous activity they identified high priority or high value areas of where the employee could improve performance or where they wanted the employee to accept a new responsibility. The next step is how to create performance improvement goals.
2. PPT Distribute **training instrument 19** as you display **slide 8-35**. State that the purpose of stating goals *positively* is to ask the performer to do more of some behavior that leads to the desired outcomes that both the employee and the coach are working to achieve. Indicate that by focusing on increasing positive behaviors and results, the coach is encouraging the performer to do more of something rather than focusing on doing less of something else.
3. Let the participants know that it's not enough to ask employees to stop doing something—focusing on ending bad behaviors or results doesn't necessarily give the performer an idea of what is expected of him or her. Emphasize that the purpose of this activity is to shift away from focusing on undesirable behaviors and toward what the performer should be doing more of.
4. PPT Show **slide 8-35** and note that these positive improvement goals should be behaviorally specific and focus on *increasing* specific behaviors. Walk the group through the examples on the slide and **training instrument 19**. Before moving into the application phase of this activity, ask if the participants have any questions about developing behaviorally specific, positive improvement goals.
5. After addressing participants' questions, assign two or three of the negatively stated performance goals to each table group. Give the groups about five minutes to develop behaviorally specific, positive improvement goals for their assigned negative goals. Indicate that, given the limited amount of details in the negatively stated goals, they will need to invent or create positive behaviors to complete the exercise.
6. After about five minutes, invite the table groups to share their positively stated, behaviorally specific improvement goals. If the same goals were assigned to different groups (which is recommended), compare and contrast the different approaches or assumptions that the groups made. Encourage participants to make notes on the instrument regarding possible answers for the goals that their group wasn't assigned. Note that the answers that the groups offer may be helpful when they develop their own performance improvement goals for their chosen employee later in the workshop.

continued on next page

Learning Activity 27. Establishing Positive Performance Improvement Goals, *continued*

7. Honor and celebrate positively stated improvement goals and add your own touches to refine or focus any improvement goals that might benefit from your perspective.

DEBRIEFING

Conclude the activity by making the following points:

- It's insufficient to tell a performer that he or she needs to stop doing something. An effective coach needs to suggest positive improvement goals that communicate what the performer is expected to do more of.
- Positively stated improvement goals also need to be behavior and outcome specific. They need to describe the behaviors and outcomes in specific language such that the performer knows precisely what is expected.
- Establishing positive improvement goals is a shared responsibility that involves the coach working closely with the performer in sketching out expectations for improvement. Using the mutual learning mindset and insights from Goal Theory (both from previous workshops and learning activities) make it essential that employees are involved in goal setting rather than the coach imposing these improvement goals.

Learning Activity 28. Performance Planning and Development—Developing Performance Goals

OBJECTIVES

The objectives of this learning activity are to
- involve participants in developing positive, behaviorally specific improvement or development goals for an employee
- give participants feedback on the clarity and specificity of these goals.

MATERIALS

The materials needed for this activity are
- Handout 14: The Purpose and Characteristics of Effective Performance Measures (which participants received as part of learning activity 19 in the Goal Setting workshop)
- Training Instrument 12: Performance Planning and Development Worksheet

- Training Instrument 19: Establishing Positive Performance Goals Application
- PPT PowerPoint slide 8-36

- flipchart pages and markers, if desired.

TIME

 45 minutes

PREPARATIONS

- Participants should already have a partially completed training instrument 12 from previous learning activities.

INSTRUCTIONS

1. Begin the activity by noting that they have been slowly working through their Performance Planning and Development Worksheet **(training instrument 12)** by defining great performance and describing key job and organizational responsibilities and have developed SMART goals for many of the responsibility areas. They also identified ways to measure Great Performance Outcomes and assessed a specific employee, in terms of maintaining, improving, accepting new responsibilities, or developing the job in a new direction. More recently, they analyzed the possible *causes* limiting performance or growth and they developed some initial *process* goals for the coaching conversation.
2. PPT Suggest that it's now time for them to focus on developing positive improvement or development goals for their chosen employee. Display **slide 8-36** as you ask participants to turn to Part F of their worksheet **(training instrument 12)**. Tell them to focus on developing one or two specific *positive* performance improvement or development goals. Note that the form provides room for up to four of these goals, but that in the time that they have available today, you want them to focus on just one or two improvement or development goals.
3. Encourage participants to use the example positive performance improvement goals from the previous activity. Ask them to also draw ideas about SMART goals and performance measures from the Performance Goal Setting Workshop that they recently attended.
4. Discuss the importance of identifying specific behaviors and outcomes that the employee might engage in or accomplish to achieve each performance improvement or development goal. Encourage them to refer to the answers given on **training instrument 19** in the previous activity.
5. Give participants about 10 minutes to develop one or two specific high value or high priority performance *improvement* or *development* performance goals. Ask them to also develop ways to measure each goal, drawing from **handout 14** on the characteristics of effective measures from learning activity 19 in the Goal Setting Workshop. Encourage participants to call you over if they have questions or are struggling with the activity. Provide a time-check at approximately five minutes to let participants know that they need to be moving toward developing another goal.
6. After about 10 minutes, call time and ask them to find their partner from earlier and spend the next 10 minutes (five minutes each) sharing and giving feedback on each other's performance improvement or development goals, measures,

continued on next page

Learning Activity 28. Performance Planning and Development—Developing Performance Goals, *continued*

and behaviors. Encourage the partners to provide feedback on the extent to which the goals, measures, and behaviors meet the SMART goals test and that the goals will be helpful in giving direction to the employee who is expected to meet these goals.

7. After about 10 minutes, reconvene the larger group. Ask them how the activity went, what they found most difficult, and what questions they have about establishing positive performance improvement or development goals. As with previous personal planning segments, if people express frustration or confusion, try to respond to the issue raised by providing additional examples, clarifying the process, or offering to assist them following the workshop. As time permits, you may want to ask one or two participants to share examples of the positive performance improvement or development goals, measures, and behaviors that they developed.

8. Conclude the activity by noting that the Performance Planning and Development Worksheet that they have been working with is an important thinking and planning tool to help them prepare for the face-to-face Performance Coaching Conversation or the Annual Performance Analysis and Planning Conversation with their employee. Reiterate that this worksheet, though a planning tool for the manager, should be developed with the active participation of the employee. Reiterate that they need to use the mutual learning mindset as they approach this planning work and be prepared to significantly modify their plans once they engage their performer in a face-to-face conversation. Note that though the coach will do his or her homework by filling in this worksheet in advance of the coaching conversation, the final version of this worksheet should be done *with* the active participation of the employee.

9. Note that Parts G and H of this worksheet haven't yet been completed. Indicate that these two sections of the worksheet are used as the coach takes his or her final steps leading up to the Performance Coaching Conversation or Annual Performance Analysis and Planning Conversation.

DEBRIEFING

Conclude the activity by making the following points:
- Setting positive performance improvement or development goals is a critical step for a coach to take when preparing for the face-to-face Performance Coaching Conversation or Annual Performance Analysis and Planning Conversation. Going into these one-on-one interactions with the performer with clear *outcome* goals is essential in order to prepare the way for communicating these expectations to the performer.
- Though you have developed these goals on your own here today, you will need to actively engage your employees in identifying and developing these and other improvement or development goals. Effective coaching is participatory, with the employee taking the lead role in the process—especially within the Performance Coaching Conversation or the Annual Performance Analysis and Planning Conversation that we'll explore in the follow-along workshop.

Learning Activity 29. The Performance Management Quiz

OBJECTIVES

The objective of this learning activity is to
- get participants thinking about the role and purpose of performance management and performance reviews within this process.

MATERIALS

The materials needed for this activity are
- Training Instrument 20: Performance Management Quiz

- PPT PowerPoint slides 9-7 and 9-8

TIME

🕐 10 minutes

PREPARATIONS

- Training instrument 20 should be placed in front of each participant chair before they enter the training room.

INSTRUCTIONS

1. 🔍 Introduce this activity by indicating to participants that you'd like to gauge their current knowledge about some aspects of performance management, performance coaching, performance reviews, and performance coaching conversations by giving them a quiz. Note that some of the quiz questions have been addressed by previous workshops and others are new to the current workshop. Ask participants to work by themselves and to take about four minutes to answer the 10 questions on **training instrument 20**.
2. PPT After about four minutes, call participants' attention back to the front of the room as you display **slides 9-7 and 9-8**. As you click each question, ask participants to shout out what they think the right answers are.
3. Note general agreement when multiple voices suggest a common response. As you note the general agreement answers, make notations on your page of their responses. You will reference their answers again toward the end of the workshop.
4. After completing the 10 quiz questions and gathering (and making note of) their thoughts about what the right answers are, suggest to participants that they should keep the quiz handy throughout the day and be on the lookout for the "correct" answers. Indicate to the group that one of the last activities of the day will be to review this quiz again to see if their answers are any different than now.

DEBRIEFING

Wrap up the activity by making the following points:
- The goal of starting the day with the Performance Management Quiz is to have you consider some important aspects of performance management and performance reviews, including the frequency of reviews or conversations, the role of the coach, who does the talking, and so forth.
- Be on the lookout for the "correct" answers and make notations as we move through today's material.

Learning Activity 30. Performance Reviews From the Dark and Light Sides

OBJECTIVES

The objectives of this learning activity are to
- enable participants to identify characteristics of performance reviews that either undermine or reinforce the provision of effective feedback and healthy performance conversations
- enable participants to identify specific actions and strategies that the coach can take to facilitate effective performance coaching conversations or performance reviews.

MATERIALS

The materials needed for this activity are
- Training Instrument 21: Performance Reviews From the Dark and Light Side
- PPT PowerPoint slide 9-9
- flipchart paper and markers.

TIME

🕐 30 minutes

PREPARATIONS

- Training instrument 21 should be ready for distribution.
- Prepare two flipchart pages, one titled "Reviews From the Dark Side" and the other titled "Reviews From the Light Side."

INSTRUCTIONS

1. Introduce this activity by noting to participants that as you begin the exploration of the face-to-face Performance Coaching Conversation, it might be instructive to tap into the collective experience in the room regarding what works and what clearly doesn't work about conducting performance reviews.
2. PPT Distribute **training instrument 21** as you display **slide 9-9**. Ask participants to first work by themselves in responding to the two experiences: one a "Dark Side" experience with performance reviews and the other a "Light Side," or positive, experience. Give them about three minutes to complete the instrument on their own.
3. After about three minutes, ask participants to turn to their table partners and discuss their response to the Dark and Light Side review experiences. Ask them to strive to identify a short list of five or six characteristics or factors that contributed to either a Dark or Light Side review. Give the groups about seven minutes to discuss and finalize their key characteristics list.
4. After about seven minutes, reconvene the large group and invite participants to first identify the common characteristics for the Dark Side review. Record these on the prepared flipchart page.
5. Next, turn to the other flipchart and record the Light Side characteristics. After both flipchart pages are complete and you have recorded all of the key characteristics of both the Dark and Light Sides, ask participants to identify the most important "take-away" from this exercise.

DEBRIEFING

Wrap up the activity by making the following points:
- Performance reviews get a bad reputation for a reason. They are often done in ways (that you have identified here) that undermine the very intention of the review, which is to increase the performer's commitment to the goals and work and to move performance to a new level.
- There is a better way to conduct reviews—an approach that builds upon many of the ideas that you have listed here under the Light Side. There are specific actions that both the coach and the performer can take that can significantly improve the quality and outcomes of traditional performance reviews.
- The transformational alternative to the traditional review that you will learn today—what we call the Performance Coaching Conversation and the Annual Performance Analysis and Planning Conversation—attempts to avoid the problems of the Dark Side review and embrace the strategies of the Light Side.

Learning Activity 31. Common Errors of Traditional Reviews

OBJECTIVES

The objectives of this learning activity are to
- enable participants to identify the common types of errors that occur in the traditional performance review
- engage participants in identifying ways to reduce these sources of error by preparing for and restructuring the way that performance coaching and performance review sessions are conducted.

MATERIALS

The materials needed for this activity are

- Handout 16: Tools for Documenting Performance (optional, as participants received this handout in a previous learning activity)
- Handout 22: Actions for Reducing Rating Errors
- Training Instrument 22: Common Errors in Performance Reviews
- Training Instrument 23: Actions to Reduce Errors in Performance Reviews
- PPT PowerPoint slides 9-10 through 9-12
- flipchart paper and markers.

TIME

25 minutes

PREPARATIONS

- Training instruments 22 and 23 and handout 22 should be ready for distribution.
- Handout 16 is optional for distribution (participants received this handout in a previous learning activity).
- Prepare two flipchart pages titled "Coach Actions for Reducing Errors" and "Employee Actions for Reducing Errors."
- Develop your own list of actions for reducing these common errors and be prepared to add these to the list that participants generate during the exercise.

INSTRUCTIONS

1. Transition from the previous learning activity by noting that one of the causes of a poor performance review is that the review or rating process itself is prone to errors. Indicate that in this activity participants will learn some of the most common errors in performance reviews and identify some specific actions that both the coach and the performer can take to reduce or eliminate these errors. Emphasize that because it is essential that a review accurately measures and discusses the employee's performance, an effective coach must work to reduce the possibility of its being wrong.
2. PPT Distribute **training instrument 22** as you display **slide 9-10**. Gradually click through each of the common review errors. With each error, give an example from your own experience of how and why the error occurs and its impact on the coach's final assessment of the employee's performance.
3. Ask participants if they have questions about any of these errors and their role in undermining the quality and accuracy of the traditional performance review. Redirect questions to other participants whenever possible and then offer your own answers to the questions raised.
4. PPT Distribute **training instrument 23** as you display **slide 9-11** and make the point that there are a variety of actions that a coach and a performer can take to reduce or eliminate many of these errors. Ask the table groups to take the next five minutes to identify specific coach and employee actions for reducing and eliminating these common errors.

continued on next page

Learning Activity 31. Common Errors of Traditional Reviews, *continued*

5. After about five minutes, reconvene the group and ask participants to first identify actions that a coach or supervisor can take to reduce these common errors. Record the suggested actions on the prepared flipchart page. Add your own suggestions to the participant-generated list on the flipchart. These might include such things as:
   a. have employees rate themselves
   b. conduct performance coaching conversations more frequently
   c. discuss performance issues as they occur rather than waiting until the review to raise them
   d. ensure that the coach reviews all performance dimensions, not just a few high profile or high impact areas
   e. work at relationship building with the performer long before the review occurs
   f. have clear performance standards and evaluate the performer against these standards rather than comparing him or her to other performers
   g. use objective measures of performance—measures that are not influenced by the coach's interpretation or bias
   h. to avoid both the recency and the halo/horn effect, document performance throughout the year and discuss each performance incident with the performer at the time of the documentation
   i. maintain a portfolio folder that holds examples of the employee's work throughout the performance period.

6. After completing the first flipchart, ask the groups to share actions that the performer could take to reduce these common errors. Record their responses on the prepared flipchart. Add your own suggestions to the participant-generated list. These suggestions might include such things as:
   a. the employee rates him or herself
   b. the employee identifies performance issues as they arise to ensure that the coach is aware of them
   c. the employee asks for more frequent coaching conversations
   d. the employee documents his or her own performance in formal ways—such as maintaining a portfolio of performance results throughout the year
   e. the employee develops performance measures in concert with the coach
   f. the employee develops a strong working relationship with the coach such that there is open, honest, and frequent communication.

7. [ ] Distribute **handout 22**, which contains the ideas that you shared with the group. Indicate that these are only a few ideas and that they should add to the list in this handout any idea from their group discussion or the flipchart lists that they find especially helpful.

8. [PPT] [ ] Display **slide 9-12**, reminding participants of the importance of formal methods for documenting performance throughout the performance period. Briefly summarize these approaches to documentation, reminding the participants that this topic was discussed in the workshop on Diagnosing Performance Problems and that they should reference **handout 16** for more information on these tools.

DEBRIEFING

Wrap up the activity by making the following points:
- Accuracy in assessing an employee's performance is critically important to the coach in order for him or her to be most effective in guiding the employee toward great performance.
- These seven common errors can all be reduced or eliminated if both the coach and the employee take proactive steps before and during the performance period to ensure that their performance coaching conversations focus on hard data of what the employee has accomplished.

Learning Activity 32. The Purposes of Performance Reviews

OBJECTIVES

The objectives of this learning activity are to
- engage participants in exploring the multiple purposes of the performance review
- identify the importance of "unbundling" these multiple purposes to ensure that these multiple purposes are accomplished within the Great Performance Management Cycle.

MATERIALS

The materials needed for this activity are
- Handout 23: The Purposes of Performance Reviews
- Handout 24: Reframing the Traditional Review
- Handout 25: Unbundling the Process
- 🖉 Training Instrument 24: Identifying the Purposes of Performance Reviews
- PPT PowerPoint slides 9-13 through 9-21 or slides 10-21 through 10-29
- flipchart paper and markers, if desired.

TIME

🕐 35 minutes

PREPARATIONS

- Training instrument 24 and handouts 23 and 24 should be ready for distribution.
- Prepare your own set of responses to the purposes of the review for each individual or group on training instrument 24. You should ensure that any formally defined purposes that the organization has established are incorporated into your list of purposes. You may also choose to document these formal purposes in a summary handout to distribute to participants at the end of the activity.

INSTRUCTIONS

1. PPT Display **slide 9-13** or **10-21** as you ask the group: *What is the purpose of the performance review?* Invite people to offer their responses to this question. You may hear such responses as:
   - to give feedback to the performer
   - to develop the performer's potential
   - to develop a performance improvement plan
   - to establish a basis for annual raises
   - to hold the person accountable for performance.

2. Honor the ideas people have offered. Note that, so far in this workshop, they have explored characteristics of effective and ineffective performance reviews, discussed some common rating errors in traditional performance reviews, and identified some actions that both the coach and performer can take to reduce these errors. Indicate that it's time for the group to identify the core purposes of the performance review. Suggest to the group that before introducing the core skills for conducting effective Performance Coaching Conversations, it is important to gain a better understanding of what we are trying to accomplish with them.

3. 🖉 PPT Distribute **training instrument 24** as you display **slide 9-14 or 10-22**. Assign each small group one of the individuals or groups from the instrument and ask them to work in their groups to identify the purpose, value, and importance of an effective review process for their assigned individual or group. Give the small groups approximately six minutes to complete this. Provide a time-check at about the half-way mark in the small group activity.

continued on next page

Learning Activity 32. The Purposes of Performance Reviews, *continued*

4. After about six minutes, reconvene the large group and work through participant ideas for each individual or group. As the groups report their ideas, encourage participants to fill in the noted purposes offered by each group. Honor and reinforce many of the critical purposes that the groups have identified.

5. PPT After the purposes of the review for each individual or group are identified, distribute **handout 23** as you display **slides 9-15 through 9-18** or **10-23 through 10-26**. Note that you have created two groups of purposes: one for the individual performer and coach level (summarized in slides 9-15 and 9-16 or 10-23 and 10-24) and one for the team, department, and organization level (summarized in slides 9-17 and 9-18 or 10-25 and 10-26). Ask participants if they have any questions about these two groupings of the goals of the performance reviews.

6. PPT Display **slide 9-19 or 10-27** as you distribute **handout 24**. Refer to the earlier learning activities on reviews from the Dark Side and problems with rating errors. The traditional review does not address the goals that have been discussed. Also, as noted in slide 9-19 or 10-27 and handout 24, it fails to address the problems on the left-hand side of the handout or achieve the higher purpose on the right-hand side.

7. PPT Suggest that, for this reason, it is critical that the review process be unbundled and dealt with through three separate but linked methods. Display **slide 9-20 or 10-28** and distribute **handout 25**. Provide a brief overview of the three methods and the associated goals of each.

8. PPT Display **slide 9-21 or 10-29**. Ask participants to review **handout 25** on their own and to note anything that isn't clear or anything that is particularly useful or helpful to them in reframing and unbundling the process. Give participants about three or four minutes to review this handout.

9. After about three or four minutes, reconvene the large group and ask people for their reactions and questions and to share anything that they found especially useful about the unbundling. Honor participant contributions and reinforce key points offered. Redirect questions to other participants first, and then offer your own responses.

DEBRIEFING

Wrap up the activity by making the following points:

- The traditional performance review is challenged in part because we expect too much of it. We have too many goals and outcomes that we are trying to accomplish through this single process.
- The key to solving this "one size fits all" problem is to "unbundle" the process and separate out Critical Incident Coaching Conversations and Performance Coaching Conversations from the formal review process and form.
- The focus of Performance Coaching Conversations is to move the employee toward great performance, strengthen employee commitment to the job and the organization, and build a strong partnership for performance with the coach.
- The focus of the traditional performance review is on completing the required forms, rating performance dimensions and overall performance, and linking performance to specific individual and organizational outcomes.

Learning Activity 33. The Great Performance Management Cycle and the Performance Coaching Conversation

OBJECTIVES

The objectives of this learning activity are to
- remind participants of the GPM Cycle and its employee-centered process
- identify the roles that both the Performance Coaching Conversation and the Annual Performance Analysis and Planning Conversation play within this cycle.

MATERIALS

The materials needed for this activity are

- [ ] Handout 14: The Great Performance Management Cycle (optional, as participants likely received this handout in earlier workshops)

- PPT PowerPoint slide 9-22

- flipchart paper and markers, if desired.

TIME

10 minutes

PREPARATIONS

- Participants should already have handout 14, which was shared with them in the Developing a Coaching Relationship Workshop.

INSTRUCTIONS

1. PPT [ ] Display **slide 9-22** and remind participants of the key steps of the Great Performance Management Cycle. If desired, refer to **handout 14** to go over details about each step of this important process. Emphasize the importance of defining great performance and then briefly walk through each of the following steps of the process.
2. Click on the slide to reveal the "Performance Coaching Conversation" animation, how it links to each of the steps of the GPM Cycle, the sources for defining great performance, and the reinforcing loop of providing logical consequences for performance.
3. Emphasize that the Performance Coaching Conversation is designed to be the major method for engaging an employee within the GPM Cycle and in the pursuit of great performance.
4. Suggest that Performance Coaching Conversations need to occur frequently within the GPM Cycle to ensure that the performer stays on track throughout the performance period and, most importantly, that the coach stays involved in the employee's progress toward his or her goals.
5. Indicate that the Annual Performance Analysis and Planning Conversation plays the same role within the GPM Cycle as the more frequent Performance Coaching Conversations, but with a slightly different focus. Indicate that the differences between the Performance Coaching Conversations and the Annual Performance Analysis and Planning Conversation will be explored later in today's workshop.

DEBRIEFING

Wrap up the activity by making the following point:
- The GPM Cycle is the focus for all Performance Coaching Conversations and the Annual Performance Analysis and Planning Conversation. This employee-centered process is the foundation upon which the coach and the employee forge a strong partnership for performance.

Learning Activity 34. Active Listening and the Values, Assumptions, and Behaviors of the Mutual Learning Mindset

OBJECTIVES

The objectives of this learning activity are to
- introduce the skills of whole body and active listening using the mutual learning mindset and within the Performance Coaching Conversations and the Annual Performance Analysis and Planning Conversation
- practice active listening.

MATERIALS

The materials needed for this activity are

- Handout 8: Unilateral Control and Mutual Learning Mindsets (optional, as participants likely received this handout in earlier workshops)
- Handout 9: Values and Behaviors for Mutual Learning (optional, as participants likely received this handout in earlier workshops)
- Handout 26: Whole Body Listening
- Handout 27: The Four Behaviors of Active Listening
- Training Instrument 25: Active Listening Application

- PPT PowerPoint slides 9-23 through 9-27

- flipchart paper and markers, if desired.

TIME

🕐 45 minutes

PREPARATIONS

- Participants should already have handouts 8 and 9, which were shared with them in the Developing a Coaching Relationship Workshop.
- Handouts 26 and 27 and training instrument 25 should be ready for distribution.

INSTRUCTIONS

1. Transition into this activity by letting the participants know that they will soon learn about the transformational Performance Coaching Conversation and the Annual Performance Analysis and Planning Conversation. Indicate that before learning more about the structure of these coaching conversations, you'd like them to focus on a skill that is fundamental to their success and to the coach's ability to bring a mutual learning mindset into his or her performance partnerships. This is the skill of active listening.
2. PPT ⬜ Display **slide 9-23** as you emphasize that active listening takes place within the larger framework of the mutual learning mindset. Call attention to Enacting Behaviors within the mindset and note that listening plays a central role throughout. Refer to the second page of **handout 8** and the governing values and enacting behaviors on **handout 9**. Stress that all of the active listening done by a coach is done based on the pursuit of the governing values of valid information, free and informed choice, personal commitment to decisions made, empathy, and transparency.
3. PPT ⬜ Display **slide 9-24** and distribute **handout 26**. Walk participants through the 10 characteristics of whole body listening. Give examples whenever possible to demonstrate each whole body listening characteristic (for example, *We have one mouth and two ears for a reason: We should talk half as much as we listen—and its starts by simply stopping talking!*). Ask participants if they have any questions about what whole body listening is and why it's important. Stress that the objective of whole body listening is to surface and explore the assumptions, reasoning, and intents of the other person and, based on what is heard, extract the true meaning of what the speaker is saying.

continued on next page

Learning Activity 34. Active Listening and the Values, Assumptions, and Behaviors of the Mutual Learning Mindset, *continued*

4. **PPT** 🗐 Indicate that whole body listening comprises four active listening skills. Display **slide 9-25** as you distribute **handout 27**. Walk participants through a high level overview of the four skills. Use your own examples whenever possible to deepen participant understanding. Note that all four skills utilize the enacting behaviors of the mutual learning mindset and, as a result, are essential to the effectiveness of a coach as he or she works with a performer.

5. Summarize these four skills in the following way: Drawing out and clarifying involve gathering valid information and data from the employee, whereas reflecting and paraphrasing involve verifying what the listener has heard with the speaker to ensure that true understanding of the speaker's meaning has been achieved. Ask participants if they have any questions about these four skills. Answer those that you can by providing additional examples of how a skill might be used. Demonstrate any of the four skills if requested by participants.

6. 🔗 **PPT** Distribute **training instrument 25** as you display **slide 9-26**. State that for the next 30 minutes or so they will have the opportunity to practice each of these four skills as well as the overall skill of whole body listening.

7. 🔗 Tell participants that they should follow the instructions on **training instrument 25**. Ask them to get into groups of three people. Inform them that there will be three rounds and that each member of their trio will take turns playing the listener, the speaker, and the observer.

8. Once everyone is in a group of three, give directions for the first round: Ask one person in the trio to be the speaker, another the listener, and the third person the observer. Indicate to the participants that the speaker in each group is to talk about something that is real, important, and somewhat unresolved for them. Ask the listeners to use whole body listening, the four active listening skills, and the mutual learning mindset as they listen. Ask the observers to focus their attention on how the listener listens, and, using the observer's notes section on the second page, to be prepared to give feedback to the listener at the conclusion of the first round. Indicate that each round will last approximately seven minutes. Encourage the trios to move their chairs and position themselves in such a way as to maximize whole body listening. Answer any questions about the process and then direct the trios to begin. Give a time-check at about the half-way mark in the first round.

9. Call time for the first round. Ask the observers in each trio to lead the debriefing process. Encourage them to follow the order for this debriefing as listed under the Observer's Role: the listener first debriefs his or her own effectiveness as a listener, then the speaker gives his or her observations, and finally the observer gives his or her feedback. Allow about four or five minutes for debriefing round one.

10. Ask participants to rotate their roles for the next two rounds. Use a similar process for rounds two and three—including a five minute debrief after each.

11. 👁 **PPT** Following the third round's debrief, reconvene the large group and call for reactions. Display **slide 9-27**. Ask all or some of the following questions:

   • *What went well with your use of whole body and active listening skills?*
   • *What didn't go as well? What skills were more difficult or awkward?* [*Note:* participants will often say that reflecting and paraphrasing seem formulaic and contrived. Acknowledge that it can sometimes be a challenge to essentially repeat back what we have heard without being patronizing. Ask: *Why is it still important that we find a way to do this?* The reason, of course, is that these two "awkward" skills are the only means for verifying that what we heard is what the person intended us to hear. It enables us to truly understand what the other person has said. If participants want suggested alternative ways to reflect or paraphrase, ask other participants to suggest some language, and then offer your own ideas.]
   • *What did you learn about yourself?*
   • *How many of you, as listeners, found yourselves trying to solve the problem or offer advice?* [Acknowledge that this is normal, but that they must work hard to resist this temptation. Remind them that their goal is to extract meaning from the speaker—not offer their sage advice!]
   • *How did it feel, as a speaker, to really be listened to?*

12. Facilitate a discussion in response to many or all of these questions, noting the power that listening has to validate another person's experience and even, in some cases, their worth—just by paying attention. Note that active listening is not therapy, but being heard—perhaps for the first time in weeks—is indeed very therapeutic! Note how it felt to be

continued on next page

Learning Activity 34. Active Listening and the Values, Assumptions, and Behaviors of the Mutual Learning Mindset, *continued*

listened to by another person. Suggest to them that these four active listening skills—informed by the mutual learning mindset—are perhaps the most important skills that they can master as a coach.

DEBRIEFING

Wrap up the activity by making the following points:

- Active listening enables the listener to hear the perspective of another person, and the skills of active listening—drawing out, clarifying, reflecting, and paraphrasing—open a window to understanding and appreciation that are central to mutual learning.
- The mutual learning mindset is the foundation of these active listening skills. The goal of listening within the performance partnership of the coach and the employee is not just hearing what is said, but also developing understanding and empathy for one another's perspective. When we have understanding and empathy, mutual learning becomes possible, a strong performance partnership results, and great performance can be achieved.

Learning Activity 35. The Performance Coaching Conversation and the Annual Performance Analysis and Planning Conversation

OBJECTIVES

The objectives of this learning activity are to
- introduce the methodology of the Performance Coaching Conversation and the Annual Performance Analysis and Planning Conversation
- enable participants to explore modifications to the conversation to better meet their requirements
- emphasize the importance of conducting frequent and ongoing Performance Coaching Conversations.

MATERIALS

The materials needed for this activity are
- Handout 28: The Performance Coaching Conversation
- Handout 29: Evolutionary vs. Revolutionary Performance Management
- PPT PowerPoint slides 9-28 through 9-30 or 10-30 through 10-32
- flipchart paper and markers, if desired.

TIME

🕐 40 minutes

PREPARATIONS

- You should revisit chapter 2 of this book and study handout 24 so that you know the process thoroughly. Discuss the handout with trusted peers in human resources or elsewhere and anticipate likely questions from participants. Be prepared to give examples of how various parts of the conversation might flow in a face-to-face interaction between a coach and an employee.
- Handout 28 should be ready for distribution.

INSTRUCTIONS

1. This activity strives to integrate all of what the participants have learned, from the roles of the coach, to the Great Performance Management Cycle, the mutual learning mindset and its associated values and behaviors, and active listening. The Performance Coaching Conversation and the Annual Performance Analysis and Planning Conversation are introduced in this activity to give coaches a step-by-step process of preparing for and successfully conducting an effective one-on-one conversation with each of the performers on their team.
2. The purpose of these Performance Coaching Conversations is to develop understanding, strengthen the performance partnership, and move the employee's efforts toward great performance.
3. PPT Display **slide 9-28 or 10-30** as you distribute **handout 28**. Highlight that there are five phases to the conversation. Click through each of the five phases, mentioning briefly what happens within each one.
4. PPT Indicate that you would like them to take the next 10 minutes or so to read through this process and develop an understanding of the general structure and flow of both preparing for and conducting the conversation. Display **slide 9-29 or 10-31** and ask them to reflect on these questions as they review the conversation handout. Reiterate that they will have about 10 minutes to read the handout and consider the questions on slide 9-29 or 10-31. Provide a time-check at about the half-way mark. Gauge how much additional time people may require by observing the progress that a variety of individuals are making through the handout.
5. PPT After about 10 minutes, ask participants to discuss their reactions to the Performance Coaching Conversation model and the questions on **slide 9-29 or 10-31** in their small groups. Give the groups about eight minutes for this discussion.
6. 🗣 PPT After about eight minutes, reconvene the large group and ask the groups to report the results from their discussions. Walk through the questions on **slide 9-29** or **10-31** as you solicit reactions, comments, and questions from participants.

continued on next page

Learning Activity 35. The Performance Coaching Conversation and the Annual Performance Analysis and Planning Conversation, *continued*

7. Ask participants why the coach encourages the employee to go first in this process. Encourage a discussion before making your concluding remarks on this issue. State that the employee is responsible for his or her own performance within the GPM Cycle and that, by asking the employee to go first, the coach is encouraging a thoughtful self-assessment. Suggest that if the coach were to present his or her analysis first—which the coach could certainly do if that's what the employee prefers—the employee's own analysis might be eclipsed by the coach's perspective. Further, indicate that if the coach's view contains constructive feedback, the employee may become defensive rather than adopt a mutual learning mindset. Conclude by emphasizing that by having the employee go first, the coach strengthens employee ownership for his or her own performance and reduces the possibility of the employee becoming defensive. Note that, within this framework, the employee should do most of the talking—suggest from 70 to 90 percent of the time—depending on the issues that the employee and the coach are exploring together.

8. Note that this core process is used for both the frequent Performance Coaching Conversations that they should be having with their direct reports as well as for the foundation of their Annual Performance Analysis and Planning Conversations. Call attention to the value of completing a preliminary performance review form prior to the conversation and the value of completing the review form following the conversation based on what is learned during the conversation.

9. Ask participants why completing the form shouldn't be done at the time of the conversation. Agree with the responses as much as possible and note that their goal is to prevent the form and the rating that they give the employee from getting in the way of the performance conversation. Note that this same principle applies in respect to discussion of the salary implications of their performance ratings. Suggest that these too need to be discussed at least one day after the Performance Coaching Conversation, specifically to keep the focus of the conversation on learning, growth, and improvement.

10. Finally, ask participants how frequently Performance Coaching Conversations should be conducted with an employee and who should initiate a coaching conversation. Hear responses to these two questions. Verify those that reinforce the points you want to make. Suggest that both the coach and the employee can initiate a coaching conversation. If either believes that a conversation would be useful, then the conversation happens. State that, in general, the issue of frequency depends on competence and confidence levels of the performer, the performance progress or problems that the employee is experiencing, and the coaching role that the coach has chosen for this employee. Coaching conversations can occur based on fixed calendar dates, specific performance incidents that need to be discussed, or either party suggesting that it would be good to chat about performance. Conclude this point by suggesting that the more formal *annual* conversation should occur at least once each year—and perhaps more often based on performance—and that the less formal Performance Coaching Conversations should occur as needed, with the coach and the employee mutually deciding upon an appropriate frequency.

11. Suggest to participants that following a specific employee performance problem, event, or incident, a coaching conversation should occur right away rather than waiting even for the more frequently occurring Performance Coaching Conversation. In these circumstances, the coach intervenes immediately to provide feedback to the performer on the incident, clarify or redefine performance expectations, explore causes of the incident, and discuss corrective actions that the employee might take. Note that, in these circumstances, the coach uses the mutual learning mindset to explore the employee's point of view of what just occurred, its causes, and possible actions by the employee and the coach to bring performance results back into alignment with expectations. Indicate that these "on the spot" coaching conversations, although less formal and structured than as spelled out in **handout 28**, should still be employee-centered and focus on positive performance improvement goals.

12. Stress that these "on the spot" coaching conversations should happen as close to the performance incident and results as possible to ensure that the actions, behaviors, and results of the performer are easily recalled. Suggest that these critical incident coaching conversations are subsequently discussed in the more formal Performance Coaching Conversations and the Annual Performance Analysis and Planning Conversation.

13. PPT ⬜ Display **slide 9-30 or 10-32** as you distribute **handout 29**. Note that the traditional once-a-year performance review, represented by John's performance line, helps boost performance following the review, but that,

continued on next page

Learning Activity 35. The Performance Coaching Conversation and the Annual Performance Analysis and Planning Conversation, *continued*

    between reviews, there may be few occasions when performance improves on its own. This "revolutionary" approach to reviews calls for a significant improvement once a year, but tends to ignore performance in the months in between.

14. Call attention to the "evolutionary" approach, represented by the rapidly rising performance curve for Susan. Note that the incremental improvements and adjustments throughout the year enable the performer to self-correct and continually improve results. Suggest that this evolutionary approach is due to the frequent Performance Coaching Conversations that occur as scheduled or whenever necessary in response to specific performance events. The goal of the evolutionary approach to performance management is ongoing continuous improvement—with the employee taking the lead. Note that the Annual Performance Analysis and Planning Conversation occurs on key dates established for the formal review process. Suggest that some organizations may choose to make this formal process happen two or three times a year to ensure that their managers are actively managing performance.

15. State as well that if the formal process remains an annual one for the organization as a whole, for some performers, the Annual Performance Analysis and Planning Conversation may need to happen two or three times a year—driven by the need for certain employees to accelerate more quickly toward meeting expectations.

DEBRIEFING

Wrap up the activity by making the following points:

- The Performance Coaching Conversation offers a transformational approach for guiding the performance discussion with an employee. By inviting the employee to take the lead in his or her own self-assessment and then encouraging the employee to take the lead in presenting his or her own analysis and action plans, the conversation puts employees at the center of their performance review.
- The Performance Coaching Conversation should be conducted as frequently as required to provide an employee the direction and support that he or she needs. These conversations can be initiated by the coach or by the employee and in response to specific performance events or according to a set schedule.
- The Annual Performance Analysis and Planning Conversation provides an opportunity to complete a more formal review process *following* the Performance Coaching Conversation. Key performance evaluation forms are completed and discussed at a follow-up meeting to the initial conversation.

Learning Activity 36. The Performance Coaching Conversation—Behavior Modeling

OBJECTIVES

The objectives of this learning activity are to
- demonstrate how to facilitate the Performance Coaching Conversation
- enable participants to develop a practical understanding of how the conversation flows.

MATERIALS

The materials needed for this activity are
- ☐ Handout 28: The Performance Coaching Conversation

- PowerPoint slide 9-31

- flipchart paper and markers, if desired.

TIME

🕐 35 minutes

PREPARATIONS

- Participants should already have handout 28, which was shared in the previous activity.
- As with the previous activity, you should revisit chapter 2 of this book and thoroughly study and understand the structure and flow of the Performance Coaching Conversation. Because you will be modeling the conversation in front of the group, it is essential that, prior to the workshop, you role play the process with another person who knows the process almost as well. Encourage your sparring partner to challenge you throughout the conversation. It is essential that you maintain the mutual learning mindset throughout the role-play, which is demonstrated by being genuinely curious and empathetic, listening actively, gathering valid data, testing assumptions, suspending judgments, and so forth.
- You will need a volunteer from the group—or someone from outside the training session—who is willing to play the role of the employee in this scenario. The benefit to using someone outside the group is that you can rehearse key issues to be explored during the coaching conversation.
- Finally, you will need to invent or create at least an outline of a realistic scenario that describes a performance situation with an employee that you will use during the role-play. A detailed write-up is not required if both you and the volunteer are comfortable inventing or creating issues and ideas as you go. This scenario is made easier if you can work through the conversation with your partner prior to the workshop. It is also critically important that you know what your goal, as a coach, is in this scenario. Don't start the coaching conversation role play without knowing what you want to accomplish as a coach with this fictitious employee.

INSTRUCTIONS

1. Transition from the previous activity by acknowledging that the Performance Coaching Conversation might at first seem intimidating because there is a lot to remember. Indicate that you'd like to model an example Performance Coaching Conversation in front of the group. Note that your goal is to let them see how the actual conversation might flow in a real interaction. Encourage them to think through what they would actually say and do in the situation that you play out for them, especially because they will be role playing the process in the next activity.
2. Set up the role-play situation by introducing your partner (especially if your partner is from outside the group) and providing some general background on the situation.
3. Before you begin, make a point of saying that, as in a real conversation, the unexpected will always happen and that, while you will try to do the right thing when and if this occurs, you may slip up and say the wrong thing.
4. PPT Display **slide 9-31**. Encourage the group to be aware of what you are saying that works and what doesn't and how you respond when the unexpected happens. Ask them to consider how they themselves might respond at various

continued on next page

Learning Activity 36. The Performance Coaching Conversation—Behavior Modeling, *continued*

times during the role-play. Indicate that you may stop the role-play at various times to ask the group to comment on what just happened or to explain your reasoning in doing or saying specific things.

5. ☐ Refer to **handout 28**. Direct participants to focus on the beginning "script" in Part C of the handout. Begin the role-play. Try to follow the "script" beginning in Part C of the conversation. Stop occasionally when something goes wrong and ask the group what happened and their ideas on how to respond. You can also stop the role-play when you want to explain or emphasize a key point that the group should understand. For variation, invite someone from the group to take your place and try their hand at role-playing part of the conversation. Make sure that you "rescue" them when appropriate and step back into the role play if it seems appropriate. If desired, stop and replay the various parts of conversation to work through a difficult spot or to offer another way to respond to the employee's comments.

6. After you complete the role-play, commend your volunteer for doing such a great job. Ask the larger group to comment on and react to the role-play. Ask them to consider such questions as:
   - *What did I do that seemed to go well?*
   - *Would you have done anything differently from what I did at various times? When and what would you do?*
   - *Do you have a better sense now of the flow of the conversation?*
   - *Are you ready to do this yourself?*

DEBRIEFING

Wrap up the activity by making the following points:
- Navigating the Performance Coaching Conversation for the first time can be challenging. There is a lot to remember. That's why it's important that coaches are deeply familiar with the process and that they actually role-play one or two conversations with someone who can give them feedback before they try this new approach with their employees.
- Note that even if they don't role-play a specific Performance Coaching Conversation in advance to become more familiar with the process, if they bring a mutual learning mindset into their existing Performance Coaching Conversations, they will benefit. Encourage the participants to at least practice their active listening skills and the other enacting behaviors of the mutual learning mindset.

Learning Activity 37. Practicing the Performance Coaching Conversation—Participant Role Plays

OBJECTIVES

The objective of this learning activity is to
- enable participants to practice navigating the Performance Coaching Conversation.

MATERIALS

The materials needed for this activity are
- 📄 Handout 28: The Performance Coaching Conversation

- Training Instrument 12: Performance Planning and Development Worksheet

- PPT PowerPoint slides 9-32 and 9-33

- flipchart paper and markers, if desired.

TIME

⏱ 50 minutes

PREPARATIONS

- Participants should already have handout 28, which was shared in the previous activity.
- Participants should have the partially completed training instrument 12, the Performance Planning and Development Worksheet.

INSTRUCTIONS

1. Transition from the previous activity by suggesting that it's now time for them to try their hand at navigating the Performance Coaching Conversation.
2. 🔗 Ask participants to locate **training instrument 12**, the Performance Planning and Development Worksheet. Note that in previous workshops they have completed sections A through F of this worksheet as they reflected upon the performance of one of their direct reports. Tell them that in this activity they will translate the performance goals that they identified on this worksheet into a coaching conversation with this employee.
3. 📄 Ask participants to locate **handout 28**. Suggest to them that they can use the sample language that begins in Part C to start their coaching role play. Ask participants to find a partner in the room. This partner could be someone who knows of this performance situation very well or not at all. Give the group a couple of minutes to locate someone with whom to role-play their respective situation.
4. 📄 Note that there will be two role-play rounds. One of them will play the role of the coach and the other will play the role of employee in round one. After a debriefing, round two will begin with the roles reversed. Encourage the coaches to have **handout 28** available for reference and to not be afraid of referring to it often as they move through the conversation. Tell them that they should begin the coaching interview with the opening script in Part C, page 3, of the handout.
5. Before starting round one, ask the designated coach to spend the next five minutes reviewing, with the "employee," the improvement areas from Parts A, B, and C of the worksheet and the performance goals identified in Parts E and F. The person playing the role of the employee should generally understand the broad outlines of the position and some of the performance improvement goals identified by the coach. After about five minutes, call time and ask the coach to begin the coaching conversation with the employee. Tell them that they have about 10 minutes to role-play their coaching conversation. Give a time-check at about the half-way mark.
6. PPT After about 10 minutes, call time. Display **slide 9-32** and ask the coach to debrief his or her performance first and then have the "employee" provide feedback on what worked and what didn't work. Give participants about five minutes for the debriefing.

continued on next page

Learning Activity 37. Practicing the Performance Coaching Conversation—Participant Role Plays, *continued*

7. Ask the partners to now switch roles for round two. Use the same process. Tell them that, as with round one, they will have five minutes to brief the "employee" on the situation and about 10 minutes to role-play this new coaching conversation. Give a time-check at about the half-way mark.

8. **PPT** After about 10 minutes, call time. Refer to **slide 9-32** again and again ask the coach to debrief his or her performance first and then have the "employee" provide feedback on what worked and what didn't work. Give participants about five minutes for the debriefing.

9. After the second round's debriefing, reconvene the larger group and ask for their general reactions.
   - *What went well with your conversations?*
   - *What didn't go well?*
   - *What would you do differently if you could do it over again?*
   - *Do you have a better sense now—after trying it yourself—of the flow of the conversation?*
   - *Are you ready to do this yourself in the real world?*

10. End this activity by commending them for being willing to role-play the Performance Coaching Conversation. Acknowledge the difficulty of understanding and mastering a new process. Encourage them to begin trying out the process in small steps, using active listening and integrating the mutual learning mindset and its enacting behaviors.

11. **PPT** Display **slide 9-33**. Ask participants what the Deming quote means to them. Respond to and agree with the comments offered and add your own interpretation: If we want our employees to tell us the truth, then we need to create an environment that is free of fear. When we use the mutual learning mindset and are genuinely curious and interested in their perspective, we will hear what we need to hear in order to help our employees move toward great performance.

DEBRIEFING

Wrap up the activity by making the following points:
- The Performance Coaching Conversation model presents a transformational approach for engaging our employees in taking responsibility for their own performance. Through these frequent conversations, both the employee and coach will learn what they need to learn to enable great performance through their mutual efforts.
- Please feel free to call on me if you are struggling with ways to use the tools you have learned throughout this series, most especially the Performance Coaching Conversation. I am here to offer suggestions and insights to help you move your performers to the next level.

Learning Activity 38. The Organization's Expectations and Obligations for Documenting Performance Conversations

OBJECTIVES

The objective of this learning activity is to
- review the organization's expectations and processes for documenting the annual performance review
- link the Great Performance Management Cycle, the Performance Coaching Conversation, and the Annual Performance Analysis and Planning Conversation learned in this workshop and throughout the entire series to the organization's formal performance review processes and forms.

MATERIALS

The materials needed for this activity are
- documents related to your organization's formal performance review process—including forms, worksheets, key dates for completing reviews, and so forth
- PowerPoint slides 9-34 or 10-33 and others, as necessary, to lead the group through a discussion of the organizations performance review processes and forms
- flipchart paper and markers, if desired.

TIME

🕐 40 minutes

PREPARATIONS

- Any documents and forms describing or used within the organization's performance review processes should be ready for distribution.
- The director of human resources should work with you in preparing for this session and should attend this session to listen to participant questions and respond to issues as they arise.

INSTRUCTIONS

1. Transition from the previous activity by indicating that the organization has specific expectations for how the formal performance review process should work.
2. **PPT** This activity should involve presenting the materials for review and then asking participants to come up with questions about the review expectations in small groups, followed by questions and answers regarding the expectations for this process. Display **slides 9-34** or **10-33** (and others as appropriate to your organization) as you describe your organization's performance review process and expectations.
3. The human resources director can also play a role in the workshop by responding to questions, recording unanswered questions, and agreeing to follow up with individuals or the group as a whole on specific issues.

DEBRIEFING

Wrap up the activity by making the following point:
- The Performance Coaching Conversation model presented in today's workshop has an important role to play in the formal performance review process discussed in this activity. It is up to you to bring the Performance Coaching Conversation and the mutual learning mindset into the more formal process to ensure that your employees understand what is expected of them and feel supported in moving toward achieving their Great Performance Outcomes.

For Further Reading

Adult Learning and Training Program Design/Evaluation

ASTD. *ASTD Handbook for Workplace Learning Professionals.* Alexandria, Virginia: ASTD Press, 2008.

ASTD. *ASTD Trainer's Toolkit: Evaluation Instruments.* Alexandria, Virginia: ASTD Press, 1991.

Biech, Elaine. *ASTD's Ultimate Train-the-Trainer: A Complete Guide to Training Success.* Alexandria, Virginia: ASTD Press, 2009.

Broad, Mary, and John Newstrom. *Transfer of Training.* Reading, Massachusetts: Addison-Wesley, 1992.

Brookfield, Stephen D. *Understanding and Facilitating Adult Learning.* San Francisco: Jossey-Bass, 1991.

Carliner, Saul. *Training Design Basics.* Alexandria, Virginia: ASTD Press, 2003.

Eitington, Julius E. *The Winning Trainer*, 3rd edition. Houston, Texas: Gulf, 1996.

Hodell, Chuck. *ISD From the Ground Up: A No-Nonsense Approach to Instructional Design.* Alexandria, Virginia: ASTD Press, 2007.

Kirkpatrick, D. L. *Evaluating Training Programs: The Four Levels*, 2nd edition. San Francisco: Berrett-Koehler, 1994.

McArdle, Geri. *Training Design and Delivery: A Guide for Every Trainer, Training Manager, and Occasional Trainer,* 2nd edition. Alexandria, Virginia: ASTD Press, 2007.

Phillips, Jack, and Patricia Pulliam Phillips. *Beyond Learning Objectives: Develop Measurable Objectives That Link to the Bottom Line.* Alexandria, Virginia: ASTD Press, 2008.

———. *ROI at Work.* Alexandria, Virginia: ASTD Press, 2005.

Phillips, Jack, and Ron Stone. *How to Measure Training Results.* Alexandria, VA: ASTD Press, 2002.

Phillips, Jack. *Return on Investment in Training and Performance Improvement Programs: A Step-By-Step Manual for Calculating the Financial Return on Investment*, 2nd edition. Burlington, Massachusetts: Butterworth-Heinemann, Gulf Professional, 2003.

Phillips, Patricia Pulliam. *Return on Investment Basics.* Alexandria, Virginia: ASTD Press, 2006.

Stolovitch, Harold D., and Erica J. Keeps. *Telling Ain't Training.* Alexandria, Virginia: ASTD Press, 2001.

Renner, Peter Franz. *The Instructor's Survival Kit: A Handbook for Teachers and Adults*, 2nd edition. Vancouver, B.C., Canada: Training Associates, 1989.

Rothwell, William J. *Adult Learning Basics.* Alexandria, Virginia: ASTD Press, 2008.

Russell, Lou. *The Accelerated Learning Fieldbook.* San Francisco: Jossey-Bass/Pfeiffer, 1999.

Performance Management and Performance Reviews

Bacal, Robert. *How to Manage Performance: 24 Lessons for Improving Performance.* New York: McGraw-Hill Companies, 2004.

———. *The Manager's Guide to Performance Reviews.* New York: McGraw-Hill, 2004.

Bianco-Mathis, Virginia, Cynthia Roman, and Lisa Nabors. *Organizational Coaching: Building Relationships and Programs That Drive Results.* Alexandria, Virginia: ASTD Press, 2008.

Falcone, Paul, and Wandi Sachs. *Productive Performance Appraisals*, 2nd edition. New York: American Management Association, 2007.

Falcone, Paul. *2600 Phrases for Effective Performance Reviews: Ready-to-Use Words and Phrases That Really Get Results*. New York: American Management Association, 2005.

Harvard Business Review. *Harvard Business Review on Appraising Employee Performance*. Cambridge, Massachusetts: Harvard Business School Press, 2005.

Langdon, Ken, and Christina Osborne. *Essential Managers: Performance Reviews*. Middlesex, United Kingdom: Doring Kindersley, 2001.

Lee, Christopher D. *Performance Conversations: An Alternative Approach to Appraisals*. Tucson, Arizona: Fenestra Books, 2006.

Maurer, Rick. *Feedback Toolkit: 16 Tools for Better Communication in the Workplace*. Portland, Washington: Productivity Press, 1994.

Oberstein, Sophie. *10 Steps to Successful Coaching*. Alexandria, Virginia: ASTD Press, Co-Published with Berrett-Koehler Publishers, 2009.

Willmore, Joe. *No Magic Bullet: Seven Steps to Better Performance*. Alexandria, Virginia: ASTD Press, 2009.

General Organizational Management and Development

Argyris, Chris. *Knowledge for Action: A Guide to Overcoming Barriers to Organizational Change*. San Francisco: Jossey-Bass, 1993.

Argyris, Chris, Robert Putnam, and Diana McLain Smith. *Action Science*. San Francisco: Jossey-Bass, 1985.

Argyris, Chris, and Donald Schön. *Theory in Practice*. San Francisco: Jossey-Bass, 1974.

Burley-Allen, Madelyn. *Managing Assertively: A Self-Teaching Guide*. New York: John Wiley and Sons, 1995.

Deming, W. Edwards. *Out of the Crisis*. Cambridge, Massachusetts: Massachusetts Institute of Technology Press, 1989.

Fisher, Roger, William L. Ury, and Bruce Patton. *Getting to Yes: Negotiating Agreement Without Giving In*, 2nd edition. New York: Houghton Mifflin Harcourt, 1991.

Gerard, Glenna, and Linda Ellinor. *Dialogue at Work: Skills at Leveraging Collective Understanding*. Waltham, Massachusetts: Pegasus Communications, 2001.

Isaacs, William. *Dialogue and the Art of Thinking Together*. New York: Doubleday, 1999.

Kohn, Alfie. *Punished by Rewards: The Trouble With Gold Stars, Incentive Plans, A's, Praise, and Other Bribes*. New York: Houghton Mifflin Company, 1993.

Kouzes, James M., and Barry Z. Posner. *The Leadership Challenge*, 4th edition. San Francisco: Jossey-Bass, 2007.

Miller, John G. *QBC! The Question Behind the Question: What to Really Ask Yourself*. Denver, Colorado: Denver Press, 2001.

Patterson, Kerry, Joseph Grenny, Ron McMillan, and Al Switzler. *Crucial Conversations: Tools for Talking When Stakes Are High*. New York: McGraw-Hill, 2002.

Patterson, Kerry, Joseph Grenny, Ron McMillan, and Al Switzler. *Crucial Confrontations: Tools for Resolving Broken Promises, Violated Expectations, and Bad Behavior*. New York: McGraw-Hill, 2005.

Ryan, Kathleen D., and Daniel K. Oestreich. *Driving Fear Out of the Workplace*. San Francisco: Jossey-Bass, 1991.

Schwarz, Roger. *The Skilled Facilitator (New and Revised)*. San Francisco: Jossey-Bass, 2002.

Scott, Susan. *Fierce Conversations: Achieving Success at Work and in Life One Conversation at a Time.* New York: Berkley, 2004.

Ury, William. *Getting Past No: Negotiating Your Way From Confrontation to Cooperation*. New York: Bantam Books, 1993.

Other

Locke, Edwin, and Gary Latham, "Building a Practically Useful Theory of Goal Setting and Task Motivation," American Psychologist (2002), volume 57, number 9, p. 707.

Thorndike, E. L. "A constant error on psychological rating." *Journal of Applied Psychology, IV* (1920): 25–29.

Van Der Zee, Han. *Measuring the Value of Information Technology*. Hershey, Pennsylvania: IRM Press, 2003, 5.

West, Thomas G., and Grace Starry West (ed. and trans.). *Four Texts on Socrates: Plato's Euthyphro, Apology, and Crito and Aristophanes' Clouds*. Ithaca, New York: Cornell University Press, 1998.

About the Authors

Jeffrey and Linda Russell are founders and co-directors of Russell Consulting, Inc., headquartered in Madison, Wisconsin (www.RussellConsultingInc.com). For more than 20 years, Russell Consulting has provided consulting and training services in leadership, strategic thinking and planning, leading change, employee quality of worklife surveys, organizational development, performance coaching, and performance management. Their diverse list of clients includes *Fortune* 500 companies, small businesses, social or nonprofit organizations, and government agencies.

Jeff's bachelor of arts in humanism and cultural change and master of arts in industrial relations are both from the University of Wisconsin. He serves as an adjunct faculty member for the University of Wisconsin—teaching for the Small Business Development Center, the Wisconsin Certified Public Manager Program, and a number of other certification programs with University of Wisconsin campuses. Jeff is a frequent presenter at local, state, regional, and international conferences.

Linda's bachelor of arts is in social work from the University of Wisconsin. She has completed graduate work in rehabilitation counseling, also at the University of Wisconsin. Linda specializes in designing and implementing job engagement and quality of worklife surveys and in facilitating team and organizational development interventions.

Jeff and Linda together have authored six additional books, including *Leading Change Training* (ASTD Press, 2003), *Strategic Planning Training* (ASTD Press, 2005), and *Change Basics* (ASTD Press, 2006). They publish *Workplace Enhancement Notes,* a journal of tips for leading organizations.

Within their vision to help create and sustain great organizations, Russell Consulting, Inc., integrates theory, research, and "real-world" experience in their daily consulting and training practice. Jeff and Linda help their clients find practical solutions in a world that too often offers strategies that are long on hype and short on substance.

Readers who want to know more about Jeff and Linda and their work or would like to subscribe to their workplace journal are encouraged to visit them at www.RussellConsultingInc.com or to send them an email at RCI@RussellConsultingInc.com. Please contact them with questions about the ideas presented in this book or to arrange for RCI's consulting or training services.

Index

A

Actions for Encouraging Employee Ownership *(Handout 6)*, 181–182

Actions for Reducing Rating Errors *(Handout 22)*, 201

Actions to Reduce Errors in Performance Reviews *(Training Instrument 23)*, 246

active listening, 325–327

Active Listening and the Values, Assumption, and Behaviors of the Mutual Learning Mindset, 325–327

Active Listening Application *(Training Instrument 25)*, 248–249

activities. *See* learning activities

adapting PowerPoint slides, 166

"Aha!" Sheet *(Training Tool 3)*, 170, 254

annual performance analysis, planning, 328–330

annual performance analysis/ planning, performance coaching, one-day workshop, 129–148
  agenda, 134–138
  CD materials, 133
  materials, 131–133
    for instructor, 131–132
    for participants, 132–133
  objectives, 131
  PowerPoint slides, 139–148
  preparations, 133–134
    before workshop, 133–134
    day of workshop, 134

appraisal vs. learning, 21

assumptions, 325–327

assumptions supporting mutual learning, 33–35
  empathy, 34
  free choice, 34
  internal commitment to decisions, 34
  transparency, 34
  valid information, 34

B

before training, support of transfer of training, 56

behavior modeling, 331–332

behaviors of mutual learning mindset, 325–327

behaviors supporting mutual learning, 35–39
  action planning, 38
  assumptions, identification of, 36
  behavioral patterns, critical reflection, 39
  beliefs, critical reflection, 39
  decision making, 38
  focus on interests vs. positions, 37–38
  judgment, suspension of, 36
  patterns of behavior, critical reflection, 39
  reasoning, 37
  sharing relevant information, 36
  understanding, 37
  whole, understanding of, 39
  words, shared meaning, 38

Building Employee Ownership for Great Performances *(Training Instrument 6)*, 219

C

Case Studies—Unilateral Control vs. Mutual Learning *(Learning Activity 9)*, 277–278

Cause/Effect Diagram *(Handout 21)*, 200

Cause/Effect Diagram Application *(Training Instrument 18)*, 240

Causes of Performance Problems, The *(Training Instrument 17)*, 239

CD. *See* compact disk materials and use

Characteristics of Effective Measures *(Learning Activity 19)*, 297

checking boxes vs. understanding, 22

coach, defined, 260–261

Coaching Cases—Using the Right Coaching Role *(Learning Activity 4)*, 266–267

coaching relationship, one-day workshop, 69–89
  agenda, 73–76
  CD materials, 72
  materials, 70–71
    for instructor, 70–71
    for participants, 71
  objectives, 70
  PowerPoint slides, 77–89
  preparations, 72–73
    before workshop, 72
    day of workshop, 72–73

coaching role, 266–267

Common Errors in Performance Reviews *(Training Instrument 22)*, 245

Common Errors of Traditional Reviews *(Learning Activity 31)*, 320–321

compact disk materials, 165–174
  computer requirements, 165–166
  contents, 165
  printing from CD, 166
  use of, 165–166
compact disk materials and use, 72, 93, 112, 133, 151, 165–174
Components of Performance and 85/15 Rule, The (Handout 19), 198
computer requirements, compact disk materials, 165–166
concepts, shared meaning, 38
contents of compact disk materials, 165
critical reflection, 39
culture of organization, 43–44
culture, performance management assessment and, 43–49

D

decisions, shared meaning, 38
defining great performance, 286–287
Defining Great Performance (Handout 5), 180
Defining Great Performance Application (Training Instrument 11), 226–227
defining great performance outcomes, 10–13
Defining Great Performance Outcomes (Learning Activity 12), 284–285
Defining Job Responsibilities (Training Instrument 13), 235
Defining Performance Accountabilities (Learning Activity 14), 288–289
Definition of a Coach (Handout 1), 176
design of training programs, 58–59
Developing Effective Measures—Case Application (Learning Activity 20), 298
developing evaluation methods, 64–67
Developing SMART Goals (Learning Activity 16), 292–293

diagnosing employee performance problems, developing improvement plans, one-day workshop, 109–127
  agenda, 113–117
  CD materials, 112
  materials, 110–111
    for instructor, 110–111
    for participants, 111
  objectives, 110
  PowerPoint slides, 118–127
  preparations, 112–113
    before workshop, 112
    day of workshop, 113
Diagnostic Tools for Exploring Causes of Performance Problems (Learning Activites 25), 308–310
diagnostic tools, performance problems, 308–310
documenting performance, 335
Documenting Performance (Training Instrument 16), 238
Dynamic Nature of the Coaching Relationship, The (Handout 3), 178
dynamic partnership for performance, 18

E

effective measures, characteristics of, 297
effects of training program, assessing, 63–64
employee-centered alternative to traditional review, 24–29
  agreement, 26–28
  employee preparations, 25–26
  following up, 28–29
  manager preparations, 24–25
employee performance
  development-assessing, 311–313
  documenting, 303–304
employee role within partnership, half-day workshop, 149–164
  agenda, 153–155
  CD materials, 151
  materials, 150–151

  for instructor, 150–151
  for participants, 151
  objectives, 150
  PowerPoint slides, 156–164
  preparations, 151–153
    before workshop, 151–152
    day of workshop, 152
Establishing Positive Performance Goals (Training Instrument 19), 241
Establishing Positive Performance Improvement Goals (Learning Activity 27), 314–315
evaluation, 63–67
  assessing effects of training program, 63–64
  judgment vs. learning, 21
  Kirkpatrick's levels, 63–64
  methods development, 64–67
  strategies, 65–66
evaluation vs. learning, 21
events, shared meaning, 38
Evolutionary vs. Revolutionary Performance Management (Handout 29), 212
examination of performance review, 19–29
examples of great performance outcomes, 12
experience, in support of mutual learning, 37

F

financial implication focus vs. learning, 21–22
focus groups, 44–45
focus on past vs. improvement for future, 20
following training, support of transfer of training, 57–58
forms vs. understanding, 22
foundation, effective performance coaching, 30–40
Four Skills of Active Listening, The (Handout 27), 206–207
fundamentals of adult learning, 51–54

G

gathering information on organizations, 44–45
  focus groups, 44–45
  online, paper surveys, 45
  structured interviews, 44
goal setting, 262–263
  purpose of, 282–283
Goal Setting (Learning Activity 2), 262–263
Goal Theory of Motivation, The (Handout 11), 189
Goals of Performance Coaching, The (Handout 15), 193–194
Goals of Performance Coaching, The (Learning Activity 22), 301–302
great performance management cycle, 10–17
Great Performance Management Cycle, The (Handout 4), 179
Great Performance Management Cycle, The (Learning Activity 5), 268–271
Great Performance Management Cycle and the Performance Coaching Conversation, The (Learning Activity 33), 324
great performance outcomes, 284–285
  defining, 10–13

H

half-day workshop, employee role within partnership, 149–164
  agenda, 153–155
  CD materials, 151
  materials, 150–151
    for instructor, 150–151
    for participants, 151
  objectives, 150
  PowerPoint slides, 156–164
  preparations, 151–153
    before workshop, 151–152
    day of workshop, 152

handouts
  Actions for Encouraging Employee Ownership (6), 181–182
  Actions for Reducing Rating Errors (22), 201
  Cause→Effect Diagram (21), 200
  Components of Performance and the 85/15 Rule, The (19), 198
  Defining Great Performance (5), 180
  Definition of a Coach, The (1), 176
  Dynamic Nature of the Coaching Relationship, The (3), 178
  Evolutionary vs. Revolutionary Performance Management (29), 212
  Four Skills of Active Listening, The (27), 206–207
  Goal Theory of Motivation, The (11), 189
  Goals of Performance Coaching, The (15), 193–194
  Great Performance Management Cycle, The (4), 179
  Ladder of Inference, The (10), 188
  Nine-Plus-One Performance Diagnostic Checklist (20), 199
  Performance Accountabilities (13), 191
  Performance Coaching Conversation, The (28), 208–211
  Purpose and Characteristics of Effective Performance Measures, The (14), 192
  Purposes of Performance Reviews, The (23), 202
  Reframing the Traditional Review (24), 203
  Role of the Coach in Shaping Great Performance, The (7), 183
  Roles of the Performance Coach, The (2), 177
  Tools for Documenting Performance (16), 195
  Unbundling the Process (25), 204
  Unilateral Control and Mutual Learning Mindsets (8), 184–185
  Using the Performance Gap to Drive Improvement (17), 196
  Values and Behaviors for Mutual Learning (9), 186–187
  What Is Great Performance? (12), 190
  Whole Body Listening (26), 205
  Why Things Go Wrong With Performance (18), 197
How Goal Setting Enables Great Performance and Applying Goal Theory (Training Instrument 10), 225

I

icons, 5–6
ideas, shared meaning, 38
Identifying Purposes of Performance Reviews (Training Instrument 24), 247
improvement plan development, diagnosing employee performance problems, one-day workshop, 109–127
  agenda, 113–117
  CD materials, 112
  materials, 110–111
    for instructor, 110–111
    for participants, 111
  objectives, 110
  PowerPoint slides, 118–127
  preparations, 112–113
    before workshops, 112
    day of workshop, 113
improving performance review, 19–29
inference, 279–281
influence by recent events vs. objective data, 23–24

information on organizations, 44–45
    focus groups, 44–45
    online, paper surveys, 45
    structured interviews, 44
infrastructure, 43–44
    performance-oriented culture, 46–48
intent, in support of mutual learning, 37
interviews, 44

J

judgment vs. learning, 21

K

Kirkpatrick's levels of training evaluation, 63–64
knowledge, in support of mutual learning, 37

L

ladder of inference, 279–281
Ladder of Inference, The *(Handout 10)*, 188
Ladder of Inference *(Learning Activity 10)*, 279–281
learning activities
    active listening, 325–327
    annual performance analysis, planning, 328–330
    assumptions, 325–327
    behavior modeling, 331–332
    behaviors of mutual learning mindset, 325–327
    coach, defined, 260–261
    coaching role, 266–267
    defining great performance, 286–287
    diagnostic tools, performance problems, 308–310
    documenting performance, 335
    effective measures, characteristics of, 297

employee performance
    development-assessing, 311–313
    documenting, 303–304
goal setting, 262–263
    purpose of, 282–283
great performance outcomes, 284–285
inference, 279–281
ladder of inference, 279–281
Learning Activity 1: What Is a Coach?, 260–261
Learning Activity 2: Goal Setting, 262–263
Learning Activity 3: Performance Coaching and the Roles of the Coach, 264–265
Learning Activity 4: Coaching Cases—Using the Right Coaching Role, 266–267
Learning Activity 5: The Great Performance Management Cycle, 268–271
Learning Activity 6: Personal Action Planning, 272
Learning Activity 7: Sharing "Aha!" Moments and Questions/Goals Review, 273
Learning Activity 8: Unilateral Control and Mutual Learning Mindsets—Two Approaches to Managing Relationships With Others, 274–276
Learning Activity 9: Case Studies—Unilateral Control vs. Mutual Learning, 277–278
Learning Activity 10: The Ladder of Inference, 279–281
Learning Activity 11: The Purpose of Goal Setting, 282–283
Learning Activity 12: Defining Great Performance Outcomes, 284–285
Learning Activity 13: Performance Planning and Development—Defining Great Performance, 286–287

Learning Activity 14: Defining Performance Accountabilities, 288–289
Learning Activity 15: Performance Planning and Development—Defining Responsibilities, 290–291
Learning Activity 16: Developing SMART Goals, 292–293
Learning Activity 17: Writing SMART Goals—Case Application, 294
Learning Activity 18: Performance Planning and Development—Developing SMART Goals, 295–296
Learning Activity 19: Characteristics of Effective Measures, 297
Learning Activity 20: Developing Effective Measures—Case Application, 298
Learning Activity 21: Performance Planning and Development—Developing Measures of Performance, 299–300
Learning Activity 22: The Goals of Performance Coaching, 301–302
Learning Activity 23: Strategies for Documenting Employee Performance, 303–304
Learning Activity 24: Why Things Go Wrong With Performance, 305–307
Learning Activity 25: Diagnostic Tools for Exploring the Causes of Performance Problems, 308–310
Learning Activity 26: Performance Planning and Development—Assessing Employee Performance, 311–313

Learning Activity 27: Establishing Positive Performance Improvement Goals, 314–315

Learning Activity 28: Performance Planning and Development—Developing Performance Goals, 316–317

Learning Activity 29: The Performance Management Quiz, 318

Learning Activity 30: Performance Reviews From the Dark and Light Sides, 319

Learning Activity 31: Common Errors of Traditional Reviews, 320–321

Learning Activity 32: The Purposes of Performance Reviews, 322–323

Learning Activity 33: The Great Performance Management Cycle and the Performance Coaching Conversation, 324

Learning Activity 34: Active Listening and the Values, Assumptions, and Behaviors of the Mutual Learning Mindset, 325–327

Learning Activity 35: The Performance Coaching Conversation and the Annual Performance Analysis and Planning Conversation, 328–330

Learning Activity 36: The Performance Coaching Conversation—Behavior Modeling, 331–332

Learning Activity 37: Practicing the Performance Coaching Conversation—Participant Role Plays, 333–334

Learning Activity 38: The Organization's Expectations and Obligations for Documenting Performance Conversations, 335

management cycle, great performance, 268–271

measures, case application, 298

measures of performance, developing, 299–300

mutual learning, 274–278

mutual learning mindset, 325–327

organization's expectations, 335

performance, 305–307

performance accountabilities, 288–289

performance coaching, 264–265, 328–330

  behavior modeling, 331–332

  goals of, 301–302

  great performance management cycle, 324

performance goals, developing, 316–317

performance management quiz, 318

performance planning, 286–287, 290–291, 295–296, 299–300, 311–313, 316–317

performance problems, causes of, 308–310

performance reviews, 319

  purposes of, 322–323

personal action planning, 272

positive performance improvement goals, 314–315

questions/goals review, 273

relationships with others, 274–276

responsibilities, defining, 290–291

role plays, performance coaching conversation, 333–334

roles of coach, 264–265

smart goals, 295–296

  developing, 292–293

  writing, 294

traditional reviews, 320–321

unilateral control, 274–278

values, 325–327

Learning Goal/Objective ➔Outcomes (Training Tool 2), 170, 253

logical consequences, performance results, 16–17

M

management cycle, great performance, 17–18, 268–271

measures, case application, 298

measures of performance, developing, 299–300

mutual learning, 274–278

Mutual Learning and Coaching Cases (Training Instrument 9), 223–224

mutual learning mindset, 30–33, 325–327

  challenges, 39–40

N

navigating through PowerPoint slides, 167

negative outcomes, 16

Nine-Plus-One Performance Diagnostic Checklist (Handout 20), 199

O

one-day workshop on diagnosing employee performance problems, developing improvement plans, 109–127

  agenda, 113–117

  CD materials, 112

  materials, 110–111

    for instructor, 110–111

    for participants, 111

  objectives, 110

  PowerPoint slides, 118–127

  preparations, 112–113

    before workshop, 112

    day of workshop, 113

one-day workshop on establishing coaching relationship, 69–89

  agenda, 73–76

  CD materials, 72

  materials, 70–71

    for instructor, 70–71

    for participants, 71

  objectives, 70

PowerPoint slides, 77–89
preparations, 72–73
before workshop, 72
day of workshop, 72–73
one-day workshop on performance coaching, annual performance analysis/planning, 129–148
agenda, 134–138
CD materials, 133
materials, 131–133
for instructor, 131–132
for participants, 132–133
objectives, 131
PowerPoint slides, 139–148
preparations, 133–134
before workshop, 133–134
day of workshop, 134
one-day workshop on performance goal setting, 91–108
agenda, 94–99
CD materials, 93
materials, 92–93
for instructor, 92–93
for participants, 93
objectives, 91–92
PowerPoint slides, 100–108
preparations, 93–94
before workshop, 93–94
day of workshop, 94
one-way communication vs. two-way dialogue, 20
online, paper surveys, 45
organization
culture of, 43–44
gathering information on, 44–45
focus groups, 44–45
online, paper surveys, 45
structured interviews, 44
organizational culture, 43–44
organizational support, 14
organization's expectations, 335
Organization's Expectations and Obligations for Documenting

Performance Conversations, The (Learning Activity 38), 335

P

paper surveys, 45
partnership, employee role within, half-day workshop, 149–164
agenda, 153–155
CD materials, 151
materials, 150–151
for instructor, 150–151
for participants, 151
objectives, 150
PowerPoint slides, 156–164
preparations, 151–153
before workshop, 151–152
day of workshop, 152
partnership for performance, 18
patterns of behavior, critical reflection, 39
performance, 305–307
performance accountabilities, 288–289
Performance Accountabilities (Handout 13), 191
performance coaching, 264–265, 328–330
annual performance analysis/planning, one-day workshop, 129–148
agenda, 134–138
CD materials, 133
materials, 131–133
for instructor, 131–132
for participants, 132–133
objectives, 131
PowerPoint slides, 139–148
preparations, 133–134
before workshop, 133–134
day of workshop, 134
behavior modeling, 331–332
goals of, 301–302
great performance management cycle, 324

Performance Coaching and the Roles of the Coach (Learning Activity 3), 264–265
Performance Coaching Conversation, The (Handout 28), 208–211
Performance Coaching Conversation and Annual Performance Analysis and Planning Conversation, The (Learning Activity 35), 328–330
Performance Coaching Conversation—Behavior Modeling, The (Learning Activity 36), 331–332
performance goal setting, one-day workshop on, 91–108
agenda, 94–99
CD materials, 93
materials, 92–93
for instructor, 92–93
for participants, 93
objectives, 91–92
PowerPoint slides, 100–108
preparations, 93–94
before workshop, 93–94
day of workshop, 94
performance goals, developing, 316–317
performance management quiz, 318
Performance Management Quiz, The (Training Instrument 20), 242–243
Performance Management Quiz, The (Learning Activity 29), 318
performance-oriented culture, infrastructure, 46–48
performance planning, 286–287, 290–291, 295–296, 299–300, 311–313, 316–317
Performance Planning and Development—Assessing Employee Performance (Learning Activity 26), 311–313
Performance Planning and Development—Defining Great Performance (Learning Activity 13), 286–287
Performance Planning and Development—Defining

Responsibilities *(Learning Activity 15)*, 290–291

Performance Planning and Development—Developing Performance Goals *(Learning Activity 28)*, 316–317

Performance Planning and Development—Developing Measures of Performance *(Learning Activity 21)*, 299–300

Performance Planning and Development—Developing SMART Goals *(Learning Activity 15)*, 295–296

Performance Planning and Development Worksheet *(Training Instrument 12)*, 228–234

performance problems, causes of, 308–310

performance reviews, 319

   purposes of, 322–323

   value of, 2–3

Performance Reviews From the Dark and Light Sides *(Learning Activity 30)*, 319

Performance Reviews From the Dark and Light Sides *(Training Instrument 21)*, 244

personal action planning, 272

Personal Action Planning, *(Learning Activity 6)*, 272

Personal Plan for Action, A *(Training Instrument 7)*, 220–221

perspective, in support of mutual learning, 37

positive outcomes, 16

positive performance improvement goals, 314–315

PowerPoint presentations, 166–167

   adapting, 166

   showing, 166–167

PowerPoint slides, 77–89, 100–108, 118–127, 139–148, 156–164

   adapting, 166

   navigating through, 167

   presentations, 166–167

   showing, 166–167

Practicing the Performance Coaching Conversation—Participant Role

Plays, *(Learning Activity 37)*, 333–334

printing from compact disk, 166

process, managing performance as, 10

process goals, strategies, development of, 13–14

Purpose and Characteristics of Effective Performance Measures, The *(Handout 14)*, 192

Purpose of Goal Setting, The *(Learning Activity 11)*, 282–283

Purposes of Performance Reviews, The *(Handout 23)*, 202

Purposes of Performance Reviews, The *(Learning Activity 32)*, 322–323

Q

questions/goals review, 273

R

reasoning, in support of mutual learning, 37

Reframing the Traditional Review *(Handout 24)*, 203

relationships with others, 274–276

research questions, 46–49

   performance management, 48–49

   performance-oriented culture, infrastructure, 46–48

   review competencies, 48–49

Responding to Threat or Embarrassment *(Training Instrument 8)*, 222

responsibilities, defining, 290–291

Responsibilities of the Performance Coach *(Training Instrument 2)*, 215

review competencies, 48–49

Role of the Coach in Shaping Great Performance, The *(Handout 7)*, 183

role plays, performance coaching conversation, 333–334

roles of coach, 264–265

Roles of the Performance Coach, The *(Handout 2)*, 177

S

Selecting Group Leaders *(Training Tool 5)*, 171, 257

Selecting the Best Coaching Roles *(Training Instrument 3)*, 216

Sharing "Aha!" Moments and Questions/Goals Review *(Learning Activity 7)*, 273

showing PowerPoint slides, 166–167

slides, PowerPoint, 77–89, 100–108, 118–127, 139–148, 156–164

   adapting, 166

   navigating through, 167

   presentations, 166–167

   showing, 166–167

smart goals, 295–296

   developing, 292–293

   writing, 294

SMART Goals and Performance Measures Application *(Training Instrument 15)*, 237

SMART Performance Goals *(Training Instrument 14)*, 236

Strategies for Documenting Employee Performance *(Learning Activity 23)*, 303–304

strategies for evaluating training program, 65–66

structured interviews, 44

support of transfer of training, 55–58

   before training, 56

   during training session, 56–57

   following training, 57–58

surveys, 45

T

teaching, facilitating, distinguished, 59–60

tips for trainers, 173–174

Tools for Documenting Performance *(Handout 16)*, 195

traditional performance review

   problems with, 20–24

   purpose of, 19–20

traditional reviews, 320–321

training instruments
Actions to Reduce Errors in Performance Reviews (23), 246
Active Listening Application (25), 248–249
Building Employee Ownership for Great Performances (6), 219
Cause→Effect Diagram Application (18), 240
Causes of Performance Problems, The (17), 239
Common Errors in Performance Reviews (22), 245
Defining Great Performance Application (11), 226–227
Defining Job Responsibilities (13), 235
Documenting Performance (16), 238
Establishing Positive Performance Goals (19), 241
How Goal Setting Enables Great Performance and Applying Goal Theory (10), 225
Identifying the Purposes of Performance Reviews (24), 247
Mutual Learning and Coaching Cases (9), 223–224
Performance Management Quiz (20), 242–243
Performance Planning and Development Worksheet (12), 228–234
Performance Reviews From the Dark and Light Sides (21), 244
Personal Plan for Action, A (7), 220–221
Responding to Threat or Embarrassment (8), 222

Responsibilities of the Performance Coach (2), 215
Selecting the Best Coaching Roles (3), 216
SMART Goals and Performance Measures Application (15), 237
SMART Performance Goals (14), 236
What Enables GREAT Performance? (5), 218
What Is a Coach? (1), 214
Which Coaching Role Is Best? (4), 217
Training Program Reaction Sheet (Training Tool 4), 171, 255–256
Training Room Configuration/Layout (Training Tool 1), 170, 252
training session, support of transfer of training during, 56–57
training tools, 170–171
"Aha!" Sheet (3), 170, 254
Learning Goal/Objective→Outcomes (2), 170, 253
Selecting Group Leaders (5), 171, 257
Training Program Reaction Sheet (4), 171, 255–256
Training Room Configuration/Layout (1), 170, 252
transfer of training, support of, 55–58
before training, 56
following training, 57–58
during training session, 56–57

U
Unbundling the Process (Handout 25), 204
unilateral control, 274–278

Unilateral Control and Mutual Learning Mindsets (Handout 8), 184–185
Unilateral Control and Mutual Mindsets—Two Approaches to Managing Relationships With Others (Learning Activity 8), 274–276
unilateral control mindset, 30–33
Using the Performance Gap to Drive Improvement (Handout 17), 196

V
value of performance reviews, 2–3
values, 325–327
Values and Behaviors for Mutual Learning (Handout 9), 186–187

W
What Enables GREAT Performance? (Training Instrument 5), 218
What Is a Coach? (Learning Activity 1), 260–261
What Is a Coach? (Training Instrument 1), 214
What Is Great Performance? (Handout 12), 190
Which Coaching Role Is Best? (Training Instrument 4), 217
Whole Body Listening (Handout 26), 205
Why Things Go Wrong With Performance (Handout 18), 197
Why Things Go Wrong With Performance (Learning Activity 24), 305–307
words, shared meaning, 38
Writing SMART Goals—Case Application (Learning Activity 17), 294